Book Markets for Children's Writers 2011

Writer's Institute
Publications

Acknowledgments

The editors of this directory appreciate the generous cooperation of the publishers who made clear their policies and practices, as well as the contributions from our instructors and students.

SUSAN TIERNEY, Editor

BARBARA COLE, Associate Editor

SHERRI KEEFE, Associate Editor

MEREDITH DESOUSA, Copy Editor

CHERYL KAUER, Research Assistant

Contributing Writers: Susan Anderson, Kristen Bishop, Caroline LaFleur, Susan Tarrant

Cover Design: Joanna Horvath
Cover illustrations supplied by iStockphoto

Contents

Contents (Cont.)

Step-by-Step through the Submissions Process

Your Publishing Strategy

strategy: the art of devising or employing
plans toward a goal

C an you imagine spending years writing and revising a picture book, novel, or nonfiction manuscript only to discover that it doesn't meet the needs of a publisher? As the writer, you may have missed the mark on any number of things, including subject matter, target audience, or differentiating yourself from the competition. If you're lucky, you may be able to address these issues with some revisions; other cases may require a complete rewrite. Writers who want to get published learn to avoid these pitfalls with the help of a good publishing strategy—one that begins long before the writing starts.

Just like any successful business, writing benefits from a bit of advance planning. As writers, we've all heard the old adage to "write what you know." Clearly, authors who are passionate and knowledgeable about a subject are high on any editor's wanted list, but there's another key ingredient to becoming a writer: Write what you can sell. Even an author who is passionate about his or her topic will produce a more marketable book if it speaks to the right audience, has a unique hook, and/or covers a subject matter that is timely and relevant. Figuring out these key ingredients ahead of time will not only help you stay focused while writing; it will also boost the marketability of your manuscript.

As a writer trying to get published, what's your strategy? To get started, review the following targets, all of which are key to tailoring your manuscript with an eye toward publication:

1 - **Target the subject.** Is your topic of personal interest and a subject you feel passionate about? An editor isn't going to be enthusiastic about a book if you're not. What type of research will make it interesting and successful? Children's editors today require first-rate, primary research.

2 - **Target the quality.** Have you done your best writing? Practiced your skills, gone to writers' conferences, taken courses, joined critique groups, or in some way worked at your craft and gained the right "equipment"?

3 - Target the audience. Can you see it clearly? What is the age? Reading level? Interest? Voice?

4 - Target the competition. Are there other books on comparable subjects? If you're writing in one genre, what else is out there? Do you have a truly different slant to offer?

5 - Target the market generally. Is your book to be trade, mass-market, religious, crossover, regional, educational?

6 - Target the individual publisher and editor. What is this particular company and editor most interested in, most successful with?

We will take you step-by-step through the process of hitting some of these targets. Only you can work on the quality, but we will coach you through subject, audience, competition, and market objectives and how to reach them. You'll come nearer and nearer to a bull's-eye with every arrow—every manuscript sent flying.

Target the Subject

Whether you're finding new ideas, developing a defined project, or searching for markets for your completed manuscript, you can improve the submission process by taking time to do fundamental research. The first step is to select an idea that interests you, that you believe will appeal to readers as much as it does to you, and then collect information about it.

This idea and research development step is an important first measure toward selling your book. A good book requires authenticity if it's fiction, and accuracy if it's nonfiction. Subject research is essential in composing the best possible manuscript, whether it's historical background for a novel, geographical information on a region or city, or current data for a scientific principle. Finding and refining your idea with research will strengthen your work, and poise it to sell.

Research resources. The Web gives writers access to libraries, research studies, museums, associations, businesses, and a seemingly endless supply of miscellaneous sites available through myriad search engines. There are also additional resources available through your local library, many of which can be accessed from home with the use of your library card. Look at:

- online encyclopedias that might provide links to more detailed pages on other sites;
- university libraries online;

- government resources like the Library of Congress, the Smithsonian, NASA;
- museum sites, such as the Metropolitan Museum of Art in New York, the British Museum, and many other world-class museums;
- the sites of smaller, more focused museums, historical sites, even corporations;
- organizations that range from the social to the arts to sports, from the local to the universal;
- journalism and research-oriented sites that lead to "experts" for interviews.

Some sites provide information about the existence of material that you'll need to get physically from the library or another source. Other sites, however, provide actual content—text, photos, and data—online.

 People are good research sources—and can be cited as such. There may be subject-area experts in your community; or, to explore a topic more generally, subscribe to a listserv about your topic to get a variety of viewpoints and opinions.

<u>**Accuracy and annotations**</u>. Websites have links to other sites. Follow the trail, the links, and keep clear notes on where you go and what you learn, so you don't lose important resources or unintentionally plagiarize. Keep a running bibliography for your submission package; even if you don't need it, it's useful for back-up and additional research. Be sure to check the *Book Markets for Children's Writers'* listings for indications of the kind of bibliographical or other research annotations targeted editors require. (See, for example, the bibliography on page 36.)

It's important to become knowledgeable about screening information that appears on the Internet. Anyone with some computer know-how can create a website, so be sure to check the credentials of every source. You can be fairly sure of the accuracy of information presented on those sites affiliated with credible organizations such as the National Education Association, NASA, the Museum of Natural History, and other educational institutions, government bodies, museums, etc.

<u>**Fiction and research.**</u> Even fiction writers may need to do some research. Is your story set in a seaside town you recall

Gateway Internet Research

Whether you're in search of an idea or searching for information about an idea, the Internet is an excellent starting point for research. The list below provides a sampling of sites that should lead to solid, high-quality resources.

• **Archives:** In addition to government sites like those of the National Archives, Library of Congress, and Smithsonian, many universities and organizations make archives available online. Among them are NewsLibrary.com; Internet Archive (www.archive.org, sound, moving images, text); Repositories of Primary Sources (www.uiweb.uidaho.edu/special-collections/Other.Repositories.html); Vanderbilt Television News Archive (http://tvnews.vanderbilt.edu); and Archives of African American Music and Culture (www.indiana.edu/~aaamc).

• **Experts:** (www.allexperts.com) All Experts is a Q&A site with volunteer experts on dozens of topics who help with research. While not updated for several years, Sources and Experts (www.ibiblio.org/slanews/internet/experts.htm) is a strong list of leads for locating scholarly experts.

• **Intute:** (www.intute.ac.uk) This excellent U.K. site deals in specialized research. Larger category areas such as agriculture, biological sciences, arts and humanities, math and engineering, psychology, and others are broken down into narrower subcategories, with many academic references.

• **NoodleTools:** (www.noodletools.com). NoodleTools offers free tools to help locate data on subjects ranging from public opinion to immigration statistics, historical censuses, crime and justice, the environment, health, and foreign nations. The site also provides guidance on learning how to use the data in graphs and statistical calculations.

• **Reference libraries:** ipl2 (www.ipl.org), Library Spot (www.libraryspot.com), and Refdesk.com (http://refdesk.com) are three strong virtual libraries that lead users to references, facts, ideas, and lists. They even answer user questions, on countless subjects.

• **Voice of the Shuttle:** (http://vos.ucsb.edu/) VOS is a highly regarded gateway database maintained by the University of California, Santa Barbara, that includes links to academic sources across topic areas in the humanities, science, law, cyberculture, religion, and business.

from childhood? What's the weather like there when your story is set? Do you need inspiration for character names for a contemporary or historical story? Internet sites such as www.newspaper-archive.com allow you to search newspapers from as far back as 1759, and are a treasure trove for interesting stories and characters. And of course, turn to print, too. Through your local library you have access to networks of other libraries that will help you borrow virtually any book you need.

Target the Audience

Developing ideas means not only putting thought and research into your topic or story, but also gathering information about the readers. Who will read this story? Who is the ultimate market? What grabs the reader?

Experts. Search out "experts" who can help you learn which books kids are reading at which ages, or what parents or educators are reading, if they're your projected audience. Talk to children's librarians and teachers about the kinds of stories and topics that currently, or universally, appeal to young readers. Ask them about curriculum needs, especially for nonfiction. Go to bookstores and speak to managers who specialize in children's books. Online, go to library and reading sites, like those for the American Library Association (ALA) and the International Reading Association (IRA).

Developmental stages. Find out what's happening developmentally at a given age, what is being studied at school, what topics or actvities spark your audience. Talk to scout leaders, coaches, and music teachers. Observe and talk to the children themselves, especially about books if you can. Go to children's websites to see the topics they cover, and watch television programming and read young people's magazines to learn more about contemporary youth culture.

Age ranges. Browse through the listings in *Book Markets for Children's Writers* to look at the ages covered and review the sample titles. Or start with the Category Index (page 563) and look under "preK" or "middle grade" or "young adult." Review the publishers listed and request their catalogues or visit their websites. Catalogues are generally free upon request with a stamped, self-addressed, 9x12 envelope. See how many titles are published in what genres, for what age ranges; it should give you a sense of that publisher's subjects and style.

Age-Targeting Resources

Child Development

- **American Library Association (ALA) and International Reading Association (IRA):** (www.ala.org and www.reading.org). These organizations will help direct you to age-appropriate writing. See the ALA's list of great websites for kids.

- **American Academy of Pediatrics:** Try the AAP's Healthy Children site (www.healthychildren.org).

- **Bright Futures:** This website (www.brightfutures.org) brings together resources from various organizations, with resources on health and development of kids and teens.

- **Child & Family WebGuide:** (www.cfw.tufts.edu) This directory evaluates and describes hundreds of child development articles and Internet sites. Topics may be searched by age range, popularity, or area of interest.

- **Search Institute:** This nonprofit organization's website (www.search-institute.org) highlights 40 developmental assets for children from grades 6 to 12.

Sites for Children and Teens

- **Research and fun:** (www.kidsclick.org) *KidsClick!* is a librarian-generated search site for children with categories such as weird and mysterious, religion and mythology, and machines and transportation. *Ask Kids* (www.askkids.com) offers a Schoolhouse learning resource section, as well as fun pages on movies, games, and images. The university-sponsored *KidSpace* and *TeenSpace* have links to sites on numerous subjects, from math and science to sports and recreation (www.ipl.org/div/kidspace and www.ipl.org/div/teen).

- **Reading:** Websites geared to young readers have proliferated. Among them are James Patterson's *ReadKiddoRead* (www.readkiddoread.com); Jon Scieszka's *Guys-read.com*, focusing on boys and literacy; *Teenreads.com*, with title lists, blogs, and reviews; and the *Library of Congress* resources and encouragement at www.read.gov/teens and www.read.gov/kids.

You might also need or want to buy a book to advance your research into what a particular segment of children is reading. Amazon.com or Barnesandnoble.com, along with other sites that help you buy books or locate out-of-print titles, have become essential tools for writers. Not only do they help you locate children's books you know you want, they give you information on readership ages. Reverse the process and begin your search at one of these sites with a designated age range and see what titles come up. Lots of humor? Nonfiction, but not the fiction you expected? Does this help you in thinking about what you want to write?

Target the Competition & General Markets

A competitive title analysis is an important part of your research. Becoming familiar with publishers' current offerings is a good way to figure out how your book can stand out from the rest. A thorough analysis will also show editors that you have the ability to judge your own book accurately.

Competitive titles. A submission package that includes information about competitive titles will have a definite advantage. It will show editors your professionalism, research skills, and dedication to your work. If you use the research well, it will indicate to the editor that you know what that particular company publishes and why your book will fit its list. Doing your competitive title research, the questions you'll need to ask are:

- What books are in print that are similar to my idea?
- Who are the publishers, and what kinds of companies are they?
- When were the competing titles published?
- How are they different in slant, format, audience, etc., from mine?
- If one or more are not different, how will I reslant my idea to make my title more distinct?

This is where you'll need to strike a balance between selecting a subject or a story that has been widely published and the challenge of giving it a new twist. The same subjects will come up over and over again, and there's a reason—a large segment of four-year-olds are always interested in trucks and always will be, for example. But how do you write another picture book on trucks and make sure it's distinct?

Competition Research Form

Title	Author	Publisher	Pub. Date	Description/Differences from My Book
Little Trucks, Big Jobs	Robert Maass	Henry Holt	August 2007	Focuses on small trucks
Trucks Roll!	George Ella Lyon	Atheneum/Richard Jackson Books	March 2007	Focuses on trucks as big and powerful, with closeup drawings
Mega Trucks	(no author listed)	Scholastic	June 2008-	An introduction to the "biggest trucks in the world"; has interactive questions
Take a Trip with Trucktown	Justin Spelvin	Simon & Schuster	March 2011	Part of Jon Scieszka's Trucktown fiction series.
Roadwork	Sally Sutton	Candlewick	January 2011	Construction slant only. Rhythmic.

Some subjects are ripe for a new spin, particularly if it's been a few years since the last book on that topic was published. To do competition research, you might check:

- bookstores, where you can ask for a list of all the books on a given subject

- *Book Markets for Children's Writers*, for an overview of companies publishing competitive books

- online booksellers, with subject and age searches

- libraries, for catalogues and the *Subject Guide to Children's Books in Print*

- publisher websites and publisher catalogues

If there are many competing titles in your subject area, focus on just four or five that you consider to be leading competitors and describe them in detail. Some online booksellers such as Amazon.com offer sales rankings, reviews, and commentary to guide you.

Market types. Use *Book Markets for Children's Writers'* Category Index to generate a list of companies that publish in the category of your book and to start you thinking about the marketplace in general. You may want to use a form like the one on page 13. Are the companies with competitive titles generally educational, trade, religious, special interest? Do they have a strong backlist of older titles that they continue to support?

The individual publisher listings in *Book Markets for Children's Writers* also give you information on how many books a company publishes each year and how many it accepts from new authors. You're another step closer to selecting the publishers to whom you'll send your submission.

Target the Publisher & Editor

Book Markets for Children's Writers is an ideal resource for aligning your work with a publisher who is looking for it. The listings in *Book Markets for Children's Writers* are updated annually, with an emphasis on finding exactly what the editor needs now.

Turn again to the Category Index on page 563, or leaf through the listings themselves, and write down those publishers with interests similar to your own, especially those you didn't find in your earlier research. You've done this in researching the field and competition as a whole, but now you need to focus on the publishers you will pursue for your book. Here's how the listings break down and how to use them best.

- **Publisher's Interests:** Does the publisher you have in mind produce books for the trade, mass market, or school and library? Does it publish fiction and/or nonfiction? Does it have a specialization, such as history, regional subjects, educational? Is your book compatible with the publisher's profile? Don't stretch to make a match—make it a close one—but if you believe you can slant your book solidly toward a publisher's needs, work toward that in pulling together your proposal. If you've written fiction that just can't be reshaped, be honest, and find a different publisher whose needs are a better fit.

- **Freelance Potential:** How many books did the publisher produce last year? Of the books published, how many came from unpublished writers? (For an idea of your odds, compare the number of submissions the publisher received last year to the number of titles it published.) What age range does it focus on? Are there particular topics or types of books it specializes in? What genres did the company publish, in fiction or nonfiction?

- **Editor's Comments:** This section reveals a publisher's current needs, and the types of manuscripts it *doesn't* want to see. It may also give you insight into preferred style or other editor preferences.

You can also keep up with current needs through many of the trade publications like *Children's Writer* newsletter (www.childrenswriter.com or 1-800-443-6078) and *Publishers Weekly* (www.publishersweekly.com). *PW* offers special feature issues on children's publishing every spring and fall, as well as an online newsletter, *Children's Bookshelf,* that covers the children's publishing industry.

Narrow your choices to 6 to 12 publishers and request their catalogues, along with their writers' guidelines. Ask a final set of questions—those in the sidebar on page 17.

You're about to pull together your submissions package. First, review the writers' guidelines, if a company has them.

Industry Insider

You can do more than subject research online. Many Internet resources are useful for getting the scoop on publishers, editors, and new books. Blogs are also a good source for news on children's publishing. Find your favorites and follow them to keep current on the industry.

- **Nathan Bransford:** (http://blog.nathanbransford.com) A blog from an agent who discusses the business, good writing, authors, inspiration, and much else.

- **Editorial Anonymous:** (http://editorialanonymous.blogspot. com) An anonymous children's book editor provides answers to editorial questions.

- **Jacket Flap:** (www.jacketflap.com). A children's book resource and social networking site for people interested in the children's book industry. Includes news, blogs, reviews, and a database.

- **Cynthia Leitich Smith:** (http://cynthialeitichsmith.blog-spot.com) An authors blog covering children's book news, with interviews, reviews, booklists, and commentary.

- **Ypulse:** (www.ypulse.com) A media and marketing site that offers insights on tweens and teens.

Read the *Book Markets for Children's Writers'* listing closely for specifications, and follow them exactly. Suppose you have completed a nonfiction book on robotics you'd like to propose to Boyds Mills Press. The Boyds Mills guidelines for submission of a nonfiction manuscript require a detailed bibliography; they also *highly recommend* an expert review and a competitive analysis of similar books on the market. You could send your submission with a bibliography only, but you'd be starting off at a disadvantage—another writer may have sent in an expert review and a competitive analysis as well. Follow any publisher's guidelines as best you can; they not only help to streamline the submission process, they also help editors to identify worthwhile submissions—both of which help you.

Take Close Aim

When you've narrowed your targeted publishers to a short list, review the individual publishers' catalogues closely or go to their websites (indicated in the listings) to find out about their overall list and specific titles—dates of publication, slant, format. With even greater focus now as you sight your target, ask:

- Is this a large house, a smaller publisher, or an independent press with 10 or fewer books published yearly?

- How many books are on its backlist?

- What audience does the publisher target?

- Are most books single titles, or does the publisher focus on series books?

- Does it aim for one or two age groups, or does it feature books for all age groups?

- Does the publisher use the same authors repeatedly, or are many different authors featured?

- Are newer authors also represented?

- Is there a mix of fiction and nonfiction books, or is there more of one than the other?

- Is there a range of subject matter? Does my book fit in their range?

- Does the publisher specialize in one or more types of books, such as picture books or easy-to-reads? Is my book one of these, or not?

- Are there books similar to yours? Too similar and too recent, so the publisher might not want duplication?

- Would your book fit in with others this house has published?

- What are the specific requirements of the writers' guidelines and how will I meet them?

Query Letters
Step-by-Step

F irst impressions are crucial in publishing, whether it's to engage your reader in the first chapter of a book, or to catch an editor's attention with an intriguing pitch. While the overall quality of your book will ultimately cinch the sale, the first hurdle is to present your project in the best light by way of a query letter.

Many editors request query letters in place of complete manuscripts. Query letters are brief (usually one page) but significant. A good query should capture the editor's interest and give a sense of your treatment of a topic. It should also convince him or her that you are the best person to write this book.

But a good query still has more work to do: It also provides important information about you as the author. A professional, well-written query lets the editor know if you've mastered the idea of a "hook," have a good grasp of your project's theme and/or plot points, and understand how and why your work is a good fit for the publisher.

The best advice:

- Be succinct, positive, enthusiastic, and interesting.

- Briefly describe your book proposal.

- Identify the publisher's needs by indicating your familiarity with titles on its list.

- Outline your qualifications to write the book.

Review the query letter samples on pages 27, 28, and 31. Note each of the following elements:

Opener: A direct, brief lead that:

- captures and holds the editor's interest (it could be the first paragraph of your book);

- tells what the subject is and conveys your particular angle or slant;

- reflects your writing style, but is at all times professional; you need not be overly formal, but do not take a casual tone.

Subject: A brief description of your proposed manuscript and its potential interest to the publisher.

Specifications: If applicable, include the following:

- your manuscript's word length;

- number and type of illustrations;

- a brief indication of the research and interviews to be done; if this list is extensive, include it on a separate page with a reference to it in your query;

- market information and intended audience; again, if you've done more extensive competition research, attach it separately.

Reader Appeal: A brief description of why your target audience will want to read your proposed book.

Credits: If you have publishing credits, list them briefly, including the publisher and the date. List magazine credits as well. Don't tell the editor you've read your book to your child's class, or that several teachers have encouraged you to send it in, or that you've taken a writing course. If you have particular qualifications that helped you write the book (e.g., you run obedience classes and have written a book on dog training), say so. Many publishers request résumés. If you're attaching one in your submissions package, your query should mention relevant credits, and then refer to the résumé.

Marketing is a primary concern in publishing, and many publishers are more willing to take a chance on an author with previous writing experience and/or professional credentials. To build up your author "platform," get smaller pieces published in a variety of outlets and network with other professionals whenever possible.

Closing: Let the publisher know if this is an exclusive or simultaneous submission.

Queries are often required for nonfiction submissions, but in the past were very uncommon in fiction. Most editors preferred to see complete manuscripts or several chapters and a synopsis for novels and early reader fiction. That has changed somewhat in recent years; some editors want a query for fiction before they'll read anything more. Here are some of the distinctions in the queries and packages for nonfiction and fiction:

Nonfiction Query Package

A nonfiction package may include:

- a query or cover letter (see page 25 for which to use);

- a synopsis (see page 32);

- a detailed outline (topical or chapter) that describes each chapter's contents (see page 34);

- alternatively, a proposal that incorporates the synopsis, outline, and other information, such as the target audience (see page 35);

- representative chapters;

- a bibliography consisting of the books, periodicals, and other sources you have already used to research the project, and those that you will use, including expert sources and interviews (see page 36);

- a résumé (see page 37).

Fiction Query Package

A fiction query package may contain any or all of the following:

- one- to two-page synopsis that briefly states the book's theme and the main character's conflict, then describes the plot, major characters, and ending;

- chapter-by-chapter synopsis consisting of one to two paragraphs (maximum) per chapter, describing the major scene or plot development of each chapter. Keep the synopsis as brief as possible. You may either single space or double space a synopsis (see page 33);

- the first three chapters (no more than 50 pages). Check the *Book Markets for Children's Writers'* listing and publisher's guidelines carefully, as some editors prefer to see only the first chapter.

Query Letter Checklist

Use this checklist to evaluate your query letter before you send it with the rest of your book proposal.

Basics:
- ❏ Address the letter to the current editor, or as directed in writers' guidelines or market listings (for example, Submissions Editor or Acquisitions Editor).
- ❏ Spell the editor's name correctly.
- ❏ Proofread the address, especially the numbers.

Opening:
- ❏ Create a hook—quote a passage from your manuscript, give an unusual fact or statistic, ask a question.

Body:
- ❏ Give a brief overview of what your book proposal is about, but do not duplicate the detailed information you give in the outline or synopsis.
- ❏ List your special qualifications or experience, publishing credits/organization memberships, and research sources.
- ❏ State whether you can or cannot supply artwork.

Closing:
- ❏ Provide a brief summation.
- ❏ Let the publisher know if this is an exclusive or simultaneous submission.

Last steps:
- ❏ Proofread for spelling and punctuation errors, including typos.
- ❏ Sign the letter.

Cover Letters

A cover letter accompanies a submitted manuscript and provides an overview of your fiction or nonfiction submission, but it does not go into the same level of detail as a query letter. A cover letter is a professional introduction to the materials attached. If you are attaching a large package of materials in your submission—a synopsis, outline, competition research, résumé, for example—you don't need a full-blown query, but a cover letter.

Cover letters range from a brief business format, stating, "Enclosed is a copy of my manuscript, (Insert Title), for your review" to something more. In a somewhat longer form, the letter may include information about your personal experience with the topic; your publication credits, if you have them; potential sources for artwork; and, if relevant, the fact that someone the editor knows and respects suggested you submit the manuscript.

A cover letter is always included when a manuscript is sent at the request of the editor or when it has been reworked following the editor's suggestions. The cover letter should remind the editor that he or she asked to see this manuscript. This can be accomplished with a simple phrase along the lines of "Thank you for requesting a copy of my manuscript, (Insert Title)." If you are going to be away or if it is easier to reach you at certain times or at certain phone numbers, include that information as well. Do not refer to your work as a book; it is a manuscript until it is published.

Many submissions are rejected because query and/or cover letters are poorly written and contain grammatical errors. Make sure your package is error-free, cleanly presented and readable, and includes an SASE (self-addressed, stamped envelope) for the publisher's reply.

Proposals

A proposal is a collection of information with thorough details on a book idea. Arguably, a query alone is a proposal, but here we'll consider the various other components that may go into a proposal package. Always consult—and follow to the letter—writers' guidelines to see what a publisher requires.

Query or cover letter. The descriptions on pages 18–22 should help you construct your query or cover letter.

Synopsis. A brief, clear description of the fiction or nonfiction project proposed, conveying the essence of the entire idea. A synopsis may be one or several paragraphs on the entire book, or it may be written in chapter-by-chapter format. Synopses should also convey a sense of your writing style, without getting wordy. See the samples on pages 32 and 33.

Outline. A formally structured listing of the topics to be covered in a manuscript or book. Outlines may consist of brief phrases, or they may be annotated with one- or two-sentence descriptions of each element. See the sample on page 34.

Note that synopses are more common for fiction than outlines. Both outlines and synopses are sometimes used to describe nonfiction, but not necessarily both in the same proposal package.

Competition/market research. The importance of researching other titles in the marketplace that might be competitive to yours was discussed earlier (pages 12–14). The presentation of this information to the editor might be in synopsis form or presented as an annotated bibliography.

Bibliography. Bibliographies are important in nonfiction submissions, yet considerably less so with fiction, except possibly when writing in a genre such as historical fiction. A well-wrought bibliography can go a long way toward convincing an editor of the substance behind your proposal. Include primary sources, which are a necessity in children's nonfiction; book and periodical sources; Internet sources (but be particularly careful these are well-established); and expert sources you've interviewed or plan to interview. For format, use a style reference such as *Chicago Manual of Style, Modern Language Association (MLA) Handbook*, or one of the major journalist references by organizations such as the *New York Times* or Associated Press. See the sample on page 38.

   __Résumé/publishing credits.__ Many publishers request a list of publishing credits or a résumé with submissions. The résumé introduces you to an editor by indicating your background and qualifications. An editor can judge from a résumé if a prospective writer has the necessary experience to research and write material for that publishing house. The résumé that you submit to a publisher is different from one you would submit when applying for a job, because it emphasizes writing experience, memberships in writing associations, and education. Include only those credentials that demonstrate experience related to the publisher's editorial requirements, not all of your work experience or every membership. In the case of educational or special interest publishers, be sure to include pertinent work experience.

   No one style is preferable, but make sure your name, address, telephone number, and email address (if you have one) appear at the top of the page. Keep your résumé short and concise—it should not be more than a page long. If you have been published, those credits may be included on the one page, or listed on a separate sheet. See the sample on page 37.

   __Sample chapters or clips.__ As well-written as a query or even a synopsis might be, nothing can give an editor as clear a sense of your style, slant, and depth of the work you are proposing, or can do, than sample chapters or clips of published work. One of the obvious dilemmas of new writers is that they may not have clips, or they may be few and not suitable to a given proposal. But sample chapters, almost always the first and perhaps one or two others that are representative, help an editor make a judgment on your abilities and the project, or determine how to guide you in another direction—and toward a sale.

Query Letter v. Cover Letter

When to use a query letter:

☐ Always when a query is the specific requirement in the publisher's writers' guidelines.

☐ When you are including no other attached information; the query should be specific, but not exceed a single page.

☐ When you are attaching some additional materials, such as a synopsis or sample chapter.

When to use a cover letter:

☐ When an editor has requested that you send a specific manuscript and it is attached. The cover letter is a polite, professional reminder to the editor.

☐ When you have had previous interactions with an editor, who will know who you are. Perhaps you've written something for the editor before, or you had a conversation at a conference when the editor clearly suggested you send your work.

☐ When your proposal package is comprehensive, and explains your book completely enough that a cover letter is all that is needed to reiterate, very briefly, the nature of the proposal.

How to Write a Synopsis

How often have you decided to buy a book (or not buy it) based on its jacket or flap copy? This promotional copy has similar qualities to the synopsis, a boiled-down version of your book, anywhere from one to five pages, that highlights the major plot points and characters. In essence, the synopsis is an important sales tool that should convince an editor to take a chance on your work.

Whether your book is fiction or nonfiction, the synopsis does the same job: It informs editors of the complete plot of your fiction book or the complete scope of your nonfiction book, and helps them to determine if they are interested in reviewing the manuscript. Note that the description is *complete*. Although a query letter for fiction usually only alludes to the ending for purposes of enticing the editor, a synopsis should answer all questions and show an editor that your project has a well thought-out story arc.

A **fiction synopsis** should describe:
- What your characters want
- What obstacles they face in getting what they want
- How they solve the problem

A **nonfiction synopsis** should describe:
- The main point of the book
- The content of your supporting argument
- Why you are the best person to write the book

Writing a synopsis often poses a challenge: How much detail should you include? As you write about the pivotal scenes or major points of your manuscript, try to strike a balance between including too much detail and not enough. For example, avoid in-depth character descriptions or detailed accounts of every scene, but do mention a particular characteristic if it will help the reader to better understand the character's actions. A synopsis that is all generalizations will do little to entice the editor and/or make your manuscript stand out.

Remember, the synopsis should show off your skills as a writer and storyteller, so the same techniques you used to write the story are just as handy for crafting a synopsis that sells.

Sample Query Letter – Fiction

Street Address
City, State Zip
Telephone Number
Email Address
Date

Beth Parker
Mountain Press Publishing
P.O. Box 2399
Missoula, MT 59806

Dear Ms. Parker:

Opener/ Hook

Would you be willing to look at my 32-page picture book manuscript entitled *Where's Blind Tom Today?* It is based on the true story of a horse that played a role in building the transcontinental railroad from Omaha, Nebraska, to Promontory Point, Utah. This tale about an obscure, all-American "horse hero" has child appeal and would be marketable to adult "trainiacs"

Synopsis

at the nearly 300 railroad museums in the United States with bookstores/gift shops. It is not anthropomorphized, and the title's query was the telegraph operators' way of asking how many miles of track had been laid each day.

Market Analysis

Currently, there are no children's books about Blind Tom on the market. Other titles about the building of the railroad are chapter books for older readers, such as *The Transcontinental Railroad* by Elaine Landau (Franklin Watts, 2005) and *Railroad Fever* (National Geographic Books, 2004). *Full Steam Ahead* by Blumberg and *10-Day Mile* by Fraser were both published in 1996 and are now out of print.

Experience

I have several books in stores now. *Patriots in Petticoats: Heroines of the American Revolution* (Random House) was named one of the best children's books of the year by the Bank Street College of Education in New York. *Lewis & Clark: A Prairie Dog for the President* (Random Step Into Reading) has sold more than 130,000 copies and is recommended by the Lewis & Clark Trail Association.

I am a professional member of the Society of Children's Book Writers and Illustrators, Women Writing the West, the Albuquerque chapter of Sisters in Crime, Southwest Writers, the Alamos Historical Society, and the New Mexico Book Association.

Sincerely,

Shirley Raye Redmond

Sample Query Letter – Nonfiction

Street Address
City, State Zip
Telephone Number
Email Address
Date

Morning Glory Press
6595 San Haroldo Way
Buena Park, CA 90620

Dear Ms. Lindsey:

Opener/ Hook — Reading is the cornerstone of education. Children who read well are more likely to be successful students. Parents want their children to become good readers, but they often don't know the steps to take to make this dream a reality. My 5,200-word self-help manuscript, *Listen to Me, I Can Read: Tips Mom and Dad Can Use to Help Me Become a Lifelong Reader*, is a practical guide for parents to use with children from birth to young adulthood. The humorous text is written from the perspective of a child. The advice is divided into four categories: baby and toddler, preschooler, little kid reader, and big kid reader.

Subject/ Reader Appeal —

Credits/ Special Experience — I worked as a classroom teacher and later as a librarian in an elementary school for twenty-seven years. Recently, I have conducted workshops on literacy, instructing parent volunteers, teaching assistants, and teachers. I am also an author of children's picture books and make numerous school presentations. If this manuscript is accepted for publication, I will market it through schools, workshops, and educational conventions.

Parents often request information, such as the tips in this manuscript, to use with their children, and teachers request the same information to pass along to parents. Several markets exist for this type of book. Many hospitals give packages to parents of newborns. This book would be a great addition to those packages. When children enter kindergarten and preschool, parents are invited to an open house in which they are given educational packages. Head Start programs, Montessori schools, and day care centers may also be interested, as well as gift shops. I know of no other book on the market that deals with the subject of literacy using the fresh approach of this manuscript: a child appealing to the parents. The federally funded "No Child Left Behind Act" requires schools to make literacy a top priority. Many schools would endorse this book.

Closing — If this manuscript meets your editorial needs, please contact me at the following:

Sincerely,

Nancy Kelly Allen

28

Sample Cover Letter – Nonfiction

Street Address
City, State Zip
Telephone Number
Email Address
Date

Attn: Children's Book Division
Tate Publishing
127 East Trade Center Terrace
Mustang, OK 73604

To Whom It May Concern:

Opener/ Subject

Have you ever watched a dog while it sleeps? Do you wonder if a dog has dreams just like you and I? Enclosed is a manuscript that offers a humorously entertaining approach to this interesting question. Every page of this book allows for vibrant illustrations that will surely appeal to any child's imagination.

Market/ Appeal

The title of my book is *WHAT DO DOGS DREAM ABOUT?* It contains 150 words with a projected target age of 4–8 years. Professional artwork from an established artist is available depending on your interest in the style depicted in the attached, rough illustrations.

Closing

Thank you for considering my manuscript. I am enclosing a self-addressed, stamped envelope for your convenience in replying.

Sincerely,

Mike Dyson

Enc: SASE

Sample Cover Letter – Fiction

Street Address
City, State Zip
Telephone Number
Email Address
Date

Karen Fisk
Associate Children's Book Editor
Tilbury House Publishers
2 Mechanic Street #3
Gardiner, ME 04345

Dear Ms. Fisk:

Opener/
Hook — Enclosed please find my 1,030-word picture book entitled THE LUNCH
THIEF. It is a contemporary realistic story about an eleven-year-old boy
named Rafael who gets justifiably angry with "the new kid" at school who
steals lunches. However, this story is really about learning how to make a
Synopsis — friend rather than punish an enemy. I think it will be a good fit for your list,
appealing to children and parents both as a story and as a "lesson" in looking beyond appearances.

Closing — Thank you for taking the time to read my work. Please feel free to contact
me if you are interested. Enclosed is an SASE for your reply only. It is not
necessary to return the manuscript.

Sincerely,

Experience — Anne C. Bromley
Member, SCBWI San Diego Chapter

Enc: manuscript
    SASE

Sample Query Letter – Fiction

Street Address
City, State Zip
Telephone Number
Email Address
Date

Emma Dryden, Associate Publisher
Margaret K. McElderry Books
Simon & Schuster Children's Publishing Division
1230 Avenue of the Americas
New York, NY 10020

Dear Ms. Dryden,

Opener/
Subject

I would very much like you to meet Jamie and Kyle, two brothers with a solid friendship and a shared passion for their make-believe cowboy world. Just when the boys think their backyard "cattle drive" is under control, the neighbors' dog invades their territory. While Bogie's friendly presence is fun at first, the dog proceeds to hog the cowboys' bedrolls, and sinks his teeth into Kyle's

Synopsis

favorite toy. How will the boys handle this "coyote" in their midst? And how will they protect their ranch from another invasion?

This picture book, COWPOKES, COWS AND COYOTES, portrays kids making their own fun and cooperating in creative ways. And tarnation! It's just full o' fun cowboy words to boot! I am very hopeful that you would find it has the right tone and matches the quality of other books on your list. I should alert you that this is a multiple submission, but I will have it under consideration by just a few publishers at any one time.

Experience

I have published articles in *Boys' Quest*; *Wee Ones*; *Cecil Child*; *Babybug*; and *Dragonfly Spirit*.

Closing

My manuscript is complete and ready to be sent should you be interested in looking at it. I have enclosed an SASE for your convenience.

Sincerely,

Lisa Bierman

Sample Synopsis – Nonfiction

Name   Address, Telephone, Email

Storms

Chapter One: How Storms Form

Defines a storm as a mass of rapidly moving air that redistributes
energy from the sun's heat. Discusses air currents, including the Jet Stream,
and their patterns of movement across the Earth. Explains that storms begin
when warm, moist air meets cold, dry air and discusses the role that the
sharp boundary, or front, formed at this meeting place has in the creation of
storms.

Chapter Two: Rainstorms, Snowstorms, and Thunderstorms

Provides information about clouds and their moisture, explaining how
rain, snow, and hail are produced. Describes the processes by which thunder
and lightning are created. Talks about weather forecasting and storm
watches and warnings. Discusses how winds influence the severity of
storms, identifying the terms gale, blizzard, and cyclone.

Chapter Three: Hurricanes and Typhoons

Explains that hurricanes and typhoons are tropical cyclones. Talks about
the formation of hurricanes and typhoons as well as "the eye of the storm."
Discusses the effects of these storms on the environment. Gives examples
of major hurricane damage and reports on scientists' attempts to study and
predict the severity of hurricanes. As part of this discussion, provides
information about the hurricane naming system, the Saffir-Simpson
Damage-Potential Scale, hurricane watches and warnings, and hurricane
safety.

Chapter Four: Tornadoes

Defines the term tornado and reports that they are the product of
middle-latitude storms as opposed to tropical storms. Describes the
formation of a tornado and mentions some of the most significant tornadoes
in history. Discusses scientists' attempts to study and predict the severity of
tornadoes, providing information about storm chasers, the Fujita Tornado
Intensity Scale, tornado watches and warnings, and tornado safety.

Sample Synopsis – Fiction

TWO MOON PRINCESS
by Carmen Ferreiro

Wishing to be the heir her father the king has always wanted, Princess Andrea trains to be a knight. But the king laughs at her efforts and sends her to her mother to be made into a lady. Andrea sulks. She finds the ladies' company boring, their manners puzzling. To make matters worse, the queen, offended by Andrea's behavior, forbids her to attend the ball that her sisters claim would have changed her view of the world. Andrea has had enough, and when that very night she learns of the existence of a parallel universe, she happily leaves her parents' castle and crosses the door into the other world: present day California.

Andrea loves California and wants to stay forever. But when by mistake she returns to her kingdom and brings a Californian boy with her, the balance of her world is upset and war breaks out. Andrea leaves the castle once more in search of the enemy king, don Julian. While she tries to convince him to negotiate, don Julian is shot trying to protect her. Bound by her conscience to save his life, Andrea defies her father and, swallowing her pride, asks her mother for help.

In a desperate effort to end the war, Andrea puts her life at risk by taking don Julian back to his kingdom. Although her plan succeeds and she has gained her parents' respect, Andrea is haunted by the cruelties of the battle she has witnessed and her grief for don Julian. She questions her wish to be a warrior, and finally accepts her role as a lady. However, the unexpected arrival of don Julian at the castle shatters her apathy and reawakens her dreams. But this time Andrea knows that leaving will not solve her problems, and she refuses to run away. Instead she confronts her mother and openly fights for the right to be herself.

Sample Outline – Nonfiction

SWEAT THE SMALL STUFF:
STRATEGIES FOR WINNING SCIENCE PROJECTS
Outline

INTRODUCTION

CHAPTER 1: "Why Do I Have to Learn This Stuff?"
The Benefits of Participating in Science Research and Science Fairs
Opportunities Beyond School or Local Competition

CHAPTER 2: In the Beginning
Questions to Ask Yourself to Evaluate a Topic
Pitfalls to Avoid: Is My Project Possible? Is It Safe?
ISEF Categories

CHAPTER 3: There's a Method to this Madness
Basic Definitions of the Elements of a Project
Keeping an Exact Record—the Logbook
Recording the Results

CHAPTER 4: Who, What, Where, When, and How
How to Write Your Research Paper
Knowing When to Stop
Putting It Together in One Page: The Abstract

CHAPTER 5: Murphy's Law of Science Research: If Anything Can Go Wrong, It Will
Establishing a Timeline
Using Proper Safety
Have a Back-up Plan

CHAPTER 6: What's Green, Glows in the Dark, and Is Growing on My Project?
Using Sterile Technique
Inoculation Techniques
Precautions When Working with Biological Hazards

CHAPTER 7: Data Isn't Just a Star Trek Character
Statistics

CHAPTER 8: Misteaks, Mistaxe, Mistackes, Mistakes
Common Errors

Sample Proposal – Nonfiction

Name
Address
City, State Zip
Date

Proposal for Millbrook Press
"Invisible Invaders: New and Dangerous Infectious Diseases"

By the middle of the 20th century, it seemed like most infectious diseases were a thing of the past. However, over the past 30 years, nearly three dozen new or re-emerging infectious diseases have started to spread among humans. Each year, 1,500 people die of an infectious disease, and half of those people are children under five years old. In the United States alone, the death rate from infectious disease has doubled since 1980.

Invisible Invaders: New and Dangerous Infectious Diseases will be an addition to the Medical Library, the Millbrook/Twenty-First Century Press series on health issues. The Centers for Disease Control and Prevention and the National Institute of Allergy and Infectious Diseases have identified 35 emerging or re-emerging diseases as serious threats to human health. The book will cover the infectious diseases with the greatest real and potential impact to Americans. It will discuss why so many infectious diseases are threatening world health and where the diseases come from. The alarming appearance of new strains of organisms that are becoming ever more resistant to antibiotics will be covered, as will the potential use of deadly microbes and bioterrorism.

One children's book about epidemics that was published in 2000 blithely announced the eradication of smallpox in the world. Yet today, the government is making contingency plans to vaccinate millions of Americans should a bioterrorist release a deadly virus. Other books fail to mention Hantavirus, West Nile Virus, or Severe Acute Respiratory Syndrome, diseases recently threatening the health and lives of Americans. Clearly, a new children's book on the subject of infectious diseases is needed.

Invisible Invaders will consist of about 25,000 words, or approximately 115 pages of text interspersed with art. It will be written for children ages 7–10 to fit into the Medical Library series format. Each section will include information about the origin and spread of the disease, its symptoms, and treatment. With knowledge comes the power to help prevent or avoid these diseases, so the text will also cover appropriate steps that young readers can follow to decrease their risk. Case studies and pertinent sidebars enhance the text.

The author will use the latest information from prestigious organizations like the CDC, World Health Organization, National Institutes of Health, the American Public Health Association, the Infectious Diseases Society of America, and the Institute of Medicine.

Sample Bibliography

Bibliography

Blind Tom

The Great and Shining Road: The Epic Story of the Transcontinental Railroad
John Hoyt Williams
Times Books, Random House, NY 1988

The Horse in America
Robert West Howard
Follett Publishing Company
Chicago and New York, 1965

The American Heritage History of Railroads
Oliver Jensen
Bonanza Books, NY 1975

American Railroads
John F. Stover
University of Chicago Press
2nd edition 1997

American Railroads of the Nineteenth Century: A Pictorial History in Victorian Wood Engravings
Jim Harter
Texas Tech Univ. Press, Lubbock, 1998

Nothing Like It in the World
Stephen Ambrose
Simon & Schuster, NY 2000

Sample Résumé

Ann Purmell
Address
Telephone Number
Email

Experience
- Writer of inspirational and children's literature.
- Freelance journalist and feature writer for *Jackson Citizen Patriot* (Michigan), a Booth Communications daily. Affiliate newspapers throughout Michigan carry my articles.
- Freelance writer for *Jackson Magazine,* a monthly business publication.
- Guest lecturer for Children's Literature and Creative Writing classes at Spring Arbor College, Spring Arbor, Michigan.
- Performs school presentations for all grade levels.

Publications/Articles
Published numerous articles, including:
- "Prayers to the Dead," *In Other Words: An American Poetry Anthology* (Western Reading Services, 1998).
- "Promises Never Die," *Guideposts for Teens* (June/July 1999). Ghost-written, first-person, true story.
- "Teaching Kids the Financial Facts of Life," *Jackson Citizen Patriot* (July 20, 1999). An interview with Jayne A. Pearl, author of *Kids and Money.*
- "New Rules for Cider? Small Presses Might Be Put Out of Business," *Jackson Citizen Patriot* (December 12, 1999).
- "Jackson Public Schools Prepare for Change: Technology, Ideas Shaping Education," *Jackson Magazine* (December 1999). An interview with Dan Evans, Superintendent of Jackson Public Schools.

Education
- B.S., Nursing, Eastern Michigan University.
- Post-B.A. work, elementary education, Spring Arbor College.
- Highlights Foundation Chautauqua Conference, summer 1999.

Sample Manuscript Pages

Title Page

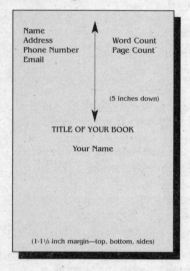

Name
Address
Phone Number
Email

Word Count
Page Count

(5 inches down)

TITLE OF YOUR BOOK

Your Name

(1-1½ inch margin—top, bottom, sides)

New Chapter

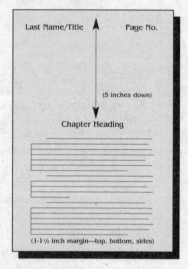

Last Name/Title

Page No.

(5 inches down)

Chapter Heading

(1-1½ inch margin—top, bottom, sides)

Following Pages

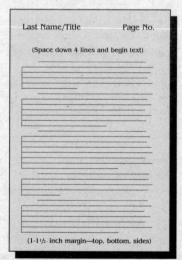

Last Name/Title

Page No.

(Space down 4 lines and begin text)

(1-1½ inch margin—top, bottom, sides)

Manuscript Preparation

Prepare and mail your manuscript according to the following guidelines:

- Use high-quality 8½x11 white bond paper.

- Double-space manuscript text; leave 1- to 1½-inch margins on the top, bottom, and sides. (See page 38.)

- Send typewritten pages or letter-quality printouts. You may send a computer disk if the publisher requests one.

- *Title Page.* In the upper left corner, type your name, address, phone number, and email address.

  In the upper right corner, type your word count, rounded to the nearest 10 to 25 words. For anything longer than a picture book, you may also type the number of pages. (Don't count the title page.) Center and type your title (using capital letters) about 5 inches from the top of the page with your byline two lines below it.

  Start your text on the next page. (Note: if this is a picture book or board book, see pages 41–42.)

- *Following Pages.* Type your last name and one or two key words of your title in the upper left corner, and the page number in the upper right. Begin new chapters halfway down the page.

- *Cover Letter.* Include a brief cover letter following the guidelines on page 22.

Mailing Requirements

- Assemble pages unstapled. Place cover letter on top of title page. Mail in a 9x12 or 10x13 manila envelope. Include a same-sized SASE marked "First Class." If submitting to a publisher outside the U.S., enclose an International Reply Coupon (IRC) for return postage.

- To ensure that your manuscript arrives safely, include a self-addressed, stamped postcard the editor can return upon receipt.

- Mail your submissions First Class or Priority. Do not use certified or registered mail.

Email Submissions

Publishers are increasingly open to receiving submissions and queries through email; in some cases it is their preferred method of submission. Whatever your personal preference may be, read publishers' guidelines carefully to determine the best way to contact them. If you do submit by email, prepare your query as carefully as if it was a traditional "mail in." Pay special attention to style and presentation, elements that are often overlooked in email submissions. Other things to consider are:

- **_File attachments._** Some publishers prefer that the body of the email be used as a cover letter, with supporting documents—including the synopsis, outline, etc.—attached as separate files. In other cases, queries may be included in the main body of the email.

- **_Electronic format._** Rich text format (RTF) and Microsoft Word are most commonly used for sending documents electronically; postscript and PDF files are also sometimes accepted. If you're not computer savvy, take time to learn what these options are and what your target publisher wants.

- **_Contact information._** Don't forget to include your contact information—traditional mailing address and telephone as well as email address—in the body of your email, as well as the full title of your work. If your email has attachments, briefly describe the attachments by file name as part of your cover letter.

- **_Subject line._** To ensure that your email is read, follow the publisher's guidelines for describing the content of your message, which sometimes includes the title of your work and/or your name, i.e. 'Submission—My Bestseller,' or the word 'Query,' as well as other information.

Email queries should be shorter than traditional "paper" queries, so that they fit on an editor's computer screen with minimal scrolling. To make sure your message is readable in most email programs: 1) use block-style paragraphs rather than indents, 2) break up large paragraphs into smaller chunks for easy reading, and 3) avoid using any special fonts or formatting.

Picture Book Submissions

Most editors will accept a complete manuscript for a picture book without an initial query. Because a picture book text may contain as few as 20 words and seldom exceeds 1,500 words, it is difficult to judge if not seen in its entirety. Do not submit your own artwork unless you are a professional artist; editors prefer to use illustrators of their own choosing.

Prepare the manuscript following the guidelines for the title page on page 38. Drop down four lines from the byline, indent, and begin your manuscript on the title page. Type it straight through as if it were a short story. Do not indicate page breaks.

Keep in mind that description is conveyed largely through illustrations, not text. Keep descriptive details to a minimum, and make sure that your manuscript provides a variety of lively illustration opportunities.

The average picture book is 32 pages, although it may be as short as 16 pages or as long as 64 pages, depending on the age of the intended audience. To make a dummy for a 32-page book, take eight sheets of paper, fold them in half, and number them as the sample indicates; this will not include the end papers. (Each sheet makes up four pages of your book.) Lay out your text and rough sketches or a brief description of the accompanying illustrations. Move these around and adjust your concept of the artwork until you are satisfied that words and pictures fit together as they should.

Do not submit your dummy unless the editor asks for it. Simply submit your text on separate sheets of paper, typed double-spaced, following the format guidelines given on page 38. If you do choose to submit artwork as well, be sure to send copies only; editors will rarely take responsibility for original artwork. Be sure to include a self-addressed, stamped envelope (SASE) large enough for the return of your entire package.

Picture Book Dummy

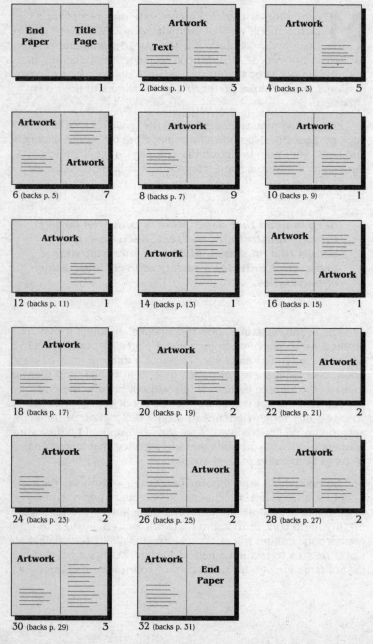

Step-by-Step through the Business of Publishing

Book Contracts

Once an editor is interested in buying your work, he or she will send a book contract for your review and signature. While book contracts vary in length and precise language from publisher to publisher, the basic provisions of these contracts are generally similar. All writers should understand publishing contract standards, know enough to acknowledge an offer as appropriate, and recognize when there may be room to negotiate. Remember, the agreement isn't complete until you sign the contract.

In Plain English

The best advice for your first contract reading is not to let the legal terminology distract you. A book contract is a complex legal document that is designed to protect you and the publisher. It defines the rights, responsibilities, and financial terms of the author, publisher, and artist (when necessary).

Because some publishers issue standard contracts and rarely change wording or payment rates for new writers, you may not need an agent or a lawyer with book-publishing experience to represent you in the negotiation of the contract. But if you choose to negotiate the contract yourself, it is advisable that you read several reference books about book contracts and have a lawyer, preferably with book-contract experience, look it over prior to signing the agreement.

In either case, you should be familiar enough with the basic premises of the contract to communicate what items you would like to change in the document. For your protection, reread the contract at every stage of negotiation.

In the following section, you'll find a primer on the basic provisions of a book contract. If a statement in your contract is not covered or remains unclear to you, ask the editor or an attorney to "translate" the clauses into plain English.

Rights and Responsibilities

A standard book contract specifies what an author and a publisher each agree to do to produce the book and place it in the marketplace. It explicitly states copyright ownership, royalty, advance, delivery date, territorial and subsidiary rights, and other related provisions.

Grant of Rights

A clause early in the contract says that, on signing, the author agrees to "grant and assign" or "convey and transfer" to the publisher all or certain specified rights to a book. You thus authorize, or license, the publisher to publish your work.

Subsidiary rights are negotiated in a contract. These rights include where a book is distributed, in what language it is printed, and in what format it is published. While most publishers want world English-language rights, some publishers will consent to retaining rights only in the United States, the Philippines, Canada, and U.S. dependencies. With the United Kingdom now part of the European Community, more and more publishers want British publication rights, in English, so they can sell books to other members of the European Community.

Other subsidiary rights often included in contracts are:

Reprint Rights: These consist of publishing the work in magazines (also known as serial rights), book club editions, and hardcover or paperback versions.

Mechanical Rights: These cover audio and video cassettes, photocopying, filmstrips, and other mechanical production media.

Electronic or Computer Rights: These include rights to cover potential use on software programs, multimedia packages, CD-ROMs, online services, etc.

Dramatic Rights: These include versions of the work for film, television, etc.

Translation Rights: These allow a work to be printed in languages other than English.

If you don't have an agent, you may want to assign a publisher broad rights since you may not have the necessary connections or experience to sell them on your own.

If possible, seek a time limit that a publisher has to use subsidiary rights. That way certain rights will revert to you if the publisher has not sold them within a specific period.

Copyright Ownership

According to the Copyright Term Extension Act of 1998, you now own all rights to work you created during or after 1978 for your lifetime plus 70 years, until you choose to sell all or part of the copyright in very specific ways. According to this law, your idea is not copyrighted; it is your unique combination of words—how you wrote something—that this law protects and considers copyrighted. A separate clause in a book contract states that you retain the copyright in your name.

Once you complete your manuscript, your work is protected. You don't need to register your work, published or unpublished, with the United States Copyright Office. In most contract agreements, a publisher is responsible for registering the published version of your work. Writers who provide a copyright notice on their submitted manuscript may be viewed as amateurs by many editors. However, registration does offer proof of ownership and a clear legal basis in case of infringement. If you decide to register your work, obtain an application form and directions on the correct way to file your copyright application. Write to the Library of Congress, Copyright Office, 101 Independence Ave. S. E., Washington, DC 20559-6000 or download them in Adobe Acrobat format at: www.copyright.gov/forms. Copyright registration fees range from $35 to $65.

If you have registered your unpublished manuscript with the Library of Congress, notify your publisher of that fact once your book is accepted for publication.

Manuscript Delivery

A publishing contract sets a due date by which you must complete and deliver an acceptable manuscript of the length specified in your contract. This clause allows a publisher time to request editorial changes, permits editing of the manuscript with your review and approval, establishes editorial schedules, and indicates how many author's alterations (also known as editorial changes) you may make without cost after the book has been typeset.

Warranty and Indemnification

You will be asked to ensure that the manuscript is your original work; that it contains nothing libelous, obscene, or private; and that it does not infringe on any copyright. The clause also stipulates that the author must pay the publisher's court costs and damages should it be sued over the book. This should not be an issue to the author who has exercised reasonable caution and written in good faith.

Though publishers are often reluctant to change this provision, you should still seek to limit the scope of warranty clauses. Include the phrase "to the best of the writer's knowledge" in your warranty agreement. Don't agree to pay for client's damages or attorney's fees, and put a ceiling on your liability—perhaps the fee agreed upon for the assignment.

Also remember that many publishers carry their own insurance and can sometimes include writers under their house policy.

Obligation to Publish

The publisher agrees to produce and distribute the book in a timely manner, generally between one and two years. The contract should specify the time frame and indicate that if the publisher fails to publish the book within that period, the rights return to you (reversion of rights) and you keep any money already received.

Option

The option clause requires the author to offer the publisher the first chance at his or her next book. To avoid a prolonged decision-making process, try to negotiate a set period for the publisher's review of a second book, perhaps 60 or 90 days from submission of the second manuscript. Also stipulate that the publisher acquire your next book on terms to be mutually agreed upon by both parties. In this way, you have room to negotiate a more favorable deal.

Payment

Calculations for the amount of money an author receives as an advance or in royalties are fairly standardized.

Advance: An advance is money the writer receives in a lump sum or installments when a manuscript is accepted or delivered. It is like a loan paid "against" royalties coming from anticipated profits.

Royalty: A royalty is a percentage of sales paid to the author. It is based either on a book's retail price or on net receipts (the price actually received by the publisher), and it may be fixed or arranged on a sliding scale. For example, standard royalty may be 10% for the first 5,000 copies, 12.5% for the next 5,000 copies, and 15% thereafter. Royalties range anywhere from 2% to 10% or higher, depending on the publisher and the author's publishing history.

Depending on the extent of artwork and who supplied it to the publisher, author and artist may divide royalties or the artist may be paid a flat fee.

Accounting Statements: The publisher must provide the author with earning statements for the book. Most companies provide statements and checks semiannually, three or more months after each accounting period ends. Be sure to determine exactly when that is. For example, if the accounting periods end June 30 and December 31, you should receive statements by October 1 and April 1.

Flat Rate: Instead of paying royalties, some book packagers and smaller publishers offer a fixed amount or flat rate in return for all rights or as part of a work-for-hire agreement. This amount is paid upon completion of the book.

Traditionally, work-for-hire means that the publisher becomes the 'author' of the work for copyright purposes. More prevalent among school and library publishers and book packagers, this type of agreement has advantages and disadvantages that you should weigh before signing.

Before You Sign . . .

The explanations presented here include suggestions for a reasonable and (we hope) profitable approach to your book contract. Every situation presents distinct alternatives, however. Your agreement with a publisher must be undertaken in good faith on both sides and you should feel comfortable with the deal you strike. When in doubt, consult an expert for advice.

You can find additional information about copyrights and publishing law in *The Copyright Handbook: What Every Writer Needs to Know* (tenth ed.) by Stephen Fishman (Nolo Press, 2008), *The Writer's Legal Guide* (third edition) by Tad Crawford (Allworth Press, 2002), and *Every Writer's Guide to Copyright and Publishing Law* by Ellen Kozak (Owl Books, 2004).

A Note About Self, Subsidy, and Co-op Publishing Options

When you self-publish your book, you assume the cost of and responsibility for printing and distributing your book. In contrast, subsidy presses handle—for a fee—the production and, to some degree, the marketing and distribution of a writer's book. Co-op or joint-venture publishers assume responsibility for marketing and distribution of a book, while the author pays some or all of the production costs.

A newer incarnation of self-publishing is print on demand (POD), a type of printing technology that allows companies to print and bind your book in a matter of minutes. This makes it easy and cost-effective to publish books individually or in small lots, rather than investing in print runs of hundreds of books—letting you publish your work on a shoestring. POD books, however, are more expensive to produce than books done by traditional offset printing.

Another technology that's appeared as a result of the Internet boom is electronic books. Authors can publish their work without the cost of printing and binding by distributing their books in the form of computer files—Adobe PDF files are typically used.

Aside from the actual production of your book, marketing is an integral part of the self-publishing process. Many large booksellers—and consumers—are wary of buying self-published titles, making sales and marketing an even bigger hurdle. Self-published authors must handle all marketing and promotional tasks on their own, which can be complex and costly. The most common marketing options include targeted direct mail advertising, web advertising, and sending out review copies. Electronic books benefit from services such as Booklocker.com, which distributes ebooks for a modest fee.

Based on your own needs and expectations, you may choose to try one of these approaches. If you do, exercise caution. Be sure you understand the terms of any contract, including exactly how much you will be required to pay, the marketing and distributing services the publisher is promising (if any), and the rights you are retaining. Also, check out *Dan Poynter's Self-Publishing Manual: How to Write, Print, and Sell Your Own Book* (Para Publishing, 2008) for a good overview of self-publishing. If you decide to take this route, it is advisable to consult a lawyer before entering into any arrangement.

Postage Information

When you send a manuscript to a publisher, always enclose a return SASE with sufficient postage; this way, if the editor does not want to use your manuscript, it can be returned to you. To help you calculate the proper amount of postage for your SASE, here are the U.S. postal rates for first-class mailings in the U.S. and from the U.S. to Canada.

Ounces	8½x11 Pages (approx pgs)	U.S. 1st-Class Postage Rate	U.S. to Canada
5	21–25	$1.56	$2.07
6	26–30	1.73	2.33
7	31–35	1.90	2.59
8	36–40	2.07	2.85
9	41–45	2.24	2.85
10	46–50	2.41	2.85
11	51–55	2.58	2.85
12	56+	2.75	3.83

How to Obtain Stamps

People living in the U.S., Canada, or overseas can acquire U.S. stamps through the mail from the Stamp Fulfillment Service Center: call 800-STAMP-24 (800-782-6724) to request a catalogue or place an order. For overseas, the telephone number is 816-545-1000. You pay the cost of the stamps plus a postage and handling fee based on the value of the stamps ordered, and the stamps are shipped to you. Credit card information (MasterCard, VISA, and Discover cards only) is required for fax orders. The fax number is 816-545-1212. If you order through the catalogue, you can pay with a U.S. check or an American money order. Allow 3–4 weeks for delivery.

Frequently Asked Questions

How do I request a publisher's catalogue and writers' guidelines?

Write a brief note to the publishing company: "Please send me a recent catalogue and writers' guidelines. If there is any charge please enclose an invoice and I will pay upon receipt." The publisher's website, if it has one, offers a faster and less expensive alternative. Many companies put their catalogues, or at least their latest releases and their writers' guidelines, on the Internet.

Do I need an agent?

There is no correct answer to this question. Some writers are very successful marketing their own work, while others feel more comfortable having an agent handle that end of the business. It's a personal decision, but if you decide to work through an agent, be an "informed consumer." Get a list of member agents from the Association of Authors' Representatives, 676A 9th Avenue, #312, New York, NY 10036 or check it out online at www.aar-online.org.

I need to include a bibliography with my book proposal. How do I set one up?

The reference section of your local library can provide several sources that will help you set up a bibliography. A style manual such as the *Chicago Manual of Style* will show you the proper format for citing all your sources, including unpublished material, interviews, and Internet material.

What do I put in a cover letter if I have no publishing credits or relevant personal experience?

In this case you may want to forego a formal cover letter and send your manuscript with a brief letter stating, "Enclosed is my manuscript, (Insert Title), for your review." For more information on cover letters see page 22.

I don't need my manuscript returned. How do I indicate that to an editor?

With the capability to store manuscripts electronically, some writers keep postage costs down by enclosing a self-addressed stamped postcard (SASP) saying, "No need to return my manuscript. Please use this postcard to advise me of the status of my manuscript. Thank you."

Do I need to register or copyright my manuscript?

Once completed, your work is automatically protected by copyright. When your manuscript is accepted for publication, the publisher will register it for you.

Should I submit my manuscript on disk?

Do not send your manuscript on disk unless the publisher's submission guidelines note that this is an acceptable format.

When a publisher says "query with sample chapters," how do I know which chapters to send? Should they be chapters in sequence or does that matter? And how many should I send?

If the publisher does not specify which chapters it wishes to see, then it's your decision. Usually it's a good idea to send the first chapter, but if another chapter gives a flavor of your book or describes a key action in the plot, include that one. You may also want to send the final chapter of the book. For nonfiction, if one chapter is more fully representative of the material your book will cover, include that. Send two to three but if the guidelines state "sample chapter" (singular), just send one.

How long should I wait before contacting an editor after I have submitted my manuscript?

The response time given in the listings can vary, and it's a good idea to wait at least a few weeks after the allocated response time before you send a brief note to the editor asking about the status of your manuscript. If you do not get a satisfactory response or you want to send your manuscript elsewhere, send a certified letter to the editor withdrawing your work from consideration and requesting its return. You are then free to submit the work to another publishing house.

A long time ago, in 1989, I was fortunate enough to have a picture book published. If I write a query letter, should I include that information? It seems to me that it may hurt more than it helps, since I have not published anything since that.

By all means include it, though you need not mention the year it was published. Any publishing credit is worth noting, particularly if it is a picture book, because it shows you succeeded in a highly competitive field.

How do I address the editor, especially if she is female (e.g., Dear Miss, Dear Ms., Dear Mrs., Dear Editor-in-Chief, or what)?

There is no accepted preference, so the choice is really yours, but in general Ms. is used most frequently. Do use the person's last name, not his or her first. Before you decide which title to use, make sure you know if the person you are addressing is male or female.

If a publisher does not specify that "multiple submissions" are okay, does that imply they are not okay?

If a publisher has a firm policy against multiple submissions, this is usually stated in its guidelines. If not mentioned, the publisher probably does not have a hard and fast rule. If you choose to send a multiple submission, make sure to indicate that on your submission. Then it's up to the publisher to contact you if it prefers not to receive such submissions.

Publishing Terms

Advance: initial payment by publisher to author against future sales

Agent: professional who contacts editors and negotiates book contracts on author's behalf

All rights: an outright sale of your material; author has no further control over it

Anthropomorphization: attributing human form and personality to things not human, for example, animals

Backlist: list of publisher's titles that were not produced this season but are still in print

Beginning readers: children ages 4 to 7 years

Book contract: legal agreement between author and publisher

Book packager/producer: company that handles all elements of producing a book and then sells the final product to a publisher

Book proposal: see **Proposal**

Caldecott Medal: annual award that honors the illustrator of the current year's most distinguished children's book

CD-ROM: (compact-disc read-only memory) non-erasable electronic medium used for digitalized image and document storage

Clean-copy: a manuscript ready for typesetting; it is free of errors and needs no editing

Clip: sample of a writer's published work. See also **Tearsheet**

Concept book: category of picture book for children 2 to 7 years that teaches an idea (i.e., alphabet or counting) or explains a problem

Contract: see **Book contract**

Co-op publishing: author assumes some or all of the production costs and publisher handles all marketing and distribution; also referred to as "joint-venture publishing"

Copyedit: to edit with close attention to style and mechanics

Copyright: legal protection of an author's work

Cover letter: brief introductory letter sent with a manuscript

Disk submission: manuscript that is submitted on a computer disk

Distributor: company that buys and resells books from a publisher

Dummy: a sample arrangement or "mock-up" of pages to be printed, indicating the appearance of the published work

Electronic submission: manuscript transmitted to an editor from one computer to another through a modem

Email: (electronic mail) messages sent from one computer to another via a modem or computer network

End matter: material following the text of a book, such as the appendix, bibliography, index

Final draft: the last version of a polished manuscript ready for submission to an editor

First-time author: writer who has not previously been published

Flat fee: one-time payment made to an author for publication of a manuscript

Front matter: material preceding the text of a book, such as title page, acknowledgments, etc.

Galley: a proof of typeset text that is checked before it is made into final pages

Genre: category of fiction characterized by a particular style, form, or content, such as mystery or fantasy

Hard copy: the printed copy of a computer's output

Hi/lo: high-interest/low-reading level

Imprint: name under which a publishing house issues books

International Reply Coupon (IRC): coupon exchangeable in any foreign country for postage on a single-rate, surface-mailed letter

ISBN: International Standard Book Number assigned to books upon publication for purposes of identification

Letter-quality printout: computer printout that resembles typed pages

Manuscript: a typewritten, or computer-generated document (as opposed to a printed version),

Mass-market: books aimed at a wide audience and sold in supermarkets, airports, and chain bookstores

Middle-grade readers: children ages 8 to 12 years

Modem: an internal or external device used to transmit data between computers via telephone lines

Ms/Mss: manuscript/manuscripts

Newbery Medal: annual award that honors the author of that year's most distinguished children's book

Outline: summary of a book's contents, usually nonfiction, often organized under chapter headings with descriptive sentences under each to show the scope of the book

Packager: see **Book Packager**

Pen name/pseudonym: fictitious name used by an author

Picture book: a type of book that tells a story primarily or entirely through artwork and is aimed at preschool to 8-year-old children

PreK: children under 5 years of age; also known as preschool

Proofread: to read and mark errors, usually in typeset text

Proposal: detailed description of a manuscript, usually nonfiction, and its intended market

Query: letter to an editor to promote interest in a manuscript or idea

Reading fee: fee charged by anyone to read a manuscript

Reprint: another printing of a book; often a different format, such as a paperback reprint of a hardcover title

Response time: average length of time for an editor to accept or reject a submission and contact the writer with a decision

Résumé: short account of one's qualifications, including educational and professional background and publishing credits

Revision: reworking of a piece of writing

Royalty: publisher's payment to an author (usually a percentage) for each copy of the author's work sold

SAE: self-addressed envelope

SASE: self-addressed, stamped envelope

Self-publishing: author assumes complete responsibility for publishing and marketing the book, including printing, binding, advertising, and distributing the book

Simultaneous submission: manuscript submitted to more than one publisher at the same time; also known as a multiple submission

Slush pile: term used within the publishing industry to describe unsolicited manuscripts

Small press: an independent publisher that publishes a limited or specialized list

Solicited manuscript: manuscript that an editor has asked for or agreed to consider

Subsidiary rights: book contract rights other than book publishing rights, such as book club, movie rights, etc.

Subsidy publishing: author pays publisher for all or part of a book's publication, promotion, and sale

Synopsis: condensed description of a fiction manuscript

Tearsheet: page from a magazine or newspaper containing your printed story or article

Trade book: book published for retail sale in bookstores

Unsolicited manuscript: any manuscript not specifically requested by an editor; "no unsolicited manuscripts" generally means the editors will only consider queries or manuscripts submitted by agents

Vanity press: see **Subsidy publishing**

Whole language: educational approach integrating literature into classroom curricula

Work-for-hire: work specifically ordered, commissioned, and owned by a publisher for its exclusive use

Writers' guidelines: publisher's editorial objectives or specifications, which usually include word lengths, readership level, and subject matter

Young adult: children ages 12 years and older

Young reader: the general classification of books written for readers between the ages of 5 and 8

Gateway to
the Markets

Biographies
at Their Best

By Peggy Thomas

T he shelves holding the children's biographies at
Barclay Elementary in Brockport, New York, are messy
and clearly picked over. Librarian Suzanne Shearman
straightens them and tells me, "More. We need more biographies, not just of famous people, but also about men and
women children haven't heard of yet." My mind spins. That
is a clarion call that any writer likes to hear.

In this disconcerting climate of library closings, school
budget cuts, and an ever-changing publishing industry, how
are children's biographies faring? John Riley, owner of Morgan Reynolds Publishing, which produces approximately 20
to 30 young adult biographies a year, acknowledges that the
book market is tight. "We are discovering, however, that
high-quality biographies as well as other titles are holding
up."

Emily Mitchell, Senior Editor at Charlesbridge Publishing,
also mentions budget constraints but adds, "Books with cur-
ricular hooks are more likely to attract those diminishing dol-
lars." David H. Dilkes, Managing Editor at Enslow Publishers,
sees "more demand for biographies of pop culture celebri-
ties and other current cultural figures."

Creating that high-quality, curriculum-hooking biography
that is in demand takes research: research to select an
appropriate subject, to find primary sources, and to discover
the story behind the person.

Likely and Unlikely Suspects

Not everyone is worthy of a new children's biography. Bookshelves are filled with the usual suspects—presidents, heroes, and geniuses—but there is always room for one more on a famous subject, if the book approaches the subject in a fresh and different way. An endless supply of George Washington biographies walk across library and school shelves. I never intended to add to that supply until I stumbled upon a fact few children know: Washington loved being a farmer. In *Farmer George Plants a Nation,* I showed his love of country reflected in his love of farming. That slant appealed to Carolyn Yoder, Editor of Calkins Creek Books, an imprint of Boyds Mills Press, and Senior Editor, History, for *Highlights for Children.* "I not only want to see the subject's story," says Yoder, "but also the author's take on it—what she or he is going to tell me, how the portrait is painted. A fresh approach is essential."

Mitchell agrees. Charlesbridge has picture book biographies in the works about Mark Twain and Emily Dickinson, two well-known and often chronicled writers. *Bambino and Mr. Twain,* by P. I. Maltbie, and *Emily and Carlo,* by Marty Rhodes Figley, caught Mitchell's eye because of their unusual viewpoints. "Each one looks at the writer through the lens of their relationship with a beloved pet." The lesson for writers interested in taking on a biography may be to look at the lesser-known aspects of a famous person's life.

When the curriculum leads to an entire grade reporting on a subject such as inventors, librarians like Shearman need to offer biographies of men and women other than the popular Thomas Edison and Henry Ford. Some publishers, like Enslow and Morgan Reynolds, answer the call with biography series in which famous names sit alongside unfamiliar ones. Enslow's Genius at Work! Great Inventor Biographies profiles Les Paul and George Ferris, among others. Although not as famous as Edison, these inventors have what Mitchell at Charlesbridge calls the "cool" factor because they are "notable enough in some kid-friendly way." Les Paul invented the electric guitar and Ferris gave us the ferris wheel.

The Charlesbridge title and Sibert Honor book, *The Day-Glo Brothers,* by Chris Barton, is a prime example. It tells the story of relatively unknown entrepreneurs Joe and Bob Switzer. The cool factor is in their invention of Day-Glo paint, which is used in every aspect of life from sports to health and safety to toys. Their story also has the added element of magic; one of the brothers was a magician.

The biographies offered by Morgan Reynolds are primarily proposed by editors in-house and closely reflect what schools and libraries need. For these editors, the determining factor is whether a person's contribution to a field is significant enough to make the book worthwhile. One relatively unknown figure that Morgan Reynolds chose to feature is Bayard Rustin. "Rustin," Riley says, "was an extremely important figure in the civil rights movement. Martin Luther King considered him to be indispensable because of his organizational talent and his long experience working with labor unions." *No Easy Answers: Bayard Rustin and the Civil Rights Movement,* by Calvin Craig Miller, earned the Carter G. Woodson Award, given annually for the most distinguished social science book for young readers depicting ethnicity in the U.S.

Alive and Well

Biographies are not all about dead people. "Many popular contemporary figures are worthwhile projects because they encourage students to read," says Ben Rosenthal, Associate Editor at Enslow. Young sports figures like Shaun White

60

and Dave Mirra easily capture boys' interest, and Lisa Rondinelli Albert's biography of Stephenie Meyer was a timely topic for girls following Meyer's blockbuster novel, *Twilight*.

Enslow believes in putting a positive spin on contemporary biographies. The series Sports Stars Who Give Back promotes the importance of community service and shows readers how to do the same. People who are in the news are good topics but, says Dilkes, "It's important to balance someone's popularity with the amount of material already published."

At Morgan Reynolds, Riley says, "We try to make sure the subjects we choose are not flash in the pans, which is why we haven't done current pop stars." The company does publish books on prominent current personalities in business, politics, arts, and sports.

Misinformation, the Kiss of Death

No matter who your subject is, Yoder advises, "There is really no other way you can uncover a personality without him or her speaking." In other words, use primary sources, which can include diaries, letters, period newspaper articles, photos, newsreels, and interviews.

"Primary sources in a biography help set the character in time and place," says Rosenthal. "They give the book more authenticity." To help students get a fuller picture of a time period, Enslow biographies usually feature photos of primary source artifacts as well as images of documents.

"It is also important to include how a person was perceived by the press, family, and enemies," says Yoder, although she cautions, "The biographer needs to know what to do with all that information, which tends to be biased or purposely incomplete. Primary sources cannot be taken at face value." When submitting a biography to Calkins Creek, writers must include a detailed bibliography.

"Misinformation is the kiss of death," comments Riley, who believes primary sources are critical. "We often tell writers to check and triple check their information and their sources."

Mitchell is editing *Music Was It: Young Leonard Bernstein,* a biography that includes family photos, college lecture notes, and early scores of the composer and conductor. Author Susan Goldman Rubin's ability "to work with primary source material like this, in addition to (her) personal interviews conducted with Bernstein's family and friends, helped her bring Lenny's personality to life on the page." Mitchell believes that Rubin's work is a great model for students doing their own research.

"I like to see that the author has already started gathering primary source material, or at least knows where it can be found and (ideally) how much it's likely to cost to access or reproduce," Mitchell says. "It's always good to see that the author has made connections to the right people and garnered their enthusiasm for the project. It makes it easier for me to pitch the proposal to my bosses."

Editors at Enslow and Morgan Reynolds concur. "In the first draft of a manuscript or an author's outline," says Rosenthal, "I like to make sure authors have a good source base." In addition to primary sources, that would include recent, preferably scholarly, secondary sources and high-quality websites.

A Good Story

Besides accurate research, a biography must read like a good story told in a clear narrative arc, and feature strong characters. "It should tell us something about the person more than just born, lived, died," says Mitchell.

"A good biography goes beyond discussing the nuts and bolts of a person," says Rosenthal. "Obviously, a standard chronology of a person is essential. All the important moments and dates need to be discussed. But a biography that displays the subject's humanity and what they were like as a person makes the book interesting."

To achieve that, Riley often tells his authors, "Write like a storyteller as much as possible. Think about pacing and when to stop the chronological progressions to discuss an important point or an event."

Start out strong. "A good biography for young readers needs to have a hook chapter that will make the child want to keep reading," says Dilkes. "I guarantee you the youngster is more likely to check out or purchase the book that starts with an exciting scene or anecdote rather than background information."

Mix humor, tragedy, and triumph to bring a real character to life.

Rosenthal suggests mixing humorous, tragic, and triumphant anecdotes to bring the character to life. One example he gives is *Elizabeth Cady Stanton: Woman Knows the Cost of Life,* by Deborah Kent, who included this story: Stanton could not get her sons to stop cursing at the dinner table, so she invited several prominent male figures over one evening. All through dinner, Stanton and her friends cursed. Her sons were so embarrassed that they promised to stop swearing if she did. Including a funny story like this reminds readers  that an otherwise solemn-looking figure in an old black-and-white photo was a real person with emotions and a sense of humor.

"Another way to make a biography unique is to break down myths," says Rosenthal. In the Enslow biography *Billy the Kid: It Was a Game of Two and I Got There First,* author Paul B. Thompson mentions legends about Billy that sprang up over time and explains how they came to be and why they are not true.

Biographies do not have to span a person's entire life. Mitchell says, "Because our books are not part of a series, we have more freedom to tailor the tone, focus, format, and illustration style of each book to fit the subject in question. We are not looking for every biography to cover the same aspects of the subject's life, and we're not tied to a particular structure."

Biography Markets

- **Calkins Creek:** Publishes books on American history. Editor Carolyn Yoder welcomes queries and full manuscripts for biographies. The guidelines are those for Boyds Mills Press, available on the website. Unsolicited submissions are welcome. For biographies and other nonfiction, include a detailed bibliography; a review by an expert on the subject, if possible; an explanation of marketplace competition; and a list of art or photos (and permissions information, if applicable). Regular mail submissions only. Titles include *Noah Webster: Weaver of Words, Sybil's Night Ride,* and *Jeannette Rankin: Political Pioneer.*

- **Charlesbridge Publishing:** Writers submitting a biography manuscript must follow Charlesbridge's general submission guidelines, found on the website. Unsolicited manuscripts must be sent as exclusive submissions. Nonfiction submissions should include a detailed proposal, chapter outline, and three chapters. Regular mail only. Biography titles include *Akira to Zoltan: Twenty-Six Men Who Changed the World, Amelia to Zora: Twenty-Six Women Who Changed the World, Into the Deep: The Life of Naturalist Explorer William Beebe,* and *Margaret Chase Smith: A Woman for President.*

- **Enslow Publishers:** Although most biography projects start in-house, writers may present ideas for new series or titles to fit into an ongoing series. To be considered for biography assignments, send a résumé. Among its many series are African-American Biographies, American Rebels, Authors Teens Love, Awesome Values in Famous Lives, Great Minds of Ancient Science and Math, Heroes of Racing, Hispanic Biographies, Holocaust Heroes and Nazi Criminals, Internet Biographies, Rebels of Rock, and Sports Leaders.

- **Morgan Reynolds Publishing:** Biographies are developed in-house and writers are selected for each project. Submit a résumé and writing samples to be considered for future projects. Biography series include American Business Leaders, American Originals (writers), Civil Rights Leaders; Civil War Generals, Classical Composers, European Queens, Political Profiles, Profiles in Science, Social Critics and Reformers, and Women Adventurers.

In other words, do not tell all the same stories. Look for different ones. In *Farmer George Plants a Nation,* I mention Washington's years as a general in the Revolutionary Army and his work as the first president of our nation, but only as they related to his time away from Mount Vernon. Freezing in a tent on a battlefield, he wrote home about his spring lambs, and at his presidential desk Washington designed a 16-sided barn.

With the right research into curriculum-hooking characters who have a kid-friendly story to tell, you just may be able to fill those library shelves with biographies that children will enjoy and benefit from for years to come.

Lights! Camera! Action-Adventure Novels!

By Katherine Swarts

E very summer the blockbusters arrive. Usually crammed with nonstop action and quirky characters with little psychological depth, these movies are as big as they are because of the audience's natural love of story. Almost every moviegoer—and adventure reader—is motivated to know the answer to "What happened next?"

Action-adventure stories for young people appeal to the voracious reader and to the reluctant reader. When an exciting story combines with a few levels of character and introspection (Harry and Hermione, and Bella and Edward are frequently mentioned successful models), the book may be irresistible. A prospective adventure writer needs to be a good judge of how long a story should run, but even more, of how the action should flow.

Pacing the Plot

"Start late—close to the action—and end early—soon after the resolution," is the advice of Rachelle Delaney, author of *Ship of Lost Souls* (HarperCollins Canada). "I tend to write slow beginnings, which I always have to rewrite in later drafts."

"Cut all narration, dialogue, plot tangents, and secondary characters not essential to the story," says

Pam Glauber, Associate Editor at Holiday House. "Read the manuscript aloud; you'll get a better sense of pacing. If you've been talking for ten minutes and your protagonist hasn't reached the next step in his or her journey, it's time to start cutting."

In all but the shortest adventure books, occasional pauses are necessary to let readers catch their breath. "Be careful of following one breathless action scene with another without any moments of pause," says Liesa Abrams, Execu-

"Let the truly thrilling moments stand out. Think in terms of natural balance, as in music."

tive Editor of Aladdin, an imprint of Simon & Schuster. "It can become desensitizing without dips and jumps to make the truly thrilling moments stand out. I advise my writers to think in terms of natural balance, as in music." Aladdin has published such titles as *Pendragon*, by D.J. MacHale, and *Fablehaven*, by Brandon Mu.

Conversely, pauses must not bring the story to a premature standstill. "Balance character and plot development," says Stephanie Hedlund, Editorial Director of ABDO Publishing's Spotlight and Magic Wagon imprints. "Recover from an intense scene by giving a character's background, emotions, and reactions in two to three sentences or paragraphs." ABDO publishes, among other series, the Ghostly Graphic Adventures, and the Adventures of Marshall & Art.

Chapters, the most natural breaks, traditionally are evenly spaced and end at a strong *what happens next*? points—either imminently threatening situations or apparent impasses.

"Chapter endings are important" for building suspense, says Ron Hatch, Director of the Canadian literary publisher Ronsdale Press. To retain a smooth flow, those endings must be "a series of mini-climaxes leading up to the final climax."

On Many Fronts

Adventure books feature high tension and an expanding of the protagonist's horizons. Beyond that, stories can take the form of many genres: fantasy, historical, even humor. Subcategories of adventure can be subject to trends and fads.

"I really don't think anyone should write with trends in mind," says Delaney. "By the time you've churned out a book about sexy goblins—seriously, the phrase 'sexy goblin book' was in a *Publishers Weekly* article about emerging trends at the Bologna Book Fair—publishers will be looking for books about sexy leprechauns. Write what interests you, amazes you, delights you, keeps you awake at night. If you feel passionately about it, there are readers out there who will feel the same."

Abrams agrees: "I hate talking about the next big thing. It's impossible to truly predict a phenomenon, and no writer should ever write to a trend anyway. When editors receive cover letters that proclaim a manuscript to be *Twilight* meets *Gossip Girl,* we glaze over; we want something that is fresh and special in its own right."

General categories may be worth considering, however, if they fit your taste. "Young adult paranormal romances continue to be in demand," says Glauber. "Perhaps the popularity of the Percy Jackson series will incite a Greek myth trend among middle-grade adventure novels."

"For ages 8 to 12," says Hedlund, "mystery and historical adventures sell well. With the success of films such as *Avatar* and *Sherlock Holmes,* fantasy and detective adventures will be a huge part of the market for the foreseeable future."

Perhaps the most important point is to match your interests to the publisher's. No contemporary-romance publisher wants a hard-science novel set in the thirty-fifth century, no matter how good the story in itself. Most publishing houses are very specific about what they do and do not want. At Ronsdale, for example, Hatch says, "We only do history and problem novels." Its *Journey to Atlantis,* by Philip Roy, is a sea adventure involving history and myth.

The Making of an Adventurer

A story's central problem, or another key plot element, is often where adventure writers start planning their fiction, and a compelling plot is indeed vital. If a book is to have staying power, however, the characters should be equally well-developed.

"Every great book, no matter the genre," says Abrams, should be character-driven. If the action doesn't stem from a specific character's needs and flaws, readers won't invest in even the most stunning scenes." Readers who empathize with a protagonist share the character's driving desires: "We care about Frodo's epic adventure to destroy the one ring because he cares about protecting the shire."

"You never really know someone until you've seen them in a crisis," says Delaney. "One of the best ways to develop characters is to put them in crisis and see how they react. Interesting characters with relationships and inner struggles elevate any plot to a higher level. *The Hunger Games,* by Suzanne Collins, is an excellent example."

Character becomes especially important in series. Significant growth in the protagonist is a major element in most stories, yet if the same hero is to carry dozens or even hundreds of plots, he cannot realistically change all that much. "For unlimited series," says Hedlund, "the reader needs to connect to a character, such as Joey DeAngelo of Magic Wagon's Ghostly Graphic Adventures series, and want to read all of his adventures." Writers who like the greater depth of stories involving significant human change, but also the appeal of recurring characters, might consider creating a series protagonist with a fairly stable personality who can be a catalyst for change in guest stars.

Generally, it is better not to be too series-minded when creating a first novel. Editors hesitate to risk more than a one-time shot on an untried author. "I don't think there's anything wrong with having a series in the back of your head," says Delaney, but the book "needs to stand on its own and should be pitched as such." Often, editors "judge series potential by the first book's sales."

A Universe of Approaches

Not every writer can create a series character like Superman or Nancy Drew, whose basic appeal holds through decades of changing times. Even editors who specialize in series are wary about premature assurances of indefinite sequels.

"ABDO looks for characters or story lines that can be featured in four to six books," says Hedlund. "Each book needs a resolution, and something to entice the reader to continue with the next book, such as the continuing battle against evil in Magic Wagon's Tommy Bomani: Teen Warrior series."

In a series or as a stand-alone, the graphic novel is a variation on the adventure novel that continues to gain ground. "In graphic novels," says Hedlund, "sentences and paragraphs are much shorter, and character development is more reliant on dialogue and art." A balanced pace matters here, too: "Several panels of talking will bore the reader, but a full page of fight panels may be overwhelming."

Another subgenre, which might be called educational fiction, teaches nonfiction concepts through sidebars or interactive puzzle formats by which readers can help move the action forward. An example is *The Crystal Connection*, by Tanya Lloyd Kyi (Walrus Books/Whitecap Books), a middle-grade mystery with sidebars consisting of related science experiments. The U.K.'s Usborne Publishing originated the Puzzle Adventure Books a generation ago, and has re-issued some. Each page spread invites readers to figure out a picture puzzle; the solution is at the back of the book.

Other adventure stories have nonfiction appendices: "Holiday House backmatter often includes source notes and additional historical information," notes Glauber. An example is Alison Lloyd's *Year of the Tiger*, a middle-grade adventure about ancient China.

More frequently, educational qualities simply blend into the plot. "The historical facts I remember best I learned from novels," says Delaney. "But mixing fact and fiction is a fine art; the author can't sound pedantic. For excellent examples, read *Catherine Called Birdy*, by Karen Cushman, or *Chains*, by Laurie Halse Anderson."

Whether or not they deliberately intend their adventure novels to teach, all writers need to know the real world facts about their settings. "Underlying nonfiction elements must be thoroughly researched and verified," says Glauber. "Become an authority on the topic; it gives you credibility and helps avoid embarrassing mistakes."

Look to successful and experienced writers—and also to the bad examples. "Read popular stories as well as poorly reviewed ones," says Hedlund. "Take notes on how and when character development and background information are placed, in successful and not-so-successful stories. By doing research, you improve your own writing."

Adventures of Another Sort

Most people associate adventure with high physical stakes: a quest for treasure; a battle against evil; an exploration of unmapped territory. But in some adventures, the dangers are more abstract.

"Of all the adventures humankind has undertaken," says Dale Carlson, President of Bick Publishing House and author of two YA science fiction novels (*The Human Apes* and *The Mountain of Truth*), "the most difficult, the most frightening, is the inner voyage. The ongoing adventure of understanding ourselves (individually and as a species), and changing ourselves through that understanding, is more frightening and exciting than any invented adventure. And the ending

Adventure Markets

Many publishers offer adventure titles, both fiction and nonfiction. Here are a select few.

- **ABDO Publishing:** PreK to age middle-grade.
- **Action Publishing:** Picture books to YA.
- **Aladdin:** PreK to middle-grade, Simon & Schuster imprint.
- **Bick Publishing:** Science fiction adventure for teens.
- **Boyds Mills:** Toddler books to YA.
- **Cedar Fort:** Inspirational fiction, 8 to 18.
- **Chaosium:** Publisher of role-playing games, and related adventure, fantasy, and horror books.
- **Chronicle Books:** All ages and formats.
- **Clarion Books:** Picture books, chapter books, novels.
- **Egmont USA:** Thrillers are a particular interest.
- **Gumboot Books:** Canadian; environmental focus.
- **HarperCollins:** Its many imprints offer adventure in various forms and for many ages.
- **High Noon:** Books for struggling readers.
- **Holiday House:** Fiction and nonfiction, ages 4 to 18.
- **Just Us Books:** African American experience and history.
- **Wendy Lamb:** Random House imprint of middle-grade and YA fiction.
- **Medallion Press:** Genre fiction, including adventure.
- **Mondo Publishing:** Reluctant readers.
- **Napoleon & Company:** Canadian, ages 5 to 18.
- **Peter Pauper:** Specialty publisher that includes adventure books on its list.
- **Pioneer Drama:** Adventure plays, ages 4 to 18.
- **Rayve Productions:** Self-help publisher that has a list of children's books, including adventures.
- **Razorbill:** A YA imprint of Penguin.
- **Reagent Press:** Small press, ages 4 to 12.
- **Ronsdale Press:** Canadian, middle-grade and YA fiction.
- **Smith & Sons:** Imprint of Smith and Kraus, building its adventure, fantasy, and science fiction list.
- **Stone Arch:** Reluctant reader fiction imprint of Capstone.
- **TokyoPop:** Graphic novels, ages 5 to 18.

remains mysterious and unknown. It is this inner adventure our books invite readers to undertake."

Then there is the picture book adventure that involves no real danger at all, simply exciting new experiences such as small children find everywhere. Many picture books let kids vicariously realize the dream of escaping adult supervision to see what else the world offers: Examples include Maurice Sendak's classic *Where the Wild Things Are* (Harper & Row); *Barn Dance!* by Bill Martin Jr. and John Archambault (Henry Holt); *Piggy Wiglet,* by David L. Harrison (Boyds Mills Press); and *I'm Really Not Tired,* by Lori Sunshine (Flashlight Press). In all these, the protagonist returns safely home at the end—a night's or day's worth of adventure being sufficient for small children who still crave the ultimate security of adult protection.

Ultimately, all of life is as much an adventure as we make it; the younger we are, the better we seem to understand this.

Have Fun with Nonfiction for Early Readers

By Joanne Mattern

Years ago, when I was working as a staff writer and editor at Troll Communications, the president of the company said to me, "You can write about any subject for even the youngest children, provided you find the right approach." Her words stuck with me, and over the course of my writing career I discovered just how true they are.

Readers ages five to eight have a huge range of books and subject matter to choose from, and the overall quality of the writing is high. This age level provides special challenges and rewards for writers, despite the deceptive words that often describe it: *easy, beginning, early*. Interpret those words wisely. They describe books that lay an important foundation for literacy and readers growing in capabilities and interests.

Curiosity Rocks!

Nonfiction for early readers is as much fun to write as to read, if it is done well. April Pulley Sayre, an award-winning children's book author of more than 55 titles, identifies curiosity as the main reason she finds writing nonfiction for beginning readers a pleasure. "This is such a curious age, an open-to-the-world age," she says. "What they love is what I love."

Vijaya Bodach, author of *How do Toys Work?* (Macmillan/ McGraw Hill) and Capstone series such as Books for Young Mathematicians, as well as many magazine articles, agrees: "At this age, everything is exciting and fun. Kids are learning about the world they live in and are naturally curious about why the sky is blue, why cats purr, or why dead plants come back to life." It is a bonus, Bodach says, that "writing for this age group allows me to satisfy my own curiosity as well."

Being the reader's first teacher appeals strongly to Dana Rau, an award-winning author who has published nonfiction for Marshall Cavendish Benchmark (*Nature's Cycles: Animals*), Cherry Lake Publishing (*It's Cool to Learn About Countries: Nigeria*), and Capstone's Compass Point Books (*Our Solar System: Black Holes*). "When you write for very young readers, you have the honor of being the first one to introduce them to a topic," she says.

Lyn Sirota enjoys surprising children with information that changes the way they look at the world. In her 14 nonfiction animal and nature books, and her many articles for periodicals such as *Science News, Highlights,* and *Ladybug,* she has found, "The most fun is discovering those nuggets of information that just make kids say 'Wow!' Or getting them to realize that an animal they had a bad impression of isn't so bad after all. I enjoy helping them to see the other side. It's like watching their minds open to different possibilities."

Early reader books even allow authors to cultivate their own childhood interests and fun. Amy Hansen, author of *Bugs & Bugsicles: Insects in the Winter* (Boyds Mills Press), says, "With the younger kids, I get to share my enthusiasms. I used the word *bugsicle* to describe frozen bugs. I don't get to go around making up words in older writing!"

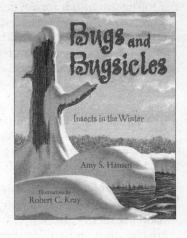

Editors share in the fun. Lori Shores, Assistant Editor of nonfiction at Capstone Press, has edited a variety of books for beginning and reluctant readers from preschool to fifth grade. She says, "Children are curious about the world around them. They have a natural wonder and fascination about everything. Working on children's nonfiction keeps me connected to that. In a way, the topics become brand-new again for me. The best part is that I know kids will also be fascinated about a topic when they read the books."

Bonnie Hinman, author of 20 nonfiction books including *We Visit Panama* (Mitchell Lane), loves how children are so open to learning. "Everything is new to this audience, and exciting. They love learning about almost anything if the information is presented in an absorbing manner."

Not All Fun and Games

The openness of children five to eight is balanced by the challenges of writing for early readers. Foremost among them is a young child's limited reading and comprehension skills as compared to those of more established, older elementary and middle-grade readers.

"One of the biggest challenges is distilling down complex information into a form young children can understand," says Rau. "You can't assume they have prior knowledge about a topic. You work with limited word count and vocabulary. You have to find a creative way to introduce your topic in their language." Hansen agrees, saying simply, "I have to remember what kids know and what they don't know."

Editors of young nonfiction are keenly aware of the possibilities and the limitations. "A lot of hard work goes into the simplest books," Capstone's Shores says. "Explaining high-level concepts in a way that children will understand is seldom easy."

Carol Hinz, Editorial Director of Millbrook Press, says, "Distilling complex concepts into something accessible for young readers can be tricky for writers and editors alike. Sticking to a limited vocabulary and keeping reading levels low is another big challenge." Tamar Mays, Senior Editor of the I Can Read! Books at HarperCollins, concurs: "The biggest challenge is how to present topics in a manner that makes sense to the young reader."

Editor's Advice

- **Carol Hinz, Editorial Director of Millbrook Press:** "I want writers to know that nonfiction is a lot of fun. Follow your passion. When you are genuinely interested in a topic, it will show through in your writing."
- **Luana Mitten, Editor in Chief, Rourke Publishing:** "Writing nonfiction for younger readers is the *best!* Learn everything you can about young readers' interests and what works in text to support children who are learning to read. Reading both nonfiction books for kids and reviews of these books is one way to gather info."
- **Jonathan Rosenbloom, Editor, Time Learning Ventures:** "Have fun with the writing; it's okay to be humorous if appropriate."

Ultimately, creativity is the key to success, but tried-and-true writing techniques help creativity succeed.

Many authors report that using comparisons is a great way to make complicated subject matter relevant to young readers. Numbers and measurements, for instance, can be meaningless to children who cannot put them in context. Hansen solves this problem by "finding examples of what kids know. So, if I need to say a water pipe has a 100-inch diameter, I say it is big enough for the tallest basketball player to stand up inside." That is a comparison children can instantly visualize and comprehend.

Melissa Stewart, whose 100-plus books about science and nature include *Ants* (National Geographic Readers), says, "I often rely on comparisons to make an idea relevant to children's daily experiences. For example, in a book I'm working on now, I tell readers that if they had a tongue as long as a frog's, they could use it to wash out their belly buttons. What kid wouldn't love that tidbit?"

Playing with words is another way to keep young readers focused and interested. Stewart often uses language devices like alliteration, rhythm, and repetition. "If text is pleasing to the ear, young children will enjoy it more."

Sayre agrees. "I use a lot of rhythm and onomatopoeia in my writing. I don't really think about it. It just happens because I love the sound of energetic language." Young readers love that sound too.

Author Fiona Bayrock also uses language and sentence structure to make her writing

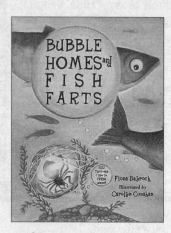

pop: "I use words to create images in my readers' heads. I do this by choosing powerful verbs and specific language. I also have fun with words where appropriate, incorporating humor, str-e-t-c-h-ing words or making them LOUD, sprinkling a few questions throughout, and using an 'Ack!', 'Who knew?', or 'No kidding!' from time to time." Bayrock has written nonfiction for Scholastic Canada, Capstone, and Charlesbridge (*Bubble Homes and Fish Farts*).

The new, a twist—something striking—is as important in a book for a kindergartener or first grader as for an adult. It's also important to remember to put yourself in the reader's shoes. "My approach to writing nonfiction for any age is to include facts or stories or ideas that caught my interest. I'm always on the lookout for quirky or unusual facts," says Hinman.

Capturing readers right away is another key. "When submitting a manuscript to a publisher, it is important that your first few paragraphs draw the reader in," says Carmen Bredeson. She offers an example from one of her many books, *Animals That Migrate* (Franklin Watts). "The chapter about red crabs begins with, 'How would you like to wake up during the night and have a crab crawling across your pillow, or even your face? That happens to some of the people who live on Christmas Island.'"

Editors appreciate writers who can face challenges with creative flair and a true understanding of their young readers. Shores says, "The text needs to be easy to understand and appropriate, but if we can't grab the reader's attention, it

Visuals Matter

Look at any nonfiction book for young readers and you will see a volume packed with photographs, illustrations, and even cartoons. These visual hooks are a key ingredient to grabbing a reader's attention and making the material more accessible and interesting.

Policies about photographs and artwork vary among publishers, with some publishers handling all the photo research in-house or commissioning illustrations themselves. Other publishers require the author to provide photos, either by taking them personally or finding them online or through other resources.

No matter what the terms of your contract are, editors always appreciate a lead to a great photo or other illustrative reference, so be sure to pass along anything you find when doing your research.

won't matter. Quirky facts and enthusiastic writing convince the reader that the subject is awesome. An editor can help with leveling the material and making sure the information is appropriate for the intended age, but the real secret is providing high-quality writing that keeps the reader interested."

Hinz, at Millbrook Press, also values authors who can focus on what matters for young readers. "A writer who is genuinely interested in a topic and has a lot of background knowledge" has qualities that go "a long way."

Just the Facts

Tackling controversial subject matter for early readers presents particular obstacles. But when a subject is a difficult one, editors and writers agree, sticking to the basics is best. Luana Mitten, Editor in Chief of Rourke, a publisher of nonfiction for young readers, says, "To borrow a line from Joe Friday, 'Just the (age-appropriate) facts, ma'am' is how we decide what should be included in the book."

Hinz advises "writers to accurately convey what happened without going into a level of detail that might be inappropriate for young readers."

The author of early reader biographies such as Scholastic News's *Jane Goodall*, Jo Kittinger thinks, "You can state some basic facts without giving too much detail or trying to moralize about the issue."

Editors also want authors to keep their personal biases out of their writing. Mitten recalls a book she recently edited on farm animals. "In the manuscript, I discovered that the writer had a definite opinion about how animals were treated on large farms versus small farms. Through the editing process and photo selections, we were able to present accurate information without opinion."

Shores adamantly agrees. "It's not the editor's or the author's place to make judgments in nonfiction. That said, it's also important to keep the focus on the reader. Some details are not going to be appropriate for children, no matter how unbiased we are."

"Generate a passion for learning with interesting books written at the right reading level, and you can create lifelong learners."

Starting Young

Writers and editors are passionate about creating nonfiction books for young readers, and with good reason. "I believe that if you can generate a passion for learning by providing interesting books at an appropriate reading level, you can create lifelong learners," says Kittinger.

At Time Learning Ventures/Time for Kids Media Group, Editor Jonathan Rosenbloom also sees a bigger responsibility. When asked what he finds the most fun about editing nonfiction for readers ages five to eight, Rosenbloom answers: "making difficult concepts understandable and accessible to young children; helping them better understand their world and their place in it; helping them feel smart; and knowing that we are helping kids to become

Publisher Information

● **Capstone Press/Compass Point Books:** Capstone is always looking for new authors for nonfiction assignments. Writers interested in writing nonfiction for the company should send a letter of interest, résumé, and writing sample to the Editorial Director, Capstone Nonfiction, 7825 Telegraph Road, Bloomington, MN 55438.

● **HarperCollins Publishers:** HarperCollins has perhaps the best known of early reader series, I Can Read. It accepts submissions only through literary agents.

● **Millbrook Press:** A Lerner Publishing imprint that focuses on classroom and library books, most in series. Check the website regularly for targeted submission needs.

● **Rourke Publishing:** Most of Rourke's writers are under "work for hire" contracts and topics are assigned by the publisher. They accept queries that provide a résumé and information on the age level and topics you are interested in writing for. All queries can be sent directly to Luana Mitten at luana@rourkepublishing.com or via snail mail to Luana Mitten, Rourke Publishing, LLC, 1701 Highway A1A, Suite 300, Vero Beach, FL 32963.

● **Time Learning Ventures/Time For Kids Media Group:** Does not accept any freelance submissions.

More Early Reader Nonfiction Publishers:

● Benchmark Books
● Boyds Mills Press
● Charlesbridge Publishing
● Clarion Books
● Darby Creek
● Dial Books
● Dorchester Publishing
● Enslow Publishers
● Harcourt
● HarperFestival
● Ideals Publications

● Innovative Kids
● Kaeden Books
● Lerner Publications
● Mitchell Lane
● PowerKids Press
● Sandlapper
● Schwartz & Wade
● Science, Naturally!
● Soundprints
● Sterling
● Paula Wiseman

confident readers and writers."

Exposure to good writing can be the start of something wonderful that has impact across children's lives. "We want children to read books, but more important, we want them to be enthusiastic about what they're learning," says Shores. It is never too early to capture a child's interest in the world and all its mysteries!

Listings

How to Use the Listings

On the following pages are 521 profiles of publishers involved in the wide range of children's publishing. More than 75 publishers, agents, and contest listings are new to the directory. These publishing houses produce a variety of material from parenting guides, textbooks, and classroom resources to picture books, photo-essays, middle-grade novels, and biographies.

Each year we update every listing through mailed surveys and telephone interviews. While we verify everything in the listing before we go to press, it is not uncommon for information such as contact names, addresses, and editorial needs to change suddenly. Therefore, we suggest that you always read the publisher's most recent writers' guidelines before submitting a query letter or manuscript.

If you are unable to find a particular publisher, check the Publishers' Index beginning on page 609 to see if it is cited elsewhere in the book. We do not list presses that publish more than 50 percent of their material by requiring writers to pay all or part of the cost of publishing. While we cannot endorse or vouch for the quality of every press we list, we do try to screen out publishers of questionable quality.

To help you judge a publisher's receptivity to unsolicited submissions, we include a Freelance Potential section in each listing. This is where we identify the number of titles published in 2010 that were written by unpublished writers, authors new to the publishing house, and agented authors. We also provide the total number of query letters and unsolicited manuscripts a publisher receives each year.

Use this information and the other information included in the listing to locate publishers that are looking for the type of material you have written or plan to write. Become familiar with the style and content of the house by studying its catalogue and a few recent titles.

Rourke Publishing

New Listing

1701 Highway A1A, Suite 300
Vero Beach, FL 32963

Editor in Chief: Luana Mitten

Who to Contact

Publisher's Interests

Rourke is a publisher of educational book series for kindergarten to grade eight. It concentrates on nonfiction series, and also publishes interactive ebooks. Rourke's series include Field Trips, Fighting Forces, the Study of Money, Action Sports, Eye on History Graphic Illustrated, and a new Factoscope science series.

Website: www.rourkepublishing.com

Website

Profile of Publisher & Readership

Freelance Potential

Published 150–200 books in 2010: many were freelance or written by contract writers, including previously unpublished authors.

Number of Books Published and Openness to Freelancers

- **Nonfiction:** Publishes picture books, 4–10 years; early readers and chapter books, 5–10 years; and middle-grade books, 9–12 years. Categories include science, social studies, reading adventures, reference, and sports.

Categories of Current Titles

- **Representative Titles:** *Hiking,* by Julie K. Lundren (grades 4–8), is one in a series about outdoor adventures. *Using Scientific Tools,* by Susan Meredith (grades 4–8), provides illustrations and explanations of tools used in a range of sciences.

Recent Titles to Study

Submissions and Payment

Query with résumé, indicating the topic and age of interest to you. Accepts hard copy or email to luana@rourkepublishing.com. Guidelines are sent to writers with their contracts. Work-for-hire, with a choice of 20 percent when the ms is approved and 80 percent after proofs, or a single payment after proofs.

How to Submit

Editor's Comments

We look for factual accuracy and objectivity, and for writers who understand the interests of children and how to write in such a way that gives them age-appropriate reading support.

Editor's Current Needs & Tips for Writers

Icon Key

 New Listing   E-publisher   Overseas Publisher

 Accepts agented submissions only

 Not currently accepting submissions

ABDO Publishing Company

8000 West 78th Street, Suite 310
Edina, MN 55439

Submissions Committee

Publisher's Interests
ABDO Publishing Company, a division of ABDO Publishing
Group, specializes in quality nonfiction for very young chil-
dren through young adults, and also publishes fiction under
its Spotlight and Magic Wagon imprints.
Website: www.abdopublishing.com

Freelance Potential
Published 450 titles in 2010: 12 were developed from unsolicited submissions. Of the 450 titles, 5 were by authors new
to the publishing house. Receives 360 queries each year.

- **Fiction:** Publishes early picture books, 0–4 years; easy-to-read
  books, 4–7 years; story picture books, 4–10 years; chapter
  books, 5–10 years; middle-grade books, 8–12 years. Categories include adventure, fantasy, fairy tales, graphic novels,
  holidays, mysteries.
- **Nonfiction:** Publishes early picture books, 0–4 years; easy-to-
  read books, 4–7 years; story picture books, 4–10 years; chapter books, 5–10 years; middle-grade books, 8–12 years; and
  young adult books, 12–18 years. Topics include animals, biography, nature, travel, geography, sciences, social studies,
  sports, history, leisure, and multicultural.
- **Representative Titles:** *The Body,* by Julie Murray (grades
  2–5), presents fascinating and utterly disgusting information
  about the human body; part of the That's Gross! A Look at
  Science series. *The Bermuda Triangle,* by Sue Hamilton
  (grades 5–9), delves into the mysteries surrounding this infa-
  mous patch of ocean; part of the Unsolved Mysteries series.

Submissions and Payment
Guidelines and catalogue available at website. Query with
résumé. No unsolicited mss. Accepts hard copy. SASE.
Response time varies. Publication period varies. Flat fee.

Editor's Comments
All books should be standards-based, in keeping with the
grade level curriculum, and thoroughly researched.

Abrams Books for Young Readers

115 West 18th Street, 6th Floor
New York, NY 10011

Editorial Department

Publisher's Interests
This imprint of Abrams Books publishes fiction and nonfiction titles (many of them award-winning and bestselling) for children and middle-grade readers.
Website: www.abramsbooks.com

Freelance Potential
Published 70 titles in 2010: all were by agented authors. Receives 1,200 queries yearly.

- **Fiction:** Publishes early picture books, 0–4 years; easy-to-read books, 4–7 years; story picture books, 4–10 years; middle-grade books, 8–12 years; and young adult books, 12–18 years. Genres include folklore, folktales, and stories about animals, nature, and the environment.
- **Nonfiction:** Publishes easy-to-read books, 4–7 years; story picture books, 4–10 years; and middle-grade books, 8–12 years. Topics include animals, history, art, and relationships.
- **Representative Titles:** *The Taming of Lola: A Shrew Story,* by Ellen Weiss (4–8 years), tells the story of a trouble-making little shrew who finally finds out what it's like on the receiving end of her behavior. *Mammoths and Mastodons: Titans of the Ice Age,* by Cheryl Bardoe (8–12 years), presents the latest research into the lives of these ancient beasts.

Submissions and Payment
Agented authors only. Writers' guidelines and catalogue available at website. Response time and publication period vary. Royalty; advance.

Editor's Comments
Due to the large volume already received, we will not review unsolicited works of fiction at this time. Please check our guidelines at the website for updates. For agented authors, please note that our current needs include girl-focused nonfiction and contemporary young adult nonfiction subjects. We will also accept other nonfiction subjects through agents.

A & C Black

36 Soho Square
London W1D 3QY
United Kingdom

Submissions Editor

Publisher's Interests

The children's division of A & C Black—a company founded
in 1807—publishes fiction, nonfiction, and teacher
resources for all reading levels. Its diverse catalogue
includes a range of topics from historical fiction and poetry
to books about science, animals, careers, and technology.
Website: www.acblack.com/children

Freelance Potential

Published 80 titles in 2010. Receives few queries yearly.

- **Fiction:** Publishes easy-to-read books, 4–7 years; chapter
  books, 5–10 years; middle-grade books, 8–12 years; and
  young adult books, 12–14 years. Genres include contemporary, historical, and science fiction; myths and legends;
  humor; and drama. Also publishes poetry.
- **Nonfiction:** Publishes easy-to-read books, 4–7 years; chapter
  books, 5–10 years; middle-grade books, 8–12 years; and
  young adult books, 12–14 years. Topics include art, design,
  technology, geography, history, music, physical education,
  sports, science, and social issues. Also publishes reference
  books and teacher resources.
- **Representative Titles:** *My First Book of Garden Bugs,* by Mike
  Unwin (4+ years), introduces kids to the creepy crawly things
  that live in the garden. *Detective Dan,* by Vivian French (7–11
  years), is the story of a young boy who tries to unravel the
  mystery of what's been happening to his lunchbox every day;
  part of the White Wolves series.

Submissions and Payment

Guidelines available. Catalogue available at website. Query
with synopsis and 2 sample chapters. Accepts hard copy.
SAE/IRC. Responds in 2 months. Publication period and payment policy vary.

Editor's Comments

Many of our books are part of guided reading series
designed for use in the classroom.

ACTA Publications

4848 North Clark Street
Chicago, IL 60640

Acquisitions Editor: Andrew Yankech

Publisher's Interests
This Christian publisher produces a variety of books and other material for children and adults seeking to expand the presence of God in their lives. ACTA has a large number of self-help books aimed at teens and parents. While its entire catalogue is Christian-themed, it prefers material that is aimed at a broadly ecumenical audience.
Website: www.actapublications.com

Freelance Potential
Published 15 titles (3 juvenile) in 2010: 1 was developed from an unsolicited submission, 1 was by an agented author, and 2 were reprint/licensed properties. Of the 15 titles, 2 were authors who were new to the publishing house. Receives 120 queries yearly.

- **Nonfiction:** Publishes story picture books, 4–10 years; and young adult books, 12–18 years. Topics include religion, parenting, divorce, grief, self-help, and history—all with a Christian theme.
- **Representative Titles:** *Catholic and College Bound: 5 Challenges and 5 Opportunities,* by George S. Szews (YA), is a guide for turning campus challenges into life-affirming examples of faith. *Someone Came Before You,* by Pat Schwiebert, addresses the surviving child of a family that has suffered a miscarriage or stillbirth.

Submissions and Payment
Guidelines and catalogue available at website. Query with table of contents, sample chapter, and market analysis. Accepts hard copy and simultaneous submissions if identified. SASE. Responds in 3–6 weeks. Publication in 9–12 months. Royalty, 10%.

Editor's Comments
We are especially interested in books for young adults on Catholic spirituality, grief, and family spirituality.

Action Publishing

P.O. Box 391
Glendale, CA 91209

Submissions Editor

Publisher's Interests
This independent publisher of children's picture books, juvenile and young adult titles, and adult trade nonfiction seeks titles that motivate and involve readers of all ages.
Website: www.actionpublishing.com

Freelance Potential
Published 4 titles (3 juvenile) in 2010: 1 was by an agented author. Of the 4 titles, 1 was by an unpublished writer and 1 was by a new author. Receives 200 queries, 850 mss yearly.

- **Fiction:** Publishes early picture books, 0–4 years; easy-to-read books, 4–7 years; story picture books, 4–10 years; chapter books, 5–10 years; middle-grade books, 8–12 years; and young adult books, 12–18 years. Genres include contemporary fiction, fantasy, and adventure.
- **Nonfiction:** Publishes middle-grade books, 8–12 years; and young adult books, 12–18 years. Topics include nature, the environment, and humor. Also publishes titles for parents.
- **Representative Titles:** *Look at the Size of That Long-Legged Ploot,* by Scott E. Sutton, is a story of adventure on the Planet of Ree that also teaches kids to treat others as you want them to treat you; part of the Family of Ree series. *Danger: Dinky Diplodocus,* by Scott E. Sutton (9–12 years), teaches about dinosaurs while engaging readers in a tale about dogs who go back in time; part of the Dinosaur Dog series.

Submissions and Payment
Guidelines and catalogue available at website. Query with outline and sample chapter; or send complete ms. Send complete ms for picture books. Accepts hard copy. SASE. Response time and publication period vary. Royalty; advance.

Editor's Comments
Unfortunately, we cannot respond to or critique each submission. If it doesn't meet our needs, we'll simply return it.

Active Parenting Publishers

1955 Vaughn Road, Suite 108
Kennesaw, GA 30144

Product Development Manager: Molly Davis

Publisher's Interests
Active Parenting Publishers delivers a variety of parenting books that provide parents with the skills to help their children survive and thrive in the changing world. Its titles cover child development issues from birth through the teen years.
Website: www.activeparenting.com

Freelance Potential
Published 4 titles in 2010. Receives 120 queries, 96 unsolicited mss yearly.

- **Fiction:** Publishes concept books, 0–4 years; story picture books, 4–10 years; middle-grade books, 8–12 years; and young adult books, 12–18 years. Offers stories about self-esteem and social issues.
- **Nonfiction:** Publishes concept books, 0–4 years; story picture books, 4–10 years; middle-grade books, 8–12 years; and young adult books, 12–18 years. Topics include gifted and special education, social issues, and parenting. Also publishes self-help titles.
- **Representative Titles:** *Taming the Spirited Child,* by Michael H. Popkin, offers strategies for understanding and taming a challenging child's behavior. *Parent's Guide,* by Michael H. Popkin, includes worksheets and activities at a 4th-grade reading level for parents who can't read English well.

Submissions and Payment
Guidelines available. Catalogue available at website. Query or send complete ms. Accepts hard copy and email submissions to cservice@activeparenting.com. SASE. Response time and publication period vary. Royalty. Flat fee.

Editor's Comments
Let us know why your idea will be successful in addressing the challenges of parenting, and how it is different from the competition. Our goal is to provide resources to build responsibility, courage, cooperation, and respect.

Adams Media Corporation

57 Littlefield Street
Avon, MA 02322

Book Proposals

Publisher's Interests
Adams Media Corporation publishes the popular Everything series of books, covering a broad range of topics of interest to adults and teens alike. Its catalogue also features reference books for studying and exam preparation.
Website: www.adamsmedia.com

Freelance Potential
Published 252 titles (1 juvenile) in 2010.

- **Nonfiction:** Publishes young adult books, 12–18 years. Topics include animals, careers, contemporary issues, fitness, health, hobbies, relationships, and social issues. Features humor, inspirational, self-help, exam-prep, and how-to books. Also publishes books for adults on business, cooking, home improvement, parenting, personal finance, women's issues, wedding planning, travel, and writing.
- **Representative Titles:** *The Everything Kids' Science Experiments Book,* by Tom Robinson, shows students how to expand their science horizons with experiments using everyday household items in surprising ways. *Fab Friends and Best Buds: Real Girls on Making Forever Friends,* by Erika V. Shearin Karres, offers tips on how to find and keep true friends, and how to recognize faux friends.

Submissions and Payment
Guidelines and catalogue available at website. Query with description of intended market, brief author biography, table of contents, and sample chapter. Accepts hard copy. SASE. No electronic submissions. Responds only if interested. Publication period varies. Royalty.

Editor's Comments
Whether you are a seasoned author or novice writer, we want to hear about your great ideas and how to market them. However, due to the volume of submissions, we cannot provide feedback on unsolicited manuscripts.

Aladdin

Simon & Schuster Children's Publishing
1230 Avenue of the Americas
New York, NY 10020

Executive Editor: Liesa Abrams

Publisher's Interests
The Aladdin imprint of Simon & Schuster offers original titles and reprints, in hardcover and paperback, for children from preschool to middle-grade, including early readers and chapter books. Aladdin Mix publishes books for tween girls that help them cross the bridge from childhood to the teen years.
Website: http://imprints.simonandschuster.biz/aladdin

Freelance Potential
Published 100 titles in 2010.

- **Fiction:** Publishes easy-to-read books, 4–7 years; story picture books, 4–10 years; chapter books, 5–10 years; and middle-grade books, 8–12 years. Genres include contemporary and historical fiction, suspense, mystery, fantasy, and adventure.
- **Nonfiction:** Publishes easy-to-read books, 4–7 years; and middle-grade books, 8–12 years. Topics include America's national monuments and natural wonders; childhood biographies of world figures; and humor.
- **Representative Titles:** *Artemis the Brave,* by Joan Holub, looks at tween issues in the dress of ancient myths. *The Secret of the Sealed Room; part of the Goddess Girl Series,* by Bailey MacDonald (8–12 years), is a mystery set in colonial Boston with the young Ben Franklin as a central character.

Submissions and Payment
Agented authors only. Does not accept unsolicited manuscripts. Response time, publication period, and payment policy vary.

Editor's Comments
Our current interests include action-adventure stories, school stories, coming-of-age stories, and humor. All submissions must come through a literary agent.

ALA Editions

American Library Association
50 East Huron Street
Chicago, IL 60611

Editorial Assistant: Megan O'Neill

Publisher's Interests

Providing librarians with the professional resources they
need to better serve their patrons and develop their careers
is the mission of ALA Editions, the publishing arm of the
American Library Association. It covers topics ranging from
children's programming to expanding digital services and
library management strategies.
Website: www.ala.org/editions

Freelance Potential

Published 30–35 titles in 2010: 1 was by an author who was
new to the publishing house. Receives 50 queries yearly.

- **Nonfiction:** Publishes professional resources for the library
  information services community. Topics include school services; acquisitions and collection development; library studies,
  issues, and trends; reference services and resources; technology; digital library operations and services; library administration and management; budgeting; fundraising; buildings
  and facilities; and children's programming.
- **Representative Titles:** *Public Libraries Going Green,* by
  Kathryn Miller, outlines ways in which libraries can join the
  green movement. *Boomers and Beyond: Reconsidering the
  Role of Libraries,* by Pauline Rothstein & Diantha Dow Schull,
  eds., explains the trends and perspectives on the library's role
  in meeting the needs of the aging population.

Submissions and Payment

Guidelines and catalogue available at website. Query with
outline, 300-word synopsis, table of contents, author bio,
and writing sample. Accepts hard copy. SASE. Responds in
6–8 weeks. Publication in 7–9 months. Royalty.

Editor's Comments

Most of our authors are library information services professionals, but we are open to writers from other areas—as long
as the research is sound and the advice is practical.

Ambassador Books

997 MacArthur Boulevard
Mahwah, NJ 07430

Acquisitions Editor: Jennifer Conlan

Publisher's Interests
Ambassador's children's titles seek to promote an understanding that children are precious in the eyes of God, and to introduce the basic concepts of living a godly life.
Website: www.ambassadorbooks.com

Freelance Potential
Published 8–10 titles in 2010: 5 were developed from unsolicited submissions. Of the 8–10 titles, 2 were by unpublished writers and 2 were by authors new to the publishing house. Receives 1,200 queries, 120 unsolicited mss yearly.

- **Fiction:** Publishes easy-to-read books, 4–7 years; story picture books, 4–10 years; and middle-grade books, 8–12 years. Genres include inspirational, religious, historical, and regional fiction; adventure; mystery; and suspense. Also publishes books about spirituality in sports.
- **Nonfiction:** Publishes easy-to-read books, 4–7 years; story picture books, 4–10 years; and middle-grade books, 8–12 years. Topics include religion, sports, and regional subjects. Also publishes self-help titles.
- **Representative Titles:** *I Can Speak Bully*, by Kevin Morrison (5–9 years), features a boy who turns an experience with a bully into a positive adventure. *Finn's Marching Band*, by Rachelle Evensen (2–5 years), teaches counting and color concepts while showing that we all have God-given gifts.

Submissions and Payment
Guidelines available. Catalogue available at website. Query with outline/synopsis, 3 sample chapters, author bio, and market analysis. Send complete ms for picture books. Accepts hard copy. SASE. Responds in 2 months. Publication in 1 year. Royalty, 8% of net.

Editor's Comments
Every book we publish fulfills our mission of encouraging a lifelong friendship with the Lord.

AMG Publishers

6815 Shallowford Road
Chattanooga, TN 37421

Acquisitions: Rick Steele

Publisher's Interests

AMG Publishers, an evangelical, non-denominational mission-focused publishing house, specializes in Bible-related nonfiction and fiction for middle-grade and young adult readers as well as adults. Its nonfiction catalogue includes books for religious educators and parents, and its fiction list features Christian-themed fantasy fiction.

Website: www.amgpublishers.com

Freelance Potential

Published 30 titles (6 juvenile) in 2010: 6 were by agented authors and 6 were reprint/licensed properties. Of the 30 titles, 9 were by unpublished writers and 11 were by new authors. Receives 1,200 queries yearly.

- **Fiction:** Publishes middle-grade books, 8–12 years; and young adult books, 12–18 years. Genres include fantasy fiction with Christian themes.
- **Nonfiction:** Publishes Bible study materials, inspirational and motivational books, Bible reference books, and books on parenting, family life, and contemporary issues.
- **Representative Titles:** *Redefining Normal,* by David Rhodes & Chad Norris (YA), is a student devotional guide designed to help teens understand the life that God has planned for them; part of the Following God for Youth and Young Adults series. *Rock Solid Families,* by Janell Rardon, is a spiritual training manual that summarizes 12 principles that spiritually strong families have in common.

Submissions and Payment

Guidelines and catalogue available at website. Query. Accepts email queries to ricks@amgpublishers.com. Response time and publication period vary. Royalty; advance.

Editor's Comments

We are in need of more juvenile and young adult fiction, and Bible studies for young adults and older readers.

Amulet Books

Abrams Books
115 West 18th Street, 6th Floor
New York, NY 10011

Publisher: Susan Van Metre

Publisher's Interests
This publisher, which brought us the *Diary of a Wimpy Kid*, focuses on books for readers ages 8 through 18. Its catalogue features novels, graphic novels, picture books, and nonfiction titles.
Website: www.amuletbooks.com

Freelance Potential
Published 30 titles in 2010: each was by an agented author. Receives 1,200 queries yearly.

- **Fiction:** Publishes middle-grade books, 8–12 years; and young adult books, 12–18 years. Genres include contemporary, historical, and science fiction; fantasy; mystery; suspense; and humor. Also publishes graphic novels.
- **Nonfiction:** Publishes middle-grade books, 8–12 years; and young adult books, 12–18 years. Topics include multicultural and ethnic issues, animals, natural history, the environment, history, and self-help.
- **Representative Titles:** *How I, Nicky Flynn, Finally Get a Life (and a Dog),* by Art Corriveau (8–12 years), is a novel about a boy who, while undergoing major life changes, finds that a rescued dog may indeed be his friend. *Anxious Hearts,* by Tucker Shaw (YA), presents an epic tale of unrequited love through a dreamlike, loose retelling of Longfellow's love poem, *Evangeline*.

Submissions and Payment
Guidelines and catalogue available at website. Agented authors only; no unsolicited mss or queries. Publication period varies. Royalty; advance.

Editor's Comments
We are proud that, since our inception in 2004, we have attracted a stellar roster of authors and published many best-selling and award-winning books. We should be contacted through your literary agent only.

Andersen Press

20 Vauxhall Bridge Road
London SW1V 2SA
United Kingdom

Submissions Editor

Publisher's Interests
Well known for its long list of high quality children's books
by award-winning authors, Andersen Press has published
such popular titles as *The Little Princess, Elmer the Patch-
work Elephant,* and *Preston Pig*. It also produces fiction
series for children and young adults.
Website: www.andersenpress.co.uk

Freelance Potential
Published 87 titles in 2010: 10 were by agented authors.
Receives 1,200 unsolicited mss yearly.

- **Fiction:** Publishes early picture books, 0–4 years; easy-to-read
  books, 4–7 years; story picture books, 4–10 years; chapter
  books, 5–10 years; middle-grade books, 8–12 years; and
  young adult books, 12–18 years. Genres include historical and
  contemporary fiction, humor, adventure, fantasy, folktales,
  horror, mystery, suspense, and romance. Also publishes
  stories about animals and sports.
- **Representative Titles:** *The Nanny Goat's Kid,* by Jeanne
  Willis, is about a nanny goat who adopts a tiger cub even
  though her sisters don't agree. *The Great Dog Bottom Swap,*
  by Peter Bently, tells a humorous tale about dogs preparing for
  a summer ball.

Submissions and Payment
Guidelines and catalogue available at website. Query with
synopsis and 3 sample chapters. Send complete ms for picture books only. Accepts hard copy. SAE/IRC. Responds in
2 months. Publication period and payment policy vary.

Editor's Comments
We have very strict word length requirements. Please refer to
our guidelines for information. We do not publish poetry or
story anthologies. Keep in mind that we receive many submissions weekly. Each submission is reviewed carefully, and
we try our hardest to respond within two months.

Annick Press

15 Patricia Avenue
Toronto, Ontario M2M 1H9
Canada

Submissions Editor: Katie Hearn

Publisher's Interests

This Canadian publisher focuses on books for children ages six through young adult. Picture books, contemporary fiction, and nonfiction fill its catalogue. Working strictly with Canadian authors, it strives to offer positive reading experiences that are self-affirming, educational, and entertaining.
Website: www.annickpress.com

Freelance Potential

Published 32 titles (12 juvenile) in 2010. Of the 32 titles, 12 were by unpublished writers and 16 were by authors who were new to the publishing house. Receives 4,000 queries yearly.

- **Fiction:** Publishes story picture books, 4–10 years; middle-grade books, 8–12 years; and young adult books, 12–18 years. Genres include contemporary fiction and humor.
- **Nonfiction:** Publishes middle-grade books, 8–12 years; and young adult books, 12–18 years. Topics include culture, history, and contemporary issues.
- **Representative Titles:** *Animal Snoops: The Wondrous World of Wildlife Spies,* by Peter Christie (9+ years), investigates how animals use secret-agent skills to find a mate, locate food, and outsmart predators. *Descent into Paradise/A Place to Live,* by Vincent Karle & Jean-Philippe Blondel (14+ years), consists of two novels that tell stories of teens dealing with social hypocrisy, stereotypes, censorship, and friendship.

Submissions and Payment

Canadian authors only. Guidelines and catalogue available at website. Query with synopsis and sample chapter. Accepts email queries to annickpress@annickpress.com. Response time, publication period, and payment policy vary.

Editor's Comments

Originality and inherent appeal are the two most important things we look for when considering submissions. Please note that we're not seeking picture books at this time.

Atheneum Books for Young Readers

Simon & Schuster Children's Publishing
1230 Avenue of the Americas
New York, NY 10020

Editorial Director: Caitlyn Dlouhy

Publisher's Interests

Hardcover and paperback books for children and teens are offered by this imprint of Simon & Schuster. It markets a variety of well-known and popular fiction and nonfiction titles for toddlers, elementary and middle school children, and young adults.
Website: www.simonandschuster.com

Freelance Potential

Published 70 titles in 2010: 42 were by agented authors. Of the 70 titles, 7 were by unpublished writers. Receives 30,000 queries yearly.

- **Fiction:** Publishes concept books, toddler books, and early picture books, 0–4 years; story picture books, 4–10 years; chapter books, 5–10 years; middle-grade books, 8–12 years; and young adult books, 12–18 years. Genres include fantasy, graphic novels, mysteries, adventure, and historical fiction.
- **Nonfiction:** Publishes story picture books, 4–10 years; chapter books, 5–10 years; middle-grade books, 8–12 years; and young adult books, 12–18 years. Topics include the environment, science, nature, sports, history, and multicultural issues. Also publishes biographies.
- **Representative Titles:** *Frindle,* by Andrew Clements (8–12 years), features a mischievous boy who creates a new word that spreads across the country, much to his surprise. *A Barnyard Collection: Click, Clack, Moo and More,* by Doreen Cronin (3–7 years), contains stories filled with fun and animal antics.

Submissions and Payment

Guidelines available. Query with outline/synopsis. Accepts hard copy. SASE. Responds in 3 months. Publication period varies. Royalty.

Editor's Comments

While we receive a large number of submissions, engaging, creative, original work will always stand out from the crowd.

Autism Asperger Publishing Company

15490 Quivira Road
Overland Park, KS 66221

Submissions: Kirsten McBride

Publisher's Interests

This independent publisher's catalogue is filled with practical resources for parents and teachers of children with autism, Asperger Syndrome, and other pervasive developmental disorders.
Website: www.asperger.net

Freelance Potential

Published 30 titles (5 juvenile) in 2010: 5 were developed from unsolicited submissions. Of the 30 titles, 25 were by unpublished writers and 25 were by authors who were new to the publishing house. Receives 240 queries yearly.

- **Nonfiction:** Publishes easy-to-read books, 4–7 years; middle-grade books, 8–12 years; and young adult books, 12–18 years. Also publishes books for teachers and parents. Topics include autism spectrum disorders, special education, and parenting.
- **Representative Titles:** *Middle School: The Stuff Nobody Tells You About,* by Haley Moss (YA), presents the story of a high-functioning autistic girl and her recommendations for fitting in. *My New School: A Workbook to Help Students Transition to a New School,* by Melissa L. Trautman, is an interactive book that addresses the difficulties of transferring to a new school.

Submissions and Payment

Guidelines and catalogue available at website. Query with table of contents, sample chapters, and author profile. Accepts hard copy. Availability of artwork improves chance of acceptance. SASE. Responds in 3–6 months. Publication in 8 months. Royalty, 10%.

Editor's Comments

Your author profile should establish your credibility for writing and selling your book. Include information on other books or articles you have written and any classes or workshops you may have led.

Avalon Books

160 Madison Avenue
New York, NY 10016

Editors

Publisher's Interests

Romance is in the air—and on the pages—at Avalon Books. It publishes mainly romance fiction for adults, much of which is suitable for older teens due to the publisher's policy prohibiting sex, violence, or profanity in its books. Avalon also publishes mysteries and Westerns, with the same prohibitions.
Website: www.avalonbooks.com

Freelance Potential

Published 60 titles in 2010. Of the 60 titles, 38 were by unpublished writers and 13 were by authors who were new to the publishing house. Receives 2,400 queries yearly.

- **Fiction:** Publishes genre fiction for adults. Genres include contemporary romance, mystery, suspense, and Westerns.
- **Representative Titles:** *Everything But a Christmas Eve,* by Holly Jacobs, tells of a matchmaking grandmother who wants to find a husband for her company's office manager. *Deadline,* by Cynthia Danielewski, follows Detective Jack Reeves as he tries to solve the murder of a local newspaper reporter, his wife's former colleague. *Outback Hero,* by Elisabeth Rose, finds a famous singer living incognito in the Australian Outback, until she is recognized by a local hero who needs her help.

Submissions and Payment

Guidelines and catalogue available at website. Query with 2- to 3-page synopsis and first 3 chapters. Accepts hard copy and simultaneous submissions if identified. SASE. Response time and publication period vary. Royalty; advance.

Editor's Comments

Our belief in the power of good stories and wholesome entertainment hasn't changed. The key to a great genre story is characterization. We look for characters who capture the reader's imagination—and that is what you should strive for. We will not accept sexual descriptions, violence, or profanity. Great writers can engage their readers without that.

Ave Maria Press

P.O. Box 428
Notre Dame, IN 46556

Acquisitions Department

Publisher's Interests
Ave Maria, a Catholic book publisher, provides a predominantly Catholic readership with religious books and materials for religious education ministry.
Website: www.avemariapress.com

Freelance Potential
Published 40 titles in 2010: 2 were by agented authors and 3 were reprint/licensed properties. Of the 40 titles, 3 were by authors who were new to the publishing house. Receives 180 queries yearly.

- **Nonfiction:** Publishes young adult books, 12–18 years. Also publishes titles for teachers, ministers, and parents. Topics include catechism, Christian living, parenting, prayer, relationships, religion, sacraments, spirituality, and youth ministry.
- **Representative Titles:** *Send Out Your Spirit,* by Michael Amodei (YA), prepares teens for the sacrament of Confirmation. *Born of the Eucharist,* by Stephen Rossetti, ed., is a compilation of spiritual recollections by priests and seminarians. *Encountering Jesus in the New Testament,* by Michael Pennock (YA), provides a scriptural and ecclesiastical foundation to explain why Jesus is the Son of the Living God.

Submissions and Payment
Guidelines and catalogue available at website. Query with résumé, synopsis, table of contents, introduction, and 1–2 sample chapters. Accepts hard copy and simultaneous submissions if identified. SASE. Responds in 6–8 weeks. Publication in 1 year. Payment policy varies.

Editor's Comments
We are looking for books on religion, spirituality, and prayers of the Catholic Church, in addition to Catholic textbooks for high school students and pastoral ministry resources. There is no fee for evaluating your query, but time constraints do not permit us to offer detailed opinions.

Bahá'í Publishing Trust

415 Linden Avenue
Wilmette, IL 60091

Director of Acquisitions: Terry Cassidy

Publisher's Interests
This publishing company, part of the National Spiritual
Assembly of the Bahá'í of the United States, produces fiction
and nonfiction books for children and young adults of the
Bahá'í faith.
Website: http://books.bahai.us

Freelance Potential
Published 10–15 titles (4 juvenile) in 2010: 10 were developed from unsolicited submissions. Of the 10–15 titles, 8
were by unpublished writers. Receives 96 queries, 60 unsolicited mss yearly.

- **Fiction:** Publishes story picture books, 4–10 years; and chapter books, 5–10 years. Genres include contemporary and historical fiction centered on the Bahá'í faith.
- **Nonfiction:** Publishes young adult books, 12–18 years. Topics
  include Bahá'í teachings, history, identity, church members,
  and social issues.
- **Representative Titles:** *Children of the Kingdom: A Bahá'í
  Approach to Spiritual Parenting,* by Daun E. Miller, conveys a
  practical approach to guiding children by moral and spiritual
  principles. *Mind, Heart, & Spirit,* by Heather Cardin, is a collection of real-life stories from educators who have struggled
  to overcome challenges in teaching children.

Submissions and Payment
Guidelines available with 9x12 SASE. Catalogue available at
www.bahaibookstore.com. Query with clips; or send com-
plete ms. Accepts email to acquisitions@usbnc.org.
Responds to queries in 1–2 weeks, to mss in 2–3 months.
Publication in 18 months. Royalty, 10%.

Editor's Comments
We look for material that will deepen the reader's Bahá'í
knowledge and understanding, and demonstrate how its
teachings and principles may be applied to daily life.

Baker's Plays

45 West 25th Street
New York, NY 10010

Managing Editor: Roxane Heinze-Bradshaw

Publisher's Interests

Baker's Plays offers school- and community-based youth and adults full-length plays, theater texts, musicals, and collections of one-acts, scenes, and monologues.
Website: www.bakersplays.com

Freelance Potential

Published 31 titles (21 juvenile) in 2010. Receives 1,000+ queries, 500 unsolicited mss yearly.

- **Fiction:** Publishes one-act and full-length plays, monologues, and skits for children's, high school, and family theater groups. Genres include comedy; mystery; folktales; fairy tales; and multicultural, religious, and historical fiction. Also publishes holiday plays, the classics, and musicals.
- **Nonfiction:** Publishes textbooks and theater resource materials for drama students and teachers. Topics include improvisation, teaching theater, acting techniques, theatrical history, and play writing.
- **Representative Titles:** *Seniors of the Sahara,* by Barbara Pease Weber, is a romantic comedy. *Kiss, Then Tell,* by Greg Cummings, is a series of romantic comedies that take place after a couple's first kiss. *Cinderella's Mice,* by Bem Morss & Justin Warner, is a new take on the Cinderella fairytale.

Submissions and Payment

Guidelines available. Query with script history, reviews, and sample pages or synopsis; or send complete ms. Prefers email submissions to publications@bakersplays.com (Microsoft Word or PDF attachments); will accept hard copy and simultaneous submissions if identified. SASE. Responds to queries in 1 month; to mss in 2–6 months. Publication period and payment policy vary.

Editor's Comments

We seek plays for youth that embrace different faiths and prefer "production-tested" plays and collections of one-acts.

Bancroft Press

P.O. Box 65360
Baltimore, MD 21209-9945

Editor: Bruce Bortz

Publisher's Interests
Bancroft Press operates under the slogan, "Books that
Enlighten." It publishes trade fiction and nonfiction on an
array of subjects, and has a youth catalogue for middle-
grade and young adult readers.
Website: www.bancroftpress.com

Freelance Potential
Published 4–6 titles (2 juvenile) in 2010. Of the 4–6 titles,
1–2 were by unpublished writers and 2–3 were by authors
who were new to the publishing house. Receives 2,000
queries, 10,000 unsolicited mss yearly.

- **Fiction:** Publishes middle-grade books, 8–12 years; and young
  adult books, 12–18 years. Genres include mystery, history,
  sports, and contemporary and multicultural fiction. Also publishes novels for adults.
- **Nonfiction:** Publishes young adult books, 12–18 years. Topics
  include sports and biography. Also publishes parenting, financial, and self-help books for adults.
- **Representative Titles:** *Mia the Meek,* by Eileen Boggess (YA),
  continues to follow the life of young Mia Fullerton, a high
  school girl who struggles to find her inner confidence; part of
  the Mia Fullerton series. *Hank,* by Arch Montgomery (YA), presents the experiences of a young man as he discovers the
  world around him; part of the Gunpowder Trilogy.

Submissions and Payment
Guidelines and catalogue available at website. Query with
résumé and 4 or 5 sample chapters; or send complete ms
with cover letter and résumé. Accepts hard copy. SASE.
Responds in 6 months. Publication period varies. Royalty,
80%; advance, $750–$5,000.

Editor's Comments
Please include your email address on the outside of your submission envelope so we can contact you with our decision.

Barbour Publishing

P.O. Box 719
Uhrichsville, OH 44683

Submissions Editor

Publisher's Interests
Barbour, a conservative Christian publishing company, offers religious and inspirational fiction and nonfiction for children. The publisher's market, though evangelical, is broad and embraces an audience from toddlers to adults. Offerings include activity books, fiction series, and self-help titles.
Website: www.barbourbooks.com

Freelance Potential
Published 150 titles (30 juvenile) in 2010.

- **Fiction:** Publishes story picture books, 3–7 years; middle-grade books, 8–12 years; and young adult books, 12–18 years. Genres include historical fiction, adventure, and mystery. Also publishes bedtime stories and Bible stories.
- **Nonfiction:** Publishes story picture books, 3–7 years; middle-grade books, 8–12 years; and young adult books, 12–18 years. Topics include biography, holidays, the Bible, inspiration, self-help, sports, puzzles, and activities.
- **Representative Titles:** *Alexis and the Arizona Escapade*, by Erica Rodgers (8–12 years), follows the adventures of girls of different backgrounds who come to learn about and accept each other; part of the Camp Club Girls series. *Armed and Dangerous*, by Ken Abraham (YA), is a book of promises that arms teens with biblical truths.

Submissions and Payment
Guidelines and catalogue available at website. Query with synopsis and 3 sample chapters. Accepts email queries to submissions@barbourbooks.com and simultaneous submissions if identified. Responds in 4–6 months. Publication period varies. Royalty; advance.

Editor's Comments
Avoid narrow theological teachings or controversial topics. All Barbour books must reflect a personal commitment to Jesus Christ. Characters should be Christian, but do not need to be saintly.

Barron's

250 Wireless Boulevard
Hauppauge, NY 11788

Acquisitions Manager: Wayne Barr

Publisher's Interests

This large publisher known for its reference and educational series, including school and study guides, also publishes in many other categories. It offers a large list of children's fiction and nonfiction, as well as family and health books.
Website: www.barronseduc.com

Freelance Potential

Published 300+ titles (75 juvenile) in 2010. Receives 3,000 queries, 1,000 unsolicited mss yearly.

- **Fiction:** Publishes concept books and toddler books, 0–4 years; easy-to-read books, 4–7 years; story picture books, 4–10 years; middle-grade books, 8–12 years; and young adult books, 12–18 years. Genres include fairy tales, fantasy, and adventure. Also publishes retold stories, graphic novels, and stories about animals.
- **Nonfiction:** Publishes toddler books, 0–4 years; easy-to-read books, 4–7 years; story picture books, 4–10 years; middle-grade books, 8–12 years; and young adult books, 12–18 years. Topics include art, activities, biography, concepts, prehistory and history, self-help, magic, bugs, and cooking.
- **Representative Titles:** *Baby's World of Colors*, by Catherine Hellier (0–3 years), features bright, active animals. *Emily's Ice Dancing Show*, by Rosalinda Kightley (3–6 years), is the story of a girl learning to skate.

Submissions and Payment

Guidelines available. Send complete ms with résumé for fiction. Query with table of contents and two sample chapters for nonfiction. Accepts hard copy and simultaneous submissions if identified. SASE. Responds to queries in 1–3 months, to mss in 6–8 months. Publication in 2 years. Royalty; advance.

Editor's Comments

Include an overview of the market you are targeting with your manuscript or proposal.

Behrman House

11 Edison Place
Springfield, NJ 07081

Editorial Department

Publisher's Interests
Offering "creative resources for the Jewish educator,"
Behrman House publishes textbooks and supplementary
classroom materials for preschool through high school. It
also produces books about Jewish life, holidays, history,
and traditions.
Website: www.behrmanhouse.com

Freelance Potential
Published 10 titles (8 juvenile) in 2010. Receives 50 queries,
50 unsolicited mss yearly.

- **Nonfiction:** Publishes early picture books, 0–4 years; chapter
  books, 5–10 years; middle-grade books, 8–12 years; and
  young adult books, 12–18 years. Topics include Judaism,
  religion, theology, prayer, holidays, the Bible, the Holocaust,
  history, liturgy, Hebrew, and ethics.
- **Representative Titles:** *Introduction to Jewish History: From
  Abraham to the Sages,* by Seymour Rossel, presents simple
  stories that highlight Jewish history. *Look at Me: I Can Celebrate Hanukkah,* by Freddie Levin & Sunny Yudkoff, introduces the holiday and its vocabulary.

Submissions and Payment
Guidelines and catalogue available at website. Prefers complete ms with author bio and table of contents; will accept
query with at least 2 sample chapters. Accepts hard copy
and simultaneous submissions if identified. SASE. Responds
in 3 months. Publication in 18 months. Royalty, 5–10%;
advance, $1,500. Flat fee.

Editor's Comments
We believe in providing educators with choices, so that they
can design an educational program that's right for them. Our
catalogue features materials that cater to different instructional methods of educators and the varied needs and learning styles of students.

Benchmark Books

Marshall Cavendish
99 White Plains Road
Tarrytown, NY 10591

Editor: Michelle Bisson

Publisher's Interests

This imprint of Marshall Cavendish focuses on the kindergarten through grade 12 school library market. It specializes in authoritative nonfiction series on curriculum topics from social studies to literature, including high-interest series on fun topics like the paranormal and sports.
Website: www.marshallcavendish.us

Freelance Potential

Published 300 titles in 2010. Of the 300 titles, 15 were by authors who were new to the publishing house. Receives 200+ queries yearly.

- **Nonfiction:** Publishes easy-to-read books, 4–7 years; chapter books, 5–10 years; middle-grade books, 8–12 years; and young adult books, 12–18 years. Topics include animals, mathematics, science, social studies, history, world cultures, American studies, human behavior, the arts, and health.
- **Representative Titles:** *Pump It Up!,* by Melissa Stewart (grades 3 and up), presents the wondrous secrets of the heart and blood; part of the Gross and Goofy Body series. *Riding,* by Dana Meachen Rau (grades K–1), uses a combination of words and pictures that introduce interesting facts and plant the seed of early literacy; part of the Benchmark Rebus: On the Move series.

Submissions and Payment

Catalogue available at website. Query with table of contents and sample chapter. Accepts hard copy. SASE. Responds in 6–8 months. Publication in 9–18 months. Flat fee.

Editor's Comments

We are particularly interested in developing book series for students in grades three through eight. Please be aware that all of our books are parts of series, and that each series includes five or six books. We are open to suggestions for other nonfiction series as well.

Bess Press

3565 Harding Avenue
Honolulu, HI 96816

Submissions Editor

Publisher's Interests
The children's list of this regional publisher features Hawaii-related fiction and textbooks for Hawaiian educators.
Website: www.besspress.com

Freelance Potential
Published 7 titles (2 juvenile) in 2010: 2 were developed from unsolicited submissions, 2 were by agented authors, and 2 were reprint/licensed properties. Of the 7 titles, 2 were by unpublished writers and 4 were by new authors. Receives 180 queries, 240 unsolicited mss yearly.

- **Fiction:** Publishes concept books, toddler books, and early picture books, 0–4 years; easy-to-read books, 4–7 years; story picture books, 4–10 years; chapter books, 5–10 years; and young adult books, 12–18 years. Genres include regional fiction, folklore, and folktales about Hawaiian life and culture.
- **Nonfiction:** Publishes concept books, toddler books, and early picture books, 0–4 years; easy-to-read books, 4–7 years; story picture books, 4–10 years; chapter books, 5–10 years; middle-grade books, 8–12 years; and young adult books, 12–18 years. Topics include Hawaiian and Pacific Island culture, language, history, natural history, literature, and biography.
- **Representative Titles:** *History of the Hawaiian Kingdom,* by Norris W. Potter, et al. (grade 7), is a textbook that details the island group's history. *The Musubi Man,* by Sandi Takayama, is a Hawaiian version of the familiar Gingerbread Man story.

Submissions and Payment
Guidelines and catalogue available at website. Query for textbooks. Send complete ms for all other books. Accepts hard copy and simultaneous submissions. SASE. Responds in 4–6 months. Publication in 6–18 months. Royalty, 5–10%.

Editor's Comments
Our interest currently lies in uniquely alternative material that crosses over from the trade to education categories.

Bethany House Publishers

11400 Hampshire Avenue South
Bloomington, MN 55438

Submissions Editor

Publisher's Interests

Touting itself as a leader in Christian fiction, Bethany House also publishes Christian-based literature, inspirational and historical fiction for children, and nonfiction that focuses on the spiritual needs of young readers.
Website: www.bethanyhouse.com

Freelance Potential

Published 86 titles in 2010: each was by an agented author. Of the 86 titles, 10 were by unpublished writers and 16 were by authors who were new to the publishing house. Receives 240–360 queries yearly.

- **Fiction:** Publishes young adult books, 12–18 years. Genres include inspirational, contemporary, and historical fiction.
- **Nonfiction:** Publishes devotionals, personal growth titles, and books dealing with contemporary issues. Also publishes biographies and parenting titles.
- **Representative Titles:** *Trailblazers: Featuring Martin Luther and Other Christian Heroes,* by Dave & Neta Jackson (YA), presents the stories of real Christian heroes through the eyes of young fictional characters. *The Purity Code,* by Jim Burns (YA), helps teens navigate the social and sexual pressures of contemporary society.

Submissions and Payment

Guidelines and catalogue available at website. Query through literary agent only. Not currently reviewing unsolicited mss. Responds in 9–12 weeks. Publication period varies. Royalty; advance.

Editor's Comments

Our mission is to help Christians apply biblical truths in all areas of life. While queries sent through agents get our attention first, you may try one of the online Christian submission services mentioned in our guidelines. These services act as liaisons between publisher and writer.

Bloomsbury USA

175 Fifth Avenue, 8th Floor
New York, NY 10010

Submissions Editor

Publisher's Interests
Bloomsbury Children's Books produces fiction in a number
of genres for children from birth through high school, in
addition to some nonfiction titles.
Website: www.bloomsburyusa.com

Freelance Potential
Published 72 titles in 2010: 71 were by agented authors. Of
the 72 titles, 9 were by unpublished writers. Receives 2,500
queries yearly.

- **Fiction:** Publishes concept books, toddler books, and early
  picture books, 0–4 years; easy-to-read books, 4–7 years; story
  picture books, 4–10 years; chapter books, 5–10 years; middle-
  grade books, 8–12 years; and young adult books, 12–18
  years. Genres include adventure, fantasy, mystery, contemporary and science fiction, and multicultural themes.
- **Nonfiction:** Publishes early picture books, 0–4 years; middle-
  grade books, 8–12 years; and young adult books, 12–18
  years. Topics include multicultural and ethnic subjects.
- **Representative Titles:** *The Geezer in the Freezer*, by Randall
  Wright (5–8 years), is a silly story about an old man who lives
  in the basement freezer next to the ice cream and leftover
  turkey. *Lady Macbeth's Daughter*, by Lisa Klein (YA), presents a
  reimagining of Shakespeare's classic in which Macbeth has a
  daughter he doesn't know being raised by three sisters.

Submissions and Payment
Guidelines and catalogue available at website. Query with
synopsis and sample chapter (or first 10 pages). Accepts
hard copy and simultaneous submissions. No SASE.
Responds if interested. Publication period varies. Royalty;
advance.

Editor's Comments
Please include a telephone number and email address with
your submission, so we may contact you if we're interested.

Blue Dolphin Publishing

P.O. Box 8
Nevada City, CA 95959

Editor: Paul M. Clemens

Publisher's Interests
Publishing books on philosophy, spirituality, nature, and self-help, Blue Dolphin also offers a catalogue of children's fiction and nonfiction on a variety of subjects.
Website: www.bluedolphinpublishing.com

Freelance Potential
Published 15–18 titles (4 juvenile) in 2010: most were developed from unsolicited submissions and 3–5 were by agented authors. Of the 15–18 titles, 8 were by unpublished writers and 10 were by authors who were new to the publishing house. Receives 3,600 queries, 3,600 unsolicited mss yearly.

- **Fiction:** Publishes easy-to-read books, 4–7 years; story picture books, 4–10 years; middle-grade books, 8–12 years; and young adult books, 12–18 years. Genres include contemporary, inspirational, spiritual, multicultural, and historical fiction; and folktales.
- **Nonfiction:** Publishes middle-grade books, 8–12 years; and young adult books, 12–18 years. Topics include science, nature, and health. Also publishes biographies.
- **Representative Titles:** *The Extraordinary Exploits of Irvin, the Handicapped Cat,* by J. Lynn Hughes (all ages), follows the adventures of an abandoned alley cat. *Call Him Father Nature,* by Patricia Topp (8–12 years), presents the life of conservationist John Muir.

Submissions and Payment
Guidelines and catalogue available at website. Query or send complete ms. Accepts hard copy, disk submissions, and simultaneous submissions if identified. SASE. Responds to queries immediately, to mss in 3–6 months. Publication in 9–12 months. Royalty, 10%.

Editor's Comments
We are especially in need of children's books on multicultural studies.

Blue Sky Press

Scholastic Inc.
557 Broadway
New York, NY 10012-3999

Editorial Director: Bonnie Verburg

Publisher's Interests
This Scholastic imprint produces a wide variety of children's fiction and nonfiction with the goal of inspiring students and cultivating their minds. It features titles for children of all ages, from birth to young adult.
Website: www.scholastic.com

Freelance Potential
Published 10–15 titles in 2010. Receives 3,000 queries each year.

- **Fiction:** Publishes toddler books and early picture books, 0–4 years; easy-to-read books, 4–7 years; story picture books, 4–10 years; chapter books, 5–10 years; middle-grade books, 8–12 years; and young adult books, 12–18 years. Genres include historical, contemporary, and multicultural fiction; folklore; fairy tales; fantasy; humor; and adventure.
- **Nonfiction:** Publishes story picture books, 4–8 years; and middle-grade books, 8–12 years. Topics include nature, the environment, and history.
- **Representative Titles:** *It's Christmas, David*, by David Shannon (4–8 years), tells the story of two brothers who travel to a volcanic island to help their aunt, only to discover she is up to no good. *How Do Dinosaurs Love Their Dogs?*, by Jane Yolen (4–8 years), uses loveable dinosaur characters to teach children how to care for their pet dogs.

Submissions and Payment
Accepts queries from previously published authors only. Query with synopsis and publishing credits. Send complete ms for picture books. Accepts hard copy. SASE. Responds in 6–12 months. Publication in 2–5 years. Royalty, 5% hardcover trade; advance.

Editor's Comments
Our products are designed to help enhance our readers' understanding of the world around them.

Borealis Press Ltd.

8 Mohawk Crescent
Nepean, Ontario K2H 7G6
Canada

Senior Editor: Frank M. Tierney

Publisher's Interests

Specializing in books by Canadian authors about the country's people, traditions, and history, Borealis Press has branched out over the years to market picture books and titles for young adults.
Website: www.borealispress.com

Freelance Potential

Published 28 titles in 2010. Of the 28 titles, 10 were by authors who were new to the publishing house. Receives 200–300 queries yearly.

- **Fiction:** Publishes story picture books, 4–10 years; and young adult books, 12–18 years. Genres include fantasy and multicultural and ethnic fiction.
- **Nonfiction:** Publishes reference titles about Canadian history. Also offers drama, poetry, and books with multicultural themes.
- **Representative Titles:** *Half of Me: An Odyssey of Understanding,* by William J. Bart (YA), is the story of a boy who, through an imaginative vision of himself, develops a perceptive understanding of what it's like to be physically challenged. *Ghost Walk,* by Shelley Awad, follows the characters through a haunted mansion as they try to solve a mystery; part of the Greenhouse Kids series.

Submissions and Payment

Guidelines and catalogue available at website. Query with outline/synopsis and sample chapter. Accepts hard copy and disk submissions. No simultaneous submissions. SAE/IRC. Responds in 3–4 months. Publication in 1–2 years. Royalty, 10% of net. Flat fee.

Editor's Comments

Books with a Canadian connection are our first preference. Children's books should convey a sense of fun, but also feature a connection to the beauty of life.

Boyds Mills Press

815 Church Street
Honesdale, PA 18431

Manuscript Submissions

Publisher's Interests
A publisher of quality children's fiction and nonfiction, Boyds Mills Press has a catalogue full of books for an audience that ranges from birth to high school.
Website: www.boydsmillspress.com

Freelance Potential
Published 100 titles in 2010: 20 were developed from unsolicited submissions, 50 were by agented authors, and 20 were reprint/licensed properties. Of the 100 titles, 8 were by unpublished writers and 20 were by new authors. Receives 2,600 queries, 15,000 unsolicited mss yearly.

- **Fiction:** Publishes concept books, toddler books, and early picture books, 0–4 years; easy-to-read books, 4–7 years; story picture books, 4–10 years; chapter books, 5–10 years; middle-grade books, 8–12 years; and young adult books, 12–18 years. Genres include adventure stories and multicultural fiction.
- **Nonfiction:** Publishes early picture books, 0–4 years; easy-to-read books, 4–7 years; story picture books, 4–10 years; chapter books, 5–10 years; and middle-grade books, 8–12 years. Topics include history, science, and nature.
- **Representative Titles:** *A Mighty Fine Time Machine*, by Suzanne Bloom (4–7 years), follows an armadillo and an aardvark as they turn an ordinary box into a time machine. *Insects: Biggest! Littlest!*, by Sandra Markle (5–7 years), spotlights 21 types of insects from around the world.

Submissions and Payment
Guidelines available at website. Query with outline/synopsis. Send complete ms for picture books only. Accepts hard copy. SASE. Response time, publication period, and payment policy vary.

Editor's Comments
For submissions of middle-grade and young adult fiction, please include the first three chapters with your synopsis.

Boynton/Cook Publishers

Heinemann
361 Hanover Street
Portsmouth, NH 03801-3912

Proposals

Publisher's Interests
This imprint of Heinemann markets textbooks and educational resource materials covering language arts and writing. It targets English teachers and students in the middle grades through college.
Website: www.boyntoncook.com

Freelance Potential
Published 10 titles in 2010. Receives 1,000 queries yearly.

- **Nonfiction:** Publishes professional books for language arts teachers. Also publishes a select number of textbooks for college students. Topics include literature, rhetoric, communications, composition, writing, and style.
- **Representative Titles:** *Stepping on My Brother's Head,* by Sondra Perl & Charles Schuster, is a college reader featuring essays that teach writing students about form, content, style, verve, and voice. *What's the Big Idea?,* by Jim Burke, presents question-driven units that motivate students to read, write, and think. *Hidden Gems,* by Katherine Bomer, helps teachers search for the intelligence and beauty in all students' writings.

Submissions and Payment
Guidelines and catalogue available at website. Query with table of contents, sample illustrations (if applicable), chapter summaries, and 3 sample chapters. Prefers email queries to proposals@heinemann.com; will accept hard copy and simultaneous submissions if identified. SASE. Responds in 6–8 weeks. Publication in 10–12 months. Royalty.

Editor's Comments
All of the proposals we receive are first reviewed by one of our editors. Those we consider to be good fits are then sent to outside readers for review. Feel free to suggest names of potential reviewers. We promise to give every proposal serious consideration and as prompt a response as possible.

Butte Publications

P.O. Box 1328
Hillsboro, OR 97123-1328

Acquisitions Editor

Publisher's Interests

This specialty publisher focuses on educating the deaf and hard of hearing. It also markets resource materials for professionals working in the fields of speech language pathology, special education, English as a Second Language, early childhood, and early intervention, as well as for parents. **Website: www.buttepublications.com**

Freelance Potential

Published 5 titles (2 juvenile) in 2010. Receives 20 queries each year.

- **Nonfiction:** Publishes resources and educational books on signing, interpreting, vocabulary, reading, writing, language skills, lipreading, and mathematics. Also publishes titles for parents who are raising deaf and hard of hearing children.
- **Representative Titles:** *Metaphor Magic,* by Katy Preston (grades K–8), is a workbook that introduces metaphors while also challenging students to interpret metaphors and create their own. *Parent-Infant Communication,* by Valerie Schuyler & Jayne Sowers (parents), presents a family-centered curriculum of listening and communication skills while guiding parents in promoting their child's language development.

Submissions and Payment

Guidelines and catalogue available at website. Query with table of contents, market analysis, and 2 sample chapters. Accepts hard copy. SASE. Responds in 6 months. Publication in 1 year. Royalty.

Editor's Comments

In your query, you must describe in detail your qualifications for writing on the subject matter you have chosen. Please identify the target audience and if there are certain organizations and institutions that might be particularly interested in the book. Successful works are written with specific readers in mind who will spend their money to buy the work.

Calkins Creek

Boyds Mills Press
815 Church Street
Honesdale, PA 18431

Manuscript Submissions

Publisher's Interests

Calkins Creek's catalogue is filled with children's books that are centered around U.S. history. An imprint of Boyds Mills Press, it accepts picture books for children over the age of eight, middle-grade and young adult novels, and nonfiction titles that provide a different look at well-known subjects.
Website: www.calkinscreekbooks.com

Freelance Potential

Published 7 titles in 2010. Receives 600 unsolicited mss each year.

- **Fiction:** Publishes story picture books, 8+ years; chapter books, 5–10 years; middle-grade books, 8–12 years; and young adult books, 12–18 years. Genres include historical fiction.
- **Nonfiction:** Publishes story picture books, 8–10 years; chapter books, 8–10 years; middle-grade books, 8–12 years; and young adult books, 12–18 years. Topics include U.S. history.
- **Representative Titles:** *Farmer George Plants a Nation*, by Peggy Thomas (8+ years), focuses on George Washington during his time as a Virginia farmer and includes excerpts from some of his writings. *The Shakeress,* by Kimberley Heuston (12+ years), features a newly orphaned girl who seeks refuge in a Shaker village to avoid working in a mill.

Submissions and Payment

Guidelines available at website. Query or send complete ms with detailed bibliography for both historical fiction and nonfiction. Accepts hard copy. SASE. Response time and publication period vary. Royalty.

Editor's Comments

History is key to our books. All submissions must be thoroughly researched. We recommend that authors rely on the most up-to-date references, and that they work with experts during the research, writing, and editing stages.

Candlewick Press

99 Dover Street
Somerville, MA 02144

Associate Publisher: Liz Bicknell

Publisher's Interests
Candlewick's award-winning list includes everything from
toddler board books and science fiction chapter books to
historical and biographical nonfiction.
Website: www.candlewick.com

Freelance Potential
Published 175 titles (170 juvenile) in 2010: 26 were developed from unsolicited submissions and 115 were by agented authors. Of the 175 titles, 1–2 were by unpublished
writers and 4–5 were by authors who were new to the publishing house. Receives 300 queries yearly.

- **Fiction:** Publishes concept books, toddler books, and early
  picture books, 0–4 years; easy-to-read books, 4–7 years; story
  picture books, 4–10 years; chapter books, 5–10 years; middle-
  grade books, 8–12 years; and young adult books, 12–18
  years. Genres include contemporary, multicultural, historical,
  and science fiction; fantasy; adventure; mystery; and humor.
- **Nonfiction:** Publishes concept books and early picture books,
  0–4 years; story picture books, 4–10 years; middle-grade
  books, 8–12 years; and young adult books, 12–18 years.
  Topics include history, nature, the environment, politics, geography, biography, and music.
- **Representative Titles:** *Flip, Flap, Fly!*, by Phyllis Root (2–5
  years), follows baby animals as they fly, swim, wiggle, and
  slide with the help of their mothers. *Swim the Fly*, by Don
  Calame (14+ years), is about three best friends who set sum-
  mertime goals of seeing a girl naked for the first time and
  swimming a 100-yard butterfly.

Submissions and Payment
Accepts submissions from agented authors only.

Editor's Comments
Our independence and passion translates into the highest
quality books possible for our readers, who have learned to
expect wonderful books from us.

Candy Cane Press

Ideals Children's Books
2636 Elm Hills Pike, Suite 120
Nashville, TN 37214

Submissions Editor

Publisher's Interests
An imprint of Guideposts, Candy Cane Press has created a niche of producing board and early picture books for children up to age four. Its fiction and nonfiction titles are all brightly illustrated and convey meaningful stories about religion, holidays, animals, and patriotism.
Website: www.idealsbooks.com

Freelance Potential
Published 4–6 titles in 2010: 2 were developed from unsolicited submissions.

- **Fiction:** Publishes board books and early picture books, 0–4 years. Genres include religion and holidays.
- **Nonfiction:** Publishes board books and early picture books, 0–4 years. Topics include animals, Bible stories, biography, and patriotic themes.
- **Representative Titles:** *Today Is Christmas!,* by P. K. Hallinan (0–4 years), introduces children to the true meaning of this holiday and why giving is better than receiving. *Little Jackie Rabbit,* by Brenda Sexton (0–4 years), tells of a baby rabbit who needs a lullaby from his mother to help him fall asleep. *What Is Halloween?,* by Michelle Adams (0–4 years), helps children understand the frightening symbols of this holiday.

Submissions and Payment
Guidelines and catalogue available at website. Send complete ms (to 200 words for board books, to 1,000 words for picture books) with list of previously published books. Accepts hard copy. SASE. Responds in 2–3 months. Publication period varies. Royalty.

Editor's Comments
We invite you to send us your work, but we discourage multiple submissions. We are always looking to expand our growing list of subjects. Review our products and let us know if you have an idea that will fit with our mission.

Capstone

151 Good Counsel Drive
P.O. Box 669
Mankato, MN 56001

Editorial Director, Fiction: Michael Dahl
Editorial Director, Nonfiction: Kay M. Olsen

Publisher's Interests

Nonfiction and fiction for emergent and reluctant readers is the specialty of this large publisher. Imprints include the nonfiction Capstone Press and Compass Point Books, and fiction imprints Picture Window Books and Stone Arch Books. (See separate listings.)
Website: www.capstonepub.com

Freelance Potential

Published 600 titles in 2010. Receives 1,200 queries yearly.

- **Fiction:** Publishes early picture books, 0–4 years; easy-to-read books, 4–7 years; story picture books, 4–10 years; chapter books, 5–10 years; middle-grade books, 8–12 years; and young adult books, 12–18 years. Genres include adventure, fantasy, horror, mystery, suspense, and graphic novels.
- **Nonfiction:** Publishes concept books and early picture books, 0–4 years; easy-to-read books, 4–7 years; chapter books, 5–10 years; middle-grade books, 8–12 years; and young adult books, 12–18 years. Topics include animals, arts and crafts, biography, social studies, geography, health, science, and math.
- **Representative Titles:** *H Is for Honk!*, by Catherine Ipcizade (6–7 years), is directed at emergent readers; part of the Alphabet Fun series. *Basketball: How It Works*, by Suzanne Slade (9–12 years), explains this sport for young readers; part of the Science of Sports series.

Submissions and Payment

Query with sample chapters, résumé, and list of publishing credits for fiction. Query with cover letter, résumé, and 3 writing samples for nonfiction. Accepts hard copy and email (fiction only) to author.sub@stonearchbooks.com. Responds in 3–5 months. Publication period varies. Flat fee.

Editor's Comments

Capstone books connect students of all ages (and their teachers and librarians) to ideas and exciting experiences.

Carolrhoda Books

Lerner Publishing Group
241 First Avenue North
Minneapolis, MN 55401

Fiction Submissions Editor

Publisher's Interests

This imprint of Lerner Publishing has been marketing fiction titles for children for more than 50 years. While its primary focus is on picture books for young children, it also offers some chapter books and novels for more advanced readers. Carolrhoda Books only accepts submissions targeted to the list of needs and subject areas posted on its website.
Website: www.lernerbooks.com

Freelance Potential

Published 20–25 titles in 2010.

- **Fiction:** Publishes story picture books, 4–10 years; chapter books, 5–10 years; middle-grade books, 8–12 years; and young adult books, 12–18 years. Genres include contemporary, historical, and multicultural fiction; and mystery.
- **Representative Titles:** *Dino-Baseball,* by Lisa Wheeler (5–9 years), features two teams of dinosaur athletes as they face off in a fast-action baseball game. *Druscilla's Halloween,* by Sally M. Walker (5–9 years), portrays an old witch with loud, creaky knees who discovers that witches can fly on brooms, thereby changing the course of witch history. *Monkey with a Tool Belt and the Noisy Problem,* by Chris Monroe (4–8 years), tells about a monkey who learns how to use tools to fix a problem.

Submissions and Payment

Guidelines available at website. Accepts targeted submissions only. Visit the website for a list of needs aimed at specific reading levels in specific subject areas, and for complete submissions information.

Editor's Comments

Before you submit your work, you must visit the website to review our submissions guidelines. It also includes suggestions on how to market your submission. Well-researched content that has been developed into a well-written, engaging story will have the best chance of acceptance.

Carson-Dellosa Publishing

P.O. Box 35665
Greensboro, NC 27425-5665

Submissions Editor: Julie Killian

Publisher's Interests
Founded by two teachers, Carson-Dellosa provides educational material and classroom resources for both teachers and parents. Its product line includes books that supplement the curricula, classroom activities, and manipulatives for preschool through grade eight.
Website: www.carsondellosa.com

Freelance Potential
Published 233 titles in 2010. Receives 150 queries yearly.

- **Nonfiction:** Publishes supplementary educational material, including activity books, resource guides, classroom material, and reproducibles, preK–grade 8. Topics include reading, language arts, mathematics, science, the arts, social studies, English Language Learners (ELL), early childhood, and crafts. Also publishes Christian education titles.
- **Representative Titles:** *Skills for Success: Reading for Understanding* (grades 1–2, 3–4, 5–6) features fiction and nonfiction passages followed by questions for the reader. *A New Trip Around the World* (grades K–5) presents geographical, factual, and cultural information about several regions of the world.

Submissions and Payment
Guidelines available at website. All work is assigned. Send résumé and writing samples. Accepts hard copy and email submissions to freelancesamples@carsondellosa.com (Microsoft Word, PDF, or plain text attachments). Responds if interested. Publication period varies. Flat fee.

Editor's Comments
We're looking for writers with expertise in the areas of math (for kindergarten through grade eight), and reading comprehension. Note that we cannot return the writing samples you submit, so please send copies only. After a review of your work, we will contact you when a project that suits your skill set becomes available.

Cartwheel Books

Scholastic Inc.
557 Broadway
New York, NY 10012

Editor: Jeff Salane

Publisher's Interests

Story picture books, toddler and concept books, and chapter books for beginning and intermediate readers are found on Cartwheel Books' list. This imprint of Scholastic features titles for children under the age of ten only.
Website: www.scholastic.com

Freelance Potential

Published 100+ titles in 2010: 20+ were reprint/licensed properties. Of the 100+ titles, 3–4 were by authors who were new to the publishing house. Receives 1,000 queries yearly.

- **Fiction:** Publishes concept books, toddler books, and early picture books, 0–4 years; easy-to-read books, 4–7 years; story picture books, 4–8 years; and chapter books, 5–10 years. Publishes humor and short stories about friendship, family, and animals.
- **Nonfiction:** Publishes concept books, toddler books, and early picture books, 0–4 years; easy-to-read books, 4–8 years; and story picture books, 4–8 years. Topics include science and mathematics.
- **Representative Titles:** *Poppleton in Winter,* by Cynthia Rylant (4+ years), features a pig who, with his friends, tries to make the most of what winter has to offer. *The Littlest Pilgrim,* by Brandi Dougherty (3+ years), features a pilgrim girl who is too little to sew or fish, but not too little to make a friend.

Submissions and Payment

Accepts submissions from agents and previously published authors only. Send complete ms. Accepts hard copy. SASE. Responds in 3–6 months. Publication period and payment policy vary.

Editor's Comments

Please be aware that we only publish titles for a young audience. Don't send manuscripts appropriate for teens or middle-grade readers.

Cedar Fort

2373 W 700 S
Springville, UT 84663

Acquisitions Editor: Jennifer Fielding

Publisher's Interests

Cedar Fort publishes fiction and nonfiction titles for older children and adults. Categories include inspirational and religious fiction, self-help, parenting, family relationships, and personal finance. Many titles are written specifically for the Latter-day Saints market; those that are geared toward a general audience must be uplifting and edifying.
Website: www.cedarfort.com

Freelance Potential

Published 115 titles (6 juvenile) in 2010. Of the 115 titles, 57 were by unpublished writers and 69–80 were by authors who were new to the publishing house. Receives 700+ unsolicited mss yearly.

- **Fiction:** Publishes middle-grade books, 8–12 years; and young adult books, 12–18 years. Genres include religious, contemporary, and historical fiction; fantasy; and adventure stories.
- **Nonfiction:** Publishes young adult books, 12–18 years. Topics include history, religion, self-help, and LDS doctrine. Also publishes books for adults.
- **Representative Titles:** *Once Upon a Time: An Adoption Story,* by Ashley Bigler, tells the sweet story of a child's journey to her "forever" family. *The Adventures of Hashbrown Jones,* by Frank Cole, is a humorous novel that follows a group of friends as they navigate the trials and tribulations of fifth grade.

Submissions and Payment

Guidelines and catalogue available at website. Send complete ms with submission form available at website. Accepts hard copy. SASE. Responds in 2–3 months. Publication period varies. Royalty; advance.

Editor's Comments

We're currently in need of books on New Testament topics, prayer, suicide prevention, autism, and Asperger's Syndrome. We welcome the chance to work with new authors.

Charlesbridge Publishing

85 Main Street
Watertown, MA 02472

Submissions Editor

Publisher's Interests

Charlesbridge publishes children's books with a goal of creating lifelong readers and learners. Its list of fiction and nonfiction titles covers a range of topics.
Website: www.charlesbridge.com

Freelance Potential

Published 44 titles in 2010: 1 was developed from an unsolicited submission and 5 were by agented authors. Receives 180 queries, 2,400 unsolicited mss yearly.

- **Fiction:** Publishes concept books, toddler books, and early picture books, 0–4 years; easy-to-read books, 4–7 years; story picture books, 4–10 years; chapter books, 5–10 years; and middle-grade books, 8–12 years. Genres include contemporary fiction, folktales, and nature stories.
- **Nonfiction:** Publishes concept books, toddler books, and early picture books, 0–4 years; easy-to-read books, 4–7 years; story picture books, 4–10 years; chapter books, 5–10 years; and middle-grade books, 8–12 years. Topics include nature, history, social studies, music, science, and multicultural themes.
- **Representative Titles:** *Flying Eagle*, by Sudipta Bardhan-Quallan (5–8 years), features a father eagle on his flight across the Serengeti to search for food for his chick. *After Gandhi*, by Anne Sibley O'Brien & Perry Edmond O'Brien (9–12 years), explores the works of Mohandas Gandhi and other nonviolent activists.

Submissions and Payment

Guidelines available at website. Query with synopsis and 3 chapters for books longer than 30 pages; send complete ms for shorter works. Accepts hard copy. No simultaneous submissions. Responds in 3 months if interested. Publication in 2–5 years. Royalty.

Editor's Comments

We are always searching for new voices, new visions, and new directions in children's literature.

Chelsea House

132 West 31st Street, 17th Floor
New York, NY 10001

Managing Editor: Justine Ciovacco

Publisher's Interests

Curriculum-based nonfiction books for middle school and high school students fill the catalogue of this publisher, an imprint of Infobase Publishing. Its areas of focus include historical and contemporary biographies, social studies, geography, science, health, and high-interest titles.
Website: www.chelseahouse.com

Freelance Potential

Published 300+ titles in 2010: 5 were developed from unsolicited submissions. Of the 300+ titles, 30 were by authors who were new to the publishing house. Receives 240+ queries yearly.

- **Nonfiction:** Publishes middle-grade books, 8–12 years; and young adult books, 12–18 years. Topics include careers, geography, government and law, health, the arts, pet care, sports, transportation, literary criticism, religion, mythology, science, and social studies. Also publishes biographies.
- **Representative Titles:** *Christopher Columbus and the Discovery of the Americas,* by Tim McNeese (grades 5–8), details the motivations and explorations of the man who discovered the New World; part of the Explorers of New Lands series. *Forensic Science: From Fibers to Fingerprints,* by Lisa Yount (grades 6–12), profiles key figures in this news-making field; part of the Milestones in Discovery and Invention series.

Submissions and Payment

Guidelines available. All books are assigned. Query with résumé and clips or writing samples for new series ideas only. Accepts hard copy and email queries to jciovacco@aol.com. SASE. Response time and publication period vary. Royalty; advance. Flat fee.

Editor's Comments

We select our authors from a wide array of professors, teachers, professional writers, freelance writers, and researchers.

Chicago Review Press

814 North Franklin Street
Chicago, IL 60610

Senior Editor: Jerome Pohlen

Publisher's Interests

Along with an award-winning line of children's activity books, Chicago Review Press's catalogue also features general non-fiction titles for the preschool through high school years, with topics such as art, math, science, history, and architecture. It also markets parenting how-to books.
Website: www.chicagoreviewpress.com

Freelance Potential

Published 60 titles (7 juvenile) in 2010. Receives 1,500 queries yearly.

* **Nonfiction:** Publishes early picture books, 0–4 years; story picture books, 4–10 years; middle-grade books, 8–12 years; and young adult books, 12–18 years. Topics include art, architecture, math, science, history, biography, geography, engineering, multicultural and ethnic issues, dream analysis, and outdoor activities. Also publishes books for parents.
* **Representative Titles:** *Africa for Kids*, by Harvey Croze (4–7 years), tells of Africa's plants, animals, tribes, and cities, and includes hands-on activities. *100 Ways to Win a Ten-Spot*, by Paul Zenon (YA), presents a humorous collection of scams, swindles, bets, and stunts using everyday objects. *The American Revolution for Kids*, by Janis Herbert, brings to life the heroes, traitors, and great thinkers of the Revolutionary War.

Submissions and Payment

Guidelines and catalogue available at website. Query with table of contents, 1–2 sample chapters, and market analysis. Accepts hard copy and simultaneous submissions if identified. SASE. Responds in 8–10 weeks. Publication in 18 months. Royalty, 7–10%; advance, $1,500–$5,000.

Editor's Comments

We rarely publish self-help or inspirational books, and we never publish fiction or poetry. Review our guidelines for the information we require with your proposal.

Children's Book Press

965 Mission Street, Suite 425
San Francisco, CA 94103

Editorial Submissions

Publisher's Interests

The multicultural and bilingual children's books in this nonprofit publisher's catalogue promote cooperation and understanding while offering children a sense of their culture, history, and importance. Its titles are written by and about people from Latino, African American, Asian/Pacific Island, and Native American communities.
Website: www.childrensbookpress.org

Freelance Potential

Published 5 titles in 2010. Receives 1,200 unsolicited mss each year.

- **Fiction:** Publishes story picture books, 4–10 years. Genres include contemporary, ethic, and multicultural fiction; and humor. Also publishes stories about immigration, family life, and relationships.
- **Representative Titles:** *Let Me Help,* by Alma Flor Ada (4–8 years), tells of a parrot that is hoping to help his family with Cinco de Mayo preparations, even if he is too young. *I Know the River Loves Me,* by Maya Christina Gonzalez (4–8 years), teaches young children to love and respect nature and the environment. *My Papa Diego and Me,* by Guadalupe Rivera Marin (6+ years), is a collection of stories by the daughter of Diego Rivera about growing up with a larger-than-life master artist.

Submissions and Payment

Guidelines and catalogue available at website. Send complete ms. Accepts hard copy and simultaneous submissions if identified. SASE. Responds in 2–3 months. Publication in 18–24 months. Royalty; advance.

Editor's Comments

Our tagline is "Many Voices, One World." We hope to make a difference in the world. Our books help equip children with a love of reading and a sense of possibility.

Children's Press

Scholastic Library Publishing
90 Sherman Turnpike
Danbury, CT 06816

Editor-in-Chief

Publisher's Interests
This imprint of Scholastic is well known for its popular book series and biographies for children of all ages. Most of its nonfiction titles cover a variety of core curriculum topics. The company is planning to take its publishing program in a new direction in the near future; please watch for an announcement in the trade press.
Website: www.scholastic.com

Freelance Potential
Published 352 titles in 2010. Receives 2,000 queries yearly.

- **Nonfiction:** Publishes concept books, 0–4 years; easy-to-read books, 4–7 years; story picture books, 4–10 years; chapter books, 5–10 years; and middle-grade books, 8–12 years. Topics include animals, arts, culture, economics, geography, history, the human body, the military, science, social studies, sports, and transportation. Also publishes biographies.
- **Representative Titles:** *Red, Blue, and Yellow Too!* (3–5 years) uses alliteration, repetition, and sing-along activities to help kids learn their colors. *Slower Than a Slug,* by Larry Dane Brimner & Deborah Zemke (preK–grade 2), tells of a race between a boy and his younger sister. *Julius Caesar,* by Denise Rinaldo, tells the life story of this famous historical figure; part of the Wicked History series.

Submissions and Payment
Agented authors only. Query with outline/synopsis and sample chapters. Responds in 2–6 months. Publication in 1–2 years. Flat fee.

Editor's Comments
We will be taking on a new direction in the coming months, so please look for updated information before preparing a query for us to review.

Christian Ed. Publishing

9260 Trade Place #100
San Diego, CA 92126

Assistant Editor: Janet Ackelson

Publisher's Interests
Christian Ed. Publishing produces youth educational materials for churches of different denominations around the world. These include curriculum materials, special program kits, and Bible-teaching crafts and activities. Founded more than 50 years ago, the company seeks to introduce readers to a personal faith in Jesus Christ and to help them grow in faith and service.
Website: www.christianedwarehouse.com

Freelance Potential
Published 84 titles in 2010. Of the 84 titles, 2 were by authors who were new to the publishing house. Receives 50 queries yearly.

- **Fiction:** Publishes religious fiction, preK–grade 12.
- **Nonfiction:** Publishes Christian education titles, Bible-based curriculum materials, and Bible club materials, grades K–12. Also publishes church-wide special event programs and Bible-teaching crafts and activities.
- **Representative Titles:** *Big Thoughts for Little People,* by Ken Taylor (3–7 years), uses the alphabet as a learning tool to teach Bible themes and verses. *The Not So Super Skyscraper,* by Janine Suter, is a rhyming book that tells kids the real story of the Tower of Babel. *Noah's Floating Animal Park,* by Janine Suter, combines humor and rhyme to help children understand the spiritual lesson of Noah's Ark.

Submissions and Payment
Catalogue available at website. Guidelines and application available via email request to jackelson@cehouse.com. All work is done on assignment. Response time varies. Publication in 12–18 months. Flat fee, $.03 per word.

Editor's Comments
We're always eager to find top-quality writers. Contact us for a freelance writer application.

Christian Focus Publishing

Geanies House, Fearn by Tain
Ross-shire IV20 ITW
Scotland
United Kingdom

Children's Editor: Catherine Mackenzie

Publisher's Interests
The children's catalogue of this publisher features books with clear Christian and biblical messages for children and families, Sunday school teachers, and youth workers.
Website: www.christianfocus.com

Freelance Potential
Published 79 titles (41 juvenile) in 2010: 6 were developed from unsolicited submissions, 6 were by agented authors, and 4 were reprint/licensed properties. Of the 79 titles, 3 were by unpublished writers and 10 were by new authors. Receives 240 queries, 240 unsolicited mss yearly.

- **Fiction:** Publishes toddler books and early picture books, 0–4 years; easy-to-read books, 4–7 years; story picture books, 4–10 years; chapter books, 5–10 years; middle-grade books, 8–12 years; and young adult books, 12–18 years. Genres include contemporary Christian fiction.
- **Nonfiction:** Publishes toddler books, 0–4 years; easy-to-read books, 4–7 years; story picture books, 4–10 years; chapter books, 5–10 years; middle-grade books, 8–12 years; and young adult books, 12–18 years. Offers Bible stories, biographies, and devotionals.
- **Representative Titles:** *Ten Boys Who Didn't Give In,* by Irene Howat (8–12 years), profiles 10 Christian martyrs. *My First Book of Bible Prayers,* by Philip Ross (4–7 years), introduces children to the Bible.

Submissions and Payment
Guidelines available at website. Query with synopsis and 3 chapters. Send complete ms for works under 10 chapters. Accepts email to Catherine.Mackenzie@christianfocus.com. Response time, publication period, and payment policy vary.

Editor's Comments
We have detailed guidelines that outline the types of books and series we publish. Please read them before submitting.

Christopher-Gordon Publishers

1420 Providence Highway, Suite 120
Norwood, MA 02062

Publisher: Susanne F. Canavan

Publisher's Interests

This specialty publisher produces books, journals, and CD-ROMs for the educational market, including teachers, administrators, and curriculum coordinators. Working with leading educators as well as up-and-coming stars, it offers titles in literacy, mathematics, science, and technology.
Website: www.christopher-gordon.com

Freelance Potential

Published 6–8 titles in 2010: 1 was developed from an unsolicited submission. Of the 6–8 titles, 4 were by authors who were new to the publishing house. Receives 50–100 queries each year.

- **Nonfiction:** Publishes professional enrichment material for educators. Topics include literacy, administration, classroom management, general education, teaching skills, mathematics, self-development, science, technology, supervision, literature, education law, and cognitive thinking.
- **Representative Titles:** *A Leader's Guide to Creating Safe Schools,* by David L. Stader, presents case studies and explanations that cover the vital aspects of school safety. *Literacy Instruction for Today's Classroom,* by Susan Nelson Wood et al., explains the resources, policies, and strategies of today's English/language arts teachers.

Submissions and Payment

Guidelines and catalogue available at website. Query with résumé, sample chapter, synopsis, table of contents, book length, and market and competition analysis. Accepts hard copy. SASE. Response time varies. Publication in 18 months. Royalty; advance.

Editor's Comments

Be sure to have a good sense of the market you are targeting. Also, keep in mind your reader as you write—a common problem is assuming they know too much or too little.

Chronicle Books

Children's Division
680 Second Street
San Francisco, CA 94107

Children's Division Editor

Publisher's Interests
Fiction and nonfiction for all ages appear on this publisher's extensive and varied list. It offers books in traditional formats, as well as board books and activity kits.
Website: www.chroniclebooks.com

Freelance Potential
Published 170 titles (90–100 juvenile) in 2010. Receives 240 queries, 12,000 unsolicited mss yearly.

- **Fiction:** Publishes concept books, toddler books, and early picture books, 0–4 years; easy-to-read books, 4–7 years; story picture books, 4–10 years; chapter books, 5–10 years; middle-grade books, 8–12 years; and young adult books, 12–18 years. Genres include contemporary, historical, and science fiction; adventure; and humor.
- **Nonfiction:** Publishes concept books, toddler books, and early picture books, 0–4 years; easy-to-read books, 4–7 years; story picture books, 4–10 years; chapter books, 5–10 years; middle-grade books, 8–12 years; and young adult books, 12–18 years. Topics include art, crafts, nature, geography, and history.
- **Representative Titles:** *Bears! Bears! Bears!,* by Bob Barner (4–8 years), presents fun facts about bears around the world. *Noonie's Masterpiece,* by Lisa Railsback (9–12 years), tells of an artistic girl who learns the importance of relationships.

Submissions and Payment
Guidelines and catalogue available at website. Query with synopsis and 3 sample chapters. Send complete ms for toddler books and picture books. Accepts hard copy and simultaneous submissions if identified. Does not return materials. Responds in 2–3 months if interested. Publication in 2 years. Payment policy varies.

Editor's Comments
Send us something that will lend our list a distinctive flair. Projects should be unique in subject matter or writing style.

Claire Publications

Tey Brook Centre, Unit 8
Great Tey, Colchester CO6 2EB
United Kingdom

Managing Editor: Noel Graham

Publisher's Interests
Educational books and teaching resources for preschool
through grade 12 comprise the catalogue of this international
publisher. It offers books on all curriculum subjects, as well
as titles on early childhood development, special and gifted
education, and teaching at home.
Website: www.clairepublications.com

Freelance Potential
Published 5 titles in 2010: each was developed from an
unsolicited submission. Of the 5 titles, 2 were by unpublished writers and 2 were by authors who were new to the
publishing house. Receives 60 queries, 24 unsolicited mss
each year.

- **Nonfiction:** Publishes books and activity kits, preK–grade 12.
  Topics include mathematics, English, ESL, science, languages,
  design and technology, early education, special needs, gifted
  education, and homeschooling.
- **Representative Titles:** *Creative Challenges* takes creative
  thinking to the next level as it presents activities to enhance
  children's creativity and thinking skills. *Creepy Crawly Poems*
  (5–8 years) features oversized, laminated science-based
  poems (with corresponding teacher's book) that can be
  extended and re-written by the class.

Submissions and Payment
Catalogue available at website. Query with résumé and clips;
or send complete ms. Accepts hard copy and email submissions to mail@clairepublications.com. SAE/IRC. Response
time varies. Publication in 1 year. Royalty, 10%.

Editor's Comments
We choose the products and books that we would like to use
in a classroom. Although we continue to review submissions
for all grade levels, our current biggest need is for material
for kindergarten through grade six.

Clarion Books

Houghton Mifflin Harcourt Publishing Company
215 Park Avenue South
New York, NY 10003

Vice President/Publisher: Dinah Stevenson

Publisher's Interests

Clarion focuses on picture books that deal with children's emotions, chapter books, and novels for kids and teens.
Website: www.hmhbooks.com

Freelance Potential

Published 35 titles in 2010: 3 were developed from unsolicited submissions, 25 were by agented authors, and 4 were reprint/licensed properties. Of the 35 titles, 3 were by unpublished writers and 11 were by new authors. Receives 480 queries, 3,600 unsolicited mss yearly.

- **Fiction:** Publishes toddler books, concept books, and early picture books, 0–4 years; easy-to-read books, 4–7 years; story picture books, 4–10 years; chapter books, 5–10 years; middle-grade books, 8–12 years; and young adult books, 12–18 years. Genres include fantasy; adventure; folklore; fairy tales; and historical, multicultural, and science fiction.
- **Nonfiction:** Publishes easy-to-read books, 4–7 years; story picture books, 4–10 years; chapter books, 5–10 years; middle-grade books, 8–12 years; and young adult books, 12–18 years. Topics include animals, nature, science, history, holidays, biography, and multicultural and ethnic issues.
- **Representative Titles:** *Flora's Very Windy Day,* by Jeanne Birdsall (5–8 years), is a picture book fantasy about sibling frustration and love. *Tyger Tyger,* by Kersten Hamilton (12+ years), is a fast-paced fantasy novel based on Celtic legend.

Submissions and Payment

Guidelines available. Query. Send complete ms for picture books only. Accepts hard copy. No SASE. Responds if interested. Publication in 2 years. Royalty.

Editor's Comments

We do not accept manuscripts from young people. Writers improve when given time to develop their skills. A novel must be superlatively written to find a place on our list.

Clear Light Publishing

823 Don Diego
Santa Fe, NM 87505

Publisher: Harmon Houghton

Publisher's Interests
This independent publisher and distributor is interested in books that provide insight into the beauty of Native American, Hispanic, and traditional cultures of the world. For children, it offers story books and youth fiction and nonfiction.
Website: www.clearlightbooks.com

Freelance Potential
Published 10–15 titles in 2010: 8–12 were developed from unsolicited submissions. Of the 10–15 titles, 7–10 were by unpublished writers and 7–10 were by new authors.
Receives 500+ unsolicited mss yearly.

- **Fiction:** Publishes story picture books, 4–10 years; middle-grade books, 8–12 years; and young adult books, 12–18 years. Genres include historical, regional, multicultural, and inspirational fiction.
- **Nonfiction:** Publishes middle-grade books, 8–12 years; and young adult books, 12–18 years. Topics include animals, nature, history, religion, multicultural subjects, folktales, social issues, health, and fitness. Also publishes biographies.
- **Representative Titles:** *The Man Who Set the Town Dancing*, by Candice Stanford, is the true story of José Tena, who popularized the folk dances of Mexico. *Watakame's Journey*, by Hallie N. Love & Bonnie Larson (9+ years), retells the creation myth of the Huichol Indian people of Mexico.

Submissions and Payment
Guidelines and catalogue available at website. Send complete ms with formal proposal. Accepts hard copy and simultaneous submissions if identified. Availability of artwork improves chance of acceptance. SASE. Responds in 3 months. Publication in 1 year. Royalty.

Editor's Comments
You must supply the artwork for your book. When submitting, please explain your motivation for writing the book.

Concordia Publishing House

3558 South Jefferson Avenue
St. Louis, MO 63118-3968

Editorial Department

Publisher's Interests
Concordia, the publishing arm of the Lutheran Church–
Missouri Synod, strives to be the provider of choice for books
and other resources that are faithful to the Scriptures and the
Lutheran Confessions. Among its offerings is a children's and
young adult list that features books on religion, faith, prayer,
and relying on God to help navigate life's challenges.
Website: www.cph.org

Freelance Potential
Published 50 titles (12 juvenile) in 2010: 1 was developed
from an unsolicited submission, 1 was from an agented
author, and 5 were reprint/licensed properties. Receives
1,500 queries yearly.

- **Nonfiction:** Publishes early picture books, 0–4 years; easy-to-
  read books, 4–7 years; story picture books, 4–10 years; middle-
  grade books, 8–12 years; and young adult books, 12–18
  years. Topics include faith, religious holidays, prayer, spirituality,
  Bible studies, social issues, and biography. Also publishes religious education resources and devotionals.
- **Representative Titles:** *Amazing Tales and Strange Stories from
  the Bible,* by Christopher Doyle, helps young readers discover
  the wonderful stories of the Bible. *Going Out, Getting Dumped,
  and Playing Mini Golf on the First Date,* by Tim Pauls (YA), contains biblically based advice on dating, sex, and marriage.

Submissions and Payment
Guidelines and catalogue available at website. All work is
assigned. Query or send résumé. Accepts hard copy. SASE.
Response time, publication period, and payment policy vary.

Editor's Comments
We are not currently considering Christian fiction, autobiographies, poetry, or children's picture books. Our aim is to
provide quality, Christ-centered resources for families, congregations, and church workers.

Contemporary Drama Service

Meriwether Publishing Ltd.
885 Elkton Drive
Colorado Springs, CO 80907

Associate Editor: Arthur Zapel

Publisher's Interests

This imprint of Meriwether Publishing offers plays, musicals, monologues, and skits for the middle grades, high schools, colleges, community theaters, and churches. It also publishes books for young people about theater.
Website: www.meriwetherpublishing.com

Freelance Potential

Published 15 titles in 2010: 5 were developed from unsolicited submissions. Of the 15 titles, 1 was by an unpublished writer and 2 were by authors who were new to the publishing house. Receives 120 queries yearly.

- **Fiction:** Publishes middle-grade plays, 8–12 years; and young adult plays, 12–18 years. Genres include drama, musicals, folktales, farce, fantasy, novelty plays, skits, adaptations, parody, social commentary, prevention plays, Christian dramas, and creative worship resources.
- **Nonfiction:** Publishes middle-grade books, 8–12 years; and young adult books, 12–18 years. Topics include public speaking, acting, improvisation, and theater arts.
- **Representative Titles:** *Let's Put on a Show!,* by Adrea Gibbs, is a beginner's theater handbook for young actors that covers the essentials of staging a theatrical show. *Jack and the Beanstalk Bandstand,* by Val R. Cheatham (grades 7–12), is a musical comedy that combines the story of the boy and the beanstalk with the musical pop culture of the 1950s.

Submissions and Payment

Guidelines and catalogue available at website. Query with outline/synopsis. Accepts hard copy and simultaneous submissions if identified. SASE. Responds in 6 weeks. Publication in 6 months. Royalty. Flat fee.

Editor's Comments

We are not accepting material designed for the elementary level. Church plays should avoid denominational slants.

Corwin Press

2455 Teller Road
Thousand Oaks, CA 91320

Editorial Director: Robert D. Clouse

Publisher's Interests
Serving the elementary through high school education community, Corwin Press markets practical and research-based resource materials that are user-friendly and hands-on. Professional development, curriculum development, and classroom practice are some of the topics covered.
Website: www.corwinpress.com

Freelance Potential
Published 260 titles in 2010. Receives 1,000+ queries yearly.

* **Nonfiction:** Publishes resource books and manuals for educators, grades K–12. Topics include administration, assessment, evaluation, professional development, curriculum development, classroom practice and management, gifted and special education, bilingual learning, counseling, school health, and educational technology.
* **Representative Titles:** *Differentiation at Work, K–5,* by Lane Narvaez & Kay Brimijoin, shows through research and experiences how differentiating instruction can reach all students in the classroom, from the struggling to the gifted. *More Best Practices for High School Classrooms,* by Randi Stone, offers ideas, lessons, projects, and units of study for math, science, language arts, social studies, music, art, and physical education.

Submissions and Payment
Guidelines and catalogue available at website. Query with prospectus; include alternative titles, rationale, and market analysis. Accepts hard copy. SASE. Response time varies. Publication in 7 months. Royalty.

Editor's Comments
We are looking for books with fresh insights, conclusions, and recommendations for action. We do not publish textbooks that simply summarize existing knowledge or books for the mass market audience. Your book should contribute to the practitioner's knowledge.

Coteau Books

2517 Victoria Avenue
Regina, Saskatchewan S4P 0T2
Canada

Managing Editor: Nik L. Burton

Publisher's Interests

Founded in 1975, Coteau Books publishes and promotes some of the best young readers' fiction, poetry, and drama written in Canada.

Website: www.coteaubooks.com

Freelance Potential

Published 15 titles (7 juvenile) in 2010: each was developed from an unsolicited submission. Of the 15 titles, 1 was by an unpublished writer and 5 were by authors who were new to the publishing house. Receives 120 queries, 240 unsolicited mss yearly.

- **Fiction:** Publishes chapter books, 5–10 years; middle-grade books, 8–12 years; and young adult books, 12–18 years. Genres include regional, historical, and contemporary fiction; mystery; suspense; and humor.
- **Representative Titles:** *Molly's Cue,* by Alison Acheson (12+ years), is the story of a young girl who aspires to be on stage but discovers that dreams aren't always what they seem to be. *Crow Boy,* by Maureen Bush (8+ years), is a fantasy fiction tale involving a magical ring, secrets to be learned from the natural world, and a sibling adventure; part of the Veil of Magic series.

Submissions and Payment

Canadian authors only. Guidelines available at website. Query with summary, writing samples, and CV; or send complete ms between May 1 and August 31. Accepts hard copy. No simultaneous submissions. SAE/IRC. Responds in 2–3 months. Publication in 1–2 years. Royalty, 10%.

Editor's Comments

Please note our new submissions timeline for children's literature, which includes young adult and young teen books. We evaluate all of the submissions that we receive, but the process takes time. Please be patient and we will get to your query or manuscript submission.

Cottonwood Press

109-B Cameron Drive
Fort Collins, CO 80525-3802

President: Cheryl Miller Thurston

Publisher's Interests

Cottonwood Press offers educators the resources they need
to engage students and make learning fun. It publishes
language arts and social studies material for use in grades
five through twelve, and includes project ideas, reproducibles, and activity books.
Website: www.cottonwoodpress.com

Freelance Potential

Published 3 titles in 2010: each was developed from an
unsolicited submission. Of the 3 titles, 2 were by authors
who were new to the publishing house. Receives 96–120
queries, 36–120 unsolicited mss yearly.

- **Nonfiction:** Publishes classroom materials for teachers, grades
  5–12. Topics include English, language arts, and social studies.
- **Representative Titles:** *Sentence CPR,* by Phyllis Beveridge
  Nissila (grades 8–12), dispenses remedies for sentences suffering from structural ailments. *Hot Fudge Monday,* by Randy
  Larson (grades 7–12), presents funny, quirky activities that
  teach the parts of speech.

Submissions and Payment

Guidelines and catalogue available at website. Query with
sample pages; or send complete ms. Accepts hard copy and
simultaneous submissions if identified. SASE. Responds in
4–6 weeks. Publication in 6–12 months. Royalty, 10%.

Editor's Comments

When you look through our catalogue, you'll notice something we think is unique about our offerings: They emphasize fun. We believe that we cannot teach students (especially
about a topic they may consider boring) unless they are
engaged—and one of the best ways to engage students is to
get them involved, interested, and laughing! If you are not
afraid to get a little silly with your projects, you are the kind
of teacher/author we want to hear from.

Covenant Communications

920 East State Road, Suite F
P.O. Box 416
American Fork, UT 84003-0416

Submissions Editor

Publisher's Interests
This is one of the largest independent publishers in the
Church of Latter-day Saints market, offering a line of children's
books that embraces the teachings of the Book of Mormon.
Website: www.covenant-lds.com

Freelance Potential
Published 80 titles (20 juvenile) in 2010: each was developed from an unsolicited submission. Of the 80 titles, 20
were by unpublished writers and 20 were by new authors.
Receives 1,200 unsolicited mss yearly.

- **Fiction:** Publishes concept books, toddler books, and early
  picture books, 0–4 years; chapter books, 5–10 years; middle-
  grade books, 8–12 years; and young adult books, 12–18 years.
  Genres include adventure, suspense, science fiction, and inspirational and historical fiction. Also publishes board books.
- **Nonfiction:** Publishes concept books and toddler books, 0–4
  years. Topics include history, religion, and regional subjects.
  Also publishes biographies, activity books, novelty and board
  books, photo-essays, and reference titles.
- **Representative Titles:** *Book of Mormon ABC,* by Amy Mullins
  & Val Bagley, is a board book that has young children learning
  the alphabet along with Book of Mormon names, places, and
  things. *Daughter of a King,* by Rachel Ann Nunes & David Lind-
  sley, is a picture book that teaches children that every girl and
  boy is a daughter or son of the Heavenly Father.

Submissions and Payment
Guidelines and catalogue available at website. Send complete ms with synopsis. Accepts disk submissions and email
to submissions@covenant-lds.com. SASE. Responds in 4–6
months. Publication in 1–2 years. Payment policy varies.

Editor's Comments
We are interested in virtually any subject that would appeal
to an LDS market and make a fresh contribution.

The Creative Company

P.O. Box 227
Mankato, MN 56002

Editor: Aaron Frisch

Publisher's Interests
Founded in 1932, the Creative Company publishes nonfiction textbooks and library books (mostly in series) for students in kindergarten through grade eight on a variety of subjects that range from sports to science. It also publishes a small number of fiction books for young children.
Website: www.thecreativecompany.us

Freelance Potential
Published 120 titles in 2010: 6 were developed from unsolicited submissions and 4 were by agented authors. Of the 120 titles, 6 were by unpublished writers. Receives 100 queries, 400 unsolicited mss yearly.

- **Fiction:** Publishes story picture books, 4–12 years. Features a wide range of genres.
- **Nonfiction:** Publishes chapter books, 5–10 years; middle-grade books, 8–12 years; and young adult books, 12–18 years. Topics include science, sports, music, history, zoology, architecture, geography, and biography.
- **Representative Titles:** *A Night on the Range,* by Aaron Frisch (grades 3 and up), finds a young boy and his dog leaving the comforts of home for their first sleep-out under the stars and encountering a nightlife they hadn't imagined. *The Energy Dilemma,* (grades 5 and up), presents the hard truths about our planet's dwindling natural resources and the need to create better alternative energy; part of the Earth Issues series.

Submissions and Payment
Guidelines available. Catalogue available at website. Query with outline and sample pages for series (4–8 titles). Send complete ms for picture books. Accepts hard copy. SASE. Responds in 3–4 months. Publication in 2 years. Flat fee.

Editor's Comments
We prefer that each author develop an entire nonfiction series, and we are open to a variety of subjects.

Creative Education & Publishing

3339 Ardley Court
Falls Church, VA 22041

Editor

Publisher's Interests
Creative Education & Publishing publishes educational books, learning games, activity books, storybooks, teacher resources, and other products for the American Muslim community. It aims to help children excel, practice their faith, and contribute to American society. The company also publishes *Omar Magazine* for children.
Website: www.creativeeducationandpublishing.com

Freelance Potential
Published 2 activity books and titles in 3 series.

- **Nonfiction:** Publishes early picture books, 0–4 years; easy-to-read books, 4–7 years; middle-grade books, 8–12 years; and young adult books, 12–18 years. Categories include character-building stories, activity books, and teacher resources.
- **Representative Titles:** *How Do We Thank Allah?* by Hanan Wehbe, is part of a series of books about a five-year-old girl from a Middle Eastern family living in a Western country. *You, Me, and We,* by Zabrina A. Bakar, is one title in a middle-grade series called Life Is an Open Secret. It is an anthology of inspirational stories told with humor.

Submissions and Payment
Email ideas to info@creativeeducationandpublishing.com.

Editor's Comments
The company's objective is to design solutions that meet the special needs of teachers in the American Muslim world, including helping them meet curriculum objectives. All publications and products reflect the local U.S. environment.

Creative Learning Press

P.O. Box 320
Mansfield Center, CT 06250

Editor: Kris Morgan

Publisher's Interests

Creative Learning Press produces engaging educational materials for gifted and talented students and how-to resources for their teachers and parents. These include textbooks, manuals, and activity books for children of all grade levels that prod youngsters to make, do, question, tinker, and delve deeper.

Website: www.creativelearningpress.com

Freelance Potential

Published 4 titles in 2010. Receives 100 queries, 100 unsolicited mss yearly.

- **Nonfiction:** Publishes textbooks, educational materials, how-to books, teaching resources, and audio cassettes for grades K–12. Topics include science, mathematics, language arts, geography, history, research skills, business, fine arts, and leadership.
- **Representative Titles:** *Light Up Your Child's Mind,* by Drs. Joseph Renzulli & Sally Reis, presents highly accessible and practical strategies to allow a child's gifts to blossom. *More Making Books by Hand,* by Peter & Donna Thomas, explains the basic steps for making and embellishing a book by hand. *The Teen Guide to Global Action* is filled with hands-on ideas for making changes locally, nationally, and internationally.

Submissions and Payment

Guidelines and catalogue available at website. Query with sample pages; or send complete ms with résumé and artwork. Accepts hard copy and email submissions to clp@creativelearningpress.com. SASE. Responds in 1 month. Publication period varies. Royalty.

Editor's Comments

We are proud to be the publisher of choice for Dr. Joseph Renzulli, the renowned educator and current director of the National Research Center of the Gifted and Talented.

Creative Teaching Press

15342 Graham Street
Huntington Beach, CA 92649

Idea Submissions

Publisher's Interests

The materials created by this publisher have been used in pre-K through eighth-grade classrooms since 1965. It offers books for emergent readers, as well as workbooks, writing charts, calendars, and materials for bulletin boards.
Website: www.creativeteaching.com

Freelance Potential

Published 84 titles (48 juvenile) in 2010; 14 were developed from unsolicited submissions. Of the 84 titles, 4 were by unpublished writers and 4 were by authors who were new to the publishing house. Receives 240–300 queries, 120–240 unsolicited mss yearly.

- **Fiction:** Publishes easy-to-read books, 4–7 years. Themes include ethnic, multicultural, and social issues; ethics and responsibility; fantasy; phonics; fluency; and writing.
- **Nonfiction:** Publishes easy-to-read books, 4–7 years; and chapter books, 5–10 years. Topics include history, social issues, science, and mathematics. Also publishes supplemental resource books for teachers.
- **Representative Titles:** *Let's Take Care of the Earth,* by Rozanne Lanczak Williams (grades K–1), uses repetitive text and illustrations that support the emergent reader. *A Teacher's Guide to Genre,* by Noel Ridge (teachers, grades 3–8), helps educators launch genre studies using sample texts, reproducible genre frames, and suggestions for mini-lessons.

Submissions and Payment

Guidelines and catalogue available at website. Prefers complete ms; will accept query with outline/synopsis. Accepts hard copy and simultaneous submissions. SASE. Response time varies. Publication period and payment policy vary.

Editor's Comments

As our name suggests, we are most interested in reviewing creative materials developed by and for teachers.

Critical Thinking Company

1997 Sherman Avenue
North Bend, OR 97459

President: Michael Baker

Publisher's Interests
Educational books and software for students in preschool through grade 12 are the specialty of this company. It produces challenging and fun material that helps develop students' critical thinking skills in reading, writing, mathematics, science, and history.
Website: www.criticalthinking.com

Freelance Potential
Published 20 titles (3 juvenile) in 2010: 10 were developed from unsolicited submissions. Of the 20 titles, 2 were by unpublished writers and 5 were by authors who were new to the publishing house. Receives 60 unsolicited mss yearly.

- **Fiction:** Publishes concept books, 0–4 years. Features stories that promote development of critical thinking skills.
- **Nonfiction:** Publishes concept and early picture books, 0–4 years; easy-to-read books, 4–7 years; and chapter books, 5–10 years. Topics include general thinking skills, grammar, spelling, vocabulary, reading, writing, mathematics, science, and history. Also publishes activity books, 8–18 years.
- **Representative Titles:** *Daily Mind Builders: Science* (grades 5–12) presents short, fun activity pages that develop important reading comprehension skills. *Balance Benders Beginning Level* (grades 2–6) is a book of balance puzzles designed to develop deductive thinking and pre-algebra skills.

Submissions and Payment
Guidelines available. Send complete ms. Accepts hard copy and Macintosh disk submissions. SASE. Responds in 6–9 months. Publication in 1–2 years. Royalty, 10%.

Editor's Comments
All of our books involve a critical thinking approach and are designed to be used as supplements to regular classroom curricula. We prefer material that can be used with class discussion.

Crossway Books

1300 Crescent Street
Wheaton, IL 60187

Editorial Administrator: Jill Carter

Publisher's Interests

Crossway Books, a not-for-profit Christian publishing house, produces Christian nonfiction and Gospel tracts. In addition to its children's catalogue featuring books of Bible stories and books that extol Christian values, Crossway publishes books on Christian parenting.
Website: www.crossway.org

Freelance Potential

Published 70 titles (5 juvenile) in 2010: 1 was by an agented author and 9 were reprint/licensed properties. Of the 70 titles, 7 were by unpublished writers and 26 were by authors who were new to the publishing house. Receives 60 queries, 60 unsolicited mss yearly.

- **Nonfiction:** Publishes story picture books, 4–10 years; middle-grade books, 8–12 years; and young adult books, 12–18 years. Topics include religion, church history, and Christian issues. Also publishes children's Bibles and books for parents.
- **Representative Titles:** *The Church History ABCs,* by Stephen J. Nichols & Ned Bustard (3–6 years), teaches children church history by introducing them to 26 heroes of faith. *God's Mighty Acts in Creation,* by Starr Meade (8–12 years), guides young readers through the six days of creation.

Submissions and Payment

Guidelines available. Reviews work submitted to First Edition or the Writer's Edge manuscript services only. Response time and payment policy vary.

Editor's Comments

Please note that we review only manuscripts submitted to First Edition or the Writer's Edge. We're interested in books that address contemporary issues facing Christians today, and books that help young Christians understand and develop an appreciation for the many ways God shows His love for us. We are not interested in children's fiction.

Crown Books for Young Readers

Random House
1745 Broadway, Mail Drop 9-3
New York, NY 10019

Assistant Editor: Allison Wortche

Publisher's Interests

This publisher, an imprint of Random House, focuses on high-quality fiction and nonfiction for children of all ages—from preschool through young adult.
Website: www.randomhouse.com/kids

Freelance Potential

Published 75 titles in 2010: 2 were developed from unsolicited submissions and 65 were by agented authors. Of the 75 titles, 6 were by unpublished writers and 27 were by authors who were new to the publishing house. Receives 1,200 queries, 3,600 unsolicited mss yearly.

- **Fiction:** Publishes story picture books, 4–10 years; middle-grade books, 8–12 years; and young adult books, 12–18 years. Genres include contemporary and historical fiction.
- **Nonfiction:** Publishes story picture books, 4–10 years; middle-grade books, 8–12 years; and young adult books, 12–18 years. Topics include science, nature, sports, history, and social issues.
- **Representative Titles:** *Kofi and His Magic,* by Maya Angelou, employs colorful photos to depict the life of a young boy in Africa. *Shipwreck at the Bottom of the World,* by Jennifer Armstrong, relays the true adventure of Ernest Shackleton and the crew of the *Endurance.*

Submissions and Payment

Guidelines and catalogue available at website. Query for nonfiction and novels. Send complete ms with cover letter for picture books. Accepts hard copy and simultaneous submissions if identified. No SASE; materials are not returned. Responds in 6 months if interested. Publication period varies. Royalty; advance.

Editor's Comments

We will not return your submission materials, nor will we notify you unless we are interested in moving forward.

CSS Publishing Company

517 South Main Street
Lima, OH 45804

Managing Editor: Becky Allen

Publisher's Interests
Serving the needs of Christian pastors, worship leaders, and
parish program planners, this publisher offers practical,
ready-to-use materials that meet the ministry needs of congregations. Sermons, children's object lessons, and pastoral
aids are some of the products in its catalogue.
Website: www.csspub.com

Freelance Potential
Published 75 titles in 2010: 50 were developed from unsolicited submissions. Of the 75 titles, 12 were by unpublished
writers and 12 were by authors who were new to the publishing house. Receives 120–240 queries, 120 unsolicited
mss yearly.

- **Nonfiction:** Publishes Christian education materials, program
  planners, children's sermons, and parenting titles. Topics
  include religious education, prayer, worship, and family life.
- **Representative Titles:** *Children's Stories from "The Village
  Shepherd,"* by Janice B. Scott, is a collection of stories featuring talking animals and imaginative characters that teaches
  lessons about faith, love, family, and God. *The Sky's the Limit,*
  by Kathy DeGraw, presents step-by-step instructions for creating a children's ministry.

Submissions and Payment
Guidelines available at website. Prefers query; will accept
complete ms. Accepts hard copy and simultaneous submissions if identified. SASE. Responds in 8 months. Publication
in 1 year. Payment policy varies.

Editor's Comments
When we review manuscripts, one question we ask is if the
material meets a real need, opens a new door, sparks a
fresh idea, or fills a gap in the life and ministry of a mainline
congregation. Our catalogue serves several different Christian denominations.

Da Capo Press

11 Cambridge Center
Cambridge, MA 02142

Editorial Director

Publisher's Interests

Featuring a wide array of books on pregnancy, parenting,
health, fitness, and relationships, Da Capo Press also publishes world history, biography, music, and sports titles. An
imprint of the Perseus Books Group, it presents "entertaining
and informative books about the way you live."
Website: www.dacapopress.com

Freelance Potential

Published 70 titles in 2010: 2 were developed from unsolicited submissions and 68 were by agented authors.
Receives 150 queries yearly.

- **Nonfiction:** Publishes nonfiction titles for adults. Topics
  include parenting, pregnancy, current events, entertainment,
  health, history, science, nature, multicultural issues, religion,
  social issues, and sports. Also publishes self-help books,
  humor, and biographies.
- **Representative Titles:** *Decoding the Heavens*, by Jo
  Marchant, tells of the hundred-year quest to decipher the
  ancient Greek computer known as the Antikythera Mechanism.
  Your Baby's First Year Week by Week, by Glade B. Curtis &
  Judith Schuler, guides parents through the social, emotional,
  and intellectual milestones of baby's first year.

Submissions and Payment

Guidelines and catalogue available at website. Query with
sample chapter, biography, and credentials. Accepts hard
copy. Availability of artwork improves chance of acceptance.
SASE. Responds in 1–2 months. Publication in 1 year. Royalty; advance.

Editor's Comments

Our catalogue proudly offers such well-known titles as Dr. T.
Berry Brazelton's *Touchpoints*, Dr. Stanley Greenspan's *The
Child with Special Needs*, and the entire line of Your Preg-
nancy books.

Darby Creek Publishing

1251 Washington Avenue North
Minneapolis, MN 55401

Submissions Editor

Publisher's Interests

Acquired last year by Lerner Publishing Group, Darby Creek
is now an imprint of one of the largest independent publishers in the U.S. Its school and library series promote reading
and language arts with high-interest fiction and creative nonfiction for kindergarten to grade nine.
Website: www.lernerbooks.com

Freelance Potential

Published 10–15 titles in 2010.

- **Fiction:** Publishes chapter books, 5–10 years; middle-grade
  books, 8–12 years; and young adult books, 12–18 years. Specializes in high-interest subjects.
- **Nonfiction:** Publishes early readers and high-interest books,
  6–9 years; middle-grade titles, 8–12 years; and young adult
  books, 12–18 years. Topics include animals, biography, history,
  science, and sports.
- **Representative Titles:** *Lay-ups and Long Shots: Eight Short
  Stories,* by David Lubar et al. (9–14 years), is a trade book
  compilation of stories that convey the spirit of sports. *Bed,
  Bats, & Beyond,* by Joan Holub (6–9 years), is a chapter book
  with funny and scary stories told to a young bat who has trouble falling asleep.

Submissions and Payment

Not accepting submissions at this time. Check website for
changes to this policy.

Editor's Comments

We will continue to build upon the Darby Creek list by
acquiring new genre fiction series for young readers, including Night Fall, a new six-book series of high-interest contemporary horror fiction. Darby Creek will also publish entertaining fiction, including both novels and chapter books, with
solid story lines for readers age 7 to 17.

DAW Books

Penguin Group
375 Hudson Street
New York, NY 10014

Submissions Editor: Peter Stampfel

Publisher's Interests

This publishing house is exclusively devoted to the creation and marketing of science fiction and fantasy novels. While it does not publish stories for children, many of its books appeal to young adult readers. DAW Books offers both paperback and hardcover mass market books, and many of its novels are published as part of series.
Website: www.dawbooks.com

Freelance Potential

Published 35 titles in 2010. Receives 1,000 unsolicited mss each year.

- **Fiction:** Publishes young adult books, 12–18 years. Genres include science fiction and fantasy.
- **Representative Titles:** *Omnitopia Dawn,* by Diane Duane, is a novel centered around a genius programmer who has created a massive multiplayer online game that has become sentient-alive. *Rift in the Sky,* by Julie E. Czerneda, features a fantasy civilization that plans to leave its current planet to create a haven of its own; part of the Stratification series. *The Magickers Chronicles: Volume 1,* by Emily Drake, depicts a war between two opposing groups of magic practitioners—one that wants to use magic only for good, and one that wants to use magic for its own purposes.

Submissions and Payment

Guidelines and catalogue available at website. Send complete ms with cover letter. Accepts hard copy. No simultaneous submissions. SASE. Responds in 3 months. Publication in 8–12 months. Royalty; advance.

Editor's Comments

We publish science fiction and fantasy novels only. Please don't send short stories, short story collections, novellas or poetry. The minimum length of the stories we publish is 80,000 words.

Dawn Publications

12402 Bitney Springs Road
Nevada City, CA 95959

Editor: Glenn Hovemann

Publisher's Interests
From bedtime stories to classroom texts and teacher guides, all of this publisher's books increase nature awareness for children and adults.
Website: www.dawnpub.com

Freelance Potential
Published 7 titles in 2010: 6 were developed from unsolicited submissions. Of the 7 titles, 2 were by unpublished writers and 3 were by authors who were new to the publishing house. Receives 2,000+ unsolicited mss yearly.

- **Nonfiction:** Publishes easy-to-read books, 4–7 years; and story picture books, 4–10 years. Topics include the environment, conservation, ecology, rainforests, animal habitats, the water cycle, the seasons, family relationships, personal awareness, and multicultural and ethnic issues.
- **Representative Titles:** *Amy's Light,* by Robert Nutt (2–10 years), is a bedtime story about fireflies and seeing the light from within. *The BLUES Go Birding Across America,* by Carol L. Malnor & Sandy F. Fuller (5–9 years), introduces children to birds and birding. *A Teacher's Guide to "How We Know What We Know About Our Changing Climate,"* by Carol L. Malnor, presents teachers with lessons, resources, and guidelines for use with the book.

Submissions and Payment
Guidelines and catalogue available at website. Send complete ms with author bio, synopsis, and publishing credits. Accepts hard copy and email submissions (Microsoft Word attachments; follow website instructions). SASE. Responds in 2–3 months. Publication in 18–24 months. Royalty; advance.

Editor's Comments
While all of our books and teachers' guides are about nature, we'd like to see more projects that focus on the wonder of nature or the dangers of not preserving it.

Deseret Book Company

57 West South Temple
Salt Lake City, UT 84101

Manuscript Acquisitions: Lisa Mangum

Publisher's Interests
Owned by the Church of Jesus Christ of Latter-day Saints,
Deseret Book Company publishes books, both fiction and
nonfiction, that reflect church values.
Website: www.deseretbooks.com

Freelance Potential
Published 150 titles (70 juvenile) in 2010: 9 were developed
from unsolicited submissions. Of the 150 titles, 18 were by
authors who were new to the publishing house. Receives
500 queries, 1,000 unsolicited mss yearly.

- **Fiction:** Publishes early picture books, 0–4 years; story picture
  books, 4–10 years; and young adult books, 12–18 years. Genres include fantasy; mystery; romance; and contemporary, historical, inspirational, and religious fiction.
- **Nonfiction:** Publishes early picture books, 0–4 years; story picture books, 4–10 years; chapter books, 5–10 years; and young
  adult books, 12–18 years. Also publishes activity, novelty, and
  board books, and biographies.
- **Representative Titles:** *How Does the Holy Ghost Make Me
  Feel?*, by Michele Leigh Carnesecca & Carol Shelley Xanthos
  (ages 4–8), teaches children how the Holy Ghost helps them
  choose to do what is right. *The Thirteenth Princess*, by Diane
  Zahler (ages 8–12), tells the story of a magic land, true love,
  and spellbound princesses.

Submissions and Payment
Guidelines and catalogue available at website. Query with
outline/synopsis, table of contents, and 2–3 sample chapters; or send complete ms. Accepts hard copy. SASE.
Responds in 2 months. Publication in 12–18 months. Royalty, 5–12% of retail.

Editor's Comments
We also have a series of books called Fiction for Youth, as
well as a line of books called Teaching Children.

Dial Books for Young Readers

Penguin Group
345 Hudson Street
New York, NY 10014

Associate Publisher: Kathy Dawson

Publisher's Interests
This imprint of Penguin Group publishes a variety of high-quality, engaging fiction and nonfiction for young readers (and pre-readers) of all ages.
Website: www.penguin.com/youngreaders

Freelance Potential
Published 49 titles in 2010: 39 were by agented authors and 9 were reprint/licensed properties. Of the 49 titles, 6 were by unpublished writers and 12 were by new authors. Receives 1,200 queries, 1,200 unsolicited mss yearly.

- **Fiction:** Publishes early picture books, 0–4 years; easy-to-read books, 4–7 years; story picture books, 4–10 years; chapter books, 5–10 years; middle-grade books, 8–12 years; and young adult books, 12–18 years. Genres include contemporary and science fiction.
- **Nonfiction:** Publishes concept books, toddler books, and early picture books, 0–4 years; easy-to-read books, 4–7 years; story picture books, 4–6 years; middle-grade books, 9–12 years; and young adult books, 12–18 years. Topics include animals, science, and social issues.
- **Representative Titles:** *Ladybug Girl at the Beach,* by Jacky Davis & David Soman (3–5 years), tells the story of two children and bravery at the beach. *The Sky Is Everywhere,* by Jandy Nelson (YA), is a novel about devastating loss and love.

Submissions and Payment
Guidelines available at website. Send ms for picture books. Query with synopsis, 10 pages, and publishing credits for longer works. Accepts hard copy. Materials are not returned. Responds in 4 months if interested. Publication period and payment policy vary.

Editor's Comments
Please note that you'll only hear from us if we are interested. We regret that we are unable to return your material.

Didax

395 Main Street
Rowley, MA 01969

Submissions

Publisher's Interests
The mission of this publisher is to help educators address individual learning styles and diverse student needs. Its catalogue is filled with educational resources and activity books for all areas of math, phonics, spelling, social studies, science, and reading comprehension.
Website: www.didax.com

Freelance Potential
Published 25 titles in 2010: 1 was by an author who was new to the publishing house.

- **Nonfiction:** Publishes reproducible activity books and teacher resources, preK–grade 8. Topics include math fundamentals, fractions, geometry, algebra, probability, problem-solving, the alphabet, pre-reading, phonics, word study, spelling, vocabulary, writing, reading comprehension, social studies, science, art, and character education.
- **Representative Titles:** *Number Grids*, by Paul Swan (grades 3–8), teaches number concepts, patterns, and problem solving by using games, grid templates, and other activities. *The Fraction Book*, by Rik Carter (grades 5–8), contains a series of worksheets on the relationships between fractions, decimals, and percentages. *Messy Math*, by Paul Swan (grades 4–7), uses math to solve real-life problems by presenting open-ended questions to get students thinking.

Submissions and Payment
Guidelines available. Query with résumé and outline. Accepts hard copy, email queries to info@didax.com, and simultaneous submissions if identified. SASE. Responds in 2 weeks. Publication in 1 year. Royalty; advance.

Editor's Comments
Teachers are our best source of ideas. We look for innovative and practical teaching tools that enrich a student's learning experience.

DK Publishing

Penguin Group
375 Hudson Street
New York, NY 10014

Assistant Editor: John Searcy

Publisher's Interests

DK Publishing strives to produce books that offer quality and authority in an attractive and accessible form. Its catalogue offers an extensive range of nonfiction children's titles for interests in every age group, plus encyclopedias and activity books. A division of Penguin Group USA, it accepts agented submissions only.

Website: www.dk.com

Freelance Potential

Published 363 titles in 2010: 10 were by agented authors and 96 were reprint/licensed properties. Receives 1,000 queries yearly.

- **Nonfiction:** Publishes concept books and toddler books, 0–4 years; easy-to-read books, 4–7 years; middle-grade books, 8–12 years; and young adult books, 12–18 years. Topics include animals, cars, trucks, numbers, letters, potty-training, manners, bedtime, families, cooking, nature, the human body, mythology, religion, history, geography, and science. Also publishes reference, activity, and sticker books.
- **Representative Titles:** *Sharks and Other Creatures of the Deep* (6+ years) looks at how fish and mammals swim, eat, and sleep in the ocean. *Hush Little Lion* is an interactive hide-and-seek book that has young children following along on the lion's adventures. *First People*, by David C. King (8+ years), traces the history of American Indians back 10,000 years.

Submissions and Payment

Guidelines available. Accepts queries through literary agents only. Responds in 6 months. Publication in 2 years. Royalty, 10%; advance, varies.

Editor's Comments

We require our writers to be experts in their fields. Books should have a combination of educational value and strong visual style.

Dorchester Publishing

200 Madison Avenue, Suite 2000
New York, NY 10016

Editorial Assistant

Publisher's Interests

Specializing in mass-market paperback fiction titles, Dorchester Publishing offers romance, horror, Westerns, and thrillers. It also offers a line of books for teens. The company is always looking to develop fresh voices that will appeal to the changing interests of its audience.
Website: www.dorchesterpub.com

Freelance Potential

Published 200+ titles in 2010: 12 were developed from unsolicited submissions and 112 were by agented authors. Of the 200+ titles, 18 were by unpublished writers and 25–30 were by authors who were new to the publishing house. Receives 3,000 queries yearly.

- **Fiction:** Publishes young adult books, 12–18 years. Genres include contemporary and science fiction, romance, and mystery. Also publishes books about paranormal activity.
- **Representative Titles:** *Tsunami Blue*, by Gayle Ann Williams, follows a radio DJ targeted by ruthless pirates for her unusual ability to predict tsunamis. *A Breath of Magic*, by Tracy Madison, tells of a girl who believes that gypsy magic may help her find the family of her dreams.

Submissions and Payment

Guidelines and catalogue available at website. Query with first 3 chapters. Accepts hard copy and email queries to submissions@dorchesterpub.com. SASE. Responds in 6–8 months. Publication in 9–12 months. Royalty; advance.

Editor's Comments

We are a small house with a big presence. Our size allows us the freedom and flexibility to adjust quickly to market changes and to take chances on projects that don't necessarily fit into neat genre categories. Please note that at the current time, we are concentrating on acquiring romance, horror, Westerns, and thrillers only.

Douglas & McIntyre Publishing Group

201-2323 Quebec Street
Vancouver, British Columbia V5T 4S7
Canada

Editorial Board

Publisher's Interests
Starting as a trade publisher deeply rooted in Pacific North-west culture, this publishing group is well known in Canada for its books on art, architecture, food and wine, and Canadian culture. Its children's books explore issues such as nature and the environment.
Website: www.douglas-mcintyre.com

Freelance Potential
Published 60 titles (3 juvenile) in 2010.

- **Nonfiction:** Publishes easy-to-read books, 4–7 years; and story picture books, 4–10 years. Topics include art, architecture, Canadian culture, First Nations art and culture, the environment, ecology, natural science, outdoor recreation, travel, geography, health, fitness, history, military history, social and political issues, biography, cooking, sports, and British Columbia and Northern Canadian regional themes.
- **Representative Titles:** *The Little Hummingbird*, by Michael Nicoll Yahgulanaas, is based on a South American indigenous story about a courageous hummingbird who saves her forest from fire. *The World Needs Your Kids,* by Craid Kielburger et al. (parents), is a guide to raising conscientious children who can help change the world.

Submissions and Payment
Guidelines and catalogue available at website. Query with outline/synopsis, sample chapter, author bio, and required cover sheet from website. Accepts hard copy. SAE/IRC. Responds in 6–8 weeks. Publication period and payment policy vary.

Editor's Comments
We are only accepting submissions for children's picture books in the areas of natural history, ecology, and the environment. If you think your project is a good match, please download our Submission Cover Sheet.

Dover Publications

31 East 2nd Street
Mineola, NY 11501-3582

Editorial Department

Publisher's Interests
Many of the books on Dover Publications' list are nonfiction titles about science topics that include hands-on experiments and projects. It also offers biographies and books on fine arts, history, and natural history.
Website: www.doverpublications.com

Freelance Potential
Published 500 titles (120 juvenile) in 2010. Of the 500 titles, 15–20 were by authors who were new to the publishing house. Receives 125 queries yearly.

- **Fiction:** Publishes reprints of children's classics and storybooks. Genres include folktales, fantasy, and fairy tales. Also publishes stories about animals.
- **Nonfiction:** Publishes story picture books, 4–10 years; middle-grade books, 8–12 years; and young adult books, 12–18 years. Topics include science, natural history, wildlife, American history, Native Americans, architecture, archaeology, literature, hobbies, and fine art. Also publishes educational titles, anthologies, biographies, coloring books, posters, sticker books, and activity books.
- **Representative Titles:** *The Code of Life,* by Alvin & Virginia Silverstein, provides a concise narrative on how DNA works and how a human cell develops. *Physics Experiments for Children,* by Muriel Mandell, includes 103 projects that demonstrate how substances are affected by energy.

Submissions and Payment
Catalogue available at website. Query with outline, table of contents, and sample chapter. Accepts hard copy. Submissions are not returned. Responds if interested. Publication period and payment policy vary.

Editor's Comments
We are guided by the philosophy that young people are naturally curious. We look for titles that spark that curiosity.

Down East Books

P.O. Box 679
Camden, ME 04843

Associate Editor: Michael Steere

Publisher's Interests
This multimedia company focuses on the state of Maine—its history, its people, its environment, and its lifestyle. Among Down East's offerings are children's fiction and nonfiction for toddlers through middle-grade students, though its emphasis is on picture books for ages 4 through 10.
Website: www.downeast.com

Freelance Potential
Published 28 titles in 2010: 10 were developed from unsolicited submissions and 3 were by agented authors. Of the 28 titles, 2 were by authors who were new to the publishing house. Receives 2,400–3,600 queries yearly.

- **Fiction:** Publishes toddler books and early picture books, 0–4 years; story picture books, 4–10 years; and middle-grade books, 8–12 years. Stories with a Maine perspective.
- **Nonfiction:** Publishes toddler books and early picture books, 0–4 years; easy-to-read books, 4–7 years; and story picture books, 4–10 years. Topics include the wildlife and the history of Maine.
- **Representative Titles:** *Counting Our Way to Maine,* by Maggie Smith (3–8 years), is a whimsical book that follows a family heading to Maine on vacation. *Moose, of Course!,* by Lynn Plourde (4+ years), tells the story of a young boy's adventures as he searches for a moose.

Submissions and Payment
Guidelines and catalogue available at website. Query with 1-page description and short author bio. Accepts hard copy and email queries to submissions@downeast.com. SASE. Responds in 3 months. Publication in 2 years. Royalty, 9–12%; advance, $300–$600.

Editor's Comments
Please note that we are no longer accepting unsolicited manuscripts. Instead, query us with a short description of your idea.

Dramatic Publishing

311 Washington Street
Woodstock, IL 60098

Submissions Editor: Linda Habjan

Publisher's Interests
Dramatic Publishing provides musicals and one-act and full-length plays to professional, stock, community, school, and children's theater groups. It also publishes resource materials and reference texts about theater arts.
Website: www.dramaticpublishing.com

Freelance Potential
Published 37 titles (9 juvenile) in 2010. Of the 37 titles, 14 were by authors who were new to the publishing house. Receives 500 unsolicited mss yearly.

- **Fiction:** Publishes full-length and one-act plays, monologues, and anthologies. Genres include drama, humor, fairy tales, and musicals. Also publishes plays with holiday themes.
- **Nonfiction:** Publishes books and resource materials. Topics include teaching theater arts, stagecraft, stage dialects, production techniques, playwriting, and audition presentations.
- **Representative Titles:** *Chocolate Soup*, by Jill Jaysen, is a musical about being a tween and coming to terms with who you are and what you believe in. *Chem Mystery*, by Caleen Sinnette Jennings, written for a young audience, follows the animals of Zooville School as they each participate in their favorite class.

Submissions and Payment
Guidelines and catalogue available at website. Send complete ms with résumé, synopsis, production history, reviews, cast list, and set and technical requirements; include CD or audio cassette for musicals. Accepts hard copy. SASE. Responds in 4–6 months. Publication in 18 months. Payment policy varies.

Editor's Comments
Due to the number of scripts we receive, we ask that you submit only one or two at a time. Please review our guidelines carefully for musical submission requirements.

The Dundurn Group

3 Church Street, Suite 500
Toronto, Ontario M5E 1M2
Canada

Assistant Editor: Allison Hirst

Publisher's Interests
Working mainly with Canadian authors, this publisher produces fiction and nonfiction titles for middle-grade students and young adults.
Website: www.dundurn.com

Freelance Potential
Published 85 titles in 2010: 10 were developed from unsolicited submissions, 18 were by agented authors, and 8 were reprint/licensed properties. Of the 85 titles, 10 were by unpublished writers and 25 were by authors who were new to the publishing house. Receives 240 queries, 600 unsolicited mss yearly.

- **Fiction:** Publishes middle-grade books, 8–12 years; and young adult books, 12–18 years. Genres include contemporary, historical, and regional fiction; mystery; and suspense. Also publishes stories about nature, the environment, and the paranormal.
- **Nonfiction:** Publishes middle-grade books, 8–12 years; and young adult books, 12–18 years. Topics include biography, current events, history, nature, the environment, the paranormal, and Canadiana.
- **Representative Titles:** *Doom Lake Holiday*, by Tom Henighan (12+ years), tells of a family that encounters an ancient curse while vacationing at the lake. *True Stories of Rescue and Survival*, by Carolyn Matthews (10+ years), presents the stories of Canada's unknown heroes, past and present.

Submissions and Payment
Guidelines and catalogue available at website. Query with résumé, synopsis (fiction), table of contents (nonfiction), and 3 sample chapters; or send complete ms. Accepts hard copy. SAE/IRC. Responds in 6 months. Publication in 1 year. Royalty; advance.

Editor's Comments
We occasionally publish science fiction books.

Dutton Children's Books

Penguin Group
345 Hudson Street
New York, NY 10014

Queries Editor

Publisher's Interests

With a publishing history that dates back to 1852, Dutton is now an imprint of the Penguin Young Readers Group. With a stated mission to create high-quality books that will transport young readers, it publishes fiction and nonfiction for children of all ages.

Website: www.us.penguingroup.com

Freelance Potential

Published 50 titles in 2010. Of the 50 titles, 7 were by unpublished writers. Receives 1,000+ queries yearly.

- **Fiction:** Publishes concept books and early picture books, 0–4 years; easy-to-read books, 4–7 years; story picture books, 4–10 years; middle-grade books, 8–12 years; and young adult books, 12–18 years. Genres include adventure, mystery, fantasy, and humor.
- **Nonfiction:** Publishes toddler books, 0–4 years; story picture books, 4–10 years; and young adult books, 12–18 years. Topics include history and nature.
- **Representative Titles:** *Ron's Big Mission,* by Corinne Naden & Rose Blue (6–8 years), is a story picture book that tells the true story of how astronaut Ron McNair peacefully desegregated his community library as a boy. *Tell Me Who,* by Jessica Wollman (10+ years), features teens discovering a machine that can tell them the future, and finding out that knowing the future comes with its own set of problems.

Submissions and Payment

Guidelines available at website. Query with synopsis and publishing credits. Accepts hard copy. SASE. Responds in 3–6 months. Publication in 1+ years. Royalty; advance.

Editor's Comments

We are proud of our many Caldecott and Newbery Medal awards. Whatever the subject, we look for books that entertain, engage, and inspire our readers.

E & E Publishing

1001 Bridgeway, #227
Sausalito, CA 94965

Submissions Editor: Eve Heidi Bine-Stock

Publisher's Interests

Publishing electronic books as well as the traditional, in-print variety, E & E's catalogue features nonfiction picture books for young children, nonfiction books for children about writing, and books for adults about how to write for children.
Website: www.EandEGroup.com/Publishing

Freelance Potential

Published 3–5 titles (2–3 juvenile) in 2010. Of the 3–5 titles, 2 were by authors who were new to the publishing house. Receives 50 queries, 200 unsolicited mss yearly.

- **Nonfiction:** Publishes concept books and early picture books, 0–4 years; and story picture books, 4–10 years. Topics include animals, nature, counting, the alphabet, and writing. Also publishes books for adults about writing children's books and other self-help topics.
- **Representative Titles:** *The Canada Goose and You,* by Jennifer S. Burrows (preK–grade 3), explains the life and characteristics of the Canada goose by relating them to the child and his world. *Bandy Bandana,* by Susan Sundwall (3–5 years), teaches children their colors, the days of the week, and other concepts through the antics of a dog and his many bandanas.

Submissions and Payment

Catalogue available at website. Query. Send complete ms for picture books only. Prefers email to EandEGroup@ EandEGroup.com; will accept hard copy. SASE. Response time and publication period vary. Royalty, 5% of retail; non-illustrated books for adults, 10% of retail.

Editor's Comments

Please note that we are no longer publishing children's fiction, nor do we handle Christian or holiday themes. We expect to see professional-quality proposals, so please be sure to prepare one that will meet our high standards.

Ebooksonthe.net

Write Words, Inc.
2934 Old Route 50
Cambridge, MD 21613

Publisher: Arline Chase

Publisher's Interests
Ebooksonthe.net produces fiction and nonfiction titles in a number of genres for young adults as well as adults. Its catalogue features both e-books and paperback books that appeal to a global audience.
Website: www.writewordsinc.com

Freelance Potential
Published 40–60 titles in 2010: 10 were by unpublished writers and 30 were by authors who were new to the publishing house. Receives 200–300 queries yearly.

- **Fiction:** Publishes young adult books, 12–18 years. Genres include contemporary, historical, inspirational, and science fiction; romance; and mystery.
- **Nonfiction:** Publishes young adult books, 12–18 years. Topics include self-help, inspirational stories, and biography.
- **Representative Titles:** *Toby Martin: Pet Detective*, by Barbara Grengs (YA), tells how Toby and her best friend search for clues to find out who's been stealing the neighborhood dogs. *Dark Elf*, by Ray Morand (YA), follows Akulina as she fights to regain honor from her people after dabbling in black magic; part of the Red Knight Chronicles series.

Submissions and Payment
Guidelines and catalogue available at website. Query with author credentials, word count, synopsis, and market analysis. Accepts email queries to arline@mail.com. Responds in 1 week. Publication in 3 months. Royalty, 40% for e-books sold from our website, 15% for paperback books; 50% of proceeds from e-books sold on subsidiary websites.

Editor's Comments
We can be a home to the homeless. If you have previously published work that you'd like to see back in print, we would be happy to consider picking it up for publication again. Please study our guidelines for format requirements.

Edcon Publishing Group

30 Montauk Boulevard
Oakdale, NY 11769

Editor-in-Chief

Publisher's Interests
With a focus on learning materials for preschool through high school, Edcon Publishing produces titles designed to improve skills in literacy, speech, and mathematics. It also offers special education materials and fiction.
Website: www.edconpublishing.com

Freelance Potential
Published 10 titles in 2010: 2 were developed from unsolicited submissions. Of the 10 titles, 2 were by unpublished writers and 1 was by an author who was new to the publishing house. Receives 120 unsolicited mss yearly.

- **Fiction:** Publishes easy-to-read books, 4–7 years; chapter books, 5–10 years; middle-grade books, 8–12 years; and young adult books, 12–18 years. Genres include science fiction, adventure, multicultural and ethnic fiction, and fairy tales. Also publishes hi/lo fiction, 6–18 years; and activity books, 6–12 years.
- **Nonfiction:** Publishes chapter books, 5–10 years; and young adult books, 12–18 years. Topics include reading comprehension, mathematics, science, and technology. Also publishes educational materials for homeschooling.
- **Representative Titles:** *Reading Step by Step* offers instruction to develop strong auditory and visual skills. *Creating Stories* helps students express ideas to build a story.

Submissions and Payment
Guidelines available with 9x12 SASE ($1.75 postage). Send complete ms. Accepts hard copy and simultaneous submissions if identified. Submissions are not returned. Responds in 1 month. Publication in 6 months. Flat fee, $300–$1,000.

Editor's Comments
High-interest/low-reading level books are always of interest to us. Review our guidelines before submitting to familiarize yourself with our needs and interests.

Edupress

401 South Wright Road
Fort Atkinson, WI 53538

Product Development Manager: Liz Bowie

Publisher's Interests
Edupress supplies teachers and homeschooling parents with standards-based language arts, math, science, and social studies materials for students in preschool through grade eight. It also produces a line of supplemental material that includes activity books, classroom games, and literacy tools.
Website: www.edupressinc.com

Freelance Potential
Published 100+ titles in 2010. Of the 100+ titles, 8+ were by authors who were new to the publishing house. Receives 20–30 queries yearly.

- **Nonfiction:** Publishes activity books and resource materials for educators, preK–grade 8. Topics include social studies, science, curriculum coordination, language arts, early learning, math, holidays, arts and crafts, and classroom decor.
- **Representative Titles:** *Main Idea: Reading Comprehension Activities* provides a range of classroom activities designed to reinforce critical reading skills and comprehension. *Brain Blasters Vocabulary Practice Cards* (grade 2) are self-checking, double-sided cards that provide students with definitions, context clues, synonyms, and antonyms for more than 400 vocabulary words.

Submissions and Payment
Guidelines and catalogue available at website. Query with résumé, targeted grade range, outline, and sample pages. Accepts hard copy email queries to lbowie@highsmith.com (with "Manuscript Submission" in subject line). SASE. Responds in 4–5 months. Publication in 1 year. Flat fee.

Editor's Comments
In the coming year, we will be focusing on unique reading and math products, as well as science and social studies material. If you are an educator and have some great ideas, we'd like to hear from you.

Eerdmans Books for Young Readers

2140 Oak Industrial Drive NE
Grand Rapids, MI 49505

Acquisitions Editor

Publisher's Interests
This publisher produces picture books, chapter books, and young adult fiction and nonfiction. It puts a premium on engaging characters, good humor, and storylines that delight. **Website: www.eerdmans.com/youngreaders**

Freelance Potential
Published 16 titles in 2010: 3 were developed from unsolicited submissions, 2 were by agented authors, and 7 were reprint/licensed properties. Of the 16 titles, 1 was by an unpublished writer and 6 were by authors who were new to the publishing house. Receives 1,200+ unsolicited mss yearly.

- **Fiction:** Publishes toddler books and early picture books, 0–4 years; easy-to-read books, 4–7 years; story picture books, 4–10 years; chapter books, 5–10 years; middle-grade books, 8–12 years; and young adult books, 12–18 years. Genres include multicultural and historical fiction, and stories about animals and nature.
- **Nonfiction:** Publishes early picture books, 0–4 years; and middle-grade books, 8–12 years. Topics include history, religion, and social issues. Also publishes biographies.
- **Representative Titles:** *Ben and the Emancipation Proclamation,* by Pat Sherman (8–12 years), is the story of a young slave who reads some very interesting news. *I See the Moon,* by Kathi Appelt (3–7 years), is a bedtime storybook that uses the moon as an illustration for God's abiding love.

Submissions and Payment
Guidelines available. Send complete ms. Accepts hard copy (marked "exclusive" on the envelope). No simultaneous submissions. SASE. Responds in 6 months. Publication period varies. Royalty.

Editor's Comments
Stories that celebrate diversity and that relate to current issues are of special interest to us at this time.

Egmont USA

443 Park Avenue South, Suite 806
New York, NY 10016

Executive Editor: Regina Griffin

Publisher's Interests
Egmont USA is the American division of a Scandinavian
company that is also one of the largest children's publishers
in the U.K. It arrived in the U.S. in 2008 and continues to
grow. Known for its picture books and high-quality fiction,
the company also places a high premium on ethics in its
books and policies.
Website: www.egmontusa.com

Freelance Potential
Published 50 books in 2010.

- **Fiction:** Publishes picture story books, 4–10 years; middle-
  grade books, 8–12 years; and young adult books, 12–18
  years. Genres include adventure, humor, multicultural and
  contemporary fiction, fantasy, and science fiction.
- **Representative Titles:** *Dangerous Neighbors,* by Beth Kephart
  (YA), is historical fiction set during the American Centennial in
  Philadelphia. *Guinea Dog,* by Patrick Jennings (9–12 years),
  tells the humorous story of a guinea pig that believes she is a
  dog. *The Cinderella Society,* by Kay Cassidy (YA), is teen chick
  lit about a 16-year-old who is always the new girl but is invited
  to join a secret club.

Submissions and Payment
Agented submissions only. Publication in 18 months. Royalty.

Editor's Comments
Our goal was to be a leading publisher in the United States
within five years across the bookstore, school, and library
markets. We have concentrated strongly on list-building, with
particular interest in high-concept books, thrillers, teen girl
fiction, and middle-grade humor.

Eldridge Publishing

P.O. Box 14367
Tallahassee, FL 32317

Editor: Susan Shore

Publisher's Interests

Since 1906, Eldridge has been publishing full-length plays, one-act plays, melodramas, holiday and religious plays, children's theater plays, and musicals of all kinds.
Website: www.histage.com; www.95church.com

Freelance Potential

Published 35 titles (23 juvenile) in 2010: 30 were developed from unsolicited submissions. Of the 35 titles, 5 were by authors who were new to the publishing house. Receives 500 unsolicited mss yearly.

- **Fiction:** Publishes full-length plays, skits, and musicals for grades 6–12. Genres include classical and contemporary drama, humor, folktales, melodrama, and Westerns. Also publishes plays with religious themes, holiday plays, and adult drama for community theaters.
- **Representative Titles:** *Promedy,* by Wade Bradford, is a comedy for school theater groups in which a group of high school students must come to the rescue of their class prom. *The Case of the Missing Homework,* by Gary H. Smith, is a one-act melodrama for elementary school students in which the hunt is on for a homework thief.

Submissions and Payment

Guidelines available. Send ms with cover letter stating play length, age ranges for actors and audience, and performance history. Include CD and sample score for musicals. Accepts hard copy and email to newworks@histage.com (Microsoft Word or PDF attachments). SASE. Responds in 2 months. Publication in 6–12 months. Royalty, 50% performances, 10% copy sales. Flat fee for religious plays.

Editor's Comments

We strongly recommend having your script workshopped, read, or performed. Scripts rewritten after this process are of a much higher caliber and, therefore, more likely to be accepted.

Elva Resa Publishing

8362 Tamarack Village, Suite 119-106
St. Paul, MN 55125

Publisher: Christy Lyon

Publisher's Interests

Elva Resa Publishing primarily focuses on books for and about military families. Its children's imprint, Alma Little, features picture books and novels on general interest and military topics for children up to age 10.
Website: www.elvaresa.com; www.almalittle.com

Freelance Potential

Published 4 titles (2 juvenile) in 2010. Of the 4 titles, 1 was by an unpublished writer and 1 was by an author who was new to the publishing house. Receives 360–3,600 queries each year.

- **Fiction:** Publishes story picture books, 4–10 years. Genres include contemporary and historical fiction, and stories about family members in the military.
- **Nonfiction:** Publishes early picture books, 0–4 years. Topics include self-help, current events, and military resources. Also publishes activity books and books for adults.
- **Representative Titles:** *Cedric and the Dragon,* by Elizabeth Raum & Nina Victor Crittenden, is about a prince who fails at dragon-slaying school but ultimately saves his kingdom. *Cathy's Animal Garden: Enter at Your Own Risk,* by Stacy Tornio & Samantha Bell, follows two boys who dodge wild animals while searching for their baseball.

Submissions and Payment

Guidelines and catalogue available at website. Elva Resa: query with outline. Accepts email queries to submissions@elvaresa.com. Alma Little: accepts targeted submissions only; see www.almalittle.com for details. Responds in 3 weeks. Publication in 12–18 months. Royalty; advance. Flat fee.

Editor's Comments

For our children's imprint, we accept submissions on a call-for-manuscript basis only. Our goal is to produce work that will make a positive difference in our readers' lives.

Encore Performance Publishing

P.O. Box 14367
Tallahassee, FL 32317

New Plays Editor: Meredith Edwards

Publisher's Interests
This publisher focuses on family-pleasing plays and musicals for performance by middle schools, high schools, colleges, community theaters, and religious institutions; and on children's theater shows to be performed by adults. It also publishes books on theater performance techniques.
Website: www.encoreplay.com

Freelance Potential
Published 5–10 titles in 2010. Receives 75 queries yearly.

- **Fiction:** Publishes full-length plays and musicals, skits, and monologue collections for grades 4–12. Genres include comedy and drama with Christian, multicultural, and ethnic themes.
- **Nonfiction:** Publishes resource titles for all ages. Topics include theater arts, acting, auditions, improvisation, stage management, set design, lighting, and makeup.
- **Representative Titles:** *The Griffin and the Minor Canon,* by Vern Adix, is a play for youth theater which embraces a message of tolerance. *Shusha and the Story Snatcher,* by Shirley Barrie, is a play for young audiences that uses the audience's help to get a favorite story returned to a young girl.

Submissions and Payment
Guidelines and catalogue available at website. Query with synopsis and production history. Accepts email queries to newworks@encoreplay.com. Responds in 2 months. Publication in 6 months. Royalty, 50% performance, 10% script.

Editor's Comments
We receive many plays each year and want to give careful attention to each one. Please do not send more than one script or collection book at a time, as flooding us with your work will not be to your benefit. Our catalogue is mailed to more than 30,000 U.S. junior and senior high schools and thousands of community theaters across the country twice each year.

Enslow Publishers

40 Industrial Road
Berkeley Heights, NJ 07922

Editor-in-Chief: Dorothy Goeller

Publisher's Interests

Curriculum-based nonfiction books have been the specialty of this family-owned company for more than 30 years. It produces high-interest, colorful titles for school-age children in a wide range of subjects, including history, science, math, sports, and technology.
Website: www.enslow.com

Freelance Potential

Published 200 titles in 2010. Receives 240 queries yearly.

- **Fiction:** Publishes middle-grade books, 8–12 years. Genres include historical fiction.
- **Nonfiction:** Publishes easy-to-read books, 4–7 years; middle-grade books, 8–12 years; and young adult books, 12–18 years. Topics include contemporary issues, health and drug education, history, government, holidays and customs, mathematics, science, technology, sports, and recreation. Also publishes biographies.
- **Representative Titles:** *Earth Shaking Science Projects About Planet Earth*, by Robert Gardner (grades 3–4), introduces students to the workings of Earth science and includes activities and experiments that can be done at home or at school. *The Locket: Surviving the Triangle Shirtwaist Fire*, by Suzanne Lieurance (grades 3–6), recounts the tragic New York City fire of 1911. *Counting in the Grasslands*, by Frederick L. McKissack, Jr. & Lisa Beringer McKissack (grades 1–3), uses the animals of the grasslands to teach children their numbers.

Submissions and Payment

Guidelines available. Catalogue available at website. Query with outline. Accepts hard copy. SASE. Responds in 1–6 months. Publication in 1 year. Royalty; advance. Flat fee.

Editor's Comments

Our books are clearly written in a way that appeals even to the most reluctant reader.

Facts On File

132 West 31st Street, 17th Floor
New York, NY 10001

Editorial Director: Laurie Likoff

Publisher's Interests
An imprint of Infobase Publishing, Facts On File produces
nonfiction reference and textbooks for the high school, academic, and public library market.
Website: www.factsonfile.com

Freelance Potential
Published 500 titles (100 juvenile) in 2010: 15 were by
agented authors and 10 were reprint/licensed properties. Of
the 500 titles, 25 were by unpublished writers and 5 were by
authors who were new to the publishing house. Receives
300 queries yearly.

- **Nonfiction:** Publishes chapter books, 5–10 years; middle-
  grade books, 8–12 years; and young adult books, 12–18
  years. Topics include history, social studies, current affairs,
  politics, government, multicultural subjects, math, science,
  and the environment. Also publishes biographies.
- **Representative Titles:** *The Great Depression and World War II*
  (grades 9 and up) goes beyond the events and notable figures
  of this period and delves into the way ordinary Americans lived;
  part of the Handbook to Life in America series. *Rock & Roll*
  (grades 6–12) celebrates this uniquely American music by profil-
  ing key personalities, performances, instruments, and social
  and historical issues; part of the American Popular Music series.

Submissions and Payment
Guidelines and catalogue available at website. Query with
résumé, sample chapter, market analysis, and marketing
ideas. Accepts hard copy, email queries to editorial@
factsonfile.com, and simultaneous submissions. SASE. Responds in 2 months. Publication in 1 year. Royalty; advance.

Editor's Comments
We're currently interested in history, science, political science,
literature, and the arts. You should be an expert or have
extensive research experience with the subject you propose.

Fairview Press

2450 Riverside Avenue
Minneapolis, MN 55454

Submissions: Steve Deger

Publisher's Interests
Fairview Press publishes self-help books for both children
and adults that address physical, emotional, and spiritual
wellness. Most of its titles are written for a lay audience by
educated professionals active within their disciplines.
Website: www.fairviewpress.org

Freelance Potential
Published 6–12 titles (1 juvenile) in 2010. Receives 600
queries yearly.

- **Nonfiction:** Publishes easy-to-read books, 4–7 years; middle-
  grade books, 8–12 years; and young adult books, 12–18
  years. Also publishes parenting titles. Topics include health;
  complementary, holistic, and integrative medicine; patient
  education; self-help; relationships; pregnancy and childbirth;
  sex education; reproductive health; diet and exercise; and
  inspiration and mindfulness.
- **Representative Titles:** *Adopted and Wondering*, by Marge
  Eaton Heegaard, uses the art process to help children understand and express their feelings about being adopted. *My
  Changing Body–Girl's Edition*, by Linda Picone, presents practical and insightful facts about the changes girls go through
  before and after puberty.

Submissions and Payment
Guidelines and catalogue available at website. Query with
outline, sample chapter, and marketing plans. Accepts hard
copy. SASE. Response time and publication period vary. Payment negotiated on a case-by-case basis.

Editor's Comments
At this time, we're particularly interested in acquiring material
on pregnancy and childbirth, health issues for young adults,
diet and exercise, and complementary/holistic/integrative
medicine. Please study our catalogue before submitting a proposal, to become familiar with the types of books we publish.

Feiwel & Friends

Macmillan
175 Fifth Avenue
New York, NY 10010

Publisher: Jean Feiwel

Publisher's Interests
Feiwel & Friends looks for books that combine quality with substance and commercial appeal. Its catalogue features an eclectic mix of fiction and nonfiction titles for children of all ages, written by both new and established authors.
Website: www.feiwelandfriends.com

Freelance Potential
Published 40 titles in 2010: each was by an agented author.

- **Fiction:** Publishes story picture books, 4–10 years; chapter books, 5–10 years; middle-grade books, 8–12 years; and young adult books, 12–18 years. Genres include humor, fantasy, thrillers, historical fiction, and stories about animals.
- **Nonfiction:** Publishes middle-grade books, 8–12 years. Topics include humor.
- **Representative Titles:** *Tyrannosaurus Drip,* by Julia Donaldson (4–8 years), tells how the plant-eating duckbill dinosaurs try to exist peacefully with the meat-eating T-Rex family that lives across the river. *Dodger and Me,* by Jordan Sonnenblick (8–12 years), is the story of a boy who befriends an imaginary oversized blue chimp that changes his life. *The President's Daughter,* by Ellen Emerson White (12+ years), is about a 16-year-old girl who doesn't want her life to change just because her mother is running for president.

Submissions and Payment
Agented authors only. Guidelines available. Response time, publication period, and payment policy vary.

Editor's Comments
We believe in "book by book publishing"—building a list book by book and sticking to the enduring categories in children's literature, such as animals, friendships both real and imaginary, sports, and school. We want to lead the way in bringing the work of distinctive and outstanding authors, illustrators, and ideas to the marketplace and to our readers.

Frederick Fell Publishers

2131 Hollywood Boulevard, Suite 305
Hollywood, FL 33020

Submissions: Barbara Newman

Publisher's Interests

First established in 1943, Frederick Fell Publishers has
carved a niche for inspirational and spiritual books for the
young adult set. This includes both fiction and nonfiction
titles. Parenting and child care books can also be found in
its catalogue. Some of its well-known authors include Og
Mandino, Harry Lorayne, and Jane Roberts.
Website: www.fellpub.com

Freelance Potential

Published 24 titles in 2010: 22 were developed from unsolicited submissions and 2 were by agented authors. Of the
24 titles, 9 were by unpublished writers and 3 were by
authors who were new to the publishing house. Receives
1,800 queries yearly.

- **Fiction:** Publishes young adult books, 12–18 years. Genres
  include inspirational and religious fiction.
- **Nonfiction:** Publishes young adult books, 12–18 years. Topics
  include spirituality and health. Also publishes books on parenting and child care.
- **Representative Titles:** *Dorothy and the Wizard's Wish,* by
  David Anthony, is the last book in the trilogy sequel to the
  movie, *The Wizard of Oz. Seven Secrets of Perfect Parenting,* by
  Shelley Herold, offers advice on raising a well-adjusted child.

Submissions and Payment

Guidelines and catalogue available at website. Query with
synopsis, table of contents, and 2 sample chapters. Accepts
hard copy and simultaneous submissions if identified. SASE.
Responds in 1 month. Publication in 9–12 months. Royalty.

Editor's Comments

Our backlist consists of over 1,500 books in 13 genres. Spiritual growth for young adults continues to be of interest to
us. We want to be a resource to this age group for spiritual
guidance and self-help advice.

Ferguson Publishing

132 West 31st Street, 17th Floor
New York, NY 10001

Editor-in-Chief: James Chambers

Publisher's Interests
Ferguson Publishing is a source of career education resources for schools and libraries. Part of Infobase (publishers of Facts on File), its titles for middle school and high school students provide up-to-date information on a variety of career fields and guidance on essential career skills.
Website: www.fergpubco.com

Freelance Potential
Published 60 titles (36–40 juvenile) in 2010. Of the 60 titles, 5 were by authors who were new to the publishing house. Receives 100–145 queries yearly.

- **Nonfiction:** Publishes middle-grade books, 8–12 years; and young adult books, 12–18 years. Topics include college planning, career exploration and guidance, and job training. Also publishes development titles and general reference books.
- **Representative Titles:** *Advertising and Public Relations,* by Stan Tymorek (grades 9 and up), provides essential information about this career field, including tips for effective communication and networking. *But What If I Don't Want to Go to College?,* by Harlow G. Unger (grades 9 and up), examines careers in 16 industry categories for students who wish to pursue educational opportunities other than college.

Submissions and Payment
Guidelines and catalogue available at website. Query with résumé, outline, and sample chapter. Accepts hard copy, email to editorial@factsonfile.com, and simultaneous submissions if identified. SASE. Responds in 3–4 weeks. Publication in 9–24 months. Payment policy varies.

Editor's Comments
Our titles are known for their accuracy, readability, and user-friendly formats. To be considered, you must be able to demonstrate a thorough knowledge of your topic. We accept proposals for stand-alone titles as well as series.

David Fickling Books

31 Beaumont Street
Oxford OX1 2NP
United Kingdom

Submissions: Matilda Johnson

Publisher's Interests
This publisher aims to "choose the very best stories we can find for people to read." Its catalogue features books for toddlers through young adults in a number of genres.
Website: www.davidficklingbooks.co.uk

Freelance Potential
Published 12 titles (6 juvenile) in 2010. Of the 12 titles, 2 were by authors who were new to the publishing house. Receives 500+ queries yearly.

- **Fiction:** Publishes toddler books, 0–4 years; story picture books, 4–10 years; chapter books, 5–10 years; middle-grade books, 8–12 years; and young adult books, 12–18 years. Genres include contemporary, historical, and science fiction; adventure; drama; fairy tales; fantasy; humor; and romance.
- **Representative Titles:** *Mistress of the Storm*, by M. L. Welsh, features a 12-year-old girl who finds a book that changes her life, but also reveals a dark family secret. *White Time*, by Margo Lanagan, is a collection of short stories about the narrow boundaries between reality and possibility. *Tall Story*, by Candy Gourlay, tells of a girl who makes several wishes, one of which is that her half-brother move in with her.

Submissions and Payment
Guidelines available at website. Query with first 3–4 chapters. Prefers email to dfbsubmissions@randomhouse.co.uk; will accept hard copy. SAE/IRC. Responds in 3 months. Publication in 1–2 years. Royalty; advance.

Editor's Comments
We like to think that our books work. By this we mean that if you pick up one of our books or give it to a child, chances are that you or they (or both) are going to be taken by it in some way—taken to tears, or to laughter, or to a world you don't want to leave. We are a story house. If you have a story that you think children will love, send it to us.

Finney Company

8075 215th Street West
Lakeville, MN 55044

President: Alan E. Krysan

Publisher's Interests

Finney Company is a trade publisher that focuses on educational books for the middle-grade and high-school levels. Its imprint, Windward Publishing, covers topics of natural history, science, and outdoor recreation.
Website: www.finneyco.com

Freelance Potential

Published 2–3 titles in 2010: 2 were developed from unsolicited submissions. Of the 2–3 titles, 2 were by unpublished writers and 2 were by authors who were new to the publishing house. Receives 36–60 queries yearly.

- **Nonfiction:** Publishes middle-grade books, 8–12 years; and young adult books, 12–18 years. Topics include natural history, science, nature, outdoor recreation, occupational guidance, careers, technical education, and interpersonal skills.
- **Representative Titles:** *A Daddy Longlegs Isn't A Spider*, by Melissa Stewart, follows a spider as it fends off predators, takes a trip down the river, and finds a safe place to lay eggs. *My Little Book of Bald Eagles*, by Hope Irvin Marston, introduces readers to a family of bald eagles as the newborns learn to take their first solo flight.

Submissions and Payment

Guidelines available at website. Query with résumé, overview, table of contents, introduction, 3 or more sample chapters, and market description. Accepts hard copy and simultaneous submissions if identified. SASE. Responds in 10–12 weeks. Publication period varies. Royalty, 10% of net.

Editor's Comments

Our principal markets are book, retail, and specialty stores. Review our catalogue to get a better idea of the types of material we publish. Please note that we do not consider submissions that are not educational.

Fitzhenry & Whiteside

195 Allstate Parkway
Markham, Ontario L3R 4T8
Canada

Children's Book Editor: Christie Harken

Publisher's Interests

In addition to a large catalogue of titles for adult readers, Fitzhenry & Whiteside publishes high-quality fiction and non-fiction for children and young adults on a variety of topics.
Website: www.fitzhenry.ca

Freelance Potential

Published 10 titles in 2010: 3 were by agented authors and 2 were reprint/licensed properties. Receives 36 queries, 360 unsolicited mss yearly.

- **Fiction:** Publishes toddler books and early picture books, 0–4 years; story picture books, 4–10 years; chapter books, 5–10 years; middle-grade books, 8–12 years; and young adult books, 12–18 years. Genres include contemporary, historical, and multicultural fiction; mystery; suspense; adventure; and romance. Also publishes poetry.
- **Nonfiction:** Publishes early picture books, 0–4 years; story picture books, 4–10 years; middle-grade books, 8–12 years; and young adult books, 12–18 years. Topics include animals, history, nature, and the environment. Also publishes biographies.
- **Representative Titles:** *The Dewpoint Show,* by Barb Howard (YA), is the story of a teen who learns from an unlikely source that actually experiencing life is much better than merely watching it happen around him. *Tim Horton,* by Don Quinlan (8+ years), profiles the life of the Stanley Cup-winning hockey player and founder of the successful donut shop chain that bears his name.

Submissions and Payment

Guidelines available at website. Query with clips. Send complete ms for picture books and poetry only. Accepts hard copy. SAE/IRC. Responds in 3 months. Publication in 1 year. Royalty; advance.

Editor's Comments

We prefer children's nonfiction texts to be related to school curriculum subjects.

Flashlight Press

527 Empire Boulevard
Brooklyn, NY 11225

Editor: Shari Dash Greenspan

Publisher's Interests
Publishing books that "explore and illuminate," Flashlight
Press offers picture books for children ages four through
eight. It looks for touching and humorous stories that
revolve around family and social situations.
Website: www.flashlightpress.com

Freelance Potential
Published 2 titles in 2010: each was developed from an
unsolicited submission. Of the 2 titles, each was by an
unpublished writer who was new to the publishing house.
Receives 1,200+ queries yearly.

- **Fiction:** Publishes easy-to-read books, 4–7 years; and story
  picture books, 4–10 years. Genres include contemporary
  fiction with themes of family and social situations.
- **Representative Titles:** *That Cat Can't Stay*, by Thad Krasnesky (4–8 years), features a mom who keeps rescuing stray
  cats even though her husband doesn't like them. *I Always,
  Always Get My Way*, by Thad Krasnesky (4–8 years), presents a
  little girl who tries to avoid punishment by creatively manipu-
  lating her parents.

Submissions and Payment
Guidelines and catalogue available at website. Query with
description of story and word count. Accepts email queries
to submissions@flashlightpress.com (no attachments).
Responds in 2–4 weeks. Publication period and payment
policy vary.

Editor's Comments
We will send you an automated reply when we receive your
query. If you don't hear from us again within a month or so,
please realize your story was not considered a fit for our
line. We publish only a handful of books each year, so we
need to be extremely selective. No chapter books, young
adult novels, early readers, or holiday stories, please.

Floris Books

15 Harrison Gardens
Edinburgh, EH11 1SH
Scotland

Commissioning Editor: Sally Martin

Publisher's Interests
As one of the largest children's book publishers in Scotland,
Floris produces picture books, storybooks, and children's
fiction. It also publishes books for adults.
Website: www.florisbooks.co.uk

Freelance Potential
Published 50 titles (20 juvenile) in 2010: 5 were developed
from unsolicited submissions, 10 were by agented authors,
and 15 were reprint/licensed properties. Of the 50 titles, 5
were by unpublished writers and 5 were by new authors.
Receives 600 queries, 300 unsolicited mss yearly.

- **Fiction:** Publishes picture books, 4–6 years; chapter books,
  7–10 years; and middle-grade books, 8–12 years. Genres
  include contemporary, multicultural, and regional fiction;
  drama; and fantasy. Also publishes board books, 0–4 years;
  and story collections, 6–10 years.
- **Nonfiction:** Publishes books for adults. Topics include children's health and development, self-help, holistic health,
  science and spirituality, and philosophy.
- **Representative Titles:** *The Big Bottom Hunt,* by Lari Don (3–6
  years), is a funny tale involving a search for the owner of a
  "bottom print." *Hoglet the Spineless Hedgehog,* by Allyson
  Marnoch (6–9 years), is a tale set in the Scottish countryside of
  a young hedgehog who doesn't have spines to protect himself.

Submissions and Payment
Guidelines and catalogue available at website. Query or send
complete ms. Agented submissions have a better chance of
acceptance. Accepts hard copy. SAE/IRC. Responds to
queries in 1 week, to mss in 3 months. Publication in 18
months. Royalty.

Editor's Comments
We are interested in submissions for our Kelpies series of
Scottish children's fiction.

Flux

Llewellyn Worldwide
2143 Wooddale Drive
Woodbury, MN 55125

Acquisitions Editor: Brian Farrey

Publisher's Interests

Flux does one thing and one thing only: It publishes high-quality novels for teens. It offers books that relate to the things teens encounter in their lives, including comedy, tragedy, ecstasy, pain, and discovery. It accepts novel-length projects only; no short stories or poetry.
Website: www.fluxnow.com

Freelance Potential

Published 24 titles in 2010. Of the 24 titles, 13 were by unpublished writers and 15 were by authors who were new to the publishing house. Receives 750 queries, 500 unsolicited mss yearly.

- **Fiction:** Publishes young adult books, 12–18 years. Genres include contemporary, realistic, and coming-of-age fiction; fantasy; and thrillers.
- **Representative Titles:** *A Blue So Dark,* by Holly Schindler (YA), paints a graphic, yet poignant, picture of a mother's mental illness and its effects on her teenaged daughter. *Choppy Socky Blues,* by Ed Briant (YA), tells the story of a boy who discovers that the father he has distanced himself from is the only person who can help him prepare for a martial arts contest.

Submissions and Payment

Guidelines and catalogue available at website. Query with synopsis and 3 chapters; or send complete ms with synopsis. Accepts email submissions to submissions@fluxnow.com (Microsoft Word attachments). Responds in 2–6 months if interested. Publication in 18–24 months. Royalty; advance.

Editor's Comments

The volume of submissions does not allow us to accept or return phone calls, email, or other inquiries, or to provide comments or feedback on unsolicited submissions. We will contact you only if we are interested in going forward with the book.

Focus on the Family
Book Development

8605 Explorer Drive
Colorado Springs, CO 80920

Director: Larry Weeden

Publisher's Interests
Focus on the Family is a Christian organization that advocates
a traditional, biblical perspective on family and marriage. Its
book development division publishes books about parenting,
family, relationships, and life challenges. It also publishes a
fiction series for children called Adventures in Odyssey.
Website: www.focusonthefamily.com

Freelance Potential
Published 15 titles (3 juvenile) in 2010: each was by an
agented author. Of the 15 titles, 1 was by an unpublished
writer and 1 was by an author who was new to the publishing house. Receives 180 queries yearly.

- **Fiction:** Publishes chapter books, 5–10 years. Publishes books
  based on Scripture.
- **Nonfiction:** Publishes young adult books, 12–18 years. Also
  publishes books for adults. Topics include family advice, marriage, parenting, relationships, encouragement for women,
  and topics for seniors.
- **Representative Titles:** *Becoming a Modern-Day Princess Jour-
  nal,* by Pam Farrel & Doreen Hanna, provides a way for girls to
  take a daily journey toward womanhood and learn to be godly
  princesses. *Have a New Kid by Friday,* by Dr. Kevin Leman,
  encourages parents to take a five-day challenge to implement
  a new parenting strategy.

Submissions and Payment
Agented authors only. Guidelines available. Query through
literary agent. Response time varies. Publication in 18
months. Payment policy varies.

Editor's Comments
Of particular interest to us are nonfiction titles on marriage
and parenting, women's issues, and grandparenting. All
books must carry our message of traditional marriage and
family values.

Formac Publishing Company

5502 Atlantic Street
Halifax, Nova Scotia B3H 1G4
Canada

Submissions Editor: Christen Thomas

Publisher's Interests

This Canadian publisher is interested in books with Canadian settings or subjects that appeal to a wide range of ages and reading interests. Its children's and teen's lists include high interest/low reading level titles.
Website: www.formac.ca

Freelance Potential

Published 50 titles (5 juvenile) in 2010: 10 were developed from unsolicited submissions, 5 were by agented authors, and 5 were reprint/licensed properties. Of the 50 titles, 5 were by unpublished writers and 10 were by authors who were new to the publishing house. Receives 50+ queries yearly.

- **Fiction:** Publishes easy-to-read books, 4–7 years; chapter books, 5–10 years; and middle-grade books, 8–13 years. Genres include humor, mystery, suspense, fantasy, adventure, historical fiction, and stories about sports.
- **Nonfiction:** Publishes middle-grade books, 8–13 years. Topics include Canadian history, multicultural and ethnic issues, the environment, and sports.
- **Representative Titles:** *Best Laid Plans,* by Christine Hart (YA), tells of a teen who is torn between working on her family's British Columbia orchard and moving away to university. *Big League Dreams,* by Richard Brignall (reading level 4.8), is the story of Canada's first inductee into the Baseball Hall of Fame.

Submissions and Payment

Canadian authors preferred. Guidelines and catalogue available at website. Query with résumé, outline, and sample chapters. Accepts hard copy and simultaneous submissions if identified. SAE/IRC. Responds in 1–12 months. Publication in 1–2 years. Royalty.

Editor's Comments

Our top priority is good writing, with believable characters, situations, and dialogue.

Free Spirit Publishing

217 Fifth Avenue North, Suite 200
Minneapolis, MN 55401-1299

Acquisitions Editor

Publisher's Interests

Free Spirit has been meeting the social and emotional needs
of kids since 1983 with self-help books and other materials.
Its books, geared toward children in preschool through grade
12, give readers the emotional and intellectual tools they need
to navigate their world, think for themselves, and succeed in
life. It also publishes books for parents and teachers.
Website: www.freespirit.com

Freelance Potential

Published 15–20 titles in 2010. Receives 1,095 queries, 450
unsolicited mss yearly.

- **Nonfiction:** Publishes toddler books and early picture books,
  0–4 years; easy-to-read books, 4–7 years; story picture books,
  4–10 years; middle-grade books, 8–12 years; and young adult
  books, 12–18 years. Topics include social skills, stress management, conflict resolution, character-building, relationships,
  and self-esteem. Also publishes titles about parenting, behavior issues, learning disorders, and gifted education.
- **Representative Titles:** *Cool Down and Work Through Anger*,
  by Cheri J. Meiners (4–8 years), helps readers build skills to
  manage their anger. *Making Differentiation a Habit,* by Diane
  Heacox, helps teachers integrate differentiation practices into
  daily teaching.

Submissions and Payment

Guidelines and catalogue available at website. Query with
résumé, outline, market analysis, and 2 or more sample
chapters. Send complete ms for early childhood books.
Accepts hard copy. SASE. Responds in 2–6 months. Publication in 1–3 years. Royalty.

Editor's Comments

Please note that we do not publish fiction or storybooks,
books with animal or mythical characters, books with religious or New Age content, biographies, or memoirs.

Samuel French, Inc.

45 West 25th Street
New York, NY 10010

Managing Editor: Roxane Heinze-Bradshaw

Publisher's Interests
Offering classic and contemporary plays and musicals for more than 175 years, Samuel French publishes works from Broadway and England's West End, as well as previously unpublished plays and musicals.
Website: www.samuelfrench.com

Freelance Potential
Published 100 titles in 2010: several were by unpublished writers and several were by authors who were new to the publishing house.

- **Fiction:** Publishes full-length and one-act plays, monologues, readings, and anthologies for theater groups of all ages. Genres include musicals; drama; comedy; farce; fantasy; thrillers; operettas; and religious, holiday, and Shakespearean plays.
- **Representative Titles:** *Rock 'n' Roll,* by Tom Stoppard, is a dramatic comedy about love, revolution, and music. *Adding Machine: A Musical,* composed by Joshua Schmidt, tells the story of a man who, after being replaced by a calculator, murders his boss and finds himself in the Elysian Fields. *Dead Man's Cell Phone,* by Sarah Ruhl, is a comedy about a woman forced to confront her own assumptions about morality, redemption, and the need to connect in a technologically obsessed world.

Submissions and Payment
Guidelines available. Query with 10-page sample and links to information about previous productions. Send complete ms through literary agents only. Prefers submissions via website; will accept hard copy and simultaneous submissions if identified. SASE. Responds to queries in 1 month, to mss in 2–3 months. Publication in 1 year. Payment policy varies.

Editor's Comments
We're proud of our reputation for publishing high-quality plays, and we're happy to discover promising new talent.

Friends United Press

101 Quaker Hill Drive
Richmond, IN 47374

Editor: Katie Wonsik

Publisher's Interests
Friends United Press is a Quaker publisher with a list that
includes Quaker history, biography, theology, spirituality,
and inspirational titles. While most of its catalogue is
designed for adults, it publishes a number of titles that are
appropriate for middle-grade and young adult readers.
Website: www.fum.org/shop

Freelance Potential
Published 2 titles in 2010: 1 was developed from an unsolicited submission. Receives 50 queries yearly.

* **Fiction:** Publishes middle-grade books, 8–12 years; and young
  adult books, 12–18 years. Genres include historical and religious fiction.
* **Nonfiction:** Publishes middle-grade books, 8–12 years; and
  young adult books, 12–18 years. Topics include Quaker
  history, theology, and biography; spirituality; peace; justice;
  African American culture; and the Underground Railroad.
* **Representative Titles:** *The Fairest Isle: History of Jamaica
  Friends,* by Mary Jones Langford, provides the history of the
  Quaker presence in Jamaica and a commentary on Quaker
  missions and local Jamaican cultures. *Where 2 or 3 Are
  Gathered. . . Someone Spills the Milk,* by Tom Mullen, takes
  a humorous look at those familiar family moments.

Submissions and Payment
Guidelines and catalogue available at website. Query with
synopsis and 2–3 chapters. Accepts hard copy and email
queries to friendspress@fum.org (Microsoft Word attachments). SASE. Responds in 3–6 months. Publication in 1
year. Royalty, 7.5%.

Editor's Comments
All books must reflect Quaker beliefs and heritage. Although
we're always interested in books on peace and social justice,
we're not currently reviewing complete manuscripts.

Front Street

Boyds Mills Press
815 Church Street
Honesdale, PA 18431

Editorial Director: Larry Rosler

Publisher's Interests
Front Street's list includes picture books and fiction for young readers, as well as novels for children in the middle grades and young adults. A division of Boyds Mills Press, it also produces some nonfiction titles for teens.
Website: www.frontstreetbooks.com

Freelance Potential
Published 25 titles in 2010. Receives 1,000 queries yearly.

- **Fiction:** Publishes story picture books, 4–10 years; middle-grade books, 8–12 years; and young adult books, 12–18 years. Genres include adventure; fantasy; humor; and multicultural, historical, contemporary, and science fiction.
- **Nonfiction:** Publishes young adult books, 12–18 years. Topics include contemporary issues. Also publishes educational titles, novelty books, and poetry collections.
- **Representative Titles:** *The Reinvention of Edison Thomas,* by Jacqueline Jaeger Houtman (8+ years), features a "science geek" who learns how to make friends when he creates an invention to control dangerous car traffic. *Warriors in the Crossfire,* by Nancy Bo Flood (11–14 years), is a story set in the South Pacific during World War II that portrays the challenges one teen boy faces to help protect his indigenous island people.

Submissions and Payment
Guidelines and catalogue available at website. Query with outline/synopsis and 1 sample chapter for nonfiction, 3 sample chapters for fiction. Accepts hard copy. SASE. Responds in 3 months. Publication in 2–3 years. Royalty; advance.

Editor's Comments
Both published and unpublished writers are welcome to submit. Because we do receive a fairly large number of submissions, we will only respond personally if we are interested in your manuscript.

Fulcrum Publishing

4690 Table Mountain Drive, Suite 100
Golden, CO 80403

Acquisitions Editor

Publisher's Interests

Fulcrum publishes an array of storybooks, novels, and non-fiction books for children ages four through young adult, as well as books for adult readers. It is not currently seeking fiction, but is still reviewing nonfiction queries—particularly in the areas of history, nature, the environment, and America's natural resources.
Website: www.fulcrum-books.com

Freelance Potential

Published 35 titles (8 juvenile) in 2010. Receives 300 queries yearly.

- **Nonfiction:** Publishes easy-to-read books, 4–7 years; middle-grade books, 8–12 years; and young adult books, 12–18 years. Topics include ecology, natural history, Native American culture, outdoor recreation, and the American West.
- **Representative Titles:** *Sand to Stone and Back Again,* by Nancy Bo Flood (4+ years), combines stunning photography and text to illustrate the life cycle of sandstone in the desert landscape of the American Southwest. *Alphabet Kingdom,* by Lauren A. Parent, uses the alphabet to introduce young children to nature's animal kingdom.

Submissions and Payment

Guidelines and catalogue available at website. Query with synopsis, sample chapters, résumé, and competition analysis. Accepts hard copy and simultaneous submissions if identified. No SASE; materials not returned. Responds in 3 months if interested. Publication in 18–24 months. Royalty; advance.

Editor's Comments

As an independent publisher, we take pride in encouraging readers—no matter what their age—to live life to the fullest and to learn something new every day. We are particularly interested in nonfiction works regarding the natural history, environment, and culture of the American Southwest.

Gibbs Smith, Publisher

P.O. Box 667
Layton, UT 84041

Editorial Assistant: Debbie Uribe

Publisher's Interests
The emphasis at Gibbs Smith is on lifestyle topics, popular culture, arts and crafts, and gift books for adults. For children, it offers fiction and nonfiction picture books, and activity books. Its subjects range from offbeat fiction to crafts and educational topics.
Website: www.gibbs-smith.com

Freelance Potential
Published 62 titles (10 juvenile) in 2010. Of the 62 titles, 2 were by unpublished writers and 1 was by an author who was new to the publishing house. Receives 1,000 queries, 500 unsolicited mss yearly.

- **Fiction:** Publishes easy-to-read books, 4–7 years; and story picture books, 4–10 years. Genres include adventure, Westerns, fantasy, folktales, and humor. Also publishes stories about animals, nature, and the environment.
- **Nonfiction:** Publishes activity books, 4–10 years. Topics include drawing, crafts, the outdoors, and holidays.
- **Representative Titles:** *Alphabad,* by Shannon Stewart, presents a hilariously wicked take on the average alphabet book. *Cooking on a Stick,* by Linda White, presents 24 easy-to-follow recipes for campfire cooking.

Submissions and Payment
Guidelines and catalogue available at website. Send complete ms for fiction. Query with outline and writing sample for nonfiction. Accepts electronic submissions via form at website only. Responds in 3 months if interested. Publication in 1–2 years. Royalty; advance.

Editor's Comments
We're currently reviewing children's activity book submissions only—no picture books. Please refer to our online submission guidelines for updates to this policy. Note that material sent via postal mail will not be read.

Gifted Education Press

10201 Yuma Court
P.O. Box 1586
Manassas, VA 20109

Editor: Maurice D. Fisher

Publisher's Interests
Gifted Education Press publishes resources for teaching
gifted and talented students. Its catalogue includes parenting
books, titles for homeschooling, textbooks, and books about
the particular needs of these special students.
Website: www.giftededpress.com

Freelance Potential
Published 10 titles in 2010: 4–8 were developed from unsolicited submissions. Of the 10 titles, 2–5 were by unpublished writers. Receives 50 queries yearly.

- **Nonfiction:** Publishes middle-grade books, 8–12 years; and
  young adult books, 12–18 years. Topics include chemistry,
  physics, biology, mathematics, social studies, language arts,
  and the humanities. Also publishes educational resources for
  parents and teachers who work with gifted students.
- **Representative Titles:** *Essential Chemistry for Gifted Students: Preparation for High School Chemistry,* by Francis T.
  Sganga (grades 4–8), is an advanced differentiated, hands-on
  science text that covers all elements of chemistry. *Golden
  Quills: Creative Thinking and Writing Lessons for Middle-
  School Gifted Students,* by R. E. Myers (grades 6–8), is a
  teacher manual and student workbook containing lessons
  designed to stimulate creative learning abilities in the language arts.

Submissions and Payment
Guidelines and catalogue available at website. Query with
1-page proposal. No unsolicited mss. Accepts hard copy.
SASE. Responds in 3 months. Publication in 3 months.
Royalty, 10%.

Editor's Comments
Please see the "Seeking Authors" section of our website to
find the latest information concerning our current needs.

David R. Godine, Publisher

9 Hamilton Place
Boston, MA 02108-4715

Editorial Department

Publisher's Interests
This publisher offers high quality fiction and nonfiction for children. Instead of producing spin-offs and commercial products, it focuses on works that many other publishers can't or won't support. It works only with agented authors. 3% self-, subsidy-, co-venture, or co-op published material. **Website: www.godine.com**

Freelance Potential
Published 30 titles in 2010: each was by an agented author. Of the 30 titles, 7 were by authors who were new to the publishing house. Receives 1,000 queries yearly.

- **Fiction:** Publishes story picture books, 4–10 years; and chapter books, 5–10 years. Genres include mystery, Westerns, historical fiction, and stories about animals and nature.
- **Nonfiction:** Publishes story picture books, 4–10 years; and chapter books, 5–10 years. Topics include study skills, camping, crafts, activities, history, and biography.
- **Representative Titles:** *The Lonely Phone Booth*, by Peter Ackerman & Max Dalton, tells an imaginary story about one of the last remaining phone booths in New York City. *Sarah and Simon and No Red Paint*, by Edward Ardizzone, is an update to this classic book about two siblings who are determined to help their father finish painting his masterpiece. *The American Girls Handy Book: How to Amuse Yourself and Others*, by Lina Beard & Adelia Beard, is filled with hands-on ideas for cooking, decorating, wax modeling, and other projects.

Submissions and Payment
Guidelines and catalogue available at website. Query through literary agent only. Response time, publication period, and payment policy vary.

Editor's Comments
Our aim is to identify the best work and to produce it in the best way possible.

Goodheart-Willcox

18604 West Creek Drive
Tinley Park, IL 60477-6243

Editor, Family & Consumer Sciences: Teresa Dec

Publisher's Interests
Specializing in textbooks for life issues and social sciences, Goodheart-Willcox publishes books that combine authoritative content, case studies, and engaging design to help students learn important life skills. It also produces teacher resource guides and software.
Website: www.g-w.com

Freelance Potential
Published 10 titles in 2010. Receives 100+ queries yearly.

* **Nonfiction:** Publishes textbooks, professional development books for teachers, and how-to titles. Topics include life management, personal development, family living, child care, child development, parenting, consumer education, food and nutrition, housing and interiors, technical trades, fashion, career education, and professional development. Also publishes instructor's guides, resource guides, and software.
* **Representative Titles:** *Strengthening Family & Self*, by Leona Johnson, is a textbook that teaches about strengthening and understanding family relationships and fulfilling career and community roles. *Working with Young Children*, by Judy Herr, speaks to students about the fields of child care service and early childhood education.

Submissions and Payment
Guidelines available. Catalogue available at website. Query with résumé, outline, sample chapter, and list of illustrations. Accepts hard copy. SASE. Responds in 2 months. Publication in 2 years. Royalty.

Editor's Comments
Many first-time authors are eager to get their book underway and immediately begin writing. This is an inefficient way to develop a textbook. The more carefully and thoroughly you research and plan, the more efficient and effective the writing process will be.

Go Teach It

522 West First Avenue
Spokane Valley, WA 99201

Submissions Editor

Publisher's Interests
Targeting educators working in kindergarten through grade 12 classrooms, this online publisher specializes in professionally edited, curriculum-based teaching units and lesson plans in downloadable formats.
Website: www.goteachit.com

Freelance Potential
Published many titles in 2010: 75% were by unpublished writers and each was by an author who was new to the publishing house. Receives 50 queries yearly.

- **Nonfiction:** Publishes teacher curricula, grades K–12. Topics include computers, current events, geography, history, math, science, technology, social issues, literature, vocabulary, and reading comprehension.
- **Representative Titles:** *Treasure Island—Complete Teaching Unit,* by Ray Mathews (grades 6–8), presents a complete lesson plan, including chapter summaries, questions, and classroom activities, for students reading the Robert Louis Stevenson classic. *If I Saw a Monster,* by Steve Denny (grades 1–3), is a literature activity packet that allows students to illustrate their own books.

Submissions and Payment
Guidelines and catalogue available at website. Prospective authors must register their interest via email at write@ goteachit.com; if accepted a personal mentor will be assigned. Response time and publication period vary. Royalty, 10–35%.

Editor's Comments
We do not publish original works unrelated to the curricula, and we prefer to publish curricula relating to established works in print, such as literary classics. Our authors must have strong writing skills, understand cross-competency education, and be able to address a variety of learning styles.

Graphia

Houghton Mifflin Harcourt
222 Berkeley Street
Boston, MA 02116

Submissions: Julie Richardson

Publisher's Interests
This imprint of Houghton Mifflin publishes young adult fiction and nonfiction that is sophisticated, funny, smart, provocative, and hopeful. In other words, its books reflect the issues and situations that teens face on a daily basis.
Website: www.graphiabooks.com

Freelance Potential
Published 10–15 titles in 2010. Of the 10–15 titles, 2–5 were by authors who were new to the publishing house. Receives 50–600 queries, 800–1,000 unsolicited mss yearly.

- **Fiction:** Publishes young adult books, 12–18 years. Genres include contemporary, historical, and science fiction; mystery; suspense; and humor.
- **Nonfiction:** Publishes young adult books, 12–18 years. Topics include history and multicultural issues.
- **Representative Titles:** *Foreign Exposure*, by Lauren Mechling & Laura Moser (13+ years), features a young woman who travels to London with a friend and takes on an exciting and glamorous internship. *The Book of Mordred*, by Vivian Vande Velde (12+ years), tells the story of King Arthur's greatest enemy through the eyes of three women who love him.

Submissions and Payment
Guidelines and catalogue available at website. Send complete ms for fiction. Query with outline and sample chapters for nonfiction. Accepts hard copy. SASE. Responds in 3 months if interested. Publication period varies. Royalty; advance.

Editor's Comments
Although we carefully consider each and every submission we receive, we regret that we cannot respond personally unless we are interested. Whether it is fiction, nonfiction, poetry, or a graphic novel, the most important factor is that our readers relate to a story's characters and situations.

Greenhaven Press

Thomson Gale
27500 Drake Road
Farmington Hills, MI 48331-3535

Administrative Assistant: Kristine Burns

Publisher's Interests

Since its flagship series was published more than 40 years ago, Greenhaven Press has been continuously producing nonfiction titles for the high school market. Its popular series cover such topics as American and world history, health and medicine, and global issues. It is an imprint of Thomson Gale.

Website: www.gale.com/greenhaven

Freelance Potential

Published 189 titles in 2010: few were by unpublished writers and 10–15 were by authors who were new to the publishing house. Receives 300–600 queries yearly.

- **Nonfiction:** Publishes young adult books, 12–18 years. Topics include contemporary social issues, biography, American and world history, geography, literature, multicultural topics, explorations of mysteries, religion, and science.
- **Representative Titles:** *Addiction,* by Wyatt Schaefer, presents a diverse collection of personal narratives from people with firsthand experience with addiction, either as a participant or a witness; part of the Social Issues Firsthand series. *Bullying and Hazing,* by Jill Hamilton, is a guide for young adults that includes facts and advice; part of the Issues That Concern You series.

Submissions and Payment

Query with résumé and list of publishing credits. All work is assigned. Response time varies. Publication in approximately 1 year. Flat fee.

Editor's Comments

We are proud to continue with our original mission of offering a wide spectrum of points of view on every topic covered in our series books. All of our work is assigned, so please review our guidelines and then contact us with your query and list of previous work.

Groundwood Books

110 Spadina Avenue, Suite 801
Toronto, Ontario M5V 2K4
Canada

Acquisitions Editor

Publisher's Interests

Fiction, nonfiction, and picture books for children of all ages
are featured in Groundwood Books' catalogue. The company
works primarily with Canadian authors, and many—but not
all—books reflect the experiences of North America's First
Peoples.
Website: www.groundwoodbooks.com

Freelance Potential

Published 36 titles in 2010. Of the 36 titles, 15 were by
authors who were new to the publishing house.

- **Fiction:** Publishes early picture books, 0–4 years; easy-to-read
  books, 4–7 years; story picture books, 4–10 years; chapter
  books, 5–10 years; middle-grade novels, 8–12 years; and
  young adult books, 12–18 years. Genres include contemporary, historical, and multicultural fiction.
- **Nonfiction:** Publishes middle-grade books, 8–12 years; and
  young adult titles, 12–18 years. Topics include contemporary
  social issues, history, language arts, science, conflict study,
  economics, politics, and multicultural studies.
- **Representative Titles:** *Emily's House,* by Niko Scharer (2–5
  years), is a rhyming tale about a girl who fills her house with
  all sorts of animals to drown out its squeaks and creaks. *The
  Big Swim,* by Cary Fagan (9–12 years), is a novel about three
  teens at summer camp, a love triangle, and a competition to
  swim across the lake.

Submissions and Payment

Guidelines and catalogue available at website. Query with
synopsis and 3 sample chapters. Accepts hard copy and
simultaneous submissions if identified. SAE/IRC. Responds
in 4–6 months. Publication period varies. Royalty; advance.

Editor's Comments

We're always open to novel-length fiction for children of all
ages, but currently we're not accepting picture books.

Group Publishing

P.O. Box 481
Loveland, CO 80539

Contract & Copyright Administration: Kerri Loesche

Publisher's Interests
Group Publishing provides relevant, biblical, fun, and practical resources for children, teens, adults, and pastors. This includes religious education material, Bible story activities, and books about teaching and mentoring children as they deepen their relationship with God.
Website: www.group.com

Freelance Potential
Published 65 titles in 2010: 1 was developed from an unsolicited submission and 1 was by an agented author. Of the 65 titles, 2 were by unpublished writers and 6 were by authors who were new to the publishing house. Receives 1,000 queries yearly.

- **Nonfiction:** Publishes Christian educational resources for all ages. Topics include children's sermons and worship ideas, Bible lessons and activities, crafts, devotions, games, plays and skits, leadership, spiritual growth, counseling, the media, current events, messages, music, retreats, and family ministry.
- **Representative Titles:** *Children's Ministry Volunteers That Stick,* by Jim Wideman, provides practical insights to help churches attract and keep volunteers. *Making Scripture Memory Fun* contains more than 80 activities that will have kids memorizing Bible verses *and* understanding them.

Submissions and Payment
Guidelines available. Query with outline, 2–3 sample chapters, and sample activities. Accepts hard copy and simultaneous submissions if identified. SASE. Responds in 3–6 months. Publication period varies. Royalty, to 10%. Flat fee.

Editor's Comments
A successful submission will get our attention if its tone is not preachy; it is based on the concepts of active and interactive learning; it avoids Christian "lingo"; it is concise; and it is filled with practical ideas that can be replicated easily.

Gryphon House

10770 Columbia Pike, Suite 201
Silver Spring, MD 20901

Editor-in-Chief: Kathy Charner

Publisher's Interests
Books for teachers and parents of infants and toddlers are
the mainstay of this publishing house. Its goal is to provide
essential learning materials that are based on current trends
and that include creative, participatory learning experiences
that enrich the lives of children.
Website: www.gryphonhouse.com

Freelance Potential
Published 20 titles in 2010: 2 were developed from unso-
licited submissions and 6 were reprint/licensed properties.
Receives 240 queries yearly.

- **Nonfiction:** Publishes books for parents and teachers working
  with children up to age 8. Topics include art, mathematics,
  science, literacy, language development, teaching strategies,
  conflict resolution, program development, and games. Also
  publishes lesson plans.
- **Representative Titles:** *Baby Smarts,* by Jackie Silberg, provides fun and easy games for babies that build a strong foundation for a future of learning. *Thinking BIG, Learning BIG,* by
  Marie Faust Evitt, connects science, math, and language learning with fun and age-appropriate activities that engage young
  imaginations.

Submissions and Payment
Guidelines available at website. Query with table of contents,
introductory material, 20–40 sample pages, market analysis,
and writing sample. Accepts hard copy. SASE. Responds in
3–4 months. Publication in 1–2 years. Payment policy varies.

Editor's Comments
We're not interested in books of paper and pencil or cutting
and pasting activities, and we do not publish any children's
books. What we do want are thoroughly researched, developmentally appropriate books that teachers will want to use on
a daily basis.

Gumboot Books

604-980 Seymour Street
Vancouver, British Columbia V6B 1B5
Canada

Editor
***
Publisher's Interests
Gumboot Books publishes children's books and educational materials for kids of all ages. Most of its titles have an environmental focus. It is currently closed to unsolicited submissions, but will review manuscripts solicited by its editors at writers' conferences or other events.
Website: www.gumbootbooks.ca

Freelance Potential
Published 15 titles (10 juvenile) in 2010: 10 were developed from unsolicited submissions. Receives 300 queries yearly.

- **Fiction:** Publishes story picture books, 4–10 years; chapter books, 5–10 years; middle-grade books, 8–12 years; and young adult books, 12–18 years. Genres include adventure; contemporary, inspirational, and multicultural fiction; fantasy; and mystery.
- **Nonfiction:** Publishes story picture books, 4–10 years; chapter books, 5–10 years; middle-grade books, 8–12 years; and young adult books, 12–18 years. Topics include entertainment, multicultural issues, nature, science, and social issues.
- **Representative Titles:** *When Chickens Fly*, by Kari-Lynn Winters, is about a chicken who has big dreams, including participating in the Snow Sports Competition. *Terrific Tuesday*, by Wendy Vale (YA), tells of a class field trip that is threatened to be canceled unless one student can discover the truth about who stole the school's money.

Submissions and Payment
Guidelines available at website. Query with bio, word count, and first and last 3 pages. Accepts hard copy. SAE/IRC. Responds in 3–6 months. Publication period varies. Royalty.

Editor's Comments
We will, periodically, be open for submissions. Please visit our website or sign up for our newsletter for periodic posting calls and updates.

Hachai Publishing

527 Empire Boulevard
Brooklyn, NY 11225

Editor: Devorah L. Rosenfeld

Publisher's Interests

Hachai Publishing focuses on high-quality children's books with Jewish subjects or contents. Its fiction and nonfiction titles, geared toward infants through age 10, impart a love of Hashem and an understanding of Judaism.
Website: www.hachai.com

Freelance Potential

Published 5 titles in 2010: 4 were developed from unsolicited submissions. Of the 5 titles, 3 were by unpublished writers and 4 were by authors who were new to the publishing house. Receives 240 queries, 240 unsolicited mss yearly.

- **Fiction:** Publishes early picture books, 0–4 years; easy-to-read books, 4–7 years; story picture books, 4–10 years; and chapter books, 5–10 years. Genres include Jewish historical fiction, folklore, and adventure.
- **Nonfiction:** Publishes concept books, 0–4 years; and story picture books, 4–10 years. Topics include the Torah, prayer, biography, mitzvos, middos, and Jewish history.
- **Representative Titles:** *Is It Shabbos Yet?*, by Ellen Emerman (2–5 years), describes the household tasks that enliven the end of the week. *Faiga Finds the Way,* by Batsheva Brandeis (7–10 years), finds a young Jewish girl looking for ways to help her impoverished family in 1825 Kiev.

Submissions and Payment

Guidelines and catalogue available at website. Query with outline and sample chapter; or send complete ms. Accepts hard copy and email to dir@hachai.com (no attachments). SASE. Responds in 2–6 months. Publication in 18–36 months. Flat fee.

Editor's Comments

In addition to providing excellent reading and storytime togetherness, your book must convey the Jewish experience for our young readers.

Hammond Publishing

Langenscheidt Publishing Group
36-36 33rd Street
Long Island City, NY 11106

Executive Editor: Nel Yomtov

Publisher's Interests

Known for its maps and atlases for more than 100 years and now a part of the German-based reference publisher Langenscheidt, Hammond has been expanding its reference and nonfiction book lists extensively for more than a year. The children's program, for ages 7 to 12, focuses on high-interest and evergreen subjects for education and trade markets.
Website: www.hammondmap.com

Freelance Potential

Published 25+ books in 2010.

- **Fiction:** Picture story books, ages 7–12. Topics include personal choices, self- and social awareness.
- **Nonfiction:** Publishes early reader books, 7–9 years; and middle-grade books, 9–12 years. Categories include biography, entertainment, environment, history, nature, science, games, puzzles, and activities.
- **Representative Titles:** *Ancient Egypt: Dead Cities, Boy Kings, Moldy Mummies and Tombs of Treasure,* by Charlie Samuels (7–10 years), is a guide to ancient Egypt with foldout maps. *Horses,* by Fran Hodgkins (8–12 years), is part of the quirky, informative, colorful Hammond Undercover series.

Submissions and Payment

Query with writing samples. Do not send complete mss. Concepts are currently being developed in-house and assigned to freelancers, as well as solicited from agents and authors. Royalty or work-for-hire, depending on the project.

Editor's Comments

Our new line is somewhat of a return to youth nonfiction, an area that was quite robust for us years ago. It includes many titles on history, science, nature, biography, and entertainment. We are now expanding the brand as we keep the core business of reference material.

Harcourt Children's Books

Houghton Mifflin Harcourt
215 Park Avenue South
New York, NY 10003

Submissions Editor

Publisher's Interests

Harcourt's catalogue offers everything from board books for toddlers to fantasy fiction for teens. An imprint of Houghton Mifflin, it has been publishing for more than 90 years and has established a reputation for producing fine literature for children.

Website: www.hmhbooks.com

Freelance Potential

Published 150–160 titles in 2010; each was by an agented author.

- **Fiction:** Publishes concept books, toddler books, and early picture books, 0–4 years; easy-to-read books, 4–7 years; story picture books, 4–10 years; chapter books, 5–10 years; and young adult books, 12–18 years. Genres include contemporary, historical, and multicultural fiction; mystery; fantasy; and suspense. Also publishes poetry and stories about sports, nature, and the environment.
- **Nonfiction:** Publishes books on all subjects, for all ages.
- **Representative Titles:** *My Vicksburg,* by Ann Rinaldi (12+ years), is a historical novel that follows a Confederate family as they flee Vicksburg during the Civil War. *Dragon Is Coming!,* by Valeri Gorbachev (3–7 years), is a picture book that offers a dramatic new twist on the Chicken Little theme.

Submissions and Payment

Agents, published authors, and members of the SCBWI only. Query. No simultaneous submissions. Accepts hard copy. SASE. Responds in 1 month. Publication in 2 years. Royalty; advance.

Editor's Comments

We pride ourselves on publishing the best children's literature. Because of the number of submissions we receive, we can only accept queries through literary agents and from previously published authors who are members of the SCBWI.

HarperCollins Children's Books

1350 Avenue of the Americas
New York, NY 10019

Associate Editor: Alyson Day

Publisher's Interests
Offering "Great Reads for All Ages," this is the publishing
house that brought us some of the classics of children's literature, including *Where the Wild Things Are* and *Goodnight
Moon*. Its list includes high-quality fiction and nonfiction for
children from preschool through high school.
Website: www.harperchildrens.com

Freelance Potential
Published 500 titles in 2010: each was by an agented
author. Receives 1,000+ queries yearly.

- **Fiction:** Publishes easy-to-read books, 4–7 years; chapter
  books, 5–10 years; middle-grade books, 8–12 years; and
  young adult books, 12–18 years. Genres include adventure;
  drama; humor; fantasy; folktales; mystery; horror; suspense;
  Westerns; and historical, contemporary, multicultural, and
  science fiction.
- **Nonfiction:** Publishes easy-to-read books, 4–7 years; chapter
  books, 5–10 years; middle-grade books, 8–12 years; and
  young adult books, 12–18 years. Topics include animals,
  science, history, geography, social studies, and biography.
- **Representative Titles:** *Scaredy-Cat, Splat!,* by Rob Scotton
  (3–7 years), is a funny tale about a cat who is just too scared
  to be scary on Halloween. *Big Nate Strikes Again,* by Lincoln
  Peirce (8–12 years), marks the return of mischief-maker Nate
  Wright, but this time he meets his match in classmate Gina.

Submissions and Payment
Agented authors only. Catalogue available at website.
Accepts hard copy. SASE. Responds in 2 months. Publication
in 18 months. Royalty; advance.

Editor's Comments
We are the proud publisher of many award-winning children's titles. Please understand that we are not a market for
beginning writers; we work with agented authors only.

HarperTeen, Eos

HarperCollins
1350 Avenue of the Americas
New York, NY 10019

Editorial Department

Publisher's Interests
Two of the HarperCollins imprints, HarperTeen and Eos, produce exciting books for teens. HarperTeen titles are lighthearted and serious, literary and commercial, but always
offer a look into what matters in teen lives, whether it's pop
culture or cultural struggles. Eos specializes in fantasy and
science fiction.
Website: www.harperteen.com; www.eosbooks.com

Freelance Potential
Published 60 titles in 2010.

- **Fiction:** Publishes young adult books, 12–18 years. Genres
  include humor, mystery, and contemporary fiction, at Harper-
  Teen. At Eos, the over-arching genres of science fiction and
  fantasy extend to urban fantasy, dystopian novels, gothic
  romance, horror, and the paranormal.
- **Representative Titles:** *Close Contact,* by Katherine Allred
  (Eos), is a futuristic romance. Robin Hobb's *Dragon Haven*
  (Eos) is a fantasy adventure about the resurgence of dragons.
  Brom's "wickedly poetic" *The Child Thief* (Eos) combines Peter
  Pan with ancient magic in a contemporary setting. *You,* by
  Charles Benoit (HarperTeen), is the tense story of a 15-year-old
  boy on the road to self-destruction.

Submissions and Payment
Accepts agented submissions only. Publication in 18–36
months. Royalty; advance.

Editor's Comments
Follow the Eos Books blog at http://outofthiseos.typepad.com
for regular updates on trends in fantasy and science fiction,
and related events. HarperTeen uses multiple media outlets to
reach teens, including online and other promotions.

Hayes School Publishing Company

321 Pennwood Avenue
Pittsburgh, PA 15221

President: Clair Hayes

Publisher's Interests
Publishing educational books and resources for preschool through grade 12, this company seeks reproducibles, workbooks, teacher planning guides, and support materials for all subjects and curricula.
Website: www.hayespub.com

Freelance Potential
Published 20–30 titles in 2010. Of the 20–30 titles, 4–5 were by unpublished writers and 2 were by authors who were new to the publishing house. Receives 360–500 queries yearly.

- **Nonfiction:** Publishes educational resource materials, grades K–12. Topics include language arts, multicultural studies, math, computer literacy, foreign language, social studies, science, health, creative thinking, handwriting, geography, and standardized testing.
- **Representative Titles:** *United States Geography,* by Claire Murphy (grades 3–6), features reproducible material designed to introduce students to basic geographical facts about the United States; includes games and puzzles. *Be a Cyber-Space Sleuth: A Student's Guide to the Internet* presents essential skills for beginning Internet use—including research, email, and safety guidelines—in a reproducible form.

Submissions and Payment
Guidelines available. Query with outline or table of contents, 3–4 sample pages, and author bio. Accepts hard copy and simultaneous submissions if identified. SASE. Responds in 2–3 weeks. Publication period varies. Flat fee.

Editor's Comments
Despite the size of our backlist, we are constantly seeking new material in all academic subject areas, especially testing and Spanish. Please note that failure to describe your book's purpose and intended audience will result in rejection.

Hazelden Publishing

P.O. Box 176
Center City, MN 55012-0176

Manuscript Coordinator

Publisher's Interests
Like its nonprofit parent company, Hazelden's focus is on alcohol and drug addiction treatment. Its books are written for professionals in the treatment field, criminal justice workers, prevention specialists, and individuals in or seeking recovery from addiction. Many of its titles target pre-teens and teens.
Website: www.hazelden.org

Freelance Potential
Published 50 titles in 2010. Receives 300 queries yearly.

- **Nonfiction:** Publishes young adult books, 12–18 years. Topics include alcohol and substance abuse, health, fitness, and social issues. Also publishes titles for parents, teachers, and professionals who work with people suffering from addiction problems.
- **Representative Titles:** *Love First: A Family's Guide to Intervention*, by Jeff Jay and Debra Jay, is a parent's guide to identifying enabling behaviors, building an intervention team, and choosing a treatment center. *Everything Changes,* by Beverly Conyers, helps families navigate the early months of addiction recovery. *Today's Gift: Daily Meditations for Families* helps families nurture and strengthen bonds.

Submissions and Payment
Guidelines and catalogue available at website. Query with outline, table of contents, 3 sample chapters, clips or writing samples, market analysis, and author credentials. Accepts hard copy. SASE. Responds in 3 months. Publication in 12–18 months. Royalty. Flat fee.

Editor's Comments
We're not interested in receiving submissions of children's books. Our mission is to provide products and services to help people recognize, understand, and overcome chemical dependency and closely related problems.

HCI Books

3201 SW 15th Street
Deerfield Beach, FL 33442

Editorial Committee

Publisher's Interests

This publisher markets the popular *Chicken Soup for the Soul* books in addition to self-help titles about personal growth and enrichment. It features parenting titles, as well as nonfiction and fiction for teens.
Website: www.hcibooks.com; www.ultimatehcibooks.com

Freelance Potential

Published 60 titles (7 juvenile) in 2010: 5 were developed from unsolicited submissions and 55 were by agented authors. Of the 60 titles, 5 were by unpublished writers and 10 were by authors who were new to the publishing house. Receives 480 queries yearly.

- **Fiction:** Publishes young adult books, 12–18 years. Genres include fantasy.
- **Nonfiction:** Publishes young adult books, 12–18 years. Topics include teen issues, health, fitness, and relationships. Also publishes self-help and parenting titles.
- **Representative Titles:** *Dead Fred, Flying Lunchboxes, and the Good Luck Circle,* by Frank McKinney & Kate Mason (YA), is a fantasy set in an underwater world where manatees talk, starfish sing, and the clownfish are practical jokers. *Get Happy Instead of Just Getting By,* by Kimberly Kirberger (YA), helps teens be happy with who they are and what they have.

Submissions and Payment

Guidelines and catalogue available at website or with 9x12 SASE ($3 postage). Query with bio, marketing data, outline, and 2–3 sample chapters. Accepts hard copy and simultaneous submissions if identified. SASE. Responds in 3–7 months. Publication in 6–12 months. Payment policy varies.

Editor's Comments

We're looking for writers who can create books that change the lives of readers.

Health Press

P.O. Box 37470
Albuquerque, NM 87176

Editor: Kathleen Frazier

Publisher's Interests

For 30 years, Health Press has been publishing books for
individuals dealing with health issues, as well as for their
friends and family members. Its children's list includes
books on an array of children's health issues, as well as
titles designed to enhance tolerance and understanding.
Website: www.healthpress.com

Freelance Potential

Published 3 titles in 2010. Of the 3 titles, 1 was by an
unpublished writer. Receives 500+ queries yearly.

- **Fiction:** Publishes concept books, 0–4 years; easy-to-read
  books, 4–7 years; middle-grade books, 8–12 years; and young
  adult books, 12–18 years. Genres include humor, adventure,
  and contemporary fiction—all with health-related themes.
- **Nonfiction:** Publishes concept books, 0–4 years; easy-to-read
  books, 4–7 years; middle-grade books, 8–12 years; and young
  adult books, 12–18 years. Topics include general health,
  disabilities, medical conditions, nutrition, and grief. Also
  publishes books for parents.
- **Representative Titles:** *Don't Laugh at Me,* by Steve Seskin &
  Allen Shamblin (6–12 years), challenges kids to create ridicule-
  free environments. *Samantha Jane's Missing Smile,* by Julie
  Kaplow & Donna Pincus (4–8 years), deals with the full range
  of emotions, questions, and worries that children have when a
  parent has died.

Submissions and Payment

Guidelines and catalogue available at website. Query with
résumé, synopsis, and 3 sample chapters. Accepts hard copy.
SASE. Response time and publication period vary. Royalty.

Editor's Comments

Most of our authors are medical or psychiatric professionals.
All work submitted for publication must be reviewed by
medical professionals.

Heinemann

361 Hanover Street
Portsmouth, NH 03801-3912

Acquisitions Editor

Publisher's Interests

Teachers of kindergarten through college are the target audience for this publisher of educational and professional resources. Its books cover all subject areas in addition to English as a Second Language and gifted and special education. **Website: www.heinemann.com**

Freelance Potential

Published 100 titles in 2010: 10 were by agented authors. Of the 100 titles, 10 were by unpublished writers. Receives 1,200+ queries yearly.

- **Nonfiction:** Publishes educational resources and multimedia material for teachers and school administrators. Topics include math, science, social studies, art education, reading, writing, ESL, bilingual education, special and gifted education, early childhood development, school reform, curriculum development, and the creative arts.
- **Representative Titles:** *What's the Big Idea?*, by Jim Burke, explains how making essential questions the center of teaching gives students dependable, transferable tools for all subjects and the real world. *Reading Ladders,* by Teri Lesesne, presents a strategy designed to foster a greater engagement with books and a lifetime of passionate reading.

Submissions and Payment

Guidelines and catalogue available at website. Query with résumé, outline, table of contents, and chapter summaries. Prefers email to proposals@heinemann.com; will accept hard copy. SASE. Responds in 6–8 weeks. Publication in 10–12 months. Payment policy varies.

Editor's Comments

We receive many submissions that reflect little or no understanding of the types of books we publish. Please review our publishing program at our website before deciding to submit your work.

Hendrick-Long Publishing

10635 Tower Oaks, Suite D
Houston, TX 77070

Vice President: Vilma Long

Publisher's Interests

This family-owned company specializes in books with a Texas historical focus for children and young adults. It welcomes proposals from authors who can help keep alive the love of Texas and its land and people.
Website: www.hendricklongpublishing.com

Freelance Potential

Published 4 titles in 2010: each was developed from an unsolicited submission. Of the 4 titles, 2 were by authors who were new to the publishing house. Receives 600 queries yearly.

- **Fiction:** Publishes middle-grade books, 8–12 years. Genres include historical and regional fiction, and folklore.
- **Nonfiction:** Publishes middle-grade books, 8–12 years; and young adult books, 12–18 years. Topics include animals, natural history, geography, and folklore related to Texas and the American Southwest. Also publishes biographies.
- **Representative Titles:** *Sam Houston: American Hero,* by Ann Fears Crawford (8+ years), tells the life story of the man who wanted to keep Texas in the Union during the Civil War. *The Ghost at the Old Stone Fort,* by Martha Tannery Jones (9+ years), presents the history of Spanish settler Gil Y'Barbo and the Old Stone Fort ruins.

Submissions and Payment

Writers' guidelines available. Query with résumé, outline/synopsis, table of contents, and 1–2 sample chapters. Accepts hard copy and simultaneous submissions if identified. SASE. Responds in 6 months. Publication in 2 years. Royalty; advance.

Editor's Comments

Texas is a unique state with rich prehistoric sites and a vivid history that stretches back centuries. Our mission is to keep the knowledge of that heritage alive.

Heuer Publishing

211 First Avenue SE
Cedar Rapids, IA 52401

Submission Contact: Geri Albrecht or Kate Wiebke

Publisher's Interests
Established in 1928, Heuer is one of the oldest publishing houses serving the educational and community theater markets. It publishes short, full-length, and 10-minute plays and monologues, as well as musicals. All of its plays are appropriate for young audiences.
Website: www.hitplays.com

Freelance Potential
Published 60 titles (45 juvenile) in 2010. Of the 60 titles, 6 were by unpublished writers and 30 were by authors who were new to the publishing house. Receives 250 queries, 2,000 unsolicited mss yearly.

- **Fiction:** Publishes plays, musicals, comedies, mysteries, and satire for children and young adults, 5–18 years.
- **Representative Titles:** *King Grisly-Beard,* by Dan Neidermyer, is the story of a princess who learns not to judge people by their appearance. *The Polar Bear Prince,* by Patrick Dorn, is a fast and funny play that has its characters, stranded near the North Pole, acting out fractured fairy tales while they await rescue.

Submissions and Payment
Guidelines and catalogue available at website. Query or send complete ms with synopsis, cast list, running time, and set requirements. Accepts submissions through the website. Responds in 2 months. Publication period varies. Royalty. Flat fee.

Editor's Comments
Our current needs include fresh and original comedies, fun parodies, and solid dramas. Murder mysteries, too, are always in demand. We no longer publish theater resources or texts. Please note that the evaluation period for plays without a production history is considerably longer than for those that have been produced.

High Noon Books

20 Commercial Boulevard
Novato, CA 94949

Acquisitions Editor

Publisher's Interests
Struggling readers are the focus of this imprint of Academic Therapy Publications. High Noon titles include leveled chapter books with carefully crafted writing to encourage reading skills, but always with highly controlled vocabulary, simple sentence structures, and subjects that draw in and excite readers.
Website: www.highnoonbooks.com

Freelance Potential
Published 20 titles in 2010.

- **Fiction:** Publishes beginning readers, 6–9 years; and phonics-based chapter books, 8–16 years. Categories include adventure, historical fiction, mystery, and science fiction.
- **Nonfiction:** Publishes beginning readers, 6–9 years; phonics-based chapter books, 8–16 years. Topics include high-interest biography, history, math, science, sports, and travel.
- **Representative Titles:** *Jen Sets Out,* by Matt Sims (9–16 years, grade 1 readability), is one of the latest sets of Sound Out Chapter Books that uses narrative to encourage reading. *Mountains,* by Lynn and Bart King (9–16 years, grade 1 readability), looks at this geographical feature; part of the What on Earth Science series.

Submissions and Payment
Query with synopsis and author bio. Accepts hard copy. SASE. Response time and publication period vary. Flat fee.

Editor's Comments
High Noon books tie in to the curriculum, are standards-based, include activities that aid in teacher assessment, and above all, engage the struggling reader whatever the age.

History Compass

25 Leslie Road
Auburndale, MA 02466

General Manager: Lisa Gianelly

Publisher's Interests
Primary source-based U.S. history books, guides, and historical fiction comprise the catalogue of this publisher. Its goal
is to provide information and stories, both compelling and
true, that give insight into our nation's history.
Website: www.historycompass.com

Freelance Potential
Published 8 titles in 2010. Of the 8 titles, 1 was by an
unpublished writer and 3 were by authors who were new to
the publishing house. Receives 50–60 queries yearly.

- **Fiction:** Publishes middle-grade books, 8–12 years; and young
  adult novels, 12–18 years. Genres include historical fiction.
- **Nonfiction:** Publishes easy-to-read books, 4–7 years; chapter
  books, 5–10 years; middle-grade books, 8–12 years; and
  young adult titles, 12–18 years. Topics include American his-
  tory. Also publishes biographies and guidebooks for adults.
- **Representative Titles:** *Children at Work,* by JoAnne Weisman
  Deitch, explains the harsh conditions under which children
  worked in mills, factories, and mines. *Daniel on the Run:
  Louisa, Will, and the Underground Railroad*, by Claiborne
  Dawes (grades 1–3), is a fictional account of a young Louisa
  May Alcott helping a fugitive slave boy escape to freedom.

Submissions and Payment
Guidelines and catalogue available at website. Query with
résumé, outline, table of contents, market analysis, and nonfiction clips. Accepts hard copy and simultaneous submissions if identified. SASE. Responds in 3 months. Publication
in 2–8 months. Royalty.

Editor's Comments
Primary source documents that tell a compelling story are
essential for our nonfiction history books. We want to see a
lot of information about you, your background, and your
project included in your query.

Holiday House

425 Madison Avenue
New York, NY 10017

Acquisitions Editor

Publisher's Interests

An independent publisher founded in 1935, Holiday House accepts children's fiction and nonfiction for kids ages four and up. It is open to a variety of genres and subject matter. **Website: www.holidayhouse.com**

Freelance Potential

Published 70 titles in 2010: most were by agented authors and 5 were reprint/licensed properties. Of the 70 titles, 3 were by unpublished writers and 3 were by new authors. Receives 1,200 unsolicited mss yearly.

- **Fiction:** Publishes toddler books and early picture books, 0–4 years; easy-to-read books, 4–7 years; story picture books, 4–10 years; chapter books, 5–10 years; middle-grade books, 8–12 years; and young adult books, 12–18 years. Genres include historical and multicultural fiction, humor, mystery, and fantasy.
- **Nonfiction:** Publishes early picture books, 0–4 years; easy-to-read books, 4–7 years; story picture books, 4–10 years; middle-grade books, 8–12 years; and young adult books, 12–18 years. Topics include history, social issues, and science. Also publishes biographies.
- **Representative Titles:** *Love-a-Duck,* by Alan James Brown (3–6 years), is the story of a little girl's favorite rubber ducky, who has some wild adventures at the park. *Frederick Douglass,* by David A. Adler (10+ years), presents the story of the former slave who became a famous orator, author, and presidential advisor.

Submissions and Payment

Guidelines and catalogue available at website. Send complete ms. Accepts hard copy. No SASE. Responds in 4 months if interested. Publication period varies. Royalty; advance.

Editor's Comments

Quality is our main criterion. We demand quality in concept, writing, and presentation.

Henry Holt Books for Young Readers

Macmillan
175 Fifth Avenue
New York, NY 10010

Submissions Editor

Publisher's Interests
Henry Holt Books for Young Readers is known for publishing quality picture books, chapter books, and novels for preschoolers through young adults. Though its genres and subjects are diverse, its common denominators are quality writing and engaging storylines.
Website: www.henryholtkids.com

Freelance Potential
Published 41 titles in 2010. Receives 12,000 queries yearly.

- **Fiction:** Publishes concept books and early picture books, 0–4 years; easy-to-read books, 4–7 years; story picture books, 4–10 years; chapter books, 5–10 years; middle-grade books, 8–12 years; and young adult books, 12–18 years. Genres include historical, multicultural, and ethnic fiction; adventure; drama; and fantasy. Also publishes poetry.
- **Nonfiction:** Publishes story picture books, 4–10 years; chapter books, 5–10 years; and middle-grade books, 8–12 years. Topics include biography, history, ethnic issues, and mythology.
- **Representative Titles:** *The Scrambled States of America,* by Laurie Keller (4–9 years), has all 50 states switching positions in order to see a different part of the country. *The Serpent Gift,* by Lene Kaaberbol (11+ years), is a fantasy novel featuring fights, bravery, danger, and illusion as the possessor of the Serpent Gift comes to a village to claim his daughter.

Submissions and Payment
Agented authors only. Catalogue available at website. Publication period and payment policy vary.

Editor's Comments
We state above that we receive 12,000 queries yearly. Due to that incredible number, we have changed our submission policy. We no longer accept unsolicited manuscripts or queries. We recommend that prospective authors find a reputable agent and submit work through that agency.

Horizon Publishers & Distributors

191 N 650 East
Bountiful, UT 84010

Submissions Editors: Duane Crowther & Jean Crowther

Publisher's Interests
Horizon publishes in several markets, from religious to general trade to specialty. Niche market titles cover Utah and surrounding regions, outdoor life, family, crafts, and how-to.
Website: www.horizonpublishersbookstore.com

Freelance Potential
Published 12 titles (4 juvenile) in 2010: 6 were developed from unsolicited submissions. Of the 12 titles, 8 were by unpublished writers and 6 were by authors new to the publishing house. Receives 100+ unsolicited mss each year.

- **Nonfiction:** Publishes chapter books, 5–10 years; middle-grade books, 8–12 years; and young adult books, 12–18 years. Also publishes activity books and educational books, 1–12 years. Topics include Latter-day Saints life, the Mormon faith, spirituality, social issues, cooking, stitchery, camping, scouting, and outdoor life. Also publishes parenting titles.
- **Representative Titles:** *Let's Learn About Tithing,* by Jan Clawson, helps children understand and appreciate the sacred law of tithing. *I Hope They Call Me on a Mission!,* by Linda K. Pfaff, suggests ways that young Latter-day Saints can prepare for future missionary service and understand the personal responsibilities that every potential missionary needs to learn.

Submissions and Payment
Guidelines and catalogue available at website. Send complete ms with résumé. Accepts hard copy. SASE. Responds in 1–3 months. Publication period varies. Royalty, 10% of wholesale.

Editor's Comments
Most of our children's books fall into the LDS category. When choosing manuscripts, we look for writing quality, suitability, uniqueness of message or approach, and marketability. Please read our guidelines before submitting.

Houghton Mifflin Books for Children

Houghton Mifflin Harcourt
222 Berkeley Street
Boston, MA 02116

Submissions Coordinator

Publisher's Interests
This large publisher of children's books is interested in works of the highest caliber only. Whether it's fiction or non-fiction, for toddlers or for young adults, a quality project can find a home here.
Website: www.hmhbooks.com

Freelance Potential
Published 60 titles in 2010: most were by agented authors and 3 were reprint/licensed properties. Receives 1,200 queries, 20,000 unsolicited mss yearly.

- **Fiction:** Publishes toddler books and early picture books, 0–4 years; easy-to-read books, 4–7 years; story picture books, 4–10 years; middle-grade books, 8–12 years; and young adult books, 12–18 years. Genres include historical and multicultural fiction and adventure.
- **Nonfiction:** Publishes middle-grade books, 8–12 years; and young adult books, 12–18 years. Topics include history, science, and nature. Also publishes biographies.
- **Representative Titles:** *Ubiquitous: Celebrating Nature's Survivors* by Joyce Sidman (6–9 years) mixes poetry, science, and art to celebrate the organisms that have overcome predators and time. *Zen and Xander Undone* by Amy Kathleen Ryan (14+ years) follows two brothers as they pursue the mystery of their mother's past.

Submissions and Payment
Guidelines and catalogue available at website. Send complete ms with author bio for fiction. Query with synopsis, sample chapters, and author bio for nonfiction. Accepts hard copy. No SASE. Responds in 3–4 months if interested. Publication period varies. Royalty; advance.

Editor's Comments
There is great competition to get published here, so be sure your submission is in its best form.

Humanics Publishing Group

12 S. Dixie Highway, Suite 203
Lake Worth, FL 33460

Acquisitions Editor: W. Arthur Bligh

Publisher's Interests
Humanics Publishing was formed in 1976 to address the
need for quality classroom materials that support parents as
the prime educator of their children. Its focus is the same
today as it continues to produce parenting and children's
books, as well as teacher resource material.
Website: www.humanicspub.com

Freelance Potential
Published 20 titles in 2010. Of the 20 titles, 15 were by
unpublished writers and 12 were by authors who were new
to the publishing house. Receives 105 unsolicited mss
each year.

- **Fiction:** Publishes concept books and toddler books, 0–4
  years. Genres include folklore and inspirational fiction.
- **Nonfiction:** Publishes teacher resource books. Topics include
  science, mathematics, art, crafts, and hobbies. Also publishes
  parenting books.
- **Representative Titles:** *Grub E. Dog,* by Al Newman, teaches
  young children the importance of personal hygiene and clean-
  liness. *Home At Last,* by Mauro Magellan, follows a worm as
  he sets out to find a better place to live. *Max the Apartment
  Cat,* by Mauro Magellan, shares the adventures of an indoor
  cat that decides to leave his apartment and tour the city.

Submissions and Payment
Guidelines and catalogue available at website. Send com-
plete ms with résumé, synopsis, and marketing plan.
Accepts hard copy and disk submissions (Microsoft Word or
WordPerfect). SASE. Response time, publication period, and
payment policy vary.

Editor's Comments
Please remember that our review process is a long one. You
may write us to inquire about the status of your manuscript,
but please don't call or email.

Hunter House Publishers

1515½ Park Street
Alameda, CA 94501-0914

Acquisitions

Publisher's Interests
Hunter House publishes books on physical, mental, and emotional health. It also produces titles on parenting and family issues, child development, and specialized teaching and counseling resources.
Website: www.hunterhouse.com

Freelance Potential
Published 10 titles (3 juvenile) in 2010: 8 were developed from unsolicited submissions. Receives 180 queries yearly.

- **Nonfiction:** Publishes activity books, 4–18+ years; and young adult books, 12–18 years. Topics include health, fitness, family, personal growth, relationships, sexuality, and violence prevention and intervention. Also publishes resources for counselors and educators, including workbooks for use with young children.
- **Representative Titles:** *Raising Each Other: A Book for Teens and Parents*, by Jeanne Brondino et al., presents a frank dialogue between parents and teens about such topics as freedom, privacy, trust, sex, and responsibility. *101 Dance Games for Children*, by Paul Rooyackers (4+ years), encourages children to interact and express how they feel in creative dance fantasies.

Submissions and Payment
Guidelines and catalogue available at website. Query with résumé, overview, and chapter-by-chapter outline. Accepts hard copy, email queries to acquisitions@hunterhouse.com, and simultaneous submissions if identified. SASE. Responds in 3–4 months. Publication in 1–2 years. Royalty.

Editor's Comments
If we have reviewed your proposal and are interested in reading more, we will request two to three sample chapters. Each chapter should address one particular concept, subject, skill, or technique.

Ideals Publications

2636 Elm Hill Pike, Suite 120
Nashville, TN 37214

Submissions Editor

Publisher's Interests

Owned by Guideposts, this company publishes a full range of books. Its children's catalogue includes fiction and nonfiction titles for infants through young adults.
Website: www.idealsbooks.com

Freelance Potential

Published 50 titles in 2010: 2–3 were developed from unsolicited submissions, 2–3 were by agented authors, and 3–4 were reprint/licensed properties. Of the 50 titles, 25 were by unpublished writers. Receives 480–600 mss yearly.

- **Fiction:** Publishes early picture books, 0–4 years; easy-to-read books, 4–7 years; story picture books, 4–10 years; chapter books, 5–10 years; middle-grade books, 8–12 years; and young adult books, 12–18 years. Genres include historical, inspirational, religious, multicultural, and seasonal fiction; folklore; and stories about animals, nature, and the environment.
- **Nonfiction:** Publishes toddler books, 0–4 years; easy-to-read books, 4–7 years; story picture books, 4–10 years; chapter books, 5–10 years; middle-grade books, 8–12 years; and young adult books, 12–18 years. Topics include animals, crafts, hobbies, geography, history, math, religion, and self-help. Also publishes biographies.
- **Representative Titles:** *How to Clean Your Room,* by Eileen Spinelli (5–8 years), provides a fun approach to a dreadful task. *Create Your Own Candles,* by Laura Check (10+ years), features safety tips and creative methods for candle-making.

Submissions and Payment

Guidelines and catalogue available at website. Send complete ms with résumé. Accepts hard copy. SASE. Responds in 3–4 months. Publication period varies. Royalty.

Editor's Comments

Although owned by Guideposts, we accept mainstream books as well as those with religious or inspirational themes.

Impact Publishers

P.O. Box 6016
Atascadero, CA 93423

Acquisitions Editor: Freeman Porter

Publisher's Interests
Impact publishes authoritative self-help books on a wide variety of personal and interpersonal matters, including parenting issues, divorce recovery, stress, personal growth, and mental health.
Website: www.impactpublishers.com

Freelance Potential
Published 65 titles (1 juvenile) in 2010: 2 were developed from unsolicited submissions. Receives 780 queries yearly.

- **Nonfiction:** Publishes middle-grade books, 8–12 years; and young adult books, 12–18 years. Also publishes books for parents and human services professionals. Topics include emotional development, self-esteem, self-expression, marriage, divorce, careers, social issues, parenting, child development and behavior, health and wellness, and practical therapy.
- **Representative Titles:** *Teen Esteem: A Self-Direction Manual for Young Adults,* by Pat Palmer & Melissa Alberti Froehner (YA), helps teens develop the skills they need to handle stress, peer pressure, sexual expression, substance abuse, and other challenges. *Calming the Family Storm,* by Gary D. McKay & Steven A. Maybell, presents anger management strategies for parents and children.

Submissions and Payment
Licensed professionals only. Guidelines and catalogue available at website. Query with résumé and sample chapters. Accepts hard copy and email queries to submissions@impactpublishers.com. SASE. Responds in 1–3 months. Publication in 1 year. Royalty, 10–15%; advance.

Editor's Comments
We publish only popular and professional psychology and self-help material written in "everyday language" by professionals with advanced degrees and significant experience in the human services field.

Incentive Publications

2400 Crestmoor Road, Suite 211
Nashville, TN 37215

Director of Development & Production: Jill Norris

Publisher's Interests
Specializing in middle school educational resources for teachers of students in kindergarten through grade 12, Incentive Publications offers both print and e-books. It features a long list of titles written by a wide array of leading author-educators who are experts in research and practical classroom know-how.
Website: www.incentivepublications.com

Freelance Potential
Published 20–30 titles in 2010. Receives 250+ queries each year.

- **Nonfiction:** Publishes teaching strategy books for all grade levels, and reproducible student materials for grades 5–9. Topics include core curriculum subjects, art, and study skills.
- **Representative Titles:** *Teaching Kids to Manage Their Own Behavior: School Dayz*, by Ron Klemp (grades 5–9), presents ideas for helping students take control of their learning experiences. *The Nuts & Bolts of Active Learning* (grades 5–9) is written by a group of award-winning educators who offer strategies to hook students on learning while fully involving their minds and bodies.

Submissions and Payment
Guidelines available at website. Query with table of contents, outline, and sample chapter. Accepts hard copy and simultaneous submissions if identified. SASE. Responds in 6–8 weeks. Publication period varies. Royalty. Flat fee.

Editor's Comments
Our mission is to impact middle-grade learners with challenging, innovative resources and provide practical, relevant strategies for educators and parents. Our books are used by teachers, administrators, and parents, including those who homeschool their children.

International Reading Association

800 Barksdale Road
P.O. Box 8139
Newark, DE 19714-8139

Book proposals

Publisher's Interests
The publishing arm of the International Reading Association produces books for literacy professionals. Its list includes titles on professional development, teacher development, assessment, lesson plans, and all aspects of literacy development for all grade levels.
Website: www.reading.org

Freelance Potential
Published 40 titles in 2010: Of the 40 titles, 5 were by unpublished writers and 20 were by authors who were new to the publishing house. Receives 100 queries yearly.

- **Nonfiction:** Publishes research-based educational titles for teachers at all levels, including preservice, teacher educators, literacy researchers, and policymakers. Topics include literacy programs, reading comprehension, reading research and practice, adolescent literacy, literacy coaching, differentiated literacy, learning/instruction, and content-area literacy.
- **Representative Titles:** *Preventing Misguided Reading,* by Jan Miller Burkins & Melody M. Croft, clarifies misunderstandings about guided reading instruction, including the teacher's role. *To Be a Boy, To Be a Reader,* by William G. Brozo, provides novel ways to boost boys' motivation to read and increase their achievement in school.

Submissions and Payment
Guidelines and catalogue available at website. Query with letter of intent, audience/market analysis, author biography, abstract, table of contents, and 1–2 sample chapters. Accepts queries via website only. Response time, publication period, and payment policy vary.

Editor's Comments
We place a premium on well-executed research. Your proposal will be evaluated by a distinguished review board of literacy professionals.

InterVarsity Press

P.O. Box 1400
Downers Grove, IL 60515

Editorial Assistant: Rachel Neftzer

Publisher's Interests
InterVarsity Press has been publishing Christian books for more than 50 years. It focuses on general interest books, Bible studies, and study guides for religious education.
Website: www.ivpress.com

Freelance Potential
Published 110 titles in 2010: 2 were developed from unsolicited submissions, 11 were by agented authors, and 13 were reprint/licensed properties. Of the 110 titles, 17 were by unpublished writers and 41 were by authors who were new to the publishing house. Receives 1,400 queries yearly.

- **Nonfiction:** Publishes biblically based, religious titles for educators, parents, and college students. Features informational, educational, how-to, and reference books.
- **Representative Titles:** *The Soul of Hip Hop,* by Daniel White Hodge, surveys the hip hop culture as a language of would-be prophets and a cultural movement with a traceable theological center. *God on Campus,* by Trent Sheppard, traces a long history of significant movements of God through college campuses and the lasting impact on the students who responded.

Submissions and Payment
Pastors, professors, or previously published authors only. Guidelines and catalogue available at website. Query with résumé, chapter-by-chapter summary, and 2 sample chapters. Accepts hard copy and simultaneous submissions if identified. SASE. Response time, publication period, and payment policy vary.

Editor's Comments
If you are a pastor or have previously authored a book with an established publisher, you may submit to the General Books Editor. If you are associated with a college or seminary and have an academic proposal, you may submit it to the attention of the Academic Editor.

Jewish Lights

P.O. Box 237
Woodstock, VT 05091

Vice President, Editorial: Emily Wichland

Publisher's Interests
Rejecting the idea that it is "just another publisher of Jewish books," Jewish Lights defines itself as a publisher of books that reflect the Jewish wisdom tradition for people of all faiths and backgrounds. Its children's catalogue includes nonfiction titles on Jewish holidays and traditions, spiritual issues, social issues, and guidance.
Website: www.jewishlights.com

Freelance Potential
Published 25 titles in 2010. Of the 25 titles, 15 were by authors who were new to the publishing house. Receives 1,000+ queries, 400 unsolicited mss yearly.

- **Nonfiction:** Publishes toddler books, 0–4 years; easy-to-read books, 4–7 years; story picture books, 4–10 years; and young adult books, 12–18 years. Topics include religious and inspirational subjects, and self-help.
- **Representative Titles:** *Tough Questions Jews Ask: A Young Adult's Guide to Building a Jewish Life,* by Rabbi Edward Feinstein (11+ years), takes young people's tough questions seriously. *What Does God Look Like?,* by Lawrence & Karen Kushner (0–4 years), brings children on an imaginative journey designed to open their minds as well as their hearts.

Submissions and Payment
Guidelines and catalogue available at website. Query with résumé, table of contents, sample chapter, and marketing plan. Send complete ms for picture books only. Accepts hard copy and simultaneous submissions if identified. SASE. Responds in 4 months. Publication in 1 year. Payment policy varies.

Editor's Comments
We apologize for our slow response process, but it is the only way we can ensure that all materials submitted receive proper consideration.

JIST Publishing

7321 Shadeland Station, Suite 200
Indianapolis, IN 46256

Acquisitions Editor: Susan Pines

Publisher's Interests

For more than 25 years, JIST has been developing self-directed books and products on job search, career exploration, occupational information, life skills, and character education. While some of its titles are directed toward adult readers, many are geared toward students in middle school or high school.
Website: www.jist.com

Freelance Potential

Published 60 titles in 2010. Receives 250 queries yearly.

- **Nonfiction:** Publishes middle-grade books, 11–12 years; and young adult books, 12–18 years. Also publishes workbooks. Topics include career exploration and assessment, occupations, job retention, job searching, character education, and career development.
- **Representative Titles:** *Pathfinder: Exploring Career and Educational Paths,* by Norene Lindsay, is a workbook designed to let students explore their values and preferences so they can make informed education and career choices. *Best College for You* teaches readers how and when to begin their college search, how to find their best fit, how to enhance their financial aid package, and how to avoid mistakes along the way.

Submissions and Payment

Guidelines and catalogue available at website. Query with outline, introduction, sample chapters, résumé, and project status. Accepts hard copy and email queries to appropriate editor (see website for addresses). SASE. Responds in 14–16 months. Publication in 9–12 months. Royalty, 8–10%.

Editor's Comments

In order for your proposal to be well received, you must do a little homework first. Peruse our extensive guidelines to ensure your proposal package includes all of the information we require. Those that do not will not be reviewed.

JourneyForth Books

1700 Wade Hampton Boulevard
Greenville, SC 29614-0060

Acquisitions Editor: Nancy Lohr

Publisher's Interests
A division of Bob Jones University Press, JourneyForth publishes Christian-themed fiction and nonfiction for children from preschool through high school.
Website: www.bjupress.com

Freelance Potential
Published 10 titles in 2010: 8 were developed from unsolicited submissions, 1 was by an agented author, and 1 was a reprint/licensed property. Of the 10 titles, 1 was by an unpublished writer and 1 was by an author new to the publishing house. Receives 144 queries, 420 mss yearly.

- **Fiction:** Publishes early picture books, 0–4 years; easy-to-read books, 4–7 years; chapter books, 5–10 years; middle-grade books, 8–12 years; and young adult books, 12–18 years. Genres include historical, biblical, and Christian fiction; animal adventure; mystery; and fantasy.
- **Nonfiction:** Publishes chapter books, 5–10 years; middle-grade books, 8–12 years; and young adult books, 12–18 years. Topics include spiritual growth. Also publishes biographies.
- **Representative Titles:** *River of Danger,* by Denise Williamson (9–12 years), tells of a Native American boy who tries to dispel the white men's stories about God. *Farmer Dillo Counts His Chickens,* by Jesse Adams (0–4 years), introduces children to numbers as they help Farmer Dillo find all of his escaped chickens.

Submissions and Payment
Guidelines available. Query with résumé, synopsis, and 5 sample chapters; or send complete ms. Accepts hard copy and simultaneous submissions if identified. SASE. Responds in 3 months. Publication in 18–24 months. Royalty, negotiable.

Editor's Comments
Early chapter books and middle readers are our current biggest needs.

The Judaica Press

123 Ditmas Avenue
Brooklyn, NY 11218

Editor: Norm Shapiro

Publisher's Interests

Founded in 1963, the Judaica Press publishes children's books that find that delicate balance between teaching important lessons of Jewish culture, history, and customs, while still being fun and enjoyable. Its catalogue includes both fiction and nonfiction for children of all ages.
Website: www.judaicapress.com

Freelance Potential

Published 20–25 titles in 2010. Of the 20–25 titles, 2–4 were by authors who were new to the publishing house. Receives 100 queries, 90 unsolicited mss yearly.

- **Fiction:** Publishes early picture books, 0–4 years; easy-to-read books, 4–7 years; story picture books, 4–10 years; and young adult books, 12–18 years. Genres include historical, religious, and contemporary fiction; mystery; and suspense.
- **Nonfiction:** Publishes story picture books, 4–10 years. Topics include Jewish traditions, Torah stories, the Hebrew language, crafts, and hobbies.
- **Representative Titles:** *Penina's Adventure at Sea,* by Miriam Walfish, follows a Jewish girl growing up in London who finds adventure aboard a ship bound for New York; part of the Jewish Girls Around the World series. *The Gift of Friendship,* by Chani Altein (5–9 years), is a tale of 10-year-old Esther and the bond she makes with an extraordinary new friend.

Submissions and Payment

Catalogue available at website. Query with outline; or send complete ms. Accepts hard copy. Availability of artwork improves chance of acceptance. SASE. Responds in 3 months. Publication in 1 year. Royalty.

Editor's Comments

We place an emphasis on compelling stories and interesting nonfiction that share the Jewish perspective with readers. We are open to any topic that will interest our core audience.

Just Us Books

356 Glenwood Avenue, 3rd Floor
East Orange, NJ 07017

Submissions Manager

Publisher's Interests

For nearly two decades, Just Us Books has been publishing books for children and young adults that reflect the diversity of African American history, heritage, and experiences. Its catalogue includes fiction, nonfiction, and biographies.
Website: www.justusbooks.com

Freelance Potential

Published 4–6 titles in 2010. Receives 1,000+ queries yearly.

- **Fiction:** Publishes concept books, 0–4 years; easy-to-read books, 4–7 years; story picture books, 4–10 years; chapter books, 5–10 years; middle-grade books, 8–12 years; and young adult books, 12–18 years. Genres include adventure; mystery; and contemporary, historical, multicultural, and ethnic fiction—all featuring African American characters or themes.
- **Nonfiction:** Publishes middle-grade books, 8–12 years. Topics include African American history, culture, social issues, and biography.
- **Representative Titles:** *The Secret Olivia Told Me,* by N. Joy (4–8 years), tells what happens when a girl lets slip a secret that her best friend told her. *Path To My African Eyes,* by Ermila Moodley (13–17 years), follows a South African teen as she leaves her homeland to begin a new life in California.

Submissions and Payment

Guidelines and catalogue available at website. Query with outline/synopsis and brief author biography. Accepts hard copy. SASE. Responds in 4–5 months. Publication period varies. Royalty.

Editor's Comments

We are currently accepting queries for young adult titles only. Please check our website for updates to this policy. Any query sent without a self-addressed stamped envelope will not receive a response.

Kaeden Books

P.O. Box 16190
Rocky River, OH 44116

Editor: Lisa Stenger

Publisher's Interests
Founded in 1986, this company publishes leveled books for early, emergent, and fluent readers in preschool through grade three. They are designed to help teachers guide children through their first years of the reading experience.
Website: www.kaeden.com

Freelance Potential
Published 12–20 titles in 2010: each was developed from an unsolicited submission. Receives 1,200+ unsolicited mss each year.

- **Fiction:** Publishes easy-to-read books, 4–7 years; story picture books, 4–10 years; and chapter books, 5–10 years. Genres include contemporary fiction and stories about animals.
- **Nonfiction:** Publishes easy-to-read books, 4–7 years; story picture books, 4–10 years; and chapter books, 5–10 years. Topics include animals, science, nature, nutrition, biography, careers, recreation, and social studies.
- **Representative Titles:** *Alex Plays Baseball* (Level 14) lets readers relate the difficulty of trying something new to the trouble Alex has in his first baseball game. *Busy Trucks* (Level 4) teaches students about different kinds of trucks and the role each plays in building a house.

Submissions and Payment
Guidelines and catalogue available at website. Send complete ms. Accepts hard copy. SASE. Responds in 1 year if interested. Publication period varies. Royalty. Flat fee.

Editor's Comments
Please do not submit manuscript summaries or books with religious themes, as we do not review these. We do not accept books that stereotype, demean, or present violence as acceptable behavior. Please be patient in waiting for a reply, as we receive a large number of submissions. We will contact you if we're interested.

Kane Miller

4901 Morena Boulevard, Suite 213
San Diego, CA 92117

Editorial Department

Publisher's Interests

Board books, picture books, and middle-grade fiction from around the world comprise the catalogue of this publisher, a division of EDC Publishing. Its focus is nonfiction books on uniquely American subjects, people, and history; it is also expanding its middle-grade fiction list.

Website: www.kanemiller.com

Freelance Potential

Published 43 titles in 2010: 2 were developed from unsolicited submissions and 2 were by agented authors. Of the 43 titles, 5 were by unpublished writers and 21 were by new authors. Receives 1,000+ unsolicited mss yearly.

- **Fiction:** Publishes concept books, toddler books, and early picture books, 0–4 years; story picture books, 4–10 years; chapter books, 5–10 years; and middle-grade books, 8–12 years. Genres include contemporary, historical, and multicultural fiction; adventure; humor; mystery; fantasy; and stories about animals.
- **Nonfiction:** Publishes early picture books, 0–4 years. Topics include animals, sports, history, multicultural issues, and American subjects.
- **Representative Titles:** *All About Scabs,* by Genichiro Yagyu (4–6 years), combines education, humor, and kid-friendly grossness to teach children how the body heals itself; part of the My Body Science series. *And What Comes After a Thousand?,* by Anette Bley (5–9 years), is a gentle story that conveys the concepts of love and friendship, and then loss and grieving.

Submissions and Payment

Guidelines and catalogue available at website. Send complete ms. Accepts hard copy. SASE. Responds in 3–6 weeks. Publication in 1–2 years. Royalty; advance.

Editor's Comments

We choose our books with extraordinary care and attention, publishing only the ones that speak to us and to children.

Kar-Ben Publishing

241 First Avenue North
Minneapolis, MN 55401

Publisher: Joni Sussman

Publisher's Interests
Kar-Ben Publishing produces books on Jewish themes for children and young adults. It welcomes unsolicited materials that are concise and have interesting, believable characters.
Website: www.karben.com

Freelance Potential
Published 18 titles (16 juvenile) in 2010: 16 were developed from unsolicited submissions and 2 were by agented authors. Of the 18 titles, 2 were by unpublished writers and 6 were by authors who were new to the publishing house. Receives 600–720 unsolicited mss yearly.

- **Fiction:** Publishes Jewish-themed concept books, toddler books, and early picture books, 0–4 years; story picture books, 4–10 years; and chapter books, 5–10 years. Publishes folklore, life-cycle stories, tales from the Torah, and Jewish identity and holiday stories.
- **Nonfiction:** Publishes Jewish-themed story picture books, 4–10 years; and middle-grade books, 8–12 years. Topics include Jewish identity, traditions, holidays, and doctrine. Also publishes prayer books, activity books, and board books.
- **Representative Titles:** *When I First Held You,* by Mirik Snir (3–8 years), is a lyrical lullaby celebrating the birth of a baby. *Zvuvi's Israel,* by Tami Lehman-Wilzig (3–8 years), takes readers on a tour of the cities and ancient ruins of Israel.

Submissions and Payment
Guidelines available at website. Send complete ms. Accepts hard copy, email to editorial@karben.com, and simultaneous submissions if identified. SASE. Responds in 4–6 weeks. Publication period varies. Royalty, 5–8%; advance, $500–$2,000.

Editor's Comments
Our current needs include picture books depicting Jewish summer camps, and nonfiction with ecology themes.

Key Curriculum Press

1150 65th Street
Emeryville, CA 94608

Executive Editor: Josephine Noah

Publisher's Interests
This educational publisher throws all of its support behind
its textbooks and supplemental materials, which engage students in and open their eyes to math and science and the
world around them. It also publishes resource materials for
educators of middle school and high school students.
Website: www.keypress.com

Freelance Potential
Published 100 titles in 2010. Receives 120 queries yearly.

- **Nonfiction:** Publishes middle-grade books, 8–12 years; and
  young adult books, 12–18 years. Topics include mathematics
  and science. Also publishes books for educators, software,
  and supplemental teaching materials for grades 6–12.
- **Representative Titles:** *Discovering Algebra,* by Jerald Mur-
  dock et al. (grades 8–10), gives students relatable experiences
  to help them comprehend abstract mathematical concepts.
  *Engineering the Future: Science, Technology, and Design
  Process* (grades 9–12) enhances students' comprehension of
  technology and its relation to physical science and physics.
  Living By Chemistry, by Angelica Stacy (grades 10–11), uses a
  standards-based, guided-inquiry approach to motivate students
  to think like scientists.

Submissions and Payment
Guidelines and catalogue available at website. Query with
résumé, prospectus, detailed table of contents, and 1–3
sample chapters. Accepts hard copy and simultaneous submissions if identified. SASE. Responds in 2 months. Publication period varies. Royalty, 6–10%.

Editor's Comments
We demand that our authors be committed to empowering
students to understand concepts, master skills, and find
enjoyment in learning. Prospective authors should have
years of research or teaching experience.

Key Education Publishing

9601 Newton Avenue South
Minneapolis, MN 55431

President: Sherrill B. Flora

Publisher's Interests

Teachers look to Key Education for supplemental educational materials that help in "unlocking the potential in every child," as the company's catalogue states. Its list serves preschool through third grade teachers. This publisher places special emphasis on resources for use with special learners.
Website: www.keyeducationpublishing.com

Freelance Potential

Published 30 titles in 2010. Of the 30 titles, 4 were by unpublished writers and 2 were by authors who were new to the publishing house.

- **Nonfiction:** Publishes educational resources, preK–grade 3. Features activity books, skill-and-practice materials, instructional methodology books, learning theme books, and materials for English as a Second Language (ESL) classes.
- **Representative Titles:** *Educating the Young Child with Autism Spectrum Disorders* guides teachers through introducing a child with ASD into the classroom and moving forward in the curriculum. *Building Alphabet Knowledge* (preK–K) presents reproducible activities that boost print awareness, letter recognition, phonemic awareness, and beginning phonics skills.

Submissions and Payment

Guidelines and catalogue available at website. Query with table of contents or outline, sample pages, and résumé. Accepts hard copy and email submissions to sherrie@keyeducationpublishing.com. SASE. Responds in 1–3 months. Publication in 9–12 months. Royalty. Flat fee.

Editor's Comments

To best determine if your concept would fit our needs, ask yourself if it is different from other teacher resource materials that are currently being marketed, and if it offers fresh ideas for educators. If your answer is yes, then we'd like to hear about it.

KidHaven Press

Thomson Gale
27500 Drake Road
Farmington Hills, MI 48331

Administrative Coordinator: Kristine Burns

Publisher's Interests

Specializing in titles for elementary and middle-school students, KidHaven Press features curriculum-related nonfiction books that turn history, geography, environment, and science themes into fascinating stories that appeal to kids. Some of its popular series are Innovators, Monsters, and Mysterious Encounters.
Website: http://gale.cengage.com/kidhaven

Freelance Potential

Published 20–25 titles in 2010. Receives 60+ queries yearly.

- **Nonfiction:** Publishes middle-grade books, 8–12 years. Topics include animals, biography, computers, geography, health, fitness, history, multicultural issues, nature, the environment, science, technology, and social issues.
- **Representative Titles:** *Abominable Snowman,* by Rachel Lynette, relates the fascinating characteristics, origins, and appeal of this creature; part of the Monsters series. *Foods of Australia,* by Barbara Sheen, takes a look at the geography, history, customs, celebrations, and—of course—food of this country; part of the A Taste of Culture series.

Submissions and Payment

Guidelines available; catalogue at website. Query. Accepts hard copy. SASE. Response time and publication period vary. Flat fee.

Editor's Comments

KidHaven Press is proud of the high-quality nonfiction books we publish. As always, we are looking for books that present important information through the use of vivid imagery, both in the words and the photography. Books should complement classroom instruction, foster ongoing discussions, and act as homework aids. Authors should be experienced in the topics they wish to write about, and text should be clear and easy to understand.

Kids Can Press

29 Birch Avenue
Toronto, Ontario M4V 1E2
Canada

Acquisitions Editor

Publisher's Interests
This Canadian publisher produces a variety of high-quality
fiction and nonfiction books for children up to age 10. Its
titles include picture books, poetry, and science books.
Website: www.kidscanpress.com

Freelance Potential
Published 32 titles in 2010. Receives 4,000 queries and
unsolicited mss yearly.

- **Fiction:** Publishes toddler books, 0–4 years; easy-to-read
  books, 4–7 years; story picture books, 4–10 years; chapter
  books, 5–10 years; middle-grade books, 8–12 years; and
  young adult books, 12–18 years. Genres include folklore,
  mystery, suspense, contemporary and historical fiction, and
  stories about animals.
- **Nonfiction:** Publishes easy-to-read books, 4–7 years; and
  middle-grade books, 8–12 years. Topics include animals,
  crafts, hobbies, nature, history, biography, and science.
- **Representative Titles:** *Kitten's Spring,* by Eugenie Fernandes
  (1–4 years), introduces toddlers to animals and the sounds
  they make. *Have You Ever Seen a Stork Build a Log Cabin?,*
  by Etta Kaner (4–7 years), tells kids how animals, such as
  ants, chimpanzees, and elephants, create shelter. *Girl in the
  Know,* by Anne Katz, is a manual explaining the ins and outs
  of puberty in a relaxed and conversational tone.

Submissions and Payment
Canadian authors only. Guidelines and catalogue available at
website. Query with synopsis and 3 chapters for fiction; send
complete ms for nonfiction and picture books. Accepts hard
copy and simultaneous submissions if identified. Responds
if interested. Publication period varies. Royalty; advance.

Editor's Comments
If you are a writer from Canada with a well-written manuscript or compelling book idea, please contact us.

Alfred A. Knopf Books for Young Readers

Random House
1745 Broadway, Mail Drop 9-3
New York, NY 10019

Submissions Editor

Publisher's Interests

One of the larger imprints of Random House Children's Books, Alfred A. Knopf publishes fiction for preschool children through young adult readers. Known for the caliber of its authors and artists, Knopf publishes books intended to entertain, inspire, and endure.

Website: www.randomhouse.com/kids

Freelance Potential

Published 75 titles in 2010. Of the 75 titles, 3 were by unpublished writers and 5 were by authors who were new to the publishing house. Receives 1,000+ queries and unsolicited mss yearly.

- **Fiction:** Publishes picture books, 0–8 years; middle-grade books, 8–12 years; and young adult books, 12–18 years. Genres include historical, contemporary, fantasy, science, and multicultural fiction; romance; mystery; adventure; and humor.
- **Representative Titles:** *Brisingr Inheritance, Book III,* by Christopher Paolini (12+ years), is a fantasy novel about a brave warrior and his dragon who fight to rid an evil kingdom of tyranny. *Scat,* by Carl Hiaasen (8–12 years), presents a comical mystery in which the kids of Bunny Starch's biology class most solve the mystery of her disappearance during a class trip to the Everglades.

Submissions and Payment

Guidelines and catalogue available at website. Send complete ms with cover letter for picture books. Query with synopsis and 25 pages of text for novels. Accepts hard copy and simultaneous submissions if identified. No SASE. Responds in 6 months if interested. Publication in 1–2 years. Royalty; advance.

Editor's Comments

Quality writing and engaging characters will get our attention, but be aware that competition here is fierce.

Wendy Lamb Books

Random House
1745 Broadway
New York, NY 10019

Editor: Wendy Lamb

Publisher's Interests

Created in 2002 as the first eponymous imprint of Random House Children's Books, Wendy Lamb Books publishes middle-grade and young adult fiction.
Website: www.randomhouse.com/kids

Freelance Potential

Published 14 titles in 2010: each was by an agented author. Receives 2,400 queries yearly.

- **Fiction:** Publishes middle-grade books, 8–12 years; and young adult books, 12–18 years. Genres include contemporary, historical, and multicultural fiction; mystery; adventure; and humor.
- **Representative Titles:** *Alligator Bayou,* by Donna Jo Napoli (12+ years), is a novel based on a true story about racism against Italian Americans in the South in 1899. *Seaglass Summer,* by Anjali Banerjee (8–12 years), tells the story of an 11-year-old girl who longs to be a veterinarian, and the summer she spends with a vet when she discovers just how much she has to learn. *Lawn Boy Returns,* by Gary Paulsen (9–12 years), features the adventures of a boy who makes a lot of money mowing lawns and attracts unwanted attention from the wrong kinds of people.

Submissions and Payment

Guidelines and catalogue available at website. Query with 10 ms pages and list of publishing credits. Accepts hard copy. SASE for reply only. Materials not returned. Responds in 2 months. Publication period and payment policy vary.

Editor's Comments

We recommend that prospective authors find literary agents to represent them. However, we also realize that there are some dynamite book ideas out there without representation, and we'd hate to miss out on them. We'll still review your query whether you are agented or not.

Learning Horizons

5301 Grant Avenue
Cleveland, OH 44125

Editorial Manager: Joanna Robinson

Publisher's Interests
Learning Horizons uses well-known and beloved children's characters, such as Elmo and Dora the Explorer, to help kids learn. It produces hands-on learning materials to excite, stimulate, encourage, and teach children in preschool through grade 6. All of its titles are written by professional educators and psychologists.
Website: www.learninghorizons.com

Freelance Potential
Published 20 titles in 2010. Of the 20 titles, 8 were by unpublished writers and 8 were by authors who were new to the publishing house. Receives 20–30 queries yearly.

- **Nonfiction:** Publishes story picture books, 4–10 years. Features educational and informational titles. Topics include mathematics, language arts, science, social studies, holidays, nature, and the environment. Also publishes workbooks for preK–grade 1, novelty books, and board books.
- **Representative Titles:** *Know Your Numbers* (3+ years) is a bilingual workbook that uses repetition to teach children their numbers; part of the Bilingual Wipe-off Workbook series. *Advanced Multiplication & Division* (grades 4–6) is a workbook that uses fun exercises to reinforce skills; part of the Learn on the Go series.

Submissions and Payment
Query. Accepts hard copy. SASE. Responds in 3–4 months. Publication in 18 months. Payment policy varies.

Editor's Comments
We offer workbook series on mathematics, reading comprehension, bilingual studies, writing and language arts, and geography. New writers who can offer a fresh perspective to our audience, and who are experienced in or knowledgeable about the field of early childhood education, are welcome to contact us.

Learning Resources

380 North Fairway Drive
Vernon Hills, IL 60061

Editorial Director

Publisher's Interests
Hands-on educational materials and learning toys are the
specialty of Learning Resources. All core curriculum subjects
are covered in its books, workbooks, reproducibles, and
activity kits designed for parents and teachers of kids in
preschool through grade six.
Website: www.learningresources.com

Freelance Potential
Published 85 titles in 2010. Of the 85 titles, 2 were by
unpublished writers and 2 were by authors who were new to
the publishing house. Receives 20 queries yearly.

- **Nonfiction:** Publishes educational materials, manipulatives,
  workbooks, games, and activity books, preK–grade 6. Topics
  include reading, grammar, writing, ESL, ELL, early childhood
  learning, geography, mathematics, measurement, sorting, nutrition and health, Earth and life sciences, and Spanish. Also produces teacher resources and classroom management tools.
- **Representative Titles:** *Hands-On Standards® Science* (grades
  4–5) provides complete science lessons and instructions for
  hands-on activities designed to teach the process of inquiry.
  Everyday Assessment with Reading Rods, by Jan Goldberg,
  provides a comprehensive assessment strategy using Reading
  Rods, and practical tips for incorporating the program into
  existing reading programs.

Submissions and Payment
Catalogue available at website or with 9x12 SASE ($3
postage). Query with résumé and writing sample. Accepts
hard copy. SASE. Responds in 6–12 weeks. Publication in
1–2 years. Flat fee.

Editor's Comments
To catch our interest, you should have professional education experience and your book should offer hands-on,
practical information.

Lee & Low Books

95 Madison Avenue
New York, NY 10016

Submissions Editor

Publisher's Interests
This small, independent children's publisher specializes in books that explore racial and cultural diversity for readers ages five to young adult.
Website: www.leeandlow.com

Freelance Potential
Published 12 titles in 2010: 2–3 were developed from unsolicited submissions and 2 were by agented authors. Of the 12 titles, 3 were by unpublished writers and 5 were by authors who were new to the publishing house. Receives 1,000 unsolicited mss yearly.

- **Fiction:** Publishes story picture books, 5–10 years; chapter books, 5–10 years; middle-grade books, 8–12 years; and young adult books, 12–18 years. Genres include realistic, historical, contemporary, multicultural, and ethnic fiction.
- **Nonfiction:** Publishes story picture books, 5–10 years; middle-grade books, 8–12 years; and young adult books, 12–18 years. Topics include multicultural and ethnic issues and traditions. Also publishes biographies.
- **Representative Titles:** *First Come the Zebra,* by Lynne Barasch (6–11 years), is the story of two boys from rival tribes in Africa who must overcome their differences to survive a dangerous situation. *The East-West House,* by Christy Hale (7–12 years), explores the bi-cultural childhood of a boy who would grow up to be a pioneering sculptor and designer.

Submissions and Payment
Guidelines available at website. Send complete ms. Accepts hard copy and simultaneous submissions if identified. SASE. Responds in 6 months if interested. Publication in 2–3 years. Royalty; advance.

Editor's Comments
We have a special interest in realistic and historical fiction, and in nonfiction with a distinct voice or unique approach.

Legacy Press

P.O. Box 261129
San Diego, CA 92196

Editorial Director

Publisher's Interests
Specializing in Christian-themed books and materials, Legacy Press publishes fiction and nonfiction for children as well as activity books and resources for religious education teachers.
Website: www.legacypresskids.com

Freelance Potential
Published 10 titles in 2010: 8 were developed from unsolicited submissions, 1 was by an agented author, and 1 was a reprint/licensed property. Of the 10 titles, 5 were by unpublished writers and 5 were by authors who were new to the publishing house. Receives 120 queries yearly.

- **Fiction:** Publishes middle-grade books, 8–12 years. Genres include adventure, mystery, contemporary fiction, and stories about animals—all with a Christian theme.
- **Nonfiction:** Publishes toddler books, 0–4 years; story picture books, 4–10 years; and chapter books, 5–10 years. Topics include the Bible, holidays, cooking, crafts, and hobbies. Also publishes activity books and parenting titles.
- **Representative Titles:** *The Christian Girl's Guide to Change (Inside and Out)* helps tween girls navigate the roller coaster of changes that await them in adolescence; part of the Christian Girl's Guide series. *The Un-Bunny Book* (3–12 years) is filled with reproducible activities and games that celebrate Easter with more God and less bunny.

Submissions and Payment
Guidelines and catalogue available at website or with 9x12 SASE (2 first-class stamps). Query with table of contents and first 3 chapters. Accepts hard copy. SASE. Responds in 3 months. Publication in 6–36 months. Royalty, 8%+; advance, $500+.

Editor's Comments
All books should exalt the presence of Jesus in our lives in a fun yet meaningful way.

Lerner Publications

241 First Avenue North
Minneapolis, MN 55401

Submissions Editor

Publisher's Interests
This publisher specializes in nonfiction books for the school library market. Targeting preschool through high school, it offers educational, photo-driven series that support key curriculum topics and engage the minds of young readers.
Website: www.lernerbooks.com

Freelance Potential
Published 250 titles in 2010: 5 were developed from unsolicited submissions and 50 were by agented authors. Of the 250 titles, 5 were by authors who were new to the publishing house.

- **Nonfiction:** Publishes easy-to-read books, 4–7 years; chapter books, 5–10 years; middle-grade books, 8–12 years; and young adult books, 12–18 years. Topics include ethnic and multicultural issues, nature, the environment, science, and sports. Also publishes biographies.
- **Representative Titles:** *Earthquakes*, by Sally M. Walker (grades 2–5), explains earthquakes in clear, simple language; part of the Early Bird Earth Science series. *Ancient Machines*, by Michael Woods & Mary B. Woods (grades 6–12), offers a close-up look at machines used by early civilizations; part of the Ancient Technology series.

Submissions and Payment
Guidelines and catalogue available at website. Accepts targeted submissions only. See website for a list of needs aimed at specific reading levels in specific subject areas, and for complete submission information. Response time, publication period, and payment policy vary.

Editor's Comments
Our goal is to publish children's books that educate, stimulate, and stretch the imagination; foster global awareness; encourage critical thinking; and inform, inspire, and entertain our readers.

Arthur A. Levine Books

Scholastic
557 Broadway
New York, NY 10012

Publisher: Arthur A. Levine

Publisher's Interests
This imprint of Scholastic Inc. is interested in high-quality,
literary titles for children of all ages—from the very young to
young adult. Embracing an array of genres and topics,
Levine puts an emphasis on engaging characters and literary-
quality writing.
Website: www.arthuralevinebooks.com

Freelance Potential
Published 15–20 titles in 2010: most were by agented
authors. Receives 2,600 queries, 400 unsolicited mss yearly.

- **Fiction:** Publishes story picture books, 4–10 years; chapter
  books, 5–10 years; middle-grade books, 8–12 years; and
  young adult books, 12–18 years. Genres include multicultural
  fiction and fantasy. Also publishes poetry.
- **Nonfiction:** Publishes story picture books, 4–10 years; middle-
  grade books, 8–12 years; and young adult books, 12–18 years.
  Topics include nature and animals. Also publishes biographies.
- **Representative Titles:** *Stick Man*, by Julia Donaldson (4–8
  years), introduces a new hero for the holidays, as Stick Man
  helps Santa save Christmas *and* finds his way back to his family
  tree. *Peaceful Heroes*, by Jonah Winter (9–12 years), presents
  the remarkable true stories of brave people who fought injus-
  tice through peaceful means.

Submissions and Payment
Guidelines and catalogue available at website. Send complete ms for picture books. Query for longer works and
fiction. Agented and published authors may send complete
ms for any length work. Accepts hard copy. SASE. Responds
to queries in 1 month; to mss in 6–8 months. Publication in
18–24 months. Payment policy varies.

Editor's Comments
Your query letter should be as individual as the book it
describes and the author it introduces.

Libraries Unlimited

130 Cremona Drive
Santa Barbara, CA 93117

Senior Acquisitions Editor: Barbara Ittner

Publisher's Interests

Serving library educators, librarians, and media specialists, Libraries Unlimited publishes bibliographies, reference books, library science textbooks, and professional development titles. It also publishes curriculum titles.
Website: www.lu.com; www.abc-clio.com

Freelance Potential

Published 100 titles in 2010: 7 were developed from unsolicited submissions. Of the 100 titles, 50 were by authors who were new to the publishing house. Receives 400+ queries yearly.

- **Nonfiction:** Publishes curriculum titles. Features bilingual books, grades K–6; and activity books, grades K–12. Topics include science, mathematics, social studies, whole language, and literature. Also publishes bibliographies, professional reference titles, gifted education titles, and regional books.
- **Representative Titles:** *Best Books for Children,* by Catherine Barr & John T. Gillespie, brings together information on nearly 25,000 of the best fiction and nonfiction for children in grades K–6. *Readers' Advisory for Children and 'Tweens,* by Penny Peck, details how to find books for various age groups, explores genre fiction for tweens, and offers techniques for promoting books and reading.

Submissions and Payment

Guidelines and catalogue available at website. Query with résumé, outline, methodology, sample chapter, and market analysis. Accepts hard copy. SASE. Responds in 2–3 months. Publication in 10–12 months. Royalty.

Editor's Comments

Neglecting to include your professional experience will be a deal breaker, as we publish only those authors who have served in the library science or library education fields and can share their knowledge with our readers.

Liguori Publications

1 Liguori Drive
Liguori, MO 63057-9999

Editorial Director: Jay Staten

Publisher's Interests
Liguori Publications, a Catholic book and magazine publisher, seeks to promote greater outreach to Catholics of all ages and to help them understand and celebrate the role of God in their lives. Its books for children include titles that introduce God, the Bible, and prayer, and help young readers navigate contemporary social issues.
Website: www.liguori.org

Freelance Potential
Published 40 titles in 2010: several were developed from unsolicited submissions.

- **Nonfiction:** Publishes toddler books, 0–4 years; easy-to-read books, 4–7 years; middle-grade books, 8–12 years; and young adult books, 12–18 years. Topics include prayer, catechism, Catholicism, the saints, celebrations, holy days, stewardship, youth ministry, family, divorce, sexuality, chastity, abuse, and other contemporary issues. Also publishes books for parents and religious educators.
- **Representative Titles:** *110 Fun Facts About God's Creation: Is It Animal, Vegetable, or Mineral?,* by Bernadette McCarver Snyder, presents Bible stories intermingled with entertaining facts about all of God's creatures. *Colorful Creation,* by Lucy Moore (5–9 years), is a colorfully illustrated retelling of the Creation story.

Submissions and Payment
Guidelines and catalogue available at website. Query with outline. Accepts hard copy and email submissions to manuscript_submission@liguori.org. SASE. Responds in 2–4 months. Publication in 9–18 months. Royalty.

Editor's Comments
As a rule, we do not accept fiction, poetry, biographies, autobiographies, or personal revelations. Our guidelines explain exactly what we'd like to see in your cover letter.

Linworth Publishing

P.O. Box 1911
Santa Barbara, CA 93116-1911

Publisher: Marlene Woo-Lun

Publisher's Interests
The professional development and practical concerns of librarians, media specialists, and educators are the focus of the books and resources offered by Linworth Publishing.
Website: www.linworth.com

Freelance Potential
Published 12 titles in 2010. Of the 12 titles, 3 were by authors who were new to the publishing house. Receives 120 queries yearly.

- **Nonfiction:** Publishes books for school librarians, media specialists, and teachers, grades K–12. Topics include technology, school library management, information literacy, research skills, library promotion, reading motivation, and grammar.
- **Representative Titles:** *Learning Right from Wrong in the Digital Age: An Ethics Guide for Parents, Teachers, Librarians, and Others Who Care About Computer-Using Young People,* by Doug Johnson, explains today's information technology ethics. *Bringing Mysteries Alive for Children and Young Adults,* by Jeanette Larson, presents an introduction to and guide for using various types of mysteries to engage readers and teach concepts within all subject areas.

Submissions and Payment
Guidelines and catalogue available at website. Query with résumé, outline, table of contents, sample chapter, and market analysis. Accepts hard copy, IBM disk submissions, and email queries to linworth@linworthpublishing.com. SASE. Responds in 1 week. Publication in 6 months. Royalty.

Editor's Comments
We're looking for submissions from professionals in the fields of library science, school or library administration, and media technology. Our readers are particularly asking for more resources that address the challenges they face every day.

Lion Children's Books

Wilkinson House
Jordan Hill Road
Oxford OX2 8DR
United Kingdom

Editorial Administrator: Jessica Tinker

Publisher's Interests
An imprint of Lion Hudson, Lion Children's Books publishes books that reflect Christian values or are inspired by a Christian worldview. Its list includes fiction and nonfiction that address the needs of an audience that ranges from infancy to young adulthood.
Website: www.lionhudson.com

Freelance Potential
Published 45 titles in 2010: 3 were developed from unsolicited submissions, 2 were by agented authors, and 1 was a reprint/licensed property. Receives 960 queries yearly.

- **Fiction:** Publishes early picture books, concept books, and toddler books, 0–4 years; chapter books, 5–10 years; and young adult books, 12–18 years. Genres include fairy tales, religious and inspirational fiction, and adventure.
- **Nonfiction:** Publishes toddler books and early picture books, 0–4 years; easy-to-read books, 4–7 years; story picture books, 4–10 years; middle-grade books, 8–12 years; and young adult books, 12–18 years. Topics include religion, current events, history, nature, social issues, health, and fitness.
- **Representative Titles:** *Thank You God: Daytime and Night-time Prayers for Little Children*, by Sophie Piper, provides short but memorable prayers that are themed around emotions and the events of a child's day. *My Very First Bible*, by Lois Rock, retells 20 key stories from the Old and New Testaments.

Submissions and Payment
Guidelines and catalogue available at website. Query with résumé. Accepts hard copy. SAE/IRC. Responds in 3 months. Publication period and payment policy vary.

Editor's Comments
We look for books that introduce children to God and the Bible, and books that foster an awareness of the wonderful world that we share.

Little, Brown and Company
Books for Young Readers

Hachette Book Group
237 Park Avenue
New York, NY 10017

Publisher: Megan Tingley

Publisher's Interests

Little, Brown and Company's children's division develops and markets picture books, chapter books, and teen titles. Its extensive catalogue includes everything from alphabet books for toddlers to novels with cutting-edge themes for adolescents.

Website: www.lb-kids.com or www.lb-teens.com

Freelance Potential

Published 150 titles in 2010: each was by an agented author.

- **Fiction:** Publishes toddler books, 0–4 years; picture books, 4–8 years; easy-to-read books, 4–7 years; chapter books, 5–10 years; and young adult books, 12–18 years. Genres include fantasy, contemporary, and multicultural fiction. Also publishes stories about the holidays.
- **Nonfiction:** Publishes books with trade market potential. Topics include multicultural issues, history, self-help, and sports.
- **Representative Titles:** *The Very Fairy Princess,* by Julie Andrews & Emma Walton Hamilton, features a girl who spends her days practicing to be a fairy princess—dressing in royal attire, honing her flying skills, and looking for problems to solve. *Strawberry Hill,* by Mary Ann Hoberman, is the story of a girl who is worried about her family's move to a new home, until she learns the pretty name of the street she will be living on.

Submissions and Payment

Accepts submissions from agented authors only. Publication period varies. Royalty; advance.

Editor's Comments

While we're always interested in high-quality writing that features engaging characters and story lines, we can only review submissions that are made through literary agents. Unsolicited submissions are returned unopened or recycled.

Little Simon

Simon & Schuster Children's Publishing
1230 Avenue of the Americas
New York, NY 10020

Editorial Department

Publisher's Interests
This division of Simon & Schuster focuses on the very
youngest readers, engaging them with colorful picture
books, board books, pop-up and lift-the-flap books, and
other novelty formats. The purpose is to make reading fun
for both young children and their parents.
Website: http://kids.simonandschuster.com

Freelance Potential
Published 65 titles in 2010: 20 were by agented authors and
15 were reprint/licensed properties. Receives 200 queries
each year.

- **Fiction:** Publishes concept books and toddler books, 0–4
  years. Features stories about animals, holidays, trucks and
  automobiles, families, and the weather. Also publishes board
  books, 0–4 years; and pop-up books, 4–8 years.
- **Representative Titles:** *Room for a Little One: A Christmas
  Tale,* by Martin Waddell (3–7 years), is a board book that tells
  about the animals in the stable who make room for one more
  little one on the night of Jesus's birth. *Mouse's First Day of
  School,* by Lauren Thompson (2–6 years), follows the adventures of a mouse who spends a day at school after acciden-
  tally stowing away in a backpack.

Submissions and Payment
Accepts queries through literary agents only. Publication in
2 years. Royalty; advance. Flat fee.

Editor's Comments
Our books are designed to delight the young readers who
hold them in their hands, while also bringing a smile to the
faces of the parents who read with them. We're looking for
titles that are clever and engaging. Because we receive so
many submissions, we are only able to review queries that
come through literary agents.

Little Tiger Press

1 The Coda Centre
189 Munster Road
London SW6 6AW
United Kingdom

Submissions Editor: Stephanie Stahl

Publisher's Interests

Specializing in picture and novelty books for children up to
age 7, Little Tiger Press features a diverse list of award-
winning books. Its brightly illustrated titles share exciting
stories and inspiring messages with young readers as they
develop and grow in confidence.
Website: www.littletigerpress.com

Freelance Potential

Published 63 titles (63 juvenile) in 2010. Of the 63 titles,
1 was by an unpublished writer and 4 were by authors
who were new to the publishing house. Receives 3,500
unsolicited mss yearly.

- **Fiction:** Publishes concept books and early picture books, 0–4
  years; and story picture books, 3–7 years. Genres include contemporary and classical fiction. Also publishes board books.
- **Representative Titles:** *The Special Christmas Tree,* by Catherine Walters & Simon Taylor-Kielty (1–3 years), tells the story of
  animal friends who set off to find tree decorations during a
  snowstorm. *Bright Stanley and the Cave Monster,* by Matt
  Buckingham (3–7 years), features a fish and his friends who
  explore a dark cave with lots of strange shadows. *The Great
  Monster Hunt,* by Norbert Landa & Tim Warnes (4–7 years),
  follows the great adventures of four animal friends as they
  embark on a scary monster hunt.

Submissions and Payment

Guidelines available at website. Send complete ms with brief
cover letter. Accepts hard copy. Material is not returned.
Responds via email in 3 months. Publication period and payment policy vary.

Editor's Comments

Try to look at several of our published books before sending
your material to get a feel for what we like. Please be patient
while awaiting a response from us.

Living Ink Books

AMG Publishers
6815 Shallowford Road
Chattanooga, TN 37421

Acquisitions: Rick Steele

Publisher's Interests
Fiction and nonfiction books for middle-grade and young
adult readers fill the youth catalogue of this AMG imprint. It
publishes nonfiction titles designed to help parents and religious educators get children into the Bible and grow with
Christ in their lives. It also publishes exciting, Christian-
themed fiction.
Website: www.amgpublishers.com

Freelance Potential
Published 30 titles (5 juvenile) in 2010: 6 were by agented
authors and 6 were reprint/licensed properties. Of the 30
titles, 9 were by unpublished writers and 11 were by authors
who were new to the publishing house. Receives 1,200
queries yearly.

- **Fiction:** Publishes middle-grade books, 8–12 years; and young
  adult books, 12–18 years. Genres include fantasy fiction with
  Christian themes.
- **Nonfiction:** Publishes Christian issue-oriented books and Bible
  references for parents, educators, and other adults. Topics
  include Bible study, family issues, relationships, and parenting.
- **Representative Titles:** *Raising Responsive Children,* by Judy
  Rossi, addresses moms' realities and responsibilities in their
  parenting. *Angela's Answer,* by Pat Matuszak (YA), is an adventure tale of a girl who tries to reveal a secret hidden in her
  town; part of the Angel Light series.

Submissions and Payment
Guidelines and catalogue available at website. Query with
synopsis and author bio. Accepts hard copy and email
queries to ricks@amgpublishers.com. SASE. Response time
and publication period vary. Royalty; advance.

Editor's Comments
We are interested in publishing more middle-grade fiction
and young adult fantasy fiction.

Lobster Press

1620 Sherbrooke Street West, Suite C & D
Montreal, Quebec H3H 1C9
Canada

Assistant Editor: Meghan Nolan

Publisher's Interests
Lobster Press is dedicated to publishing the work of Canadian authors for children of all ages. Its catalogue includes picture books, short novels for young readers, motivational nonfiction, and engaging young adult novels.
Website: www.lobsterpress.com

Freelance Potential
Published 23 titles in 2010. Of the 23 titles, 2 were by unpublished writers and 4 were by authors who were new to the publishing house. Receives 2,000 queries yearly.

- **Fiction:** Publishes toddler books, 2–4 years; story picture books, 4–10 years; middle-grade books, 8–12 years; and young adult books, 12–18 years. Genres include contemporary fiction, fantasy, and humor.
- **Nonfiction:** Publishes early picture books, 2–4 years; story picture books, 4–10 years; middle-grade books, 8–12 years; and young adult books, 12–18 years. Topics include history, science, nature, health, sports, travel, music, and social issues.
- **Representative Titles:** *Don't Worry, Joey,* by Addie Meyer Sanders (1–7 years), follows 5-year-old Joey as he tries to tame his worries about being away from home for the first time. *A Bloom of Friendship: The Story of the Canadian Tulip Festival,* by Anne Renaud (9–12 years), tells the true story of how the festival was created.

Submissions and Payment
Canadian authors only. Guidelines and catalogue available at website. Query with résumé and synopsis. Send complete ms for picture books. Accepts email submissions to LobsterPressSubmissions@gmail.com. Responds if interested. Publication period varies. Royalty, 5–10%.

Editor's Comments
Please see our guidelines at our website for details about our most recent editorial call.

James Lorimer & Company

317 Adelaide Street West, Suite 1002
Toronto, Ontario M5V 1P9
Canada

Children's Book Editor: Faye Smailes

Publisher's Interests

This publisher works with Canadian authors to create fiction and nonfiction titles for children and teens. All books have a Canadian topic or theme.
Website: www.lorimer.ca

Freelance Potential

Published 25 titles (17 juvenile) in 2010: 3 were developed from unsolicited submissions and 1 was a reprint/licensed property. Of the 25 titles, 2 were by unpublished writers and 4 were by authors who were new to the publishing house. Receives 240 queries, 120 unsolicited mss yearly.

- **Fiction:** Publishes chapter books, 7–9 years; middle-grade books, 10–13 years; and young adult books, 13–18 years. Genres include realistic, issue-based, contemporary, historical and sports-themed fiction; mystery; suspense; adventure; graphic novels; and humor.
- **Nonfiction:** Publishes middle-grade books, 8–12 years; and young adult books, 12–18 years. Topics include multicultural subjects, nature, sports, and contemporary social studies.
- **Representative Titles:** *Harley's Gift*, by Beth Pollock (6–10 years), tells the story of a Toronto girl who wants only one thing for Christmas: peace between her mother and grandmother. *Image: Deal with It from the Inside Out*, by Kat Mototsune (9+ years), addresses the costs of conforming to social images.

Submissions and Payment

Canadian authors only. Guidelines available. Prefers query with outline and sample chapters; will accept complete ms. Accepts hard copy and simultaneous submissions if identified. SASE. Responds in 3–4 months. Publication period varies. Royalty; advance.

Editor's Comments

We believe in supporting the Canadian writer, and in preserving the Canadian culture and voice through books.

Lucent Books

Thomson Gale
27500 Drake Road
Farmington Hills, MI 48331-3535

Administrative Assistant: Kristine Burns

Publisher's Interests
This imprint of Thomson Gale supports the middle school curriculum with nonfiction books that are seen as valuable tools for conducting research and sharpening critical thinking skills. Its popular series include Technology 360, Crime Scene Investigations, and Hot Topics.
Website: www.gale.cengage.com/lucent

Freelance Potential
Published 110 titles in 2010: 3 were by unpublished writers and 10 were by authors who were new to the publishing house. Receives 100 queries yearly.

- **Nonfiction:** Publishes middle-grade books, 8–12 years; and young adult books, 12–18 years. Topics include contemporary social issues, biography, history, geography, health, science, and sports.
- **Representative Titles:** *ADHD*, by Barbara Sheen (YA), offers young readers insight into the causes, treatment, and prevention of this disorder; part of the Diseases and Disorders series. *Crime Scene Investigations: The 9/11 Investigation*, by Craig E. Blohm (YA), reveals how forensic science unravels clues in the smallest bits of evidence. *Auschwitz*, by Don Nardo (YA), introduces readers to this World War II prison camp; part of the World History series.

Submissions and Payment
Query with résumé and list of publishing credits. All work is assigned. Response time varies. Publication in 1 year. Flat fee.

Editor's Comments
Our books provide divergent points of view on controversial social, political, and economic topics. Our goal is to present complex ideas and events in a way that middle-school students will understand, but with depth and objectivity. Send us a query and we may consider giving you the assignment.

Mage Publishers

1032 29th Street NW
Washington, DC 20007

Submissions Editor: Amin Sepehri

Publisher's Interests
Mage publishes books of Persian literature, history, arts, and culture for English-speaking readers of all ages. Its list includes translations, historical texts, and contemporary works written in English. For children, it publishes books about Persian folktales, legends, and history.
Website: www.mage.com

Freelance Potential
Published 4–5 titles in 2010. Of the 4–5 titles, 1 was by an author who was new to the publishing house. Receives 50 queries, 25 unsolicited mss yearly.

- **Fiction:** Publishes children's tales and legends from Persia.
- **Nonfiction:** Publishes books on Persian literature, culture, history, and life. Also publishes books for adults on Persian cooking, architecture, music, history, poetry, and literature.
- **Representative Titles:** *Happy Nowruz: Cooking with Children to Celebrate the Persian New Year,* by Najmieh Batmanglij, is a guide to customs and cooking for a festival that celebrates the Earth, the arrival of spring, and the rebirth of nature. *Inside Iran: Women's Lives,* by Jane Howard, features personal stories of Iranian women and historical perspectives from a British journalist who lived and raised her family in Iran.

Submissions and Payment
Guidelines and catalogue available at website. Query or send complete ms with brief biographical statement. Accepts hard copy. SASE. Responds in 1–3 months. Publication in 9–15 months. Royalty; advance.

Editor's Comments
Though most of our catalogue's content features titles for adults, we are interested in receiving more proposals for books for children. Books on Persian history, notable figures, culture, and tales written especially for young readers would be well-received here.

Magical Child Books

Shades of White
301 Tenth Avenue
Crystal City, MO 63019

Acquisitions Editor

Publisher's Interests

A small, niche publisher, Magical Child publishes children's fiction about Earth-based religions. It looks for contemporary characters, imaginative stories, accurate descriptions of the practices of Earth religions, and themes with a strong Pagan world view.
Website: http://magicalchildbooks.com

Freelance Potential

Published 1–3 titles in 2010. Of the 1–3 titles, 1 was by an author who was new to the publishing house. Receives 4,000+ queries, 1,000+ unsolicited mss yearly.

- **Fiction:** Publishes story picture books, 4–10 years; early readers, 4–7 years; chapter books, 5–10 years; and middle-grade books, 9–13 years. Genres include contemporary, magical lore, holidays, and folklore.
- **Nonfiction:** Publishes biographies, 5–12 years.
- **Representative Titles:** *Smoky and the Feast of Mabon,* by Catherynne M. Valente (4–8 years), is an autumn equinox story that gently explains the cycle of the seasons. *Rabbit's Song,* by S. J. Tucker and Trudy Herring (4–8 years), is an imaginative rendering of the traditional trickster tale.

Submissions and Payment

Query via the website form, or send complete ms, to 1,000 words, for picture books; for older books, submit sample chapters. Include a résumé, review of competitive titles, and why your book is unique. Royalty; advance.

Editor's Comments

We like stories that have modern-day children as main characters, and with the elements of magical lore associated of the Earth religions. Do not send fairy tales or folklore unrelated to Pagan themes. Our list is currently very Wicca-oriented and we'd like to get manuscripts with accurate depictions of Asatru or Druidism.

Magination Press

750 First Street NE
Washington, DC 20002-4242

Acquisitions Editor

Publisher's Interests
Magination Press, a publishing arm of the American Psychological Association, calls the titles in its catalogue "self-help
books for kids, and the adults in their lives." It publishes
books that help children and families understand feelings
and deal with whatever challenges they may face.
Website: www.maginationpress.com

Freelance Potential
Published 12 titles in 2010: 3 were developed from unso-
licited submissions and 2 were reprint/licensed properties.
Receives 800 unsolicited mss yearly.

- **Fiction:** Publishes picture books and easy-to-read books, 4–8
  years; story picture books, 4–10 years; and middle-grade
  books, 8–12 years. Stories address psychological concerns.
- **Nonfiction:** Publishes story picture books, 4–10 years; middle-
  grade books, 8–12 years; and young adult books, 12–18
  years. Topics include divorce, ADHD/ADD, learning disabilities,
  depression, death, anxieties, self-esteem, and family matters.
  Also publishes workbooks.
- **Representative Titles:** *The Bald-Headed Princess,* by Maribeth
  R. Ditmars (8–13 years), is the story of a girl who doesn't let
  cancer stop her from being what she is—a soccer princess. *My
  Anxious Mind,* by Michael A. Tompkins & Katherine A. Mar-
  tinez (YA), is a teen's guide to managing anxiety and panic.

Submissions and Payment
Guidelines available at website. Send complete ms with
résumé, synopsis, and market analysis. Accepts hard copy.
SASE. Responds in 4–6 months. Publication in 2–3 years.
Royalty.

Editor's Comments
We are currently interested in receiving nonfiction books on
a variety of psychological topics for middle-school readers
and teens.

Master Books

P.O. Box 726
Green Forest, AR 72638

Assistant Editor: Craig Froman

Publisher's Interests
Part of New Leaf Publishing Group since 1996, this imprint
focuses on Creation-based nonfiction and educational materials, and fiction for all ages.
Website: www.masterbooks.net

Freelance Potential
Published 25 titles (11 juvenile) in 2010: 13 were developed
from unsolicited submissions, 3 were by agented authors,
and 1 was a reprint/licensed property. Of the 25 titles, 5
were by unpublished writers and 3 were by new authors.
Receives 1,080–1,200 queries yearly.

- **Fiction:** Publishes story picture books, 4–10 years. Religious
  fiction, Bible stories, and stories that promote Creationism.
- **Nonfiction:** Publishes toddler books and early picture books,
  0–4 years; easy-to-read books, 4–7 years; story picture books,
  4–10 years; middle-grade books, 8–12 years; and young adult
  books, 12–18 years. Topics include science, technology, and
  animals. Also publishes Christian homeschooling materials.
- **Representative Titles:** *Dinosaurs: Stars of the Show,* by Amie
  Zordel, is the story of a little girl who discovers that dinosaurs
  actually prove the Bible was right about Creation. *Not Too
  Small at All: A Mouse Tale,* by Stephanie Z. Townsend, presents the story of a young mouse who learns that even little
  ones have a place in God's kingdom.

Submissions and Payment
Guidelines and catalogue available at website. Query. Prefers
electronic queries using proposal form at website; will accept
hard copy and email to submissions@newleafpress.net. SASE.
Responds in 3–4 months. Publication in 1 year. Royalty.

Editor's Comments
At this time, we're interested in church resources, books for
Christian education and homeschooling, and Creation-based
science materials.

Meadowbrook Press

5455 Smetana Drive
Minnetonka, MN 55343

Submissions Editor

Publisher's Interests

Meadowbrook Press specializes in poetry books for children.
It also publishes humorous and practical nonfiction books
for parents-to-be and parents of babies and young children.
Website: www.meadowbrookpress.com

Freelance Potential

Published 10 titles in 2010. Receives 100 queries yearly.

- **Nonfiction:** Publishes concept books, 0–4 years; and middle-
grade books, 8–12 years. Topics include toilet training, school,
party games, and arts and crafts. Also publishes poetry, nurs-
ery rhymes, and activity books; and books on pregnancy,
childbirth, child care, breastfeeding, and parenting.
- **Representative Titles:** *I Hope I Don't Strike Out! And Other
Funny Sports Poems,* by Bruce Lansky, is an anthology of
humorous poems for and about kids playing all sorts of
sports. *The Arts & Crafts Busy Book,* by Trish Kuffner, offers
how-to instructions for simple and affordable arts and crafts
activities for toddlers and preschoolers. *The Breastfeeding
Diaries* is a collection of the diary entries of nursing moms
chronicling their funniest misadventures.

Submissions and Payment

Guidelines and catalogue available at website. Query.
Accepts hard copy and simultaneous submissions if identified. No SASE. Responds only if interested. Publication in 2
years. Royalty; advance.

Editor's Comments

We're still interested in submissions of poetry for children.
We are not accepting adult fiction or poetry, nor are we
accepting children's fiction. We are always seeking material
that we can edit, design, and promote to its full commercial
potential, so tell us why you think there is a market for your
submission, and how you can help to promote your book.

Medallion Press

1020 Cedar Avenue, Suite 216
St. Charles, IL 60174

Acquisitions Editor: Helen Rosburg

Publisher's Interests
In addition to its long list of genre fiction for adults, Medallion Press also publishes a collection of young adult novels and Christian fiction. It has recently added a nonfiction category for adult readers that is open to submissions from agented authors only.
Website: www.medallionpress.com/index.html

Freelance Potential
Published 21 titles in 2010. Of the 21 titles, 6 were by unpublished writers and 8 were by authors who were new to the publishing house. Receives 500 queries yearly.

- **Fiction:** Publishes young adult books, 12–18 years. Genres include mainstream, contemporary, historical, and science fiction; fantasy; adventure; mystery; thriller; suspense; romance; and horror.
- **Nonfiction:** Publishes titles for adults.
- **Representative Titles:** *Starlight & Promises,* by Cat Lindler, is a historical romance featuring a search for a saber-toothed tiger, a missing uncle, and love. *Stress Fracture,* by D. P. Lyle, finds a crime scene investigator working on a case very close to his heart—the brutal slaying of his friend.

Submissions and Payment
Guidelines and catalogue available at website. Query with word count, 2- to 5-page synopsis, first 3 chapters, and list of publishing credits. Accepts email queries to submissions@medallionpress.com. Responds in 6–8 months. Publication in 2–3 years. Royalty; advance.

Editor's Comments
We have recently expanded our publishing categories, and we have reopened our young adult category. We're exacting in our query requirements, so prospective authors are advised to follow our guidelines closely. Queries that do not adhere to our guidelines will not be reviewed.

Meriwether Publishing

885 Elkton Drive
Colorado Springs, CO 80907

Associate Editor: Arthur L. Zapel

Publisher's Interests
Theatre arts textbooks, plays, and stagecraft books are all
found in the catalogue of this publisher. Its titles target
middle-grade and high school students.
Website: www.meriwether.com

Freelance Potential
Published 11 titles (9 juvenile) in 2010: 7 were developed
from unsolicited submissions and 4 were by agented
authors. Of the 11 titles, 2 were by unpublished writers and
7 were by authors who were new to the publishing house.
Receives 240 queries, 180 unsolicited mss yearly.

- **Fiction:** Publishes middle-grade books, 8–12 years; and young
  adult books, 12–18 years. Genres include drama, comedy,
  and musicals; one-act plays; monologues; dialogues; and
  folktales.
- **Nonfiction:** Publishes middle-grade books, 8–12 years; and
  young adult books, 12–18 years. Topics include acting, direct-
  ing, auditioning, improvisation, public speaking, interpersonal
  communication, debate, mime, clowning, storytelling, costum-
  ing, stage lighting, and sound effects.
- **Representative Titles:** *Let's Put on a Show!,* by Adrea Gibbs
  (YA), gives young actors the what, where, when, and how of
  staging a show. *Staging Musicals for Young Performers,* by
  Maria Novelly & Adele Firth, is a step-by-step guide for putting
  on a show within any budget.

Submissions and Payment
Guidelines available at website. Query with outline and sam-
ple chapter for books. Send complete ms for plays. Accepts
hard copy and simultaneous submissions if identified. SASE.
Responds in 4–6 weeks. Publication in 6 months. Royalty.
Flat fee.

Editor's Comments
Please include a market analysis with your submission.

Milkweed Editions

1011 Washington Avenue South, Suite 300
Minneapolis, MN 55415

Editors

Publisher's Interests
This not-for-profit press specializes in works of fiction for
young readers, as well as adult literary nonfiction that
focuses on the relationship between nature and humans.
Website: www.milkweed.org

Freelance Potential
Published 17 titles (4 juvenile) in 2010: 1 was developed
from an unsolicited submission, 5 were by agented authors,
and 2 were reprint/licensed properties. Of the 17 titles, 3
were by unpublished writers and 7 were by authors who
were new to the publishing house. Receives 1,200 unsolicited
mss yearly.

- **Fiction:** Publishes middle-grade books, 8–13 years. Genres
  include historical, multicultural, and ethnic fiction; and stories
  about nature. Also publishes poetry.
- **Representative Titles:** *The Linden Tree,* by Ellie Mathews,
  tells of a farm family of the 1940s coping with the sudden
  death of their mother. *No Place,* by Kay Haugaard, is the story
  of 12-year-old Arturo who inspires his sixth-grade classmates
  to help him turn a vacant lot into a playground. *Water Steps,*
  by A. LaFaye, tells how a young girl must face her fear of the
  sea when her adoptive parents move into a house on Lake
  Champlain for the summer.

Submissions and Payment
Guidelines available at website. Send complete ms. Accepts
electronic submissions through Submissions Manager at
website only. Responds in 1–6 months. Publication in 2
years. Royalty, 6% of list price; advance, varies.

Editor's Comments
We're particularly in need of submissions of multicultural or
ethnic stories. Please note that we do not publish picture
books or children's nonfiction. For young readers, we offer
middle-grade fiction only.

Millbrook Press

Lerner Publishing
241 First Avenue North
Minneapolis, MN 55401

Submissions

Publisher's Interests
This imprint of Lerner Publishing Group focuses on books for classroom and homeschool use. Its list focuses on curriculum topics, including math, science, social studies, and language arts. Most of its books are published in series.
Website: www.lernerbooks.com

Freelance Potential
Published 60 titles in 2010.

- **Nonfiction:** Publishes concept books and toddler books, 0–4 years; middle-grade books, 8–12 years; and young adult books, 12–18 years. Topics include the arts, sports, social studies, history, math, science, nature, the environment, and crafts. Also publishes biographies.
- **Representative Titles:** *Your Body Battles a Cold,* by Vicki Cobb (grades 2–5), explains how the human body heals itself and fights off intruders; part of the Body Battles series. *Vanishing From Grasslands & Deserts,* by Gail Radley (grades 5–8), examines the situations of endangered or threatened animals living in this environment; part of the Vanishing From series. *Foul Play: Sports Jokes that Won't Strike Out,* by Rick Walton & Ann Walton, lets readers take a break from academics and enjoy some light reading with sports-related comedy.

Submissions and Payment
Guidelines and catalogue available at website. Accepts targeted submissions only. See website for list of needs at specific reading levels and in specific subject areas. Response time, publication period, and payment policy vary.

Editor's Comments
Due to significant increases in volume, we no longer accept unsolicited submissions. However, we continue to seek targeted submissions depending on our subject needs during any given publication period. Please see our guidelines for our current needs, if any.

Mirrorstone Books

Wizards of the Coast
P.O. Box 707
Renton, WA 98057-0707

Submissions Editor

Publisher's Interests

Launched in 2004, Mirrorstone Books publishes fantasy fiction for ages four through young adult. It focuses exclusively on novels inspired by the lore of the Dungeons & Dragons game. Series proposals and stand-alone titles are not considered, but freelance assignments are available on a work-for-hire basis.

Website: www.mirrorstonebooks.com

Freelance Potential

Published 10 titles in 2010: 5 were by agented authors. Of the 10 titles, 1 was by an unpublished writer and 1 was by an author who was new to the publishing house. Receives 360 queries yearly.

- **Fiction:** Publishes story picture books, 4–10 years; chapter books, 5–10 years; middle-grade books, 8–12 years; and young adult books, 12–18 years. Genres include medieval, mystical, heroic, epic, and light fantasy fiction.
- **Representative Titles:** *The Shadowmask,* by R. A. Salvatore & Geno Salvatore, furthers the story of young Maimun's quest to find the Stone of Tymora and the magic that rightfully belongs to him; part of the Stone of Tymora trilogy. *Why It Sucks to Be Me,* by Kimberly Pauley, follows the adventures of a teen girl whose parents are vampires.

Submissions and Payment

Guidelines and catalogue available at website. Submit writing sample only; include 3 sample chapters of a completed novel for middle-grade or young adult readers and a 1- to 2-page synopsis. Accepts hard copy. SASE. Responds in 4 months. Publication period varies. Flat fee.

Editor's Comments

We cannot judge your work from a query letter only; you must send a writing sample to be properly considered for an assignment for one of our series titles.

Mitchell Lane Publishers

P.O. Box 196
Hockessin, DE 19707

Publisher: Barbara Mitchell

Publisher's Interests

The books from Mitchell Lane target children who do not like to read. In order to capture the attention of these readers, Mitchell Lane publishes engaging nonfiction on high-interest topics such as entertainment and sports, pop culture, and science. This publisher works with established authors on a work-for-hire basis.
Website: www.mitchelllane.com

Freelance Potential

Published 77 titles in 2010. Of the 77 titles, 3 were by authors who were new to the publishing house. Receives 360 queries yearly.

- **Nonfiction:** Publishes easy-to-read books, 4–7 years; chapter books, 5–10 years; middle-grade books, 8–12 years; and young adult books, 12–18 years. Topics include animals, natural disasters, biography, sports, mythology, art, history, poets, playwrights, science, music, health and fitness, and multicultural topics.
- **Representative Titles:** *How You Can Use Waste Energy to Heat and Light Your Home* (grades 3–6) explains this alternative energy source; part of the Tell Your Parents series. *Kanye West* (grades 4–8) profiles the famous and sometimes controversial rapper; part of the Blue Banner Biography Contemporary Pop Entertainers V series.

Submissions and Payment

Guidelines and catalogue available at website. Work-for-hire only. Query with unedited writing sample, résumé, and publishing credits. Accepts hard copy. Material is not returned. Responds if interested. Publication period varies. Flat fee.

Editor's Comments

We will be expanding our subject list to include community service and volunteering, environmental topics, genealogy, and the Middle East.

Mondo Publishing

980 Avenue of the Americas
New York, NY 10018

Editorial Director

Publisher's Interests

The Mondo Publishing catalogue includes literacy materials
for grades K–5, as well as professional development materials for language arts teachers and literacy program educators. Its titles cover programs for phonics, comprehension,
oral language, writing, reluctant readers, intervention, and
comprehensive solutions for core reading instruction.
Website: www.mondopub.com

Freelance Potential

Published 30 titles in 2010.

- **Fiction:** Publishes easy-to-read books, 4–7 years; story picture
  books, 4–10 years; chapter books, 5–10 years; and middle-grade books, 8–12 years. Genres include contemporary and
  historical fiction; science fiction; fantasy, mystery; folktales;
  adventure; and humor.
- **Nonfiction:** Publishes early picture books, 0–4 years; story picture books, 4–10 years; and young adult books, 12–18 years.
  Topics include science, nature, animals, the environment, history, music, crafts, hobbies, and language arts.
- **Representative Titles:** *A Manual of House Monsters,* by
  Stanislav Marijanovic (grade 3), shows the funny and fantastic
  side of everyday life at home. *Growing Radishes and Carrots,*
  by Faye Bolton & Diane Snowball (grade 1), presents a simple,
  colorfully illustrated how-to growing guide for very young vegetable gardeners.

Submissions and Payment

Query. Accepts hard copy. SASE. Response time varies. Publication in 1–3 years. Royalty.

Editor's Comments

We are interested in submissions of both fiction and nonfiction material for emerging and reluctant readers. Work that
can be included in any of our existing series is welcome, as
well as new, stand-alone books.

Moose Enterprise Book and Theatre Play Publishing

684 Walls Road
Sault Ste. Marie, Ontario P6A 5K6
Canada

Owner/Publisher: Richard Mousseau

Publisher's Interests

The titles produced by this small, independent publisher include fiction and nonfiction for children and young adults, as well as theatrical plays of all lengths. 1% self-, subsidy-, co-venture, or co-op published material.
Website: www.moosehidebooks.com

Freelance Potential

Published 6 titles in 2010: each was developed from an unsolicited submission. Of the 6 titles, 1 was by an unpublished writer and 6 were by authors who were new to the publishing house. Receives 240 queries yearly.

- **Fiction:** Publishes chapter books, 5–10 years; middle-grade books, 8–12 years; and young adult books, 12–18 years. Genres include adventure, drama, fantasy, historical and science fiction, humor, horror, mystery, suspense, and Westerns.
- **Nonfiction:** Publishes middle-grade books, 8–12 years; and young adult books, 12–18 years. Topics include local, Canadian, and military history. Also publishes biographies.
- **Representative Titles:** *Blackthorn Island,* by Maria Monaco (YA), is a fantasy fiction tale involving the collision between the humans of the island and the trolls and fairies that live beneath it. *Swamp Gators: Clayton and Gilmore,* by Dolly Dunn (4–8 years), tells the story of an old and wise alligator that forms a bond with a lost baby gator.

Submissions and Payment

Guidelines and catalogue available at website. Query with 2–3 sample chapters, brief author bio, and publishing credits. Accepts hard copy. SAE/IRC. Responds in 1 month. Publication in 1 year. Royalty, 10–30%.

Editor's Comments

We consider it our mandate to assist up-and-coming writers and to provide the public access to the authors' work. We happily work with first-time authors as well as professionals.

Morgan Reynolds

620 South Elm Street, Suite 387
Greensboro, NC 27406

Associate Editor: Adrianne Loggins

Publisher's Interests

Specializing in nonfiction series and individual titles for young adults, Morgan Reynolds publishes high-quality, appealing books that complement school curricula. It covers such topics as science, social studies, literature, music, and American history.
Website: www.morganreynolds.com

Freelance Potential

Published 30 titles (11 juvenile) in 2010: 2–3 were developed from unsolicited submissions. Of the 30 titles, 3 were by unpublished writers and 4 were by authors who were new to the publishing house. Receives 120 queries, 60 unsolicited mss yearly.

- **Nonfiction:** Publishes young adult books, 12–18 years. Topics include history, music, science, business, feminism, and world events. Also publishes biographies of notable figures in those subject areas.
- **Representative Titles:** *Xtreme Athletes: David Beckham* presents the life story of this well-known soccer star. *The Mail Must Go Through: The Story of the Pony Express* by Margaret Ran recaptures this important piece in the history of the American West.

Submissions and Payment

Guidelines and catalogue available at website. Published authors, query with outline and sample chapter; unpublished authors, send complete ms. Accepts hard copy and simultaneous submissions if identified. SASE. Responds to queries in 1 month, to mss in 1–3 months. Publication in 12–18 months. Payment policy varies.

Editor's Comments

We continue to add new titles to our ongoing series; single titles are also welcome. Your work must be thoroughly researched before you submit it to us.

Mott Media

1130 Fenway Circle
Fenton, MI 48430

Editorial Contact: Joyce Bohn

Publisher's Interests

Founded in 1974, this educational publisher focuses on Christ-based books for use in classrooms, religious education, and homeschool settings, as well as books for teachers. Its titles emphasize a return to classic curricula that doesn't push God out of the learning process.
Website: www.mottmedia.com

Freelance Potential

Published 10 titles in 2010. Of the 10 titles, each was by a new author. Receives 3 queries yearly.

- **Fiction:** Publishes chapter books, 5–10 years; middle-grade books, 8–12 years; and young adult books, 12–18 years. Genres include contemporary and historical fiction, adventure, and mystery.
- **Nonfiction:** Publishes chapter books, 5–10 years; middle-grade books, 8–12 years; and young adult books, 12–18 years. Topics include animals, history, humor, language arts, grammar, spelling, phonics, religion, and biography. Also publishes books for adults and educators.
- **Representative Titles:** *World History Made Simple: Matching History with the Bible,* by Ruth Beechick (YA), gives readers a knowledge of history along with a biblical worldview. *The City Bear's Adventures,* by Lee Roddy, finds 13-year-old D. J. struggling with the realization that the bear cub he has raised needs to be set free.

Submissions and Payment

Catalogue available at website. Query with outline and sample chapter; or send complete ms. Accepts hard copy and simultaneous submissions if identified. SASE. Responds in 1–2 months. Publication in 6 months. Royalty; advance. Flat fee.

Editor's Comments

Our mission has been, and will remain, the production of sound, Christ-based learning materials.

Mountain Press
Publishing Company

1301 South Third West
Missoula, MT 59801

Publisher: John Rimel

Publisher's Interests
This publisher is interested in nonfiction books focusing on
natural history, Earth science, western U.S. history, plants,
and wildlife for a general reading audience. Books for children and young adults should introduce the reader to the
factual wonders of the natural world.
Website: www.mountain-press.com

Freelance Potential
Published 12 titles (7 juvenile) in 2010: 10 were developed
from unsolicited submissions, 1 was by an agented author,
and 1 was a reprint/licensed property. Of the 12 titles, 4
were by unpublished writers and 6 were by authors who
were new to the publishing house. Receives 120–145
queries yearly.

- **Nonfiction:** Publishes easy-to-read books, 4–7 years; story
  picture books, 4–10 years; chapter books, 5–10 years; middle-
  grade books, 8–12 years; and young adult books, 12–18
  years. Topics include natural history, geology, Earth science,
  and western U.S. history.
- **Representative Titles:** *Three Dogs, Two Mules, and a Rein-
  deer,* by Marjorie Cochrane (8+ years), presents the true tales
  of animals who made a mark in Alaska's history. *You Can Be a
  Nature Detective,* by Peggy Kochanoff (5+ years), is part field
  guide and part whodunit that introduces kids to the mysteries
  of the natural world.

Submissions and Payment
Catalogue available. Guidelines available at website. Query
with table of contents, bibliography, and 2 sample chapters.
Accepts hard copy. SASE. Responds in 2 months. Publication
in 1–2 years. Royalty.

Editor's Comments
We do not publish memoirs or personal stories. All books
must be factual and thoroughly researched.

MuseItUp Publishing

14878 James
Pierrefonds, Quebec H9H 1P5
Canada

Acquisitions Editor

Publisher's Interests
Publishing eight books on its debut list in December 2010, epublisher MuseItUp plans to release six to eight books on the first of every month in the categories of young adult and adult fiction. The company is also launching MuseItYoung, for tweens ages 10 to 14.
Website: http://museituppublishing.com

Freelance Potential
Published 8 books in 2010; expects to publish 60+ in 2011. Receives 3,600 unsolicited mss yearly.

- **Fiction:** Publishes middle-grade chapter books, 10–14 years; and young adult books, 15–19 years. Genres include fantasy, mystery, suspense, science fiction, historical fiction, sports, tween and teen issues, and humor.
- **Representative Titles:** *The Secrets Revealed,* by Nick G. Giannaras (YA), is the first volume in the Christian fantasy Relics of Nanthara series. *Crimson Dream,* by David Normoyle, is also YA fantasy.

Submissions and Payment
Guidelines available at website. Send complete ms in RTF format, a short synopsis, contact info, genre, and word count. For MuseItYoung, indicate the category: Muse Tweens or Muse Sportsters. Length for tweens, 10,000–30,000 words. Responds in 3–6 weeks. Offers three-year contract. Royalty, 40% of the download price.

Editor's Comments
We would love to see more young adult, romance, and dark fiction submissions. For MuseItYoung, all manuscripts must contain protagonists that are about the same age as the target reader, and have strong plots with no lecturing or outcome/dilemma finalized by an adult.

Napoleon & Company

235-1173 Dundas Street East
Toronto, Ontario M4M 3P1
Canada

Submissions Editor: Allister Thompson

Publisher's Interests
This Canadian publisher offers picture books, biographies, and educational resources for children in elementary school through high school, as well as young adult novels. All titles relate to Canada, and all authors are Canadian. Napoleon & Company also publishes a number of books for adults, also on topics related to Canada.
Website: www.napoleonandcompany.com

Freelance Potential
Published 15 titles (6 juvenile) in 2010: 12 were developed from unsolicited submissions and 3 were by agented authors. Of the 15 titles, 10 were by unpublished writers and 4–5 were by authors who were new to the publishing house. Receives 240 queries, 180 unsolicited mss yearly.

- **Fiction:** Publishes chapter books, 5–10 years; middle-grade books, 8–12 years; and young adult books, 12–18 years. Genres include adventure, drama, humor, mystery, and historical and contemporary fiction.
- **Nonfiction:** Publishes young adult books, 12–18 years. Features biographies and educational resources.
- **Representative Titles:** *The Last Superhero,* by Kristin Butcher (9+ years), is the story of two classmates who team up to produce an adventure comic, and end up with some unexpected adventures of their own. *Under the Moonlit Sky,* by Nav K. Gill (14+ years), tells of a teen's trip to India to meet her deceased father's family.

Submissions and Payment
Canadian authors only. Guidelines available at website. Query or send complete ms. Accepts hard copy. SASE. Responds in 1 year. Publication in 2 years. Royalty; advance.

Editor's Comments
Our mission is to promote the work of Canadian authors. For new writers, fiction presents the best chance at publication.

National Council of Teachers of English

The Books Program
1111 West Kenyon Road
Urbana, IL 61801-1096

Senior Editor: Bonny Graham

Publisher's Interests
Professional resources designed to aid English language educators at all grade levels, as well as at the college level, fill this association's catalogue. Its books focus on current issues and challenges in teaching, research findings and their application to classrooms, and ideas for teaching all aspects of English. 4% co-venture published material.
Website: www.ncte.org

Freelance Potential
Published 12 titles in 2010: 8 were developed from unsolicited submissions. Of the 12 titles, 6 were by authors who were new to the publishing house. Receives 90 queries yearly.

- **Nonfiction:** Publishes books for English and language arts teachers. Topics include reading, writing, grammar, literature, poetry, rhetoric, censorship, media studies, technology, research, classroom practices, student assessment, and professional issues.
- **Representative Titles:** *What Do I Teach for 90 Minutes?*, by Carol Porter (teachers, grades 9–12), addresses both pedagogical and administrative aspects of block teaching. *Unlocking Shakespeare's Language: Help for the Teacher and Student*, by Randal Robinson (grades 7–12), outlines classroom activities that help students recognize and translate the Bard's troublesome words and syntactic patterns.

Submissions and Payment
Guidelines available at website. Query. Accepts queries through www.editorialmanager.com/nctebp. Response time varies. Publication in 18 months. Royalty.

Editor's Comments
We welcome proposals from professional educators on all topics related to professional development. We're always looking for new voices in the field, and we encourage proposals from classroom teachers, first-time authors, and veteran authors.

National Geographic Society

Children's Books
1145 17th Street NW
Washington, DC 20036-4688

Associate Editor: Kate Olesin

Publisher's Interests

The publishing division of the National Geographic Society is dedicated to books that promote the mission of the organization: to inspire people to learn about, and care about, our planet. For children, it publishes nonfiction books for preschool kids through young adult readers.
Website: www.nationalgeographic.com/books

Freelance Potential

Published 50 titles in 2010. Of the 50 titles, 5 were by authors who were new to the publishing house. Receives 100 queries yearly.

- **Nonfiction:** Publishes easy-to-read books, 4–7 years; story picture books, 4–10 years; chapter books, 5–10 years; middle-grade books, 8–12 years; and young adult books, 12–18 years. Topics include life, Earth, and general science; American and world cultures and history; animals; multicultural issues; and geography. Also publishes biographies.
- **Representative Titles:** *Coral Reefs* (4–8 years) introduces young readers to the underwater realm of coral reefs and the many species that live there; part of the Jump Into Science series. *True Green Kids,* by Kim McKay & Jenny Bonnin (10–14 years), is a collection of fun and practical ways for kids to become agents for environmental change in their world.

Submissions and Payment

Catalogue available at website. Query with outline and sample chapter. Accepts hard copy. SASE. Responds in 3–4 months. Publication period varies. Flat fee.

Editor's Comments

Our books are packed with information about our world, as we believe that education is the first step toward motivating young people to conserve and preserve. But we like our books to be more than merely informative; they should engage young people from the very first page.

Naturegraph Publishers

P.O. Box 1047
Happy Camp, CA 96039

Owner: Barbara Brown

Publisher's Interests
In business for more than 60 years, this family-owned publishing company produces well-researched fiction and nonfiction titles on natural history and Native American culture for the young adult set. Its goal is to raise awareness and increase appreciation for nature in all its forms.
Website: www.naturegraph.com

Freelance Potential
Published 2 titles in 2010: each was developed from an unsolicited submission. Of the 2 titles, 1 was by an unpublished writer. Receives 360 queries yearly.

- **Fiction:** Publishes young adult books, 12–18 years. Features books that pertain to Native American folklore.
- **Nonfiction:** Publishes young adult books, 12–18 years. Topics include Native American wildlife, birds, the environment, crafts, hiking, backpacking, outdoor skills, rocks and minerals, marine life, and natural history.
- **Representative Titles:** *Springer's Quest,* by Nina Gee, follows a salmon from the beginning to the end of its life, examining its biological and environmental aspects. *Where Wild Things Live,* by Dan Story, presents advice and tips on how and where to best find animals in the wild.

Submissions and Payment
Guidelines available at website. Query with outline and 1–2 sample chapters. Accepts hard copy and email queries to nature@sisqtel.net. SASE. Response time and publication period vary. Royalty.

Editor's Comments
Please study our guidelines and catalogue first to determine if your book will fit our publishing niche. We like well-written and researched books that are clear and easy to understand, but also appealing. We are no longer publishing books for middle-grade students.

Neal-Schuman Publishers

100 William Street, Suite 2004
New York, NY 10038

Director of Publishing: Charles T. Harmon

Publisher's Interests

Publishing books for school and public librarians, Neal-Schuman focuses on curriculum, literacy, and information science titles.

Website: www.neal-schuman.com

Freelance Potential

Published 40 titles in 2010: 10 were developed from unsolicited submissions. Of the 40 titles, 32 were by unpublished writers and 12 were by authors who were new to the publishing house. Receives 240 queries yearly.

- **Nonfiction:** Publishes resource materials for school media specialists and librarians. Topics include curriculum support, the Internet, technology, literacy skills, reading programs, collection development, reference needs, staff development, management, and communication.
- **Representative Titles:** *Teddy Bear Storytimes,* by LaDonna Yousha, is a resource guide for running successful storytimes. *Game On!,* by Beth Galloway, presents young adult librarians with the resources they need to make effective choices about video games in the library. *Staff Development Strategies that Work!,* by Georgie L. Donovan & Miguel A. Figueroa, eds., shares successful library personnel management strategies.

Submissions and Payment

Guidelines and catalogue available at website. Query with résumé, outline, and sample chapter. Prefers email queries to charles@neal-schuman.com; will accept hard copy. SASE. Responds in 2 weeks. Publication in 10–12 months. Royalty.

Editor's Comments

Proposals that get our attention are ones that relate your thorough knowledge of the subject matter at hand. Extensive personal experience in library science is an absolute plus. The length of your query matters far less than your ability to communicate your idea.

Thomas Nelson Children's Books and Education

501 Nelson Place
P.O. Box 141000
Nashville, TN 37214

Acquisitions Editor

Publisher's Interests

From children's Bibles to religious novels, this Christian publisher offers books for very young children to young adults. Common to all of its products are biblical themes, Christian values, and quality writing. 2% self-, subsidy-, co-venture, or co-op published material.
Website: www.thomasnelson.com

Freelance Potential

Published 39 titles in 2010. Receives 240 queries yearly.

- **Fiction:** Publishes toddler books and early picture books, 0–4 years; easy-to-read books, 4–7 years; story picture books, 4–10 years; and middle-grade books, 8–12 years. Genres include religious fiction.
- **Nonfiction:** Publishes concept books, 0–4 years; easy-to-read books, 0–4 years; story picture books, 4–10 years; middle-grade books, 8–12 years; and young adult books, 12–18 years. Topics include the Bible and Christianity. Also publishes Bible stories.
- **Representative Titles:** *If I Could Ask God Anything,* by Kathryn Slattery, addresses kids' curiosity with age-appropriate answers to questions about God, faith, prayer, and Christianity. *The Flowering Cross,* by Beth Ryan, is a modern-day story of how Christ's resurrection is still changing lives.

Submissions and Payment

Catalogue available at website. Accepts proposals through literary agents only. Response time and publication period vary. Royalty; advance.

Editor's Comments

Since our establishment in Edinburgh, Scotland, more than 200 years ago, our publishing program has been guided by two goals—to honor God and to serve people. We believe that we exist to inspire the world. Please note that we do not accept proposals from unagented authors.

New Harbinger Publications

5674 Shattuck Avenue
Oakland, CA 94609

Acquisitions Manager: Tesilya Hanauer

Publisher's Interests
Focusing on self-help books covering medical, mental health, and personal growth topics, this publisher also offers titles on parenting, family relationships, and child development for parents and professionals who work with children. **Website: www.newharbinger.com**

Freelance Potential
Published 50 titles (7 juvenile) in 2010: 30 were developed from unsolicited submissions, 20 were by agented authors, and 5 were reprint/licensed properties. Of the 50 titles, 38 were by unpublished writers and 30 were by authors who were new to the publishing house. Receives 600 queries each year.

- **Nonfiction:** Publishes therapeutic workbooks for children and young adults. Topics include communication, divorce, adoption, pregnancy, ADHD, autism, sensory processing disorder, depression, social anxiety, eating disorders, self-injury, and self-control. Also publishes parenting titles.
- **Representative Titles:** *Helping Your Angry Child: A Workbook for You & Your Family,* by Darlyne Gaynor Nemeth et al., teaches children and parents anger management skills. *Helping Your Child Overcome an Eating Disorder: What You Can Do at Home,* by Bethany A. Teachman et al., explains ways to communicate with a child who has an eating disorder.

Submissions and Payment
Guidelines and catalogue available at website. Query with table of contents and 1–3 chapters. Accepts hard copy and email to proposals@newharbinger.com. SASE. Responds in 4–6 weeks. Publication in 1 year. Royalty; advance. Flat fee.

Editor's Comments
We prefer to work with authors who have extensive professional experience with children in crisis.

New Hope Publishers

P.O. Box 12065
Birmingham, AL 35201-2065

Manuscript Submissions

Publisher's Interests

Offering a range of titles for children, teens, and adults, New Hope Publishers encourages and challenges its readers to live and serve in the Christian way. Among its books are inspirational fiction for school-age children, and spiritual books for teens and parents.
Website: www.newhopepublishers.com

Freelance Potential

Published 26 titles in 2010: 13 were by agented authors.

- **Fiction:** Publishes story picture books, 4–10 years; chapter books, 5–10 years; middle-grade books, 8–12 years; and young adult books, 12–18 years. Genres include inspirational fiction.
- **Nonfiction:** Publishes inspirational and spiritual books for men, women, families, and religious education teachers. Topics include spiritual growth, women's issues, parenting, prayer, relationships, mission life, Christian living, and Bible study.
- **Representative Titles:** *Lady in Waiting for Little Girls*, by Jackie Kendall & Dede Kendall, is a mother-daughter mentoring book about a girl's devotion to God. *200+ Games and Fun Activities for Teaching Preschoolers*, by Kathryn Kizer, features games, music, poems, fingerplay, and quiet activities. *Great Love (for Girls)*, by Chandra Peele & Aubrey Spears, offers pre-teen and teen girls guidance on sexual intimacy and Christian values.

Submissions and Payment

Catalogue available at website. No unsolicited submissions. Post proposal at christianmanuscriptsubmissions.com. Response time and publication period vary. Royalty. Flat fee.

Editor's Comments

We challenge Christians to do God's work. To fulfill this mission, we seek books that will help readers live out Christ's love in their homes and in their communities.

New Horizon Press

P.O. Box 669
Far Hills, NJ 07931

Submissions: Dr. Joan S. Dunphy

Publisher's Interests
New Horizon's catalogue features self-help titles for children on contemporary social and emotional issues, and books for parents on family relationships. For adults or young adults, it publishes books on true crime, social issues, self-help subjects, and true stories of real heroes.
Website: www.newhorizonpressbooks.com

Freelance Potential
Published 12 titles (2 juvenile) in 2010: 5 were developed from unsolicited submissions. Of the 12 titles, 11 were by unpublished writers and each was by an author who was new to the publishing house. Receives 1,700 queries, 1,500 unsolicited mss yearly.

- **Nonfiction:** Publishes self-help titles for children and adults on family, parenting, and relationship issues.
- **Representative Titles:** *Tommy and the T-Tops: Helping Children Overcome Prejudice,* by Frederick Alimonti & Ann Tedesco, uses a family of dinosaurs to relate the message that we must value people not for their appearance but for their character. *Troubled Childhood, Triumphant Life: Healing from the Battle Scars of Youth,* by James P. Krehbiel, offers a blueprint for transcending a turbulent childhood and achieving a productive life as an adult and a parent.

Submissions and Payment
Guidelines and catalogue available at website. Query with résumé, outline, and 2 sample chapters; or send complete ms. Accepts hard copy and email queries to nhp@ newhorizonpressbooks.com ("Attn: Ms. P. Patty" in subject line). SASE. Response time, publication period, and payment policy vary.

Editor's Comments
We're currently interested in reviewing material on coping with the suicide of a young person, or the death of a pet.

New Leaf Press

P.O. Box 726
Green Forest, AR 72638

Assistant Editor: Craig Froman

Publisher's Interests
New Leaf Press, an imprint of New Leaf Publishing Group, specializes in nonfiction religious books for children, young adults, parents, and teachers. Its catalogue includes books on topics such as Christian values and religious holidays, as well as Bible stories.
Website: www.nlpg.com

Freelance Potential
Published 20–25 titles (10 juvenile) in 2010: 2 were developed from unsolicited submissions, 1 was by an agented author, and 2 were reprint/licensed properties. Of the 20–25 titles, 4 were by unpublished writers and 3 were by authors who were new to the publishing house. Receives 1,000 queries yearly.

- **Nonfiction:** Publishes easy-to-read books, 4–7 years; story picture books, 4–10 years; middle-grade books, 8–12 years; and young adult books, 12–18 years. Topics include the Bible, Christian living, history, current events, and social issues.
- **Representative Titles:** *Big Thoughts for Little Thinkers: The Gospel,* by Joey Allen (4–8 years), presents the foundational teachings of the Christian faith in language that young children can understand. *Quizzles: In the Big Inning,* by Roger Howerton (grades 7 and up), features entertaining puzzles and word games designed to expand the reader's Bible knowledge.

Submissions and Payment
Guidelines and catalogue available at website. Query with proposal form from website. Accepts hard copy and simultaneous submissions if identified. SASE. Responds in 3 months. Publication in 12–18 months. Royalty.

Editor's Comments
We look for books that meet the needs of the Christian family and that surpass the standard for excellence in the Christian market.

New Society Publishers

P.O. Box 189
Gabriola Island, British Columbia V0R 1X0
Canada

Editor: Ingrid Witvoet

Publisher's Interests

This activist publisher advocates solutions for social change
and sustainable living. It publishes titles that educate and
motivate readers to action regarding such issues as the environment, peace, and social justice throughout the world. It
also publishes books on progressive parenting.
Website: www.newsociety.com

Freelance Potential

Published 23 titles in 2010: 6 were by unpublished writers
and 14 were by authors who were new to the publishing
house. Receives 300 queries yearly.

- **Nonfiction:** Publishes middle-grade books, 8–12 years; and
  young adult books, 12–18 years. Topics include the environment, conflict resolution, social responsibility, and democratic
  behavior in young people. Also publishes parenting titles.
- **Representative Titles:** *EcoKids: Raising Children Who Care
  for the Earth,* by Dan Chiras, outlines ways parents can foster
  a love for nature in their kids and promote environmental values. *So You Love Animals,* by Zoe Weil (9–12 years), explains
  what is happening to species throughout the world and teaches
  readers the importance of caring about all animals.

Submissions and Payment

Guidelines and catalogue available at website. Query with
résumé, synopsis, table of contents, and sample chapter.
Accepts hard copy. SAE/IRC. Responds in 2–3 months. Publication in 1 year. Payment policy varies.

Editor's Comments

A large majority of the books we publish are initiated inter-
nally or are acquired through previous contact with the
author. We sometimes publish manuscripts that are wholly
unsolicited, and welcome queries from authors who share
our goal of producing "books to build a new society." Note
that we do not publish fiction.

Nimbus Publishing

3731 MacKintosh Street
Halifax, Nova Scotia B3K 5A5
Canada

Senior Editor: Patrick Murphy

Publisher's Interests

Quality nonfiction and endearing fiction titles on subjects connected to the Atlantic coastal region of Canada are the specialty of this publisher.
Website: www.nimbus.ca

Freelance Potential

Published 35 titles (15 juvenile) in 2010: 12 were developed from unsolicited submissions, 1 was by an agented author, and 3 were reprint/licensed properties. Of the 35 titles, 8 were by unpublished writers and 8 were by authors who were new to the publishing house. Receives 240 queries yearly.

- **Fiction:** Publishes toddler books, 0–4 years; easy-to-read books, 4–7 years; story picture books, 4–10 years; chapter books, 5–10 years; middle-grade books, 8–12 years; and young adult books, 12–18 years. Genres include adventure; folklore; and regional, historical, and multicultural fiction.
- **Nonfiction:** Publishes toddler books, 0–4 years; easy-to-read books, 4–7 years; story picture books, 4–10 years; and middle-grade books, 8–12 years. Topics include Atlantic Canada's geography, history, and environment.
- **Representative Titles:** *A Nova Scotia Lullaby,* by Terrilee Bulger (1–4 years), matches lyrical text with illustrations to provide a scenic tour through Nova Scotia. *Keep Out!,* by Hélène Boudreau (6–10 years), is an early reader mystery involving twin brothers and the piping plovers of Prince Edward Island.

Submissions and Payment

Guidelines available at website. Query with synopsis, bio, table of contents, and sample chapter. Accepts hard copy and simultaneous submissions. Material is not returned. Response time varies. Publication in 1–2 years. Royalty; advance. Flat fee.

Editor's Comments

We're looking for books about or involving the region's popular culture, environment, business, and multiculturalism.

NL Associates

P.O. Box 1199
Hightstown, NJ 08520-0399

President: Nathan Levy

Publisher's Interests

Specializing in educational materials and activity books, NL Associates provides "tools for master teachers and thoughtful parents." Its catalogue features books on math, science, critical thinking, writing, and multicultural issues for students in kindergarten through grade 12.
Website: www.storieswithholes.com

Freelance Potential

Published 1 title in 2010. Receives 20 queries, 50 unsolicited mss yearly.

- **Nonfiction:** Publishes educational materials and activity books for grades K–12. Topics include reading, writing, creativity, social studies, math, science, and critical thinking. Also publishes books about classroom management and special education for teachers.
- **Representative Titles:** *Bright Kids Who Can't Learn*, by Laurie Steding, is a resource for parents and teachers that offers guidance on working through the education system and becoming a child's best advocate. *Fair is Fair*, by Sharon Creedon (grades 3–12), features a collection of 30 tales of justice from around the world. *The Magical Math Book*, by Bob Longe (grades 3–8), shows how to use a variety of math principles to present demonstrations that appear to be magic.

Submissions and Payment

Query or send complete ms. Accepts hard copy. SASE. Response time, publication period, and payment policy vary.

Editor's Comments

Our company was founded by educator Nathan Levy to provide books that help make learning fun. We're always looking for unique teaching strategies that encourage the love of learning and develop critical and creative thinking skills. In addition to our books for teachers and parents, we also produce books for gifted children.

North Country Books

220 Lafayette Street
Utica, NY 13502

Publisher: Rob Igoe, Jr.

Publisher's Interests
This regional publisher focuses on the history, biography, nature, folklore, and travel opportunities in New York State. It also publishes fiction and nonfiction children's books.
Website: www.northcountrybooks.com

Freelance Potential
Published 7 titles (1 juvenile) in 2010: each was developed from an unsolicited submission. Of the 7 titles, 1 was by an unpublished writer and 3 were by authors who were new to the publishing house. Receives 48–72 unsolicited mss each year.

- **Fiction:** Publishes early picture books, 0–4 years; story picture books, 4–10 years; chapter books, 5–10 years. Themes include the folklore, history, and wildlife of New York State.
- **Nonfiction:** Publishes early picture books, 0–4 years; easy-to-read books, 4–7 years; and middle-grade books, 8–12 years. Topics include New York history, ecology, geology, cuisine, travel, recreation, art, and Native American culture. Also publishes biographies and books for adults.
- **Representative Titles:** *Champlain and the Silent One,* by Kate Messner (YA), tells the story of an Innu Indian during his tribe's battle with the Iroquois. *The Adirondacks: In Celebration of the Seasons,* by Mark Bowie, presents photo-essays on the ever-changing scenery of the Adirondack region.

Submissions and Payment
Guidelines and catalogue available at website or via email request to ncbooks@verizon.net. Send complete ms with synopsis, table of contents, and market analysis. Accepts hard copy. SASE. Responds in 1–2 months. Publication in 2–5 years. Royalty.

Editor's Comments
Please include reproductions of illustrations or photographs with your submission.

North South Books

350 Seventh Avenue, Suite 1400
New York, NY 10001

Submissions Editor

Publisher's Interests
North South Books is a publisher of quality fiction and non-fiction books for children up to age 10. It is a North American imprint of the Swiss publishing company NordSud. Currently, it is open to working with agented authors only.
Website: www.northsouth.com

Freelance Potential
Published 40 titles in 2010: each was by an agented author.

- **Fiction:** Publishes concept books, toddler books, and early picture books, 0–4 years; easy-to-read books, 4–7 years; story picture books, 4–10 years; and chapter books, 5–10 years. Genres include multicultural and contemporary fiction, adventure, drama, fairy tales, folklore, fantasy, humor, and stories about nature and the environment. Also publishes board books and novelty books.
- **Nonfiction:** Publishes early picture books, 0–4 years. Topics include animals, hobbies, crafts, humor, nature, religion, science, technology, social issues, sports, and multicultural and ethnic issues.
- **Representative Titles:** *Dinosaurs?!,* by Lila Prap (4–8 years), is a humorous tale about chickens who have a hard time believing that they are descended from dinosaurs. *Do You Still Love Me?,* by Sarah Emmanuelle Burg (3–8 years), is a tender story about two baby animals trying to sort out their feelings after witnessing their parents argue.

Submissions and Payment
Agented authors only. Publication period and payment policy vary.

Editor's Comments
We are proud to bring an international roster of stellar writers and illustrators to young readers and their parents in North America. At this time, we are working only with writers who are represented by literary agents. Check our website for changes to this policy.

O Books

The Bothy, Deershot Lodge
Park Lane, Ropley
Hampshire SO24 OBE
United Kingdom

Submissions: Trevor Greenfield

Publisher's Interests
This company takes its name from the symbol of the world,
oneness, and unity. It publishes books for children and
adults on religion and spirituality of all forms, psychology,
culture, and self-help. 2% self-, subsidy-, co-venture-, or co-
op published material.
Website: www.o-books.net

Freelance Potential
Published 200 titles in 2010: 50 were developed from unsolicited submissions and 20 were by agented authors. Of the
200 titles, 40 were by unpublished writers and 60 were by
new authors. Receives 6,000 queries yearly.

- **Fiction:** Publishes easy-to-read books, 4–7 years; story picture
  books, 4–10 years; chapter books, 5–10 years; middle-grade
  books, 8–12 years; and young adult books, 12–18 years. Genres include religious and spiritual fiction.
- **Nonfiction:** Publishes story picture books, 4–10 years; chapter
  books, 5–10 years; middle-grade books, 8–12 years; and
  young adult books, 12–18 years. Topics include spirituality,
  religion, meditation, prayer, and astrology.
- **Representative Titles:** *Relax Kids: The Wishing Star,* by Mar-
  neta Viegas, uses guided meditations based on traditional stories to introduce children to the world of relaxation. *Charming!
  If the Glass Slipper Fits,* by Gregory Dark, tells the story of
  Prince Charming's background.

Submissions and Payment
Guidelines and catalogue available at website. Query with
sample chapters. Accepts email to trevor.greenfield@
o-books.net (Microsoft Word attachments). Response time
varies. Publication in 18 months. Royalty. Flat fee.

Editor's Comments
We focus on the "mid-list"—not celebrity mass-market books
on the one hand, or highly academic works on the other.

OnStage Publishing

190 Lime Quarry Road, Suite 106J
Madison, AL 35758

Senior Editor: Dianne Hamilton

Publisher's Interests
Operating under the motto, "Where children's literature is center stage," this company publishes fiction for children ages 8 through 18.
Website: www.onstagepublishing.com

Freelance Potential
Published 2–3 titles in 2010: 1 was by an unpublished writer and 1 was by an author who was new to the publishing house. Receives 500 queries, 1,500–2,000 unsolicited mss each year.

- **Fiction:** Publishes chapter books, 5–10 years; middle-grade books, 8–12 years; and young adult books, 12–18 years. Genres include adventure; drama; fantasy; horror; mystery; suspense; and contemporary, historical, humorous, and science fiction.
- **Representative Titles:** *The Ducks and Diamonds Mystery,* by Darren J. Butler, follows two girl detectives as they unravel the mystery of the missing ducks of the Peabody Hotel; part of the Abbie, Girl Spy series. *Dear Jack, by* Tammi Sauer (YA), is the story of a 13-year-old girl who must come to terms with her mother's pregnancy and newly diagnosed breast cancer.

Submissions and Payment
Guidelines and catalogue available at website. Send complete ms for works under 100 pages. Query with 3 sample chapters and plot summary for longer works. Accepts hard copy, email queries to onstage123@knology.net (no attachments), and simultaneous submissions if identified. SASE for response only. Responds in 4–6 months. Publication in 1–2 years. Royalty; advance.

Editor's Comments
We're particularly interested in seeing books that target boys. While we do not generally publish nonfiction, we will consider nonfiction proposals.

Ooligan Press

P.O. Box 751
Portland, OR 97207

Acquisitions Committee

Publisher's Interests

Ooligan Press focuses on books that honor cultural and natural diversity. Staffed by graduate students at Portland State University, it publishes young adult and adult fiction and nonfiction—often with a Pacific Northwest perspective—as well as educational books about writing and the art of publishing.
Website: www.ooliganpress.pdx.edu

Freelance Potential

Published 3 titles (1 juvenile) in 2010. Receives 600 queries and unsolicited mss yearly.

- **Fiction:** Publishes young adult books, 12–18 years. Genres include historical and regional fiction. Also publishes collections of poetry.
- **Nonfiction:** Publishes young adult books, 12–18 years. Topics include the Pacific Northwest, writing, editing, publishing, and book arts.
- **Representative Titles:** *Ricochet River,* by Robin Cody (YA), is a coming-of-age story set in the 1960s about a group of teens preparing to break out of their small Oregon town. *Fort Clatsop: Rebuilding an Icon* retells the story of Lewis and Clark, and describes the efforts of the citizens of Astoria, Oregon, to honor their journey by rebuilding the burned replica of the explorers' Fort Clatsop.

Submissions and Payment

Guidelines and catalogue available at website. Query with outline/synopsis and brief author bio; or send complete ms. Prefers hard copy; will accept email queries to acquisitions@ooliganpress.pdx.edu (no attachments). SASE. Responds in 2–3 months. Publication period and payment policy vary.

Editor's Comments

Young adult historical fiction set in the Pacific Northwest will catch our attention first.

Orca Book Publishers

P.O. Box 5626, Station B
Victoria, British Columbia V8R 6S4
Canada

Publisher: Andrew Wooldridge

Publisher's Interests
This publisher is home to a number of award-winning and best-selling books for children, teens, and reluctant readers. Accepting work from Canadian authors only, it publishes picture books, early chapter books, novels, and nonfiction.
Website: www.orcabook.com

Freelance Potential
Published 60 titles in 2010: 30 were developed from unsolicited submissions, 30 were by agented authors, and 1 was a reprint/licensed property. Of the 60 titles, 12 were by unpublished writers and 35 were by new authors. Receives 2,000 queries, 500 unsolicited mss yearly.

- **Fiction:** Publishes toddler books and early picture books, 0–4 years; easy-to-read books, 4–7 years; story picture books, 4–10 years; chapter books, 5–10 years; middle-grade books, 8–12 years; and young adult books, 12–18 years. Genres include regional, historical, and contemporary fiction; mystery; adventure; and stories about sports.
- **Nonfiction:** Publishes middle-grade books, 8–12 years. Topics include nature and history.
- **Representative Titles:** *Queen of Disguises*, by Melanie Jackson (9–13 years), tells of a stalker who is pursuing Dinah; part of the Dinah Galloway Mystery series. *Absolute Pressure*, by Sigmund Brouwer (10+ years), tells of a boy who uncovers some mysteries while helping at his uncle's dive shop.

Submissions and Payment
Canadian authors only. Guidelines and catalogue available at website. Query with 2–3 sample chapters for novels. Send complete ms for picture books. Accepts hard copy. SASE. Responds in 2–3 months. Publication in 18–24 months. Royalty, 10% split; advance.

Editor's Comments
We do not publish seasonal stories or beginning readers.

Orchard Books

Scholastic
557 Broadway
New York, NY 10012-3999

Editor: Ken Geist

Publisher's Interests
This Scholastic imprint focuses on increasing literacy and comprehension through high-quality, engaging stories and subjects. While its catalogue is filled with books for children of all ages, its current focus is on picture books.
Website: www.scholastic.com

Freelance Potential
Published 15–20 titles in 2010. Of the 15–20 titles, 1–5 were by unpublished writers and 2–5 were by authors who were new to the publishing house. Receives 200–350 queries yearly.

- **Fiction:** Publishes concept books, toddler books, and early picture books, 0–4 years; easy-to-read books, 4–7 years; and story picture books, 4–10 years. Genres include historical, contemporary, and multicultural fiction; fairy tales; folktales; fantasy; and humor. Also publishes stories about sports, animals, and nature.
- **Representative Titles:** *Farmer Joe and the Music Show,* by Tony Mitton (3–5 years), relates the story of a farmer who realizes that the best way to liven up the farm is through music. *Bedtime for Button,* by Amber Stewart & Layn Marlow (0–3 years), tells of a daddy bear who eases the bedtime fears of his little one by telling the story of the day little Button was born.

Submissions and Payment
Query. No unsolicited mss. Accepts hard copy. SASE. Responds in 3 months. Publication period varies. Royalty; advance.

Editor's Comments
We like fun, engaging books that kids will seek out, either to enjoy alone or share with a parent. Please note that we review queries only, not complete manuscripts.

Our Sunday Visitor

200 Noll Plaza
Huntington, IN 46750

Acquisitions Editor

Publisher's Interests
This nonprofit publisher produces trade books and religious educational products that reinforce the Catholic perspective. It publishes titles for children, young adults, and parents. Our Sunday Visitor also publishes an array of titles that support a religious education curriculum serving kindergarten through grade eight.
Website: www.osv.com

Freelance Potential
Published 40 titles in 2010. Of the 40 titles, 5 were by authors who were new to the publishing house. Receives 1,300 queries yearly.

- **Nonfiction:** Publishes concept books, 0–4 years; story picture books, 4–10 years; chapter books, 5–10 years; middle-grade books, 8–12 years; and young adult books, 12–18 years. Topics include family issues, parish life, Catholic identity and practices, and the lives of saints.
- **Representative Titles:** *The Beatitudes for Children,* by Rosemarie Gortler & Donna Piscitelli, helps kids put Catholic teaching into action with child-friendly explanations and illustrations. *U Got 2 Pray,* by Fr. Stan Fortuna (YA), addresses how and when to pray, and presents hundreds of prayers for teens that fit a variety of occasions.

Submissions and Payment
Guidelines and catalogue available at website. Query with résumé and sample chapter. Accepts hard copy and simultaneous submissions if identified. SASE. Responds in 2–3 months. Publication in 1+ years. Royalty; advance. Flat fee.

Editor's Comments
We look for books and subjects that are engaged with the contemporary world yet are still faithful to what the Catholic Church teaches us. Please explain in your query why you think your book is unique.

The Overmountain Press

P.O. Box 1261
Johnson City, TN 37605

Submissions

Publisher's Interests

Founded in 1970, the Overmountain Press is primarily a publisher of Southern and Appalachian history and other nonfiction titles, though it does accept some fiction and picture books set in those regions of the U.S. Its catalogue includes titles on Revolutionary and Civil War history, as well as books about the history, culture, and lifestyle of the region's inhabitants.
Website: www.overmountainpress.com

Freelance Potential

Published 10 titles (2 juvenile) in 2010. Of the 10 titles, 2 were by authors who were new to the publishing house. Receives 500 queries yearly.

- **Fiction:** Publishes early picture books, 0–4 years; middle-grade books, 8–12 years; and young adult books, 12–18 years. Genres include folklore, folktales, mystery, and regional fiction—all pertaining to the South and Appalachian regions.
- **Nonfiction:** Publishes story picture books, 4–10 years; and chapter books, 5–10 years. Topics include southern Appalachia, regional history, and cultural issues of the region.
- **Representative Titles:** *The Banjoman,* by Tyler Norman & Jose Perez, tells the story of a wandering musician who stops his travel long enough to entertain the children of the area. *Why Are the Mountains Smoky?,* by Kent Whitaker, presents interesting facts about the southern Appalachian mountains.

Submissions and Payment

Guidelines and catalogue available at website or with 6x9 SASE ($.85 postage). Query with résumé and sample chapters. Accepts hard copy. SASE. Responds in 3–6 months. Publication in 18 months. Royalty, 15%.

Editor's Comments

With few exceptions, we are now accepting only regional (southern Appalachian) titles for our children's catalogue.

Richard C. Owen Publishers

P.O. Box 585
Katonah, NY 10536

Director of Children's Books: Richard C. Owen

Publisher's Interests
The focus of this publisher is literacy education with an emphasis on reading and writing. It produces fiction and nonfiction on a series of topics, as well as English/Spanish sets and teacher resource material.
Website: www.rcowen.com

Freelance Potential
Published 2 titles in 2010. Of the 2 titles, each was by an author who was new to the publishing house. Receives 1,000 unsolicited mss yearly.

- **Fiction:** Publishes story picture books, 4–10 years; easy-to-read books, 5–8 years; and chapter books, 5–10 years. Genres include contemporary fiction; mystery; humor; folktales; stories about animals and nature; and books about social, ethnic, and multicultural issues.
- **Nonfiction:** Publishes story picture books, 4–10 years; and easy-to-read books, 5–8 years. Topics include current events, geography, music, science, nature, and the environment. Also publishes professional books and resources for teachers.
- **Representative Titles:** *My Book*, by Marilyn Duncan (preK–grade 1), is an assessment tool that assists teachers in gathering relevant data at the beginning of the kindergarten year. *Imagination,* by Mike Thaler (grades 2–5), features a collection of humorous tales that run the gamut from contemporary to historical topics.

Submissions and Payment
Guidelines available at website. Send ms. Accepts hard copy and simultaneous submissions if identified. SASE. Responds in 3–6 months. Publication period and payment policy vary.

Editor's Comments
We believe that students become enthusiastic, independent, lifelong learners when supported and guided by skillful teachers. The books we publish support that belief.

Pacific Educational Press

6365 Biological Sciences Road
Faculty of Education, University of British Columbia
Vancouver, British Columbia V6T 1Z4
Canada

Director: Catherine Edwards

Publisher's Interests

This publishing house of the Faculty of Education at the University of British Columbia produces children's nonfiction books with teacher guides for classroom use. Topics include the arts, social studies, language arts, math, science, and First Nations and multicultural education. It also publishes professional resources for teachers.
Website: www.pep.educ.ubc.ca

Freelance Potential

Published 4 titles in 2010. Of the 4 titles, 2 were by unpublished writers and 2 were by authors who were new to the publishing house. Receives 60–120 queries yearly.

- **Nonfiction:** Publishes middle-grade books, 8–12 years; and young adult books, 12–18 years. Also publishes books for teachers, grades K–12. Topics include math, language arts, the sciences, social studies, multicultural education, and critical thinking.
- **Representative Titles:** *Teaching to Wonder: Responding to Poetry in the Secondary Classroom,* by Carl Leggo, outlines teaching strategies to engage young readers in contemporary poetry. *The Forest* (grade 1) explains about the animals and plants that thrive in the forests of the Queen Charlotte Islands; part of the Queen Charlotte Island Readers series.

Submissions and Payment

Guidelines available. Query with résumé, outline, and 2 sample chapters. Accepts hard copy and simultaneous submissions if identified. SAE/IRC. Responds in 4–6 months. Publication in 18–24 months. Royalty, 10% of net.

Editor's Comments

Though you'll still see a children's fiction section in our catalogue, we are no longer adding fiction titles. Many—but not all—of our books are written by Canadian educators on Canadian subjects designed for use in Canadian classrooms.

Pacific Press Publishing Association

P.O. Box 5353
Nampa, ID 83653

Acquisitions Editor: Scott Cady

Publisher's Interests
Pacific Press provides a wide variety of spiritually-based books that follow the beliefs of the Seventh-day Adventist Church. Its children's books, which include historical and biblical stories, help young readers connect with God.
Website: www.pacificpress.com

Freelance Potential
Published 30 titles (10 juvenile) in 2010: 2 were developed from unsolicited submissions and 1 was a reprint/licensed property. Of the 30 titles, 1 was by an unpublished writer and 1 was by an author who was new to the publishing house. Receives 180 queries yearly.

- **Fiction:** Publishes early picture books, 0–4 years; easy-to-read books, 4–7 years; story picture books, 4–10 years; chapter books, 5–10 years; and middle-grade books, 8–12 years. Genres include adventure, mystery, and suspense—all with Christian themes.
- **Nonfiction:** Publishes easy-to-read books, 4–7 years; chapter books, 5–10 years; and middle-grade books, 8–12 years. Topics include children, animals, and Seventh-day Adventist beliefs.
- **Representative Titles:** *The Day the School Blew Up,* by Seth Pierce (10–14 years), is a modern-day adventure story that shows God's love. *Don't Let Your Heart Feel Funny,* by Jerry & Kitty Thomas, tells how a boy learns to trust in God when he is feeling afraid.

Submissions and Payment
Guidelines and catalogue available at website. Query. Accepts hard copy and email queries to booksubmissions@pacificpress.com. SASE. Responds in 3 weeks. Publication in 6–12 months. Royalty, 6–12%; advance, to $1,500.

Editor's Comments
Be sure to do your research first to ensure you are not duplicating books already in print.

Parenting Press

P.O. Box 75267
Seattle, WA 98175-0267

Acquisitions: Carolyn J. Threadgill

Publisher's Interests

As its name indicates, this publisher focuses exclusively on books for parents, caregivers, and counselors. Its books are practical guides for navigating the ups and downs of raising children. It also publishes books for young children that help them understand their feelings or difficult situations.
Website: www.parentingpress.com

Freelance Potential

Published 6 titles (1 juvenile) in 2010: 2 were developed from unsolicited submissions. Of the 6 titles, 2 were by authors who were new to the publishing house. Receives 804 queries yearly.

- **Nonfiction:** Publishes concept books, 2–8 years. Also publishes books for parents and professionals. Topics include parenting, child development, problem-solving, handling emotions, abuse prevention, parent desertion, sleep issues, toilet training, safety, and guiding children to independence and responsibility.
- **Representative Titles:** *Mommy! I Have to Go Potty!*, by Jan Faull & Helen F. Neville, is a guide to understanding this important developmental period. *The Way I Feel*, by Janan Cain (2–8 years), uses whimsical verse that helps kids describe their emotions and understand that feelings are a normal part of life.

Submissions and Payment

Guidelines and catalogue available at website. Query with outline, table of contents, introduction, and 2 sample chapters. Accepts hard copy. SASE. Responds in 1 month. Publication in 18–24 months. Royalty, 4–8% of net; advance, negotiable.

Editor's Comments

Please note that we do not publish fiction, academic works, illness- or disability-based books, or personal experience narratives. We look for books that are long on information but short on judgmental attitudes.

Parkway Publishers

P.O. Box 3678
Boone, NC 28607

President: Rao Aluri

Publisher's Interests

This regional book publisher is interested in books about the history, literature, culture, travel, and tourism of western North Carolina or Appalachia; and in books by the region's authors.
Website: www.parkwaypublishers.com

Freelance Potential

Published 6 titles (2 juvenile) in 2010: each was developed from an unsolicited submission. Of the 6 titles, 3 were by unpublished writers and 5 were by authors who were new to the publishing house. Receives 60 unsolicited mss yearly.

- **Fiction:** Publishes story picture books, 4–10 years; chapter books, 5–10 years; and young adult books, 12–18 years. Genres include regional and historical fiction, folklore, mysteries, and adventure.
- **Nonfiction:** Publishes story picture books, 4–10 years; chapter books, 5–10 years; and young adult books, 12–18 years. Topics include regional history, culture, and the environment. Also publishes biographies and memoirs of regional and historical personalities.
- **Representative Titles:** *Appalachian State A to Z,* by Anne Aldridge Webb, encourages young readers and those who read to them to go through each letter of the alphabet examining different campus treasures. *An Old Salem Christmas, 1840,* by Karen Cecil Smith, tells the story of a young Moravian girl who experiences the wonder of Christmas in nineteenth-century Salem, North Carolina.

Submissions and Payment

Guidelines and catalogue available at website. Send complete ms. Accepts hard copy. SASE. Responds in 2–6 months. Publication in 6–12 months. Royalty, 10%.

Editor's Comments

We're most interested in books that appeal to children and adults alike.

Pauline Books & Media

50 St. Pauls Avenue
Boston, MA 02130-3491

Children's Editor: Christina Wegendt, FSP

Publisher's Interests
The children's titles published by Pauline Books present solid Christian values with a Catholic perspective. It accepts both fiction and nonfiction.
Website: www.pauline.org

Freelance Potential
Published 20 titles (19 juvenile) in 2010: 2 were developed from unsolicited submissions, 1 was by an agented author, and 6 were reprint/licensed properties. Of the 20 titles, 1 was by an unpublished writer and 2 were by new authors. Receives 240–420 queries yearly.

- **Fiction:** Publishes toddler books and early picture books, 0–4 years; story picture books, 4–8 years; easy-to-read books, 7–9 years; and middle-grade books, 8–12 years. Features stories that relate Christian faith and values.
- **Nonfiction:** Publishes toddler books, 0–4 years; chapter books, 5–10 years; and middle-grade books, 8–12 years. Topics include religious education, church holidays, prayer, faith, spirituality, saints, and sacraments. Also publishes religious coloring/activity books.
- **Representative Titles:** *Friend 2 Friend: Twelve Short Stories,* by Diane M. Lynch, ed. (8–12 years), presents stories that reflect true friendship. *My Scriptural Rosary,* by Lauren S. Roddy (6–8 years), teaches children how to pray the rosary.

Submissions and Payment
Guidelines available at website. Query with outline/synopsis and 2 sample chapters. Send complete ms for board books and picture books. Accepts hard copy and email to editorial@paulinemedia.com. SASE. Responds in 3 months. Publication in 2–3 years. Royalty, 5–10% of net; advance, $200–$500.

Editor's Comments
All material should be relevant to the lives of young readers and in accord with Catholic teaching and practice.

Paulist Press

997 Macarthur Boulevard
Mahwah, NJ 07430

Submissions Editor: Jennifer Conlan

Publisher's Interests
Paulist Press offers a growing selection of children's stories
and activity books on Christian and Catholic themes. Included
on its list are picture books, prayer books, chapter books,
biographies, and Catholic guidebooks.
Website: www.paulistpress.com

Freelance Potential
Published 92 titles (12 juvenile) in 2010: 9 were developed
from unsolicited submissions, 9 were by agented authors,
and 2 were reprint/licensed properties. Of the 92 titles, 46
were by unpublished writers and 46 were by authors who
were new to the publishing house. Receives 900 unsolicited
mss yearly.

- **Nonfiction:** Publishes easy-to-read books, 4–7 years; story
  picture books, 4–10 years; middle-grade books, 8–12 years;
  and young adult books, 12–18 years. Topics include blessings;
  prayers; saints; modern heroes; Bible stories; and Catholic
  traditions, holidays, and doctrine. Also publishes biographies.
- **Representative Titles:** *The Hurt*, by Teddi Doleski (6–8
  years), tells of a boy whose feelings get hurt when a friend
  calls him a name. *Moonlight Miracle*, by Tony Magliano (2–7
  years), uses the moon as an example that all humans, big and
  small, all over the world are part of one big family.

Submissions and Payment
Guidelines available at website. Send complete ms with
résumé. Accepts hard copy. SASE. Responds in 6–8 weeks.
Publication in 2–3 years. Royalty, 8%; advance, $500.

Editor's Comments
Our children's books fall under six categories, as outlined in
our guidelines. Please keep these in mind when submitting
your ideas. Please include a cover letter that summarizes
your story and describes which category and age group you
have in mind.

Paws IV Books

119 South Main Street, Suite 400
Seattle, WA 98104

Acquisitions Editor: Susan Roxborough

Publisher's Interests
Books for children in preschool through grade eight are the
focus of this publisher. As the children's imprint of Sasquatch
Books, all books have an Alaskan theme that relates to the
state's animals, environment, history, or culture.
Website: www.sasquatchbooks.com

Freelance Potential
Published 2 titles in 2010. Receives 600 queries, 540 unsolicited mss yearly.

- **Fiction:** Publishes concept books, toddler books, and early
  picture books, 0–4 years; and easy-to-read books, 4–7 years.
  Features stories about animals, nature, and the environment—
  all with Alaskan themes.
- **Nonfiction:** Publishes concept books, toddler books, and early
  picture books, 0–4 years; and easy-to-read books, 4–7 years.
  Topics include Alaskan history, culture, natural history, environment, and wildlife.
- **Representative Titles:** *Alaska's Three Bears,* by Shelley Gill
  (3+ years), offers the "real" story of the three bears, as a polar,
  grizzly, and black bear travel across the Alaskan wilderness.
  Danger, the Dog Yard Cat, by Libby Riddles, is a whimsical
  story of a cat who hangs around with sled dogs, written by the
  first female Iditarod winner.

Submissions and Payment
Guidelines and catalogue available at website. Query or send
complete ms with résumé and clips. Accepts hard copy.
SASE. Responds in 2–4 months. Publication period varies.
Royalty; advance.

Editor's Comments
We're interested in a variety of topics for young children, as
long as they embrace an Alaskan theme, such as using rein-
deer to teach counting or crafting an engaging story that
takes place in a native peoples' village.

Peachtree Publishers

1700 Chattahoochee Avenue
Atlanta, GA 30318-2112

Submissions Editor: Helen Harriss

Publisher's Interests
Picture books, chapter books, middle readers, and young
adult titles are all found in Peachtree Publishers' catalogue.
It publishes both fiction and nonfiction.
Website: www.peachtree-online.com

Freelance Potential
Published 23 titles (22 juvenile) in 2010: 1 was developed
from an unsolicited submission and 4 were reprint/licensed
properties. Of the 23 titles, 3 were by authors who were new
to the publishing house. Receives 18,000 mss yearly.

- **Fiction:** Publishes early picture books, 0–4 years; easy-to-read
  books, 4–7 years; story picture books, 4–10 years; chapter
  books, 5–10 years; middle-grade books, 8–12 years; and
  young adult novels, 12–18 years. Genres include regional,
  historical, and multicultural fiction.
- **Nonfiction:** Publishes early picture books, 0–4 years; story picture books, 4–10 years; and middle-grade books, 8–12 years.
  Topics include nature, the outdoors, travel, and recreation.
- **Representative Titles:** *Uncharted Waters,* by Leslie Bulion
  (8–12 years), tells of a boy who gets tangled in a web of lies
  while spending the summer with his uncle in a seaside cabin.
  About Marsupials: A Guide for Children, by Cathryn Sill (3–7
  years), uses detailed color illustrations to engage children in
  learning about how marsupials look, eat, and live.

Submissions and Payment
Guidelines and catalogue available at website. Query with
table of contents and 3 sample chapters; or send complete
ms. Send complete ms for picture books. Accepts hard
copy. SASE. Responds in 6 months. Publication period and
payment policy vary.

Editor's Comments
We seek powerful, affecting literature that is fun for children
to read. We don't accept science fiction or fantasy.

Pelican Publishing

1000 Burmaster Street
Gretna, LA 70053

Editorial Department

Publisher's Interests
Pelican's children's catalogue includes fiction and nonfiction for readers ages four through young adult. Though many existing titles focus on the Louisiana region, the company is open to broader regions and subjects.
Website: www.pelicanpub.com

Freelance Potential
Published 100 titles (31 juvenile) in 2010: 34 were developed from unsolicited submissions, 4 were by agented authors, and 16 were reprint/licensed properties. Of the 100 titles, 26 were by unpublished writers and 39 were by authors who were new to the publishing house. Receives 3,600 queries, 7,800 unsolicited mss yearly.

- **Fiction:** Publishes easy-to-read books, 4–7 years; middle-grade books, 8–12 years; and young adult books, 12–18 years. Genres include historical, regional, and multicultural fiction.
- **Nonfiction:** Publishes easy-to-read books, 4–7 years; and middle-grade books, 8–12 years. Topics include history, food, people, and culture; and multicultural issues.
- **Representative Titles:** *The Declaration of Independence From A to Z*, by Catherine L. Osornio (6–12 years), explains the process by which Americans gained their liberty. *Clovis Crawfish and His Friends*, by Mary Alice Fontenot (5–8 years), follows a friendly crawfish as he navigates the bayou and finds friends.

Submissions and Payment
Guidelines available. Catalogue available at website. Query with synopsis. Send complete ms for easy-to-read books only. Accepts hard copy. No simultaneous submissions. SASE. Responds in 3 months. Publication in 9–18 months. Royalty.

Editor's Comments
Queries and submissions with spelling and typographic errors will reflect unfavorably on the author.

Pembroke Publishers

538 Hood Road
Markham, Ontario L3R 3K9
Canada

Submissions Editor: Mary Macchiusi

Publisher's Interests
Practical, quality books for teachers, librarians, and parents
are the focus of Pembroke Publishers. Its catalogue includes
books on curriculum subjects, classroom management
strategies, and major issues in education.
Website: www.pembrokepublishers.com

Freelance Potential
Published 10–20 titles in 2010. Of the 10–20 titles, 1 was by
an author who was new to the publishing house. Receives
50 queries yearly.

- **Nonfiction:** Publishes chapter books, 5–10 years; and middle-
  grade books, 8–12 years. Topics include history, science, writing, and notable Canadians. Also publishes titles for educators
  about reading, writing, literacy learning, drama, the arts,
  school leadership, discipline, and working with parents.
- **Representative Titles:** *Books as Bridges,* by Jane Baskwill,
  explores the many ways to use books to increase literacy and
  create a common reading experience that extends to students'
  homes and involves their parents. *No More "I'm Done!,"* by
  Jennifer Jacobsen, shows teachers how to build writing independence and nurture young writers.

Submissions and Payment
Guidelines available. Query with résumé, outline, and
sample chapter. Accepts hard copy and simultaneous
submissions if identified. SAE/IRC. Responds in 1 month.
Publication in 6–24 months. Royalty.

Editor's Comments
Most of our authors are leading educators, psychologists, and
journalists. We place a premium on the practicality of the
data offered in a project, and demand that it provide our
readers with information that will help them in their classrooms. Though we publish on a variety of education topics,
our primary focus is on literacy.

Peter Pauper Press

202 Mamaroneck Avenue, Suite 400
White Plains, NY 10601-5376

Editorial Director: Barbara Paulding

Publisher's Interests

Peter Pauper offers specialty, gift, and art activity books for children ages four and up. It also produces stationery, journals, engagement calendars, and personal organizers for an audience made up primarily of women. Many of its products spotlight special relationships or occasions.
Website: www.peterpauper.com

Freelance Potential

Published 50 titles (10 juvenile) in 2010: 2 were developed from unsolicited submissions. Receives 60 queries, 96 unsolicited mss yearly.

- **Fiction:** Publishes story picture books, 4–10 years; and story-based activity books, 5–11 years. Genres include humor, fantasy, and adventure.
- **Nonfiction:** Publishes activity books, 3–13 years. Topics include animals, the environment, science, math, and humor.
- **Representative Titles:** *The Nutcracker Ballet,* by Mara Conlon (6+ years), allows children to read the classic story while reenacting the drama with paper dolls and a fold-out theater set. *Whoo's There* (4–9 years) invites readers to use transparent windows on the pages to project silhouette shadows on the wall as they read rhyming tales about nighttime animals.

Submissions and Payment

Guidelines available. Query with cover letter, outline, 2 sample chapters, and credentials; or send complete ms. Accepts hard copy. SASE. Responds in 3+ months. Publication period varies. Flat fee.

Editor's Comments

Because we are a specialty publisher, it is very important that you familiarize yourself with our catalogue before sending us any work. We are always looking for the next great activity book idea or series that will enchant and engage young children.

Philomel Books

Penguin Group
345 Hudson Street
New York, NY 10014

Editorial Assistant

Publisher's Interests

This imprint of Penguin Young Readers Group is dedicated to producing quality books for young people that stretch the limits of their reality, whether it is culturally, imaginatively, historically, or artistically. It offers fiction and nonfiction titles for children of all ages.
Website: www.penguingroup.com

Freelance Potential

Published 40–50 titles (25 juvenile) in 2010: 3 were developed from unsolicited submissions and 44 were by agented authors. Receives 600 queries yearly.

- **Fiction:** Publishes early picture books, 0–4 years; story picture books, 4–10 years; chapter books, 5–10 years; middle-grade books, 8–12 years; and young adult books, 12–18 years. Genres include fantasy and contemporary, historical, multicultural, and science fiction. Also publishes poetry.
- **Nonfiction:** Publishes story picture books, 4–10 years; and young adult books, 12–18 years. Publishes biographies and first-person narratives.
- **Representative Titles:** *Back of the Bus*, by Aaron Reynolds (6–8 years), recounts the story of Rosa Parks' act of defiance through the eyes of a child. *Erak's Ransom*, by John Flanagan (10+ years), follows the Rangers as they travel through the desert in search of their captured leader; part of the Ranger's Apprentice series.

Submissions and Payment

Guidelines available. Query with outline/synopsis. Accepts hard copy. SASE. Responds if interested. Publication in 1–2 years. Royalty.

Editor's Comments

We prefer to see proposals submitted through established literary agents. We do not accept unsolicited manuscripts, but we will review queries for new projects.

Phoenix Learning Resources

914 Church Street
Honesdale, PA 18431

Submissions

Publisher's Interests
The mission of Phoenix Learning Resources is to produce quality supplemental educational materials for students in preschool through high school. It publishes books in all curriculum areas, and includes titles designed for use in special education, English as a Second Language classes, and basic adult education.
Website: www.phoenixlearningresources.com

Freelance Potential
Published 43 titles in 2010. Receives 25 queries yearly.

- **Nonfiction:** Publishes textbooks and educational materials for preK–grade 12 and beyond. Also publishes books for special education and for gifted students, materials for use with ESL students, reference books, and biographies. Topics include language skills, integrated language arts, reading comprehension, math, study skills, and social skills.
- **Representative Titles:** *Sounds Right, Read, Write,* by Elske Brown & Judy Jackson (grades K–4), appears in grade-appropriate editions to guide students through the sounds and spellings of basic words. *Critical Reading and Thinking Skills* (grades 2–6) is a series of units that provide articles designed to build comprehension skills.

Submissions and Payment
Guidelines available. Catalogue available at website. Query with résumé. Accepts hard copy and simultaneous submissions if identified. SASE. Responds in 1–4 weeks. Publication in 1–15 months. Royalty. Flat fee.

Editor's Comments
We are a respected publisher of educational products used in classrooms and libraries across the U.S. As such, we are selective about the types of books we publish and the authors with whom we work. You must present us with a description of your education experience and areas of expertise.

Picture Window Books

Captsone Press
151 Good Counsel Drive
P.O. Box 669
Mankato, MN 56002

Managing Editor: Christianne Jones

Publisher's Interests
This imprint of Capstone Press focuses on high-interest fiction for preschool children through elementary school readers. It specializes in material for reluctant readers—works that weave ideas and words to captivate children's imaginations. All books are produced on a work-for-hire basis.
Website: www.capstonepub.com

Freelance Potential
Published 38 titles in 2010: 1 was by an agented author. Of the 38 titles, 2 were by unpublished writers and 8 were by authors who were new to the publishing house. Receives 360 queries yearly.

- **Fiction:** Publishes concept books and early picture books, 0–4 years; easy-to-read books, 4–7 years; and story picture books, 4–10 years. Fiction and accelerated reader titles for preK–grade 3.
- **Representative Titles:** *Katie in the Kitchen,* by Fran Manushkin (grades K–2), finds the young Katie Woo beginning to cook dinner for her mother, but strange noises lead her to think she has ghosts for dinner; part of the Katie Woo series. *Pony Brushes His Teeth,* by Michael Dahl (preK), tells the story of a pony who learns his dental hygiene from watching his dad.

Submissions and Payment
Guidelines available at website. Send résumé and writing sample only. Accepts email to author.sub@ stonearchbooks.com. Response time, publication period, and payment policy vary.

Editor's Comments
To be considered for one of our projects, send us your writing samples and tell us a little bit about your publishing experience. We'll contact you if your expertise matches our current needs.

Pilgrim Press

700 Prospect Avenue East
Cleveland, OH 44115-1100

Editorial Director: Kim Sadler

Publisher's Interests

Publishing books that connect spirituality to real life, Pilgrim Press targets church scholars and professionals, laypersons, and students. Many of its titles are used as part of religious education programs. Pilgrim Press is the publishing division of the United Church of Christ.
Website: www.thepilgrimpress.com

Freelance Potential

Published 40 titles in 2010: 23 were developed from unsolicited submissions and 1 was by an agented author. Of the 40 titles, 1 was by an unpublished writer and 12 were by authors who were new to the publishing house. Receives 200+ queries yearly.

- **Nonfiction:** Publishes educational titles of interest to religious educators, clergy, parents, and caregivers. Also publishes informational titles on religion, social issues, and multicultural and ethnic subjects.
- **Representative Titles:** *Bible Stories for All Ages,* by Margaret Kyle, offers a positive, clear, and uncomplicated presentation of some of the more complicated stories in the Bible. *Seasons Growing Faith* is a board book series for the youngest members of the church that teaches about a God of love and the foundations of the Christian faith.

Submissions and Payment

Guidelines and catalogue available at website. Query via form at website. Responds in 9–12 months. Flat fee for work-for-hire projects.

Editor's Comments

We look for authors who can write clearly and concisely and who have the credentials to write on the topic they propose. Tell us what makes your proposal compelling or unique. It is important to note that we do not publish children's or adult fiction, memoirs, autobiographies, or poetry.

Pineapple Press

P.O. Box 3889
Sarasota, FL 34230

Executive Editor: June Cussen

Publisher's Interests
This regional publisher has been producing books about
Florida since 1982. Its children's list includes fictional tales
set in the state and nonfiction books about Florida's history,
environment, and people.
Website: www.pineapplepress.com

Freelance Potential
Published 18 titles (5 juvenile) in 2010: 14 were developed
from unsolicited submissions. Of the 18 titles, 1 was by an
unpublished writer and 8 were by authors who were new to
the publishing house. Receives 1,200 queries yearly.

- **Fiction:** Publishes story picture books, 4–10 years; chapter
  books, 5–10 years; middle-grade books, 8–12 years; and
  young adult books, 12–18 years. Genres include folklore, mystery, science fiction, and historical fiction related to Florida.
- **Nonfiction:** Publishes easy-to-read books, 4–7 years; story picture books, 4–10 years; and middle-grade books, 8–12 years.
  Topics include the history, sports, wildlife, nature, and environment of Florida. Also publishes biographies.
- **Representative Titles:** *Henry Flagler, Builder of Florida,* by Sandra Wallus Sammons (9–12), is the biography of the man who
  changed Florida with his hotels and railroads. *My Florida Alphabet,* by Russell W. Johnson & Annie P. Johnson (4–8 years),
  teaches children the alphabet along with facts about Florida.

Submissions and Payment
Guidelines available at website. Query with clips, synopsis,
and sample chapter for fiction. Query with table of contents
and sample chapters for nonfiction. Accepts hard copy and
simultaneous submissions if identified. SASE. Responds in
2 months. Publication in 12–18 months. Royalty.

Editor's Comments
We publish more nonfiction than fiction, so please keep in
mind that fiction titles are less likely to be accepted.

Pioneer Drama Service

P.O. Box 4267
Englewood, CO 80155-4267

Submissions Editor: Lori Conary

Publisher's Interests
Pioneer Drama Service publishes scripts for middle school, high school, and community theater. All titles are family friendly and suitable for audiences of all ages. It also publishes books about theater, acting, and stagecraft.
Website: www.pioneerdrama.com

Freelance Potential
Published 25 titles (23 juvenile) in 2010: 10–12 were developed from unsolicited submissions. Of the 25 titles, 4 were by unpublished writers and 4 were by authors who were new to the publishing house. Receives 200–300 queries, 300–400 unsolicited mss yearly.

- **Fiction:** Publishes play scripts, 4–18 years. Genres include comedy, mystery, fantasy, adventure, folktales, and musicals.
- **Nonfiction:** Publishes theatrical textbooks and resources for children's and school theater groups.
- **Representative Titles:** *Aesop's Foibles,* by Flip Kobler & Cindy Marcus, is a play for all ages that presents some of Aesop's more famous fables in a unique but hilarious way. *Cinderella Caterpillar,* by Jim Houle, turns the age-old love story into a modern-day bug story.

Submissions and Payment
Guidelines and catalogue available at website. Prefers query; will accept complete ms with synopsis, cast list, running time, set design, prop list, and proof of production. Accepts hard copy, email submissions to submissions@ pioneerdrama.com, and simultaneous submissions if identified. SASE. Responds in 4–6 months. Publication period varies. Royalty.

Editor's Comments
All plays must be unpublished and should be accompanied by proof of production. New plays must have this fundamental field test before we offer them to our customers.

Pipers' Ash

Church Road, Christian Malford
Chippenham, Wiltshire SN15 4BW
United Kingdom

Submissions: A. Tyson

Publisher's Interests
Pipers' Ash Ltd. publishes books and New Chapbooks for all
ages. Its children's literature catalogue features endearing
tales for bedtime reading and true-to-life stories tailored for
older children and young adults.
Website: www.supamasu.com

Freelance Potential
Published 15 titles (3 juvenile) in 2010: 5 were developed
from unsolicited submissions. Of the 15 titles, 10 were by
unpublished writers and 10 were by authors who were new
to the publishing house. Receives 240 queries, 120 unsolicited mss yearly.

- **Fiction:** Publishes chapbooks, 5–10 years; middle-grade
  books, 8–12 years; and young adult books, 12–18 years.
  Genres include short stories; mystery; and contemporary,
  historical, and science fiction.
- **Nonfiction:** Publishes young adult books, 12–18 years. Topics
  include animals, crafts, hobbies, sports, and history. Also publishes biographies and poetry.
- **Representative Titles:** *Northern Lights,* by Anne Colledge
  (5–11 years), tells of the adventures of a 9-year-old deaf boy
  along the rugged coastline of northeast England. *Class War,* by
  Eric R. Brady (YA), explains how Adolf Hitler's war machine
  could not defeat a group of London school children.

Submissions and Payment
Guidelines and catalogue available at website. Query with
brief proposal (to 25 words); or send complete ms. Accepts
hard copy, disk submissions, and email to pipersash@
supamasu.com. SAE/IRC. Response time and publication
period vary. Royalty, 10%.

Editor's Comments
If sending a manuscript, please format it in either Microsoft
Word or WordPerfect.

Platypus Media

725 8th Street SE
Washington, DC 20003

President: Dia L. Michels

Publisher's Interests
An independent publisher founded in 2001, Platypus focuses on books that foster family closeness. It publishes books for children, as well as parenting titles that encourage co-sleeping, breastfeeding, and family togetherness.
Website: www.platypusmedia.com

Freelance Potential
Published 4 titles in 2010: 2 were by agented authors. Receives 180 queries, 24 unsolicited mss yearly.

- **Fiction:** Publishes concept books, 0–4 years; and middle-grade books, 8–12 years. Themes include families, family diversity, and animals.
- **Nonfiction:** Publishes concept books, toddler books, and early picture books, 0–4 years; easy-to-read books, 4–7 years; story picture books, 4–10 years; chapter books, 5–10 years; middle-grade books, 8–12 years; and young adult books, 12–18 years. Topics include family issues, science, and math. Also publishes activity books and parenting titles.
- **Representative Titles:** *I Was Born to Be a Brother,* by Zaydek Michels-Galtieri (3–7 years), depicts the many roles of a brother and the importance of nurturing and being nurtured. *Breastfeeding Facts for Fathers,* by Dia L. Michels, ed. (parents), examines the crucial role that men have in breastfeeding, answers questions, and provides tips for supportive dads.

Submissions and Payment
Guidelines and catalogue available at website. Query or send complete ms with brief author biography and marketing analysis. Accepts hard copy and simultaneous submissions if identified. SASE. Response time varies. Publication in 9–12 months. Royalty. Flat fee.

Editor's Comments
We always welcome books that celebrate the diversity of families and traditions.

Players Press

P.O. Box 1132
Studio City, CA 91614

Vice President: Robert W. Gordon

Publisher's Interests
Players Press publishes plays, musicals, and monologues for young audiences and young performers. It also publishes informational books on stage craft and the performing arts.
Website: www.ppeps.com

Freelance Potential
Published 50 titles (22 juvenile) in 2010: 1 was by an agented author and 1 was a reprint/licensed property. Of the 50 titles, 5 were by unpublished writers and 11 were by new authors. Receives 6,000+ queries yearly.

- **Fiction:** Publishes full-length and one-act plays for children, 4–18 years. Genres include drama, comedy, musicals, fairy tales, and monologues.
- **Nonfiction:** Publishes toddler books and early picture books, 0–4 years; easy-to-read books, 4–7 years; chapter books, 5–10 years; middle-grade books, 8–12 years; and young adult books, 12–18 years. Also publishes guides for educators. Topics include auditioning, theater arts, film, television, music, costume design, stage management, set construction, and theater history.
- **Representative Titles:** *Alice N'Wonderland,* by William-Alan Landes, is a magical, musical adaption of the classic tale. *Every Teacher's Friend Classroom Plays,* by Pat Jordan, is a collection of lesson plans and classic plays for teachers, librarians, and homeschoolers.

Submissions and Payment
Guidelines available. Query with proposal for books. Query with author biography, dated production flyer and program, score and CD (for musicals), and reviews for scripts. Accepts hard copy. SASE. Responds in 3–12 months. Publication in 3–24 months. Royalty, 10%; advance.

Editor's Comments
We're always on the lookout for promising new playwrights and exciting new works to add to our catalogue.

Playwrights Canada Press

215 Spadina Avenue, Suite 230
Toronto, Ontario M5T 2C7
Canada

Editorial Coordinator

Publisher's Interests
Playwrights Canada Press caters to drama production and
theater groups by offering plays of all types, as well as books
on topics such as stage management and acting technique.
It also publishes plays for young audiences. Writers must be
from Canada to submit their work.
Website: www.playwrightscanada.com

Freelance Potential
Published 35 titles (2 juvenile) in 2010: 1 was developed
from an unsolicited submission. Receives 10–15 queries
each year.

- **Fiction:** Publishes dramatic plays for elementary, middle
  school, and high school students.
- **Nonfiction:** Publishes books about acting and play production,
  and theater resources for drama teachers.
- **Representative Titles:** *Danny, King of the Basement,* by
  David S. Craig, features a boy who helps his friends while he
  searches for a home of his own. *Illegal Entry,* by Clem Martini,
  follows three teens living in a group home as they go AWOL,
  equipped with nothing but a garage door opener and a plan.

Submissions and Payment
Canadian authors only. Guidelines and catalogue available at
website. Query with synopsis and first-production information, including lists of cast and crew. Accepts hard copy and
simultaneous submissions if identified. SASE. Responds in
6–12 months. Publication in 5 months. Royalty.

Editor's Comments
Our publishing house can accept plays from Canadian citizens or landed immigrants only. You must also have had at
least one professional production in the last 10 years. Occasionally we send out a call for material for anthologies and
drama festivals; check our website for details.

Plexus Publishing

143 Old Marlton Pike
Medford, NJ 08055

Editor-in-Chief: John B. Bryans

Publisher's Interests

Incorporated in 1977, this New Jersey publisher produces books on the region's history, nature, environment, and tourism, as well as a limited number of novels set in New Jersey. While it has no dedicated children's list, many of its titles appeal to young adult readers.
Website: www.plexuspublishing.com

Freelance Potential

Published 4 titles in 2010: 1 was developed from an unsolicited submission. Of the 4 titles, 1 was by an unpublished writer and 2 were by authors who were new to the publishing house. Receives 150–300 queries yearly.

- **Fiction:** Genres include mystery, adventure, folklore, and contemporary and historical fiction—all with New Jersey settings.
- **Nonfiction:** Publishes regional field guides, reference books, and biographies. Topics include New Jersey's history, natural resources, seashore, wildlife, recreation, tourism, travel, and unique locations such as the Pine Barrens.
- **Representative Titles:** *Boardwalk Empire,* by Nelson Johnson, traces the development of Atlantic City from its humble beginning to its rebirth as an international gambling mecca. *Wrong Beach Island,* by Jane Kelly, brings a funny and reluctant sleuth to Long Beach Island to unravel a mystery.

Submissions and Payment

Guidelines and catalogue available at website. Query with synopsis, table of contents, and 3 sample chapters. Accepts hard copy. SASE. Responds in 2 months. Publication in 10 months. Royalty, 12%.

Editor's Comments

While we had previously focused on topics relating to southern New Jersey, we recently expanded our publishing program to include books on all areas of the state, as well as the Philadelphia area.

Polychrome Publishing Corporation

4509 North Francisco Avenue
Chicago, IL 60625-3808

Editorial Department

Publisher's Interests
This publishing company hopes to diversify the books found on children's bookshelves by sharing "stories of color for a colorful world." It produces multicultural fiction and nonfiction titles with an emphasis on Asian American stories from the Asian American community.
Website: www.polychromebooks.com

Freelance Potential
Published 1 title in 2010: it was developed from an unsolicited submission. Receives 300 unsolicited mss yearly.

- **Fiction:** Publishes toddler books and early picture books, 0–4 years; story picture books, 4–10 years; chapter books, 5–10 years; middle-grade books, 8–12 years; and young adult books, 12–18 years. Genres include contemporary, historical, and multicultural fiction.
- **Nonfiction:** Publishes books about Asian American culture for families and educators.
- **Representative Titles:** *Almond Cookies & Dragon Well Tea*, by Cynthia Chin-Lee (grades 1–4), is the story of a European girl and a Chinese girl sharing the stories of their heritages. *Blue Jay in the Desert*, by Marlene Shigekawa, introduces the story of the Japanese American internment through the eyes of a young boy.

Submissions and Payment
Guidelines and catalogue available at website. Send complete ms with author bio. Accepts hard copy and simultaneous submissions if identified. SASE. Responds in 3–6 months. Publication in 1–2 years. Royalty; advance.

Editor's Comments
We are interested in books that will teach children how to understand and appreciate the rich and diverse cultural heritages and experiences that may differ from their own. New authors are always welcome here.

Portage & Main Press

100-318 McDermot Avenue
Winnipeg, Manitoba R3A 0A2
Canada

Editor: Catherine Gerbasi

Publisher's Interests

Supporting the work of teachers for more than 40 years, this
education publisher produces hands-on teaching modules,
textbooks, and supplementary resource materials for use in
kindergarten through grade 12 classrooms. It also publishes
professional support titles for educators on assessment,
classroom management, and educational research. Portage
& Main markets its books in Canada, the United States, and
internationally.
Website: www.portageandmainpress.com

Freelance Potential

Published 10–15 titles in 2010.

- **Nonfiction:** Publishes educational resource books for
  teachers, grades K–12. Topics include assessment, continual
  learning, ESL, visual literacy, reading, spelling, writing, safe
  schools, social studies, mathematics, and science.
- **Representative Titles:** *Together Is Better: Collaborative
  Assessment, Evaluation & Reporting,* by Anne Davies et al.,
  shows teachers how to include parents and children in the
  assessment process. *Literature Circles: Tools and Techniques
  to Inspire Reading Groups,* by Warren Rogers & Dave Leochko,
  provides instruction and materials for setting up literature
  circles in the classroom.

Submissions and Payment

Guidelines and catalogue available at website or with
SAE/IRC ($.50 Canadian postage). Query with table of con-
tents and sample chapter; or send complete ms. Accepts
hard copy and disk submissions. SAE/IRC. Responds in
1–2 months. Publication in 6 months. Royalty, 8–12%.

Editor's Comments

We look for books that are practical, yet based on solid
theory and research. All of our authors are teachers or other
education professionals.

PowerKids Press

Rosen Publishing
29 East 21st Street
New York, NY 10010

Editorial Director: Rachel O'Conner

Publisher's Interests

High-interest nonfiction books for children in preschool
through grade eight comprise the catalogue of this Rosen
Publishing Group imprint. With titles designed for classrooms
and libraries, it seeks books that inform while provoking
curiosity and exploration of our natural and social world.
Website: www.powerkidspress.com

Freelance Potential

Published 200 titles in 2010. Of the 200 titles, 15 were by
unpublished writers and 15 were by authors who were new
to the publishing house. Receives 500 queries yearly.

- **Nonfiction:** Publishes educational materials, preK–grade 8.
  Topics include art, social studies, science, geography, health,
  fitness, sports, math, Native Americans, ancient history,
  natural history, politics and government, and multicultural
  and ethnic issues. Also publishes biographies and titles for
  special education and bilingual programs.
- **Representative Titles:** *The Life Cycle of an Owl,* by Ruth
  Thomson (grade 2), follows an owl from egg to learning to
  catch prey; part of the Learning About Life Cycles series. *How
  To Deal with Diabetes,* by Lynette Robbins (grades 2–3),
  explains the types of diabetes, its symptoms, and how to
  manage it; part of the Kids' Health series.

Submissions and Payment

Guidelines available. Catalogue available at website. Query
with outline and sample chapter. Accepts hard copy and
simultaneous submissions if identified. SASE. Responds in
3 months. Publication in 9–18 months. Flat fee.

Editor's Comments

Many of our books are parts of series. Since we are dedicated
to offering an ever-expanding array of materials that meet
students' and teachers' needs, we welcome proposals for
new titles or new series.

P & R Publishing

P.O. Box 817
Phillipsburg, NJ 08865

Editorial Director: Marvin Padgett

Publisher's Interests

With books that promote biblical understanding and godly living, P & R's list ranges from academic works advancing biblical scholarship to popular books that help lay readers grow in Christian thought. For middle-grade and young adult readers, it offers Christian and inspirational fiction and Christian-themed nonfiction on life issues.

Website: www.prpbooks.com

Freelance Potential

Published 40 titles (2 juvenile) in 2010: Of the 40 titles, 3–5 were by unpublished writers and 15–20 were by authors who were new to the publishing house. Receives 150 queries each year.

- **Fiction:** Publishes middle-grade books, 8–12 years; and young adult books, 12–18 years. Genres include inspirational and religious fiction, and fantasy.
- **Nonfiction:** Publishes middle-grade books, 8–12 years; and young adult books, 12–18 years. Topics include Christian living, counseling, theology, apologetics, Christian issues and ethics, and women's issues. Also publishes study aids.
- **Representative Titles:** *The Faithful Parent,* by Martha Peace & Stuart Scott, offers practical advice and biblical hope to parents of children of all ages. *All My Holy Mountain,* by L. B. Graham (YA), is a fantasy novel that finds warriors fighting dragons and other adversaries to free the kingdom of Kirthanin; part of the Binding of the Blade series.

Submissions and Payment

Catalogue and guidelines available at website. Query. Accepts electronic queries through website only. Responds in 1–3 months. Publication period varies. Royalty.

Editor's Comments

Please see our online guidelines for a list of categories for which we are accepting submissions.

Mathew Price

12300 Ford Road, Suite 455
Dallas, TX 75234

Publisher: Mathew Price

Publisher's Interests

Mathew Price Ltd. is now in its second year of publishing in the U.S., after many years of creating books in the U.K. Its books are targeted to the youngest readers, helping them learn language through interactive reading with their parents and families.

Website: www.mathewprice.com

Freelance Potential

Published 30 titles in 2010.

- **Fiction:** Publishes early picture books, 0–4 years; easy-to-read books, 4–7 years; and story picture books, 4–10 years. Also publishes board books, novelty books, and books in Spanish. Features stories about animals, sports, cars and vehicles, families, and holidays.
- **Nonfiction:** Publishes early picture books, 0–4 years; easy-to-read books, 4–7 years; and story picture books, 4–10 years. Topics include nature, animals, vehicles, the alphabet, and early math.
- **Representative Titles:** *Fire Engine to the Rescue,* by Steve Augarde, uses pop-ups and pull tabs to put young children into the action when the fire alarm sounds. *Soccer Crazy,* by Colin McNaughton (5–8 years), features a slightly overweight bear who suddenly has to prove himself on the soccer field when the game is tied.

Submissions and Payment

Send complete ms. Accepts email submissions to mathewp@mathewprice.com. Response time varies. Publication in 18 months. Royalty.

Editor's Comments

With innovative ideas, joyous stories, and stunning artwork, we aim to set even the youngest of readers on the path to a lifetime love of reading. Our philosophy is "education through delight."

Prometheus Books

59 John Glenn Drive
Amherst, NY 14228-2119

Editor-in-Chief: Steven L. Mitchell

Publisher's Interests

This self-proclaimed "provocative, progressive, and independent" publisher has a catalogue of intelligent nonfiction for the thoughtful layperson on such diverse subjects as atheism, philosophy, criminology, and self-help. For children, it publishes science and sexual education titles as well as books that help children explore moral and emotional issues. **Website: www.prometheusbooks.com**

Freelance Potential

Published 100 titles in 2010: 15–20 were developed from unsolicited submissions. Receives 300 queries, 400 unsolicited mss yearly.

- **Nonfiction:** Publishes easy-to-read books, 4–7 years; and middle-grade books, 8–12 years. Topics include social issues, health, sexuality, religion, politics, critical thinking, and decision-making.
- **Representative Titles:** *The Favorite Child,* by Ellen Weber Libby, shares a clinical psychologist's observations on how being a parent's "favorite child" can confer great advantages as well as emotional handicaps. *The Tree of Life: The Wonders of Evolution,* by Ellen Jackson, explains the excitement and beauty of evolution in an easy-to-read and fun manner.

Submissions and Payment

Guidelines and catalogue available at website. Query or send complete ms with résumé and bibliography. Accepts hard copy and simultaneous submissions if identified. SASE. Responds in 2–3 months. Publication in 12–18 months. Payment policy varies.

Editor's Comments

We believe that thoughtful and authoritative books do not have to be stale and boring. We respond to books that take on provocative, exciting issues in ways that will entice our readers—whatever their ages.

Pruett Publishing Company

P.O. Box 2140
Boulder, CO 80306-2140

Editor: James Pruett

Publisher's Interests

Award-winning books about the Rocky Mountain region that
appeal to outdoor enthusiasts, travelers, and lovers of history
can be found in Pruett Publishing's catalogue. It also produces textbooks for grade-school students.
Website: www.pruettpublishing.com

Freelance Potential

Published 6 titles (2 juvenile) in 2010. Receives 180 queries,
144 unsolicited mss yearly.

- **Nonfiction:** Publishes middle-grade books, 8–12 years; and
  young adult books, 12–18 years. Topics include biography,
  health, fitness, history, multicultural issues, nature, and the
  environment—all related to the Rocky Mountain West. Also
  publishes coloring and activity books for younger children.
- **Representative Titles:** *The Earth Is Enough,* by Harry Middleton, is a memoir of a boy growing up on a farm in the Ozark
  foothills. *Wild Boulder County: A Seasonal Guide to the
  Natural World,* by Ruth Carol Cushman & Stephen Tories
  (3–5 years), reveals the natural wonders of the Rocky Mountain Front Range.

Submissions and Payment

Guidelines and catalogue available at website. Query with
résumé, outline, sample chapters, and market analysis; or
send complete ms. Accepts hard copy and simultaneous
submissions if identified. SASE. Responds to queries in
2 weeks, to mss in 1–2 months. Publication period varies.
Royalty, 10–15%.

Editor's Comments

We welcome submissions about the outdoor recreation,
hiking, flyfishing, travel, history, and natural environment of
the Rocky Mountain West. First-time authors are encouraged
to send us their proposals. Be sure to include your ideas
for artwork.

Prufrock Press

5926 Balcones Drive, Suite 220
Austin, TX 78731

Submissions Editor: Lacy Compton

Publisher's Interests
Prufrock Press publishes award-winning books and educational resource material focused on gifted education, gifted children, advanced learning, and special needs learners in kindergarten through grade 12.
Website: www.prufrock.com

Freelance Potential
Published 30–35 titles (2 juvenile) in 2010. Of the 30–35 titles, 10–12 were by authors who were new to the publishing house.

- **Nonfiction:** Publishes supplemental classroom materials for gifted and advanced learners, grades K–12. Topics include math, science, social studies, language arts, thinking skills, problem-solving, research, and presentation skills. Also publishes books for teachers and parents of gifted children. Topics include differentiated instruction; teaching strategies; independent study; identifying, parenting, and counseling gifted children; and enrichment.
- **Representative Titles:** *Math and Logic Puzzles That Make Kids Think,* by Jeffrey J. Wanko & Benjamin L. Walker (grades 6–8), presents a variety of logic puzzles that lay the groundwork for further mathematic exploration. *Success Strategies for Teaching Kids with Autism,* by Wendy Ashcroft et al., provides practical advice for implementing successful programs and services for kids with autism.

Submissions and Payment
Guidelines and catalogue available at website. Query with table of contents; or send complete ms. Accepts hard copy. SASE. Responds in 2–4 months. Publication period varies. Royalty; advance.

Editor's Comments
All of our material is authored by professionals with experience in the fields of gifted or special education.

Puffin Books

Penguin Group
345 Hudson Street, 15th Floor
New York, NY 10014

Manuscript Submissions

Publisher's Interests
Children's and young adult books are the focus of Puffin, an imprint of the Penguin Young Readers Group. It publishes everything from picture books to ground-breaking middle-grade and teen fiction.
Website: www.us.penguingroup.com

Freelance Potential
Published 200 titles in 2010. Receives 500+ queries yearly.

- **Fiction:** Publishes early picture books, 0–4 years; easy-to-read books, 4–7 years; story picture books, 4–10 years; chapter books, 5–10 years; middle-grade books, 8–12 years; and young adult books, 12–18 years. Genres include historical, contemporary, and science fiction; mystery; adventure; and romance. Also publishes novelty books, 0–4 years.
- **Nonfiction:** Publishes story picture books, 4–10 years; and middle-grade books, 8–12 years. Topics include social issues and science.
- **Representative Titles:** *Drita, My Homegirl,* by Jenny Lombard (9–11 years), is a poignant story about the difficulties of leaving everything behind and the friendships that help you get through it. *Slippers at School,* by Andrew Clements (3–5 years), follows the adventure of a curious puppy who stows away in a girl's backpack to see what school is really like.

Submissions and Payment
Guidelines available. Catalogue available at website. Query with outline/synopsis. Accepts hard copy. SASE. Responds in 4–5 months. Publication in 12–18 months. Royalty, 2–6%.

Editor's Comments
We look for compelling stories that will engage young readers, and inviting, whimsical tales that will help the very young fall in love with books. The best way to put your idea in front of us is through a literary agent; but a truly great proposal will be noticed whether you are agented or not.

G. P. Putnam's Sons

Penguin Group
345 Hudson Street
New York, NY 10014

Manuscript Editor

Publisher's Interests

This publisher markets books to readers of all ages. A division of Penguin Young Readers Group, it features fiction and nonfiction in a variety of formats.
Website: www.penguin.com

Freelance Potential

Published 56 titles in 2010: 1 was developed from an unsolicited submission, 36 were by agented authors, and 5 were reprint/licensed properties. Of the 56 titles, 5 were by unpublished writers and 19 were by authors who were new to the publishing house. Receives 1,500 queries, 7,200 unsolicited mss yearly.

- **Fiction:** Publishes toddler books and early picture books, 0–4 years; story picture books, 4–10 years; chapter books, 5–10 years; middle-grade books, 8–12 years; and young adult books, 12–18 years. Genres include contemporary and multicultural fiction.
- **Nonfiction:** Publishes early picture books, 0–4 years; story picture books, 4–10 years; chapter books, 5–10 years; and middle-grade books, 8–12 years.
- **Representative Titles:** *Little Pink Pup,* by Johanna Kerby (3–5 years), tells how the runt of a pig litter is fed and nurtured by a dachshund mom. *The Julian Game,* by Adele Griffin (12+ years), features a girl who gets in trouble when she creates a fake Facebook page.

Submissions and Payment

Guidelines available. Query with synopsis and 3 sample chapters. Send ms for picture books. Accepts hard copy and simultaneous submissions. No SASE. Responds in 4 months if interested. Publication period varies. Royalty; advance.

Editor's Comments

While we cannot respond personally to submissions, we do make every effort to consider each one we receive.

Quest Books

306 West Geneva Road
P.O. Box 270
Wheaton, IL 60187

Assistant Editor: Richard Smoley

Publisher's Interests
Quest Books is committed to publishing books of intelligence, readability, and insight for the contemporary spiritual seeker. It features books on theosophy, yoga, meditation, new science and cosmology, holistic health, and spiritual traditions. Its catalogue is intended for adults, though some books are suitable for young adult readers.
Website: www.questbooks.net

Freelance Potential
Published 10 titles in 2010: 3 were developed from unsolicited submissions, 3 were by agented authors, and 1 was a reprint/licensed property. Of the 10 titles, 4 were by unpublished writers and 9 were by new authors. Receives 200 queries, 350 unsolicited mss each year.

- **Nonfiction:** Publishes self-help books. Topics include healing, spirituality, philosophy, theosophy, religion, meditation, spiritual ecology, transpersonal psychology, new science, holistic health, mysticism, mythology, and ancient wisdom.
- **Representative Titles:** *Yoga Beyond Fitness,* by Tom Pilarzyk, makes the argument for a return to yoga's roots as a spiritual practice rather than just exercise. *The World of the Dalai Lama,* by Gill Farrer-Halls, provides an inside look at the life and vision of this religious leader.

Submissions and Payment
Guidelines and catalogue available at website. Query with author biography, table of contents, introduction, and sample chapter; or send complete ms. Prefers email to submissions@questbooks.net (no attachments); will accept hard copy. SASE. Responds in 4–6 weeks. Publication period varies. Royalty; advance.

Editor's Comments
We do not accept fiction, biographies, how-to books, or academic works unsuitable for a general audience.

Rainbow Publishers

P.O. Box 261129
San Diego, CA 92196

Submissions: Daniel Miley

Publisher's Interests
Books for use in Christian religion classes, or at home, are the focus of this publisher. Activities, including crafts, games, and puzzles, help to make learning about the Bible and Christian living a fun experience for both student and teacher. All material is designed to be reproducible.
Website: www.rainbowpublishers.com

Freelance Potential
Published 16 titles in 2010. Receives 100 queries yearly.

- **Fiction:** Publishes middle-grade books, 8–12 years. Genres include inspirational and religious fiction.
- **Nonfiction:** Publishes Christian education resource materials, preK–grade 6. Topics include the Bible, religion, crafts, and hobbies. Also offers titles in series, 8+ years; and activity books, 2–12 years.
- **Representative Titles:** *Instant Bible Lessons for Toddlers* (1–3 years) enhances learning with fun activities to introduce toddlers to Bible stories. *Undercover Heroes of the Bible* (2+ years) comes in age-appropriate editions to help kids discover the stories of God's leaders. *More! Bible Crafts on a Shoe-string Budget* (5–10 years) offers step-by-step instructions for economical crafts accompanied by a Bible lesson.

Submissions and Payment
Guidelines and catalogue available at website or with a 9x12 SASE (2 first-class stamps). Query with résumé, table of contents, 2–5 sample chapters, and market analysis. Accepts hard copy and simultaneous submissions if identified. SASE. Responds in 2–8 weeks. Publication in 1–3 years. Flat fee.

Editor's Comments
We encourage writers who have experience in the religious education of children, so be sure to include that information with the submission. We are always seeking fresh ideas that capture the imagination, but that stay true to Bible teaching.

Random House Children's Books

1745 Broadway
New York, NY 10019

Submissions Editor

Publisher's Interests
The juvenile division of Random House features highly
regarded books that have won Newbery and Caldecott
honors and medals, as well as Coretta Scott King and
Michael L. Printz awards. It targets preschoolers, children
in the elementary and middle grades, and young adults.
Website: www.randomhouse.com

Freelance Potential
Published 350 titles in 2010: each was by an agented
author. Receives 1,200 queries yearly.

- **Fiction:** Publishes concept books, toddler books, and early
  picture books, 0–4 years; easy-to-read books, 4–7 years; story
  picture books, 4–10 years; chapter books, 5–10 years; middle-
  grade books, 8–12 years; and young adult books, 12–18
  years. Genres include contemporary, historical, inspirational,
  multicultural, and science fiction; adventure; drama; horror;
  mystery and suspense; fairy tales; romance; and stories about
  animals, nature, and the environment.
- **Nonfiction:** Publishes easy-to-read books, 4–7 years; story
  picture books, 4–10 years; chapter books, 5–10 years: middle-
  grade books, 8–12 years; and young adult books, 12–18
  years. Topics include animals, history, nature, the environment, adventure, and humor. Also publishes biographies.
- **Representative Titles:** *Who Will I Be, Lord?,* by Vaunda
  Micheaux Nelson (4–8 years), is a read-aloud book about the
  importance of family stories. *The Long Wait for Tomorrow,* by
  Joaquin Dorfman (12+ years), is a science fiction novel that
  explores themes of identity, high school roles, and destiny.

Submissions and Payment
Query through agent only. Publication in 18 months. Payment
policy varies.

Editor's Comments
We will only consider submissions from writers with established literary agents.

Raven Productions

P.O. Box 188
Ely, MN 55731

Editor: Johnna Hyde

Publisher's Interests

Publishing children's books about natural places is the focus of Raven Productions. Its catalogue includes both fiction and nonfiction, as well as titles for adults.

Website: www.ravenwords.com

Freelance Potential

Published 5 titles (3 juvenile) in 2010: each was developed from an unsolicited submission. Of the 5 titles, 3 were by unpublished writers and 4 were by authors who were new to the publishing house. Receives 240 unsolicited mss each year.

- **Fiction:** Publishes early picture books, 0–4 years; story picture books, 4–10 years; chapter books, 5–10 years; middle-grade books, 8–12 years; and young adult books, 12–18 years. Genres include regional, historical, multicultural, and ethnic fiction; folklore; and books about nature and sports.
- **Nonfiction:** Publishes easy-to-read books, 4–7 years; story picture books, 4–10 years; middle-grade books, 8–12 years; and young adult books, 12–18 years. Also publishes books for adults. Topics include animals, nature, science, technology, biography, history, sports, and regional subjects.
- **Representative Titles:** *Someone Walks By*, by Polly Carlson-Voiles, presents Northwoods animals in their winter habitats. *Wolf Song*, by Mary Bevis, tells of a girl who takes an evening stroll with her uncle to hear the wolves' howls.

Submissions and Payment

Guidelines available at website. Send complete ms. Accepts hard copy and disk submissions (Microsoft Word). SASE. Responds in 8–24 months. Publication in 3–5 years. Royalty, 10–15% of net.

Editor's Comments

Of special interest to us are books about children's outdoor experiences for ages three and up.

Raven Tree Press

1400 Miller Parkway
McHenry, IL 60050

Submissions

Publisher's Interests

Raven Tree Press, a division of Delta Systems Company, Inc., is an independent publisher committed to providing high-quality picture books in a variety of formats—bilingual, English only, and Spanish only.
Website: www.raventreepress.com

Freelance Potential

Published 15 titles in 2010: 2 were by agented authors. Of the 15 titles, 3 were by unpublished writers and 10 were by new authors. Receives 500 unsolicited mss yearly.

- **Fiction:** Publishes early picture books, 0–4 years; easy-to-read books, 4–7 years; and story picture books, 4–10 years. Themes include conflict resolution, family values, and multicultural and ethnic issues.
- **Representative Titles:** *Nathan Saves Summer/Nathan Rescata El Verano,* by Gerry Renert, presents, in English and Spanish, the story of a hippo who dreams of becoming a lifeguard for a small pond and the animals who vacation there each summer. *Rip Squeak and His Friends,* by Susan Yost-Filgate (4+ years), follows a little mouse, his sister, and their newfound animal friends as they encounter adventures in an abandoned summer cottage.

Submissions and Payment

Guidelines and catalogue available at website. Send complete ms with synopsis, author bio, and publishing credits. Accepts hard copy and email to raven@raventreepress.com. SASE. Responds in 1–2 months. Publication period varies. Royalty; advance.

Editor's Comments

We offer our books in a variety of formats because we believe that every child has his own learning style. But we are consistent in choosing books that feature engaging characters and stories that enthrall and amuse.

Rayve Productions

P.O. Box 726
Windsor, CA 95492

Editor: Barbara Ray

Publisher's Interests

Self-help books for adults on a range of subjects, both professional and personal, are the mainstay of Rayve Productions. It also publishes parenting books and a list of children's fiction and nonfiction that includes storybooks, folktales, and books that help children through crises.
Website: www.rayveproductions.com

Freelance Potential

Published 5 titles (1 juvenile) in 2010: 1 was developed from an unsolicited submission. Of the 5 titles, 1 was by an author who was new to the publishing house. Receives 75 unsolicited mss yearly.

- **Fiction:** Publishes easy-to-read books, 4–7 years; story picture books, 4–10 years; and chapter books, 5–10 years. Genres include contemporary, historical, multicultural, and ethnic fiction; folktales; and adventure.
- **Nonfiction:** Publishes chapter books, 5–10 years; middle-grade books, 8–12 years; and young adult books, 12–18 years. Topics include history and biography. Also publishes educational and multicultural titles for teachers and parents.
- **Representative Titles:** *Gracie Gannon: Middle School Zero,* by Mary Elizabeth Anderson (13–15 years), tells of a teen girl who, in overcoming bullying and self-doubt, comes to understand the value of family and true friendship. *Kellie's Book: The Art of the Possible,* by Kellie Greenwald (6+ years), is the autobiography of an accomplished artist with Down syndrome.

Submissions and Payment

Guidelines and catalogue available at website. Send complete ms. Accepts hard copy. SASE. Responds in 6 weeks. Publication in 1 year. Royalty, 10%; advance, varies.

Editor's Comments

We are currently focusing on career-oriented titles, but would certainly welcome an exemplary children's proposal.

Razorbill

Penguin Group
345 Hudson Street, 15th Floor
New York, NY 10014

Editorial Assistant

Publisher's Interests

This imprint of the Penguin Young Readers Group is dedicated to middle-grade and young adult books. Though it puts an emphasis on its fiction list, it also publishes a number of nonfiction titles on pop culture.
Website: www.razorbillbooks.com

Freelance Potential

Published 35–40 titles in 2010. Receives 500 queries yearly.

- **Fiction:** Publishes middle-grade books, 8–12 years; and young adult books, 12–18 years. Genres include contemporary and science fiction, mystery, suspense, and fantasy.
- **Nonfiction:** Publishes middle-grade books, 8–12 years; and young adult books, 12–18 years. Topics include adventure and pop culture.
- **Representative Titles:** *Possessions,* by Nancy Holder (YA), is a chilling tale of possession and hauntings set in an eerie boarding school in California. *I Am a Genius of Unspeakable Evil and I Want to Be Your Class President,* by Josh Lieb (YA), is a comic novel featuring a 12-year-old genius who finds out that trying to become popular in junior high is much harder than overthrowing governments. *The Teen Vogue Handbook: An Insider's Guide to Careers in Fashion,* by the editors of *Vogue* (YA), provides a real-life look at the fashion industry, and what it takes to land a job there.

Submissions and Payment

Catalogue available at website. Query. Accepts hard copy. SASE. Response time and publication period vary. Advance.

Editor's Comments

We are committed to publishing the very best in young adult and middle-grade books. We choose books that will speak to our readers on their level, and present them with stories and characters with whom they can relate. If this describes your project, then we'd like to see it.

Reagent Press Books for Young Readers

P.O. Box 362
East Olympia, WA 98540-0362

Submissions: Jeannie Kim

Publisher's Interests

Children's books and teen fiction comprise the catalogue of this imprint of Reagent Press. Genres range from contemporary to fantasy fiction, while nonfiction subjects center around nature and sports.
Website: www.reagentpress.com

Freelance Potential

Published 15–20 titles in 2010: 7 were by agented authors. Receives 1,200–1,500 queries yearly.

- **Fiction:** Publishes easy-to-read books, 4–7 years; story picture books, 4–10 years; chapter books, 5–10 years; and middle-grade books, 8–12 years. Genres include contemporary and science fiction, fantasy, mystery, suspense, adventure, fairy tales, and stories about insects and nature.
- **Nonfiction:** Publishes easy-to-read books, 4–7 years; story picture books, 4–10 years; chapter books, 5–10 years; and middle-grade books, 8–12 years. Topics include animals, sports, and multicultural and ethnic subjects.
- **Representative Titles:** *Arianna Kelt and the Wizards of Sky-hall,* by J. R. King, is a tale of the adventures of a 12-year-old reformed thief and wizard. *Buster Bee's School Days: Make New Friends,* by Robert Stanek, finds the playful Bugville Critters going to school and making new friends.

Submissions and Payment

Guidelines and catalogue available at website. Query with synopsis and author bio. Accepts email to reagentpress@aol.com. Responds in 1–6 months if interested. Publication period varies. Royalty; advance.

Editor's Comments

If you don't love independent presses and how they work, we're not the right publisher for you. We post open calls at our website that outline the types of books we're interested in during any given period.

Red Deer Press

195 Allstate Parkway
Markham, Ontario L3R 4T8
Canada

Children's Editor: Peter Carver

Publisher's Interests

Red Deer publishes juvenile and young adult fiction, non-fiction, and picture books, as well as science fiction and books about sports and contemporary issues for adults. It prefers work from Canadian authors that features Canadian themes, locations, and subjects.
Website: www.reddeerpress.com

Freelance Potential

Published 15 titles (10 juvenile) in 2010: 2 were by unpublished writers and 4 were by authors who were new to the publishing house. Receives 2,000+ unsolicited mss yearly.

- **Fiction:** Publishes story picture books, 4–10 years; middle-grade books, 8–12 years; and young adult books, 12–18 years. Genres include regional, contemporary, and ethnic fiction; adventure; fantasy; mystery; suspense; and drama.
- **Nonfiction:** Publishes activity books, field guides, and biographies, 4–18 years. Topics include Canadian nature, wildlife, First Nations, history, and personalities.
- **Representative Titles:** *Acting Up,* by Ted Staunton (9–14 years), is a comic novel about a teen boy trying to find a balance between acting in a mature manner and having fun. *The McGuillicuddy Book of Personal Records,* by Colleen Sydor (YA), tells the story of a 13-year-old boy who is obsessed with setting odd records as a way to escape being ordinary.

Submissions and Payment

Guidelines available at website. Send complete ms for picture books and YA fiction. Query with synopsis and sample chapters for other work. Accepts hard copy, email to rdp@reddeerpress.com, and simultaneous submissions. SAE/IRC. Responds in 4–6 months. Publication in 2–3 years. Royalty.

Editor's Comments

Currently, we are focusing less on picture books and more on middle-grade and young adult fiction.

Redleaf Press

10 Yorkton Court
St. Paul, MN 55117

Acquisitions Editor: Kyra Ostendorf

Publisher's Interests
Redleaf Press publishes books and other resources for educa-tors and early childhood care providers who work with chil-dren from birth to age eight.
Website: www.redleafpress.org

Freelance Potential
Published 25 titles in 2010: 24 were developed from unso-licited submissions, and 1 was a reprint/licensed property.
Of the 25 titles, 12 were by unpublished writers and 12 were by authors who were new to the publishing house. Receives 120 queries yearly.

- **Nonfiction:** Publishes curriculum, management, and business resources for early childhood professionals. Topics include math, science, language, literacy, cultural diversity, music, movement, health, safety, nutrition, child development, spe-cial needs, and teacher training and assessment.
- **Representative Titles:** *Incredible, Edible Science,* by Liz Plas-ter & Rick Krustchinsky (4–8 years), provides food activities to nurture science and literacy skills. *The Home Visitor's Manual,* by Sharon Woodward & Donna Hurley, shows how to effectively teach and support family child-care providers.

Submissions and Payment
Guidelines and catalogue available at website. Query with résumé, outline, table of contents, and sample chapters. Accepts email queries to acquisitions@redleafpress.org. Responds in 6 weeks. Publication in 18–24 months. Payment policy varies.

Editor's Comments
Please note that we do not publish books or other materials for children or for parents unless they are directly related to early child care or education issues and practices. All authors must have relevant experience in the field of early childhood education.

Resource Publications

160 East Virginia Street, Suite 290
San Jose, CA 95112

Acquisitions Editor: William Burns

Publisher's Interests

Founded in 1973, Resource Publications specializes in professional resources for pastoral ministry, religious education, and liturgical ministry. For children, it publishes books on faith formation, Christian topics, and children's liturgy. 5% self-, subsidy, co-venture, or co-op published material.
Website: www.rpinet.com

Freelance Potential

Published 6 titles in 2010: 2 were developed from unsolicited submissions. Of the 6 titles, 1 was by an unpublished writer and 1 was by a new author. Receives 60–120 queries yearly.

- **Fiction:** Publishes young adult books, 12–18 years. Genres include religious and spiritual fiction.
- **Nonfiction:** Publishes middle-grade books, 8–12 years; and young adult books, 12–18 years. Topics include prayer, religion, catechism, faith, meditations, the sacraments, and spirituality. Also publishes books on prayer and personal growth.
- **Representative Titles:** *Learning about Liturgy: Catechesis for Children and Their Families,* by Dorothy Kosinski Carola, can be used by teachers to supplement an existing catechetical program, or by parents for home teaching. *Preaching to Adults, Teens, and Children* covers all Sundays and feasts in the three-year cycle and includes reflection questions for the homilist and the church community.

Submissions and Payment

Guidelines and catalogue available at website. Query with clips. Prefers electronic queries via form at website; will accept hard copy and email queries to editor@rpinet.com. Responds in 6–8 weeks. Publication in 9–18 months. Royalty, 8% of net.

Editor's Comments

Our online project proposal form will best help us determine if your idea is a good fit for us.

Rocky River Publishers

P.O. Box 1679
Shepardstown, WV 25443

Acquisitions Editor

Publisher's Interests
Helping children cope with the myriad problems they could encounter from infancy through adulthood is the mission of Rocky River Publishers. Stress, self-esteem, substance abuse prevention, and other social challenges are tackled in books for children as well as for parents and educators.
Website: www.rockyriver.com

Freelance Potential
Published several titles in 2010. Receives 240 queries, 720 unsolicited mss yearly.

- **Fiction:** Publishes toddler books, 0–4 years; easy-to-read books, 4–7 years; story picture books, 4–10 years; and young adult books, 12–18 years. Genres include contemporary, inspirational, and educational fiction.
- **Nonfiction:** Publishes middle-grade books, 8–12 years; and young adult books, 12–18 years. Topics include drug education, self-esteem, stress, youth safety, abuse, health, disabilities, and addiction. Also publishes parenting resources.
- **Representative Titles:** *Alexandra, Keeper of Dreams,* by Mary Alice Baumgardner, is a story of a duck who is unafraid to dream even the most impossible dreams. *The Proud Little Ant,* by Wayne Walker (4–7 years), delivers a delightful message that teaches a simple lesson about pride and bragging.

Submissions and Payment
Guidelines and catalogue available at website. Query or send complete ms. Accepts hard copy. SASE. Response time and publication period vary. Royalty; advance. Flat fee.

Editor's Comments
We put a premium on creativity. Books must be educational and address situations and challenges that many children face in their lives—but that doesn't mean they can't be engaging, entertaining, and fun as well. Teaching lessons through a great story is what we are all about.

Ronsdale Press

3350 West 21st Avenue
Vancouver, British Columbia V6S 1G7
Canada

Director: Ronald B. Hatch

Publisher's Interests

Founded in 1988, Ronsdale is dedicated to publishing books from across Canada—books that give Canadians new insights into themselves and their country. It publishes fiction, regional history, biographies, and children's books—all on Canadian topics or with Canadian themes.
Website: www.ronsdalepress.com

Freelance Potential

Published 13 titles (3 juvenile) in 2010: 8 were developed from unsolicited submissions and 1 was by an agented author. Of the 13 titles, 2 were by unpublished writers and 3 were by authors who were new to the publishing house. Receives 300 queries, 1,200 unsolicited mss yearly.

- **Fiction:** Publishes middle-grade books, 8–12 years; and young adult books, 12–18 years. Genres include Canadian historical fiction. Also publishes books for adults.
- **Nonfiction:** Publishes titles for adults on politics, economics, regional history, and language.
- **Representative Titles:** *Pete's Gold,* by Luanne Armstrong (10+ years), is the story of a teen boy who spends the summer at his grandmother's farm and discovers more there than he bargained for. *Journey to Atlantis,* by Philip Roy (10+ years), follows a Newfoundland boy as he takes his homemade submarine to the Mediterranean in search of Atlantis; part of the Submarine Outlaw series.

Submissions and Payment

Canadian authors only. Guidelines and catalogue available at website. Query with sample chapter; or send complete ms. Accepts hard copy. SASE. Responds in 1–2 months. Publication in 1 year. Royalty, 10%.

Editor's Comments

Our children's books continue to win awards, and we are eager to hear from the next award-winning author.

The Rosen Publishing Group

29 East 21st Street
New York, NY 10010

Editorial Director, YA Division: Iris Rosoff

Publisher's Interests
This publisher produces educational nonfiction books on
guidance and curriculum-based subjects for students in
middle school and high school. Many of its titles are parts
of series. All work is assigned by in-house staff.
Website: www.rosenpublishing.com

Freelance Potential
Published 200 titles in 2010. Of the 200 titles, 5–10 were by
authors who were new to the publishing house. Receives 75
queries yearly.

- **Nonfiction:** Publishes middle-grade books, 10–13 years; and
  young adult books, 13–18 years. Topics include digital and
  information technology, health, science, high-interest topics,
  guidance, careers, and contemporary social issues.
- **Representative Titles:** *First Car Smarts,* by Daniel E. Harmon
  (YA), provides everything the reader needs to know about
  negotiating the deal, warranties, contracts, and loan for a car;
  part of the Get Smart with Your Money series. *Violence Against
  Women,* by Linda Bickerstaff (YA), presents information on this
  public health issue to give the reader an understanding of the
  challenges associated with it; part of the Young Woman's
  Guide to Contemporary Issues series.

Submissions and Payment
Catalogue available at website. All work is assigned. Query
with résumé. Accepts email queries to irisr@rosenpub.com.
Responds in 3 months. Publication in 9 months. Flat fee.

Editor's Comments
We will be broadening our subject areas to include twenty-
first-century literary skills regarding the digital world. All of
our books are assigned by in-house staff. Please send us a
query with a résumé outlining your areas of expertise. We
will contact you if we have an upcoming project that fits
your particular area of knowledge.

Rourke Publishing

1701 Highway A1A, Suite 300
Vero Beach, FL 32963

Editor in Chief: Luana Mitten

Publisher's Interests
Rourke is a publisher of educational book series for kinder-
garten to grade eight. It concentrates on nonfiction series,
and also publishes interactive ebooks. Rourke's series
include Field Trips, Fighting Forces, the Study of Money,
Action Sports, Eye on History Graphic Illustrated, and a new
Factoscope science series.
Website: www.rourkepublishing.com

Freelance Potential
Published 150–200 titles in 2010: many were freelance or
written by contract writers, including previously unpublished
authors.

- **Nonfiction:** Publishes picture books, 4–10 years; early readers
  and chapter books, 5–10 years; and middle-grade books, 9–12
  years. Topics include science, social studies, reading adventures, reference, and sports.
- **Representative Titles:** *Hiking,* by Julie K. Lundren (grades
  4–8), is one in a series about outdoor adventures. *Using Scientific Tools,* by Susan Meredith (grades 4–8), provides illustrations and explanations of tools used in a range of sciences.

Submissions and Payment
Query with résumé, indicating the topic and age of interest
to you. Accepts hard copy and email queries to luana@
rourkepublishing.com. Guidelines are sent to writers with
their contracts. Work-for-hire, with a choice of 20% when the
ms is approved and 80% after proofs, or a single payment
after proofs.

Editor's Comments
We look for factual accuracy and objectivity, and for writers
who understand the interests of children and how to write in
such a way that gives them age-appropriate reading support.

Royal Fireworks Press

41 First Avenue
P.O. Box 399
Unionville, NY 10988

Submissions: William Neumann

Publisher's Interests
This publisher of gifted education materials provides teachers, administrators, and parents with the resources they need to enrich and expand the experiences of gifted and talented children. It produces books on all core curriculum subjects. **Website: www.rfwp.com**

Freelance Potential
Published 100 titles in 2010. Of the 100 titles, 50 were by authors who were new to the publishing house. Receives 300 unsolicited mss yearly.

- **Fiction:** Publishes chapter books, 5–10 years; middle-grade books, 8–12 years; and young adult books, 12–18 years. Genres include contemporary, historical, Western, and science fiction; folklore; adventure; and mystery.
- **Nonfiction:** Publishes chapter books, 5–10 years; middle-grade books, 8–12 years; and young adult books, 12–18 years. Topics include creative problem solving, logic, strategy, memory enhancement, guidance, leadership, science, math, social studies, history, philosophy, the arts, and language arts. Also publishes books on the education of gifted students.
- **Representative Titles:** *The Eerie Canal,* by Jack Reber (8–12 years), is a historical novel in which students on a class trip to the Erie Canal are transported back in time and into the middle of a mystery. *Creative Encounters,* by Barbara Fisher Mizer, provides teachers with lesson plans for teaching writing.

Submissions and Payment
Guidelines and catalogue available at website. Send complete ms; include synopsis for fiction. Accepts hard copy. No simultaneous submissions. SASE. Responds in 1 month. Publication in 8 months. Royalty.

Editor's Comments
We are proud to support the efforts of homeschooling parents as well as school teachers.

Rubicon Publishing

281 Wyecroft Road
Oakville, Ontario L6K 2H2
Canada

Editorial Director: Amy Land

Publisher's Interests
Rubicon publishes educational resources designed to improve literacy and promote interest in language arts, math, and social studies. It also publishes trade fiction and nonfiction.
Website: www.rubiconpublishing.com

Freelance Potential
Published 200 titles (195 juvenile) in 2010. Of the 200 titles, 10 were by unpublished writers and 20 were by new authors. Receives 60 queries yearly.

- **Fiction:** Publishes early picture books, 0–4 years; easy-to-read books, 4–7 years; story picture books, 4–10 years; chapter books, 5–10 years; middle-grade books, 8–12 years; and young adult books, 12–18 years. Features fiction of all genres. Also publishes poetry and graphic novels.
- **Nonfiction:** Publishes early picture books, 0–4 years; easy-to-read books, 4–7 years; story picture books, 4–10 years; chapter books, 5–10 years; middle-grade books, 8–12 years; and young adult books, 12–18 years. Topics include current events, curriculum topics, entertainment, humor, social issues, sports, and multicultural and ethnic issues. Also publishes educational resources.
- **Representative Titles:** *The 10 Deadliest Sea Creatures* (grades 4–7) presents facts about these creatures; part of The 10 series. *In The Park* (grade 1) depicts the fun that can be enjoyed in the park; part of the Boldprint series.

Submissions and Payment
Catalogue available at website. All work is assigned. Query with clips. Accepts hard copy and email to submissions@rubiconpublishing.com. SASE. Response time varies. Publication in 1 year. Royalty.

Editor's Comments
All of our educational resources are assigned. Our trade books are not, but we do not publish many of those.

St. Anthony Messenger Press

28 West Liberty Street
Cincinnati, OH 45202

Editorial Director: Lisa Biedenbach

Publisher's Interests

This well-established Catholic publisher offers books and DVDs for faith formation in both children and adults. Its catalogue is filled with titles on Catholic life and identity, prayer, spirituality, Franciscanism, Scripture, saints, and Catholic heroes. It supports the ministry and charities of the Franciscan Friars of St. John the Baptist Province.
Website: www.americancatholic.org

Freelance Potential

Published 12 titles in 2010: 5 were by unpublished writers and 9 were by authors who were new to the publishing house. Receives 800 queries yearly.

- **Nonfiction:** Publishes books for parents, ministers, and religious education teachers. Topics include Christian living, personal growth, faith, the sacraments, Scripture, prayer, spirituality, the saints, marriage, family, and parenting.
- **Representative Titles:** *I Choose God,* by Chris Cuddy & Peter Ericksen (YA), features 21 testimonies in which young Catholics share their search for truth in a world increasingly free of values and lasting peace. *Love in the Little Things: Tales of Family Life,* by Mike Aquilina (parents), spins humorous stories of how God can give us a family life filled with laughter and love, and shows how moms, dads, and kids are happier when they lay down their lives for one another.

Submissions and Payment

Guidelines and catalogue available at website. Query with sample chapter and outline. Accepts hard copy. SASE. Responds in 2–3 months. Publication in 1–2 years. Royalty, 10%; advance, $1,000–$3,000.

Editor's Comments

We're interested in reviewing manuscripts that inspire, inform, and connect adult Catholic Christians so that they can better understand their faith.

Saint Mary's Press

702 Terrace Heights
Winona, MN 55987-1318

Submissions Coordinator: Linda Waldo

Publisher's Interests
The mission of Saint Mary's Press is to share the Good News
of Jesus Christ with Catholic youth aged 10 through 19. It
publishes religious education textbooks, parish and youth
ministry resources, Bibles and supplemental resources, and
teen spirituality resources.
Website: www.smp.org

Freelance Potential
Published 30 titles (15 juvenile) in 2010. Of the 30 titles, 8
were by authors who were new to the publishing house.
Receives 240 queries yearly.

- **Nonfiction:** Publishes middle-grade books, 8–12 years; and
  young adult books, 12–18 years. Topics include spirituality,
  Christianity, and the Catholic faith. Also publishes titles for
  adults who teach or minister to youth.
- **Representative Titles:** *World Religions: A Voyage of Discovery,*
  by Jeffrey Brodd (grades 11–12), helps students understand
  the people, dimensions, and principles of the world's major
  religions. *Love, Reason, and God's Story,* by David Cloutier
  (grades 12 and up), presents the basics of the history of
  Catholic teaching on sexual ethics, particularly as it has
  evolved in the last half century.

Submissions and Payment
Guidelines available at website. Query with synopsis, table
of contents, introduction, sample chapter, author bio, and
list of publishing credits. Accepts hard copy, email to
submissions@smp.org (Microsoft Word attachments), and
simultaneous submissions if identified. SASE. Responds in
2 months. Publication in 12–18 months. Royalty, 10%.

Editor's Comments
Before sending your proposal, ask yourself if your book or
resource is clearly in touch with the needs of our audience,
and whether it offers something new, significant, or unique.

Salina Bookshelf

3120 North Caden Court, Suite 4
Flagstaff, AZ 86004

Editor: LaFrenda Frank

Publisher's Interests

Salina Bookshelf is an independent publisher of textbooks, picture books, reference books, and electronic media that offer authentic depictions of Navajo life, both contemporary and traditional.
Website: www.salinabookshelf.com

Freelance Potential

Published 10 titles in 2010: 5 were developed from unsolicited submissions and 3 were reprint/licensed properties. Of the 10 titles, 2 were by unpublished writers and 6 were by new authors. Receives 120–144 unsolicited mss yearly.

- **Fiction:** Publishes toddler books and early picture books, 0–4 years; easy-to-read books, 4–7 years; story picture books, 4–10 years; chapter books, 5–10 years; middle-grade books, 8–12 years; and young adult books, 12–18 years. Genres include folklore, folktales, multicultural and ethnic fiction, and stories about nature and the environment. Also publishes bilingual Navajo/English books, 4–7 years.
- **Nonfiction:** Publishes middle-grade books, 8–12 years; and young adult books, 12–18 years. Topics include Navajo history and culture. Also publishes biographies.
- **Representative Titles:** *Frog Brings Rain,* by Patricia Hruby Powell, is a retelling of a Navajo folktale about a mysterious frog who saves a village from fire. *Proud To Be a Blacksheep,* by Roberta John, is the story of a young Navajo girl growing up off her reservation.

Submissions and Payment

Guidelines and catalogue available at website. Send complete ms. Accepts hard copy. SASE. Responds in 3 weeks. Publication in 1 year. Royalty, varies; advance, varies.

Editor's Comments

Though we have not published many novels, we are certainly open to this type of submission.

Samhain Publishing

577 Mulberry Street, Suite 1520
Macon, GA 31201

Executive Editor: Laurie Rauch

Publisher's Interests

Romance fiction is the specialty of Samhain Publishing. It features all types of romance, including fantasy, celtic, and science fiction with romantic elements. Adults are the target audience, although many of its titles appeal to young adult readers. While most of its books are published in digital format, it does produce a few titles for the print market.
Website: www.samhainpublishing.com

Freelance Potential

Published 240 titles (2–3 juvenile) in 2010. Receives 1,824 queries yearly.

- **Fiction:** Does not currently publish young adult novels, although has published them as recently as 2009 and may do so again in the future. Genres include contemporary fiction, romance, fantasy, urban fantasy, and science fiction.
- **Representative Titles:** *The Ankh of Isis,* by Christine Norris (YA), is a fantasy about a teen girl who is trying to protect a secret library of magical books from prying houseguests, one of whom is an attractive teen boy. *The Vampire . . . In My Dreams,* by Terry Lee Wilde (YA), features the entanglements of a young witch and a handsome vampire.

Submissions and Payment

Guidelines available at website. Query with 2–5 page synopsis and 3+ sample chapters. Accepts email queries to editor@samhainpublishing.com (Microsoft Word or RTF attachments) and simultaneous submissions if identified. Responds in 3–4 months. Publication period varies. Royalty, 30–40% of retail.

Editor's Comments

At this point, we are only accepting romance, erotica, and fantasy/urban and fantasy/science fiction with romantic elements. We're not currently accepting young adult titles, but check our website for updates.

Sandlapper Publishing

P.O. Box 730
Orangeburg, SC 29116

Managing Editor: Amanda Gallman

Publisher's Interests

Sandlapper's mission is to celebrate South Carolina's rich heritage through books for children and adults. It publishes nonfiction titles about the region's history, folklore, culture, recreation, and natural history.
Website: www.sandlapperpublishing.com

Freelance Potential

Published 4–6 titles (3 juvenile) in 2010. Receives 150 queries yearly.

- **Nonfiction:** Publishes easy-to-read books, 4–7 years; story picture books, 4–10 years; chapter books, 5–10 years; middle-grade books, 8–12 years; and young adult books, 12–18 years. Topics include South Carolina history, flora, fauna, travel, culture, literature, and cooking.
- **Representative Titles:** *The Mysterious Tail of a Charleston Cat,* by Ruth Paterson Chappell & Bess Paterson Shipe, uses a feline tour guide to introduce children to historic Charleston and the Ashley River Plantations. *Spirits & Legends of the South Carolina Sea Islands,* by Margie Willis Clary, explains the superstitions and spooky folktales of the region. *Brave Black Patriots,* by Idella Bodie (8+ years), provides the life stories of black Americans who served in South Carolina battles.

Submissions and Payment

Guidelines and catalogue available at website. Query with outline, résumé, and writing samples. Accepts hard copy and email queries to agallman@sandlapperpublishing.com. SASE. Responds in 2 months. Publication in 2 years. Royalty, 15% of net.

Editor's Comments

We're looking to publish inspiring and informative books that include an unusual angle or different approach to educating readers about South Carolina. The work must be well researched and show potential for strong sales.

Sasquatch Books

119 South Main Street, Suite 400
Seattle, WA 98104

Acquisitions Editor: Terence Meikel

Publisher's Interests

Books about the Pacific Northwest, Alaska, and California are the focus of this regional publisher. Its children's catalogue features nonfiction on nature and travel, as well as fiction set in the region.
Website: www.sasquatchbooks.com

Freelance Potential

Published 42 titles (7 juvenile) in 2010: 2 were developed from unsolicited submissions and 6 were by agented authors. Of the 42 titles, 10 were by unpublished writers. Receives 3,000 queries, 2,700 unsolicited mss yearly.

- **Fiction:** Publishes concept books, toddler books, and early picture books, 0–4 years; and easy-to-read books, 4–7 years. Genres include regional, historical, multicultural, and ethnic fiction, and stories about animals and nature.
- **Nonfiction:** Publishes concept books, toddler books, and early picture books, 0–4 years; easy-to-read books, 4–7 years; and young adult books, 12–18 years. Topics include the Pacific Northwest, Canada, Alaska, and California.
- **Representative Titles:** *Alaska Animal Babies,* by Deb Vanasse, shows off a variety of Alaskan animal babies and offers interesting facts about their lives. *Catwalk,* by Jasper Tomkins, follows seven cats who, when out for a walk with their owner, exhibit some very silly, un-catlike behavior.

Submissions and Payment

Guidelines and catalogue available. Query or send complete ms. Accepts hard copy. SASE. Responds in 1–3 months. Publication period and payment policy vary.

Editor's Comments

We are happy to evaluate full manuscripts or queries. What matters most to us is that the work shows the potential for capturing young readers' interest and imagination. Be sure to let us know about you as well as your project.

Scarecrow Press

4501 Forbes Boulevard, Suite 200
Lanham, MD 20706

Acquisitions Editor

Publisher's Interests
In addition to scholarly bibliographies, historical dictionaries, and reference works in the humanities, Scarecrow Press publishes books about library and information science, and how it relates to children's programming.
Website: www.scarecrowpress.com

Freelance Potential
Published 180 titles in 2010: 115 were developed from unsolicited submissions and 9 were by agented authors. Receives 1,200 queries, 240 unsolicited mss yearly.

- **Nonfiction:** Publishes handbooks, reference tools, bibliographies, historical dictionaries, library science monographs, and other scholarly and professional works. Topics include the humanities, history, geography, religion, social and multicultural issues, ancient civilizations, music, and science.
- **Representative Titles:** *Library Programs for Teens: Mystery Theater,* by Karen J. Siwak, provides complete instructions for creating a successful mystery theater program that will draw teens to the library. *Animals in Young Adult Fiction,* by Walter Hogan, examines several hundred novels and stories to explore the ways in which animals and adolescents have connected.

Submissions and Payment
Guidelines and catalogue available at website. Query with résumé, tentative titles, synopsis, table of contents, market analysis, and 2 sample chapters; or send complete ms. Accepts hard copy and email to mboggs@rowman.com (Microsoft Word attachments). SASE. Responds in 1–2 months. Publication in 6–12 months. Royalty, 8–12.5%.

Editor's Comments
We look for proposals that represent new treatments of traditional topics, original scholarship in developing areas, and cogent synthesis of existing research.

Scholastic Children's Books

Euston House
24 Eversholt Street
London NW1 1DB
United Kingdom

Editorial Department

Publisher's Interests
Dedicated to developing reading and literacy in children and supporting parents and teachers, this children's publisher creates books that educate, entertain, and motivate children of all ages.

Website: www.scholastic.co.uk

Freelance Potential
Published 200 titles in 2010: most were by agented authors. Receives 350–400 queries yearly.

- **Fiction:** Publishes concept books, toddler books, and early picture books, 0–4 years; easy-to-read books, 4–7 years; story picture books, 4–10 years; chapter books, 5–10 years; middle-grade books, 8–12 years; and young adult books, 12–18 years. Genres include contemporary and historical fiction, adventure, drama, and fantasy.
- **Nonfiction:** Publishes chapter books, 5–10 years. Topics include geography, history, math, and sports.
- **Representative Titles:** *What I Saw and How I Lied,* by Judy Blundell, is a coming-of-age tale set just after World War II that features a girl torn between her family and the GI she loves. *Havoc,* by Chris Wooding, is a fantasy novel in which a teen must return to a terrifying world inside a comic book in order to save the friend he left there.

Submissions and Payment
Guidelines and catalogue available at website. Query with outline/synopsis and 3 sample chapters. Accepts hard copy. SAE/IRC. Response time, publication period, and payment policy vary.

Editor's Comments
We receive an enormous number of proposals. To make yours stand out, be sure it is well prepared and professional. Don't get discouraged if we do not choose yours. This can be a frustrating business, but keep at it.

Scholastic Press

557 Broadway
New York, NY 10012

Senior Editor: Jennifer Rees

Publisher's Interests
As a division of publishing giant Scholastic Inc., Scholastic Press markets hardcover books in a variety of genres for the very youngest readers through young adults. Picture books, chapter books, novels, and biographies all appear on its list.
Website: www.scholastic.com

Freelance Potential
Published 40–50 titles in 2010. Receives 3,000 queries each year.

- **Fiction:** Publishes toddler books and early picture books, 0–4 years; story picture books, 4–10 years; chapter books, 5–10 years; middle-grade books, 8–12 years; and young adult books, 12–18 years. Genres include contemporary and science fiction, adventure, fantasy, humor, and mystery.
- **Nonfiction:** Publishes story picture books, 4–10 years; chapter books, 5–10 years; middle-grade books, 8–12 years; and young adult books, 12–18 years. Topics include history, nature, the environment, and multicultural subjects. Also publishes biographies and humor.
- **Representative Titles:** *Tentacles,* by Roland Smith (9–12 years), is an adventure novel featuring twins who follow their scientist uncle on an expedition to New Zealand to study a mythical sea creature. *I'm a Turkey,* by Jim Arnosky (4–8 years), provides young readers with an up-close-and-personal look at wild turkeys.

Submissions and Payment
Agented authors only. Guidelines available. Accepts hard copy. SASE. Responds in 2–3 weeks. Publication in 1–2 years. Royalty; advance.

Editor's Comments
Because we receive thousands of submissions each year, we can only accept queries from agented authors and writers we have worked with in the past.

Scholastic Trade Paperback Division

557 Broadway
New York, NY 10012

Group Publisher: Suzanne Murphy

Publisher's Interests

Scholastic's Trade Paperback Division offers a variety of chapter books and novels for readers of all ages, many of which are published in series format. It also creates nonfiction, on topics ranging from nature and science to sports. It considers submissions made through literary agents or from authors who have written for Scholastic in the past.
Website: www.scholastic.com

Freelance Potential

Published 600 titles in 2010: each was by an agented author. Receives 250 queries, 150 unsolicited mss yearly.

- **Fiction:** Publishes chapter books, 5–10 years; middle-grade books, 8–12 years; and young adult books, 12–18 years. Genres include contemporary and science fiction, fantasy, adventure, and romance. Also publishes humor, scary stories, and stories about sports, animals, and friendship.
- **Nonfiction:** Publishes books for children of all ages. Topics include animals, science, nature, and multicultural issues.
- **Representative Titles:** *Firehouse!,* by Mark Teague (preK–K), is a hilarious story about the misadventures of two children who spend a day at the firehouse learning how to be firefighters. *The Dead End,* by Mimi McCoy (grades 3–7), is a ghost story about a girl who spends a summer with her parents restoring a creepy, creaky old house.

Submissions and Payment

Accepts submissions through literary agents and from previous Scholastic authors only. SASE. Response time, publication period, and payment policy vary.

Editor's Comments

Our editors will always take a look at exciting, imaginative stories that will spark a love of reading in children and young adults. Have your agent contact us with your most creative work.

Science, Naturally!

725 8th Street SE
Washington, DC 20003

President: Dia L. Michels

Publisher's Interests

This independent press is committed to increasing science and math literacy among students. It publishes books for students and educational resources for teachers of pre-school through high school that make the topics accessible and fun.

Website: www.sciencenaturally.com

Freelance Potential

Published 4 titles in 2010: 2 were developed from unsolicited submissions. Of the 4 titles, 4 were by unpublished writers and 2 were by authors who were new to the publishing house. Receives 240 queries yearly.

- **Nonfiction:** Publishes concept books and early picture books, 0–4 years; easy-to-read books, 4–7 years; story picture books, 4–10 years; chapter books, 5–10 years; middle-grade books, 8–12 years; and young adult books, 12–18 years. Topics include science and mathematics.
- **Representative Titles:** *If My Mom Were a Platypus: Mammal Babies and Their Mothers,* by Dia L. Michels, introduces young readers to biology by showing them how several types of mammal babies eat, learn, and grow. *101 Things Everyone Should Know About Math,* by Marc Zev et al., uses a simple Q&A format and real-life situations to broaden the reader's understanding of math concepts.

Submissions and Payment

Guidelines and catalogue available at website. Query. Accepts hard copy and simultaneous submissions if identified. SASE. Response time varies. Publication in 9–12 months. Royalty. Flat fee.

Editor's Comments

We will consider publishing material that fits our mission to make science and math accessible, understandable, and fun for everyone. If your material isn't fun, it's not for us.

Scobre Press Corporation

2255 Calle Clara
La Jolla, CA 92037

Editor: Scott Blumenthal

Publisher's Interests

This publisher's mission is to foster a love of literature in children and teens who may be reluctant to pick up a book. Each of its fiction and nonfiction titles is available on two reading levels. Scobre Press markets its books to elementary, middle, and high schools across the U.S.

Website: www.scobre.com

Freelance Potential

Published 6 titles in 2010. Of the 6 titles, 2 were by unpublished writers and 4 were by authors who were new to the publishing house. Receives 10–15 queries yearly.

- **Fiction:** Publishes middle-grade books, 8–12 years; and young adult books, 12–18 years. Features stories about sports, dance, and music.
- **Nonfiction:** Publishes middle-grade books, 8–12 years; and young adult books, 12–18 years. Topics include sports, dance, music, and video games. Also publishes teacher resources.
- **Representative Titles:** *The Green,* by Justin Reichman (grades 3–5), tells the story of an overweight boy who learns through golf that he might be much more than just "the fat kid who's good for a laugh." *Emerald,* by Christine Webster (grades 3–5), features a girl who learns that making it big in the entertainment industry isn't as easy or glamorous as it seems.

Submissions and Payment

Guidelines available via email to info@scobre.com. Query. Accepts hard copy and email to info@scobre.com. SASE. Responds in 1 week. Publication in 6 months. Royalty, 12%.

Editor's Comments

To engage our audience, we need books that are realistic and incorporate elements of pop culture and the modern world. All of the protagonists in the stories we publish are young people, not adults.

Seal Press

1700 Fourth Street
Berkeley, CA 94710

Senior Editor: Brooke Warner

Publisher's Interests
Since 1976, Seal Press has grown from a small producer of
strictly feminist books to a publisher of titles that inform,
reveal, engage, delight, and support women of all ages and
backgrounds. Its books take an edgy, honest, and sometimes comedic approach to women's issues, parenting,
gender, sexuality, careers, and current affairs.
Website: www.sealpress.com

Freelance Potential
Published 25 titles in 2010: 1–2 were developed from unsolicited submissions. Receives 600 queries yearly.

- **Nonfiction:** Publishes young adult books, 12–18 years. Topics
  include health, sexuality, abuse, politics, travel, and other
  women's issues. Also publishes parenting titles and books
  for adults.
- **Representative Titles:** *Invisible Girls: The Truth About Sexual
  Abuse,* by Patti Feuereisen & Caroline Pincus, presents the
  stories of girls who have been abused and discusses the
  healing process. *Girldrive: Criss-Crossing America, Redefining
  Feminism,* by Nona Willis Aronowitz & Emma Bee Bernstein,
  profiles 127 women, from well-known feminists to women
  who don't relate to feminism at all, about the topics and
  issues that are most important to them.

Submissions and Payment
Guidelines and catalogue available at website. Query with
outline, sample chapter, and author bio. Accepts hard copy.
SASE. Responds in 6–8 weeks. Publication period and payment policy vary.

Editor's Comments
With each book, we strive to make a difference in women's
everyday lives, and to tell the truth—the real truth—about
the issues that matter most to women. If your book can be
part of that mission, we invite you to query.

Second Story Press

20 Maud Street, Suite 401
Toronto, Ontario M5V 2M5
Canada

Editorial Manager

Publisher's Interests
This Canadian publisher, founded in 1988, is dedicated to feminist-inspired books for adults and young readers. It works almost exclusively with Canadian authors.
Website: www.secondstorypress.ca

Freelance Potential
Published 15 titles (10 juvenile) in 2010. Of the 15 titles, 2 were by unpublished writers and 6 were by authors who were new to the publishing house. Receives 250 queries, 300 unsolicited mss yearly.

- **Fiction:** Publishes story picture books, 4–10 years; chapter books, 5–10 years; middle-grade books, 8–12 years; and young adult books, 12–18 years. Genres include mystery and historical, contemporary, and multicultural fiction.
- **Nonfiction:** Publishes middle-grade books, 8–12 years; and young adult books, 12–18 years. Topics include history, nature, the environment, contemporary social issues, family life, and ethics. Also publishes parenting titles.
- **Representative Titles:** *A Friend Like Zilla,* by Rachna Gilmore (8–13 years), is the story of the endearing friendship between two teen friends, one of them developmentally disabled. *An Alien in My House,* by Shenaaz Nanji (4–8 years), is a story picture book that examines the sometimes funny dynamics when different generations live under the same roof.

Submissions and Payment
Preference given to Canadian authors. Guidelines and catalogue available at website. Prefers query with outline and sample chapters; will accept complete ms. Accepts hard copy. SAE/IRC. Responds in 4–6 months. Publication period varies. Royalty; advance.

Editor's Comments
We look for books dealing with the diverse and varied aspects of the lives of girls and women.

Seedling Publications

520 East Bainbridge
Elizabeth, PA 17022

Managing Editor: Megan Bergonzi

Publisher's Interests
Seedling Publications, part of Continental Press, focuses on fiction and nonfiction leveled readers that support early literacy in students in preschool through grade two. It also publishes nonfiction resource books for parents and educators regarding mathematics, learning, and test prep.
Website: www.continentalpress.com

Freelance Potential
Published 50+ titles (40 juvenile) in 2010: 5 were developed from unsolicited submissions. Receives 240 unsolicited mss each year.

- **Fiction:** Publishes easy-to-read books, 4–7 years. Genres include fairy tales, adventure, and humor. Also publishes workbooks and stories about sports and nature.
- **Nonfiction:** Publishes easy-to-read books, 4–7 years. Topics include nature, science, technology, mathematics, animals, and multicultural subjects. Also publishes workbooks.
- **Representative Titles:** *Sherman in the Talent Show,* by Betty Erickson (grades K–2), follows a dog named Sherman as he participates in a school show; part of the Sherman Collection series. *Help Your Child Get Ready for Math* (parents) provides tips for parents to help reinforce math concepts. *Toad or Frog?* (grades K–2) introduces young readers to the amphibian world while strengthening reading skills.

Submissions and Payment
Guidelines and catalogue available. Send complete ms. Accepts hard copy and simultaneous submissions if identified. SASE. Responds in 6 months. Publication in 1 year. Payment policy varies.

Editor's Comments
Familiarity with Reading Recovery, guided reading, and other reading intervention programs will give you a sense of the kinds of materials we are seeking.

Servant Books

P.O. Box 7015
Ann Arbor, MI 48107

Editorial Director: Cynthia Cavnar

Publisher's Interests

With its mission of "nourishing the Christian mind and strengthening the Christian heart," this imprint of St. Anthony Messenger Press publishes books for young adults, parents, and religious educators on Christian living, marriage, family life, prayer, and spirituality.
Website: www.servantbooks.org

Freelance Potential

Published 14 titles in 2010: 1 was a reprint/licensed property. Of the 14 titles, 2 were by unpublished writers and 5 were by authors who were new to the publishing house. Receives 150 queries yearly.

- **Nonfiction:** Publishes young adult books, 12–18 years. Also publishes books for parents and teachers. Topics include Christian living, the sacraments, Scripture, prayer, spirituality, popular apologetics, church teaching, Mary, the saints, charismatic renewal, marriage, family life, and popular psychology.
- **Representative Titles:** *I Choose God: Stories from Young Catholics,* by Chris Cuddy & Peter Ericksen (YA), shares the testimonies of 21 young Catholics about their search for God in an ever-challenging world. *Ask the Bible Geek 2,* by Mark Hart (YA), uses equal parts wisdom and wit to answer teens' tough questions about contemporary social issues.

Submissions and Payment

Guidelines and catalogue available at website. Query with outline. Accepts hard copy. SASE. Responds in 2–3 months. Publication in 1–2 years. Royalty, 10%; advance, $1,000.

Editor's Comments

While we do publish books for young adults regarding faith and spirituality, we do not publish children's books and we will not accept proposals for religious-themed fiction. We encourage you to write in a conversational style and to offer practical advice.

Shen's Books

1547 Palos Verdes Mall, #291
Walnut Creek, CA 94597

Owner: Renee Ting

Publisher's Interests
Stories that introduce young children to the cultures of Asia
and Asian Americans are the speciality of this publisher. For
25 years it has been offering books that emphasize cultural
diversity and tolerance.
Website: www.shens.com

Freelance Potential
Published 2 titles in 2010: each was developed from an
unsolicited submission. Of the 2 titles, 1 was by an unpublished writer and 1 was by an author who was new to the
publishing house. Receives 600 unsolicited mss yearly.

- **Fiction:** Publishes story picture books, 4–10 years. Genres
  include fairy tales, folklore, and historical and multicultural
  fiction about Asia and its people.
- **Nonfiction:** Publishes story picture books, 4–10 years. Topics
  include world cultures and immigrants.
- **Representative Titles:** *Maneki Neko: The Tale of the Beckon-
  ing Cat,* by Susan Lendroth (4–8 years), retells a Japanese legend about a cat that saves a samurai's life and brings good
  fortune to a temple and its surrounding village. *The Wishing
  Tree,* by Roseanne Thong (6–10 years), is the story of a boy's
  love for his grandmother, the excitement of making wishes,
  and the futility of making unrealistic wishes.

Submissions and Payment
Guidelines available at website. Send complete ms with
author biography and publishing history. Accepts hard copy
and simultaneous submissions if identified. SASE. Responds
in 6–12 months. Publication in 18–24 months. Payment
policy varies.

Editor's Comments
We're only reviewing picture book manuscripts of fewer than
2,500 words. Remember that our focus is on introducing
children to Asian cultures.

Simon Pulse

Simon & Schuster Children's Publishing
1230 Avenue of the Americas
New York, NY 10020

Submissions Editor

Publisher's Interests

Novels and nonfiction that appeal to a teen audience are the specialty of Simon Pulse. This Simon & Schuster imprint does not shy away from edgy, contemporary issues that are relevant to today's high schoolers. It publishes original and reprint titles, as well as books in series.
Website: http://kids.simonandschuster.com

Freelance Potential

Published 100 titles in 2010. Of the 100 titles, 10 were by authors who were new to the publishing house.

- **Fiction:** Publishes young adult books, 12–18 years. Genres include contemporary, inspirational, ethnic, and multicultural fiction; mystery; suspense; fantasy; drama; and horror.
- **Nonfiction:** Publishes young adult books, 12–18 years. Topics include age-appropriate social issues.
- **Representative Titles:** *Getting Revenge on Lauren Wood,* by Eileen Cook (14+ years), is a novel about a girl who publicly humiliates her best friend so she can begin high school as one of the "it" girls—never suspecting the revenge her ex-best friend is plotting against her. *Bleeding Violet,* by Dia Reeves (14+ years), follows a girl who has a reputation for being a "freak" as she travels to a new town in Texas and discovers the town's terrifying dark secrets.

Submissions and Payment

Guidelines available. Query with outline and author biography. Accepts hard copy. SASE. Response time, publication period, and payment policy vary.

Editor's Comments

Send us ideas for books that teens want to read. The topics can be a little controversial—teen sexuality, adolescent angst, and drug use are not off limits. But the topics must be explored in a way that resonates with contemporary teens. You must be able to speak the language of your audience.

Simon & Schuster Books for Young Readers

Simon & Schuster Children's Publishing
1230 Avenue of the Americas
New York, NY 10020

Submissions Editor

Publisher's Interests

Hardcover and paperback books for children of all ages are marketed under this imprint of Simon & Schuster. It publishes picture books, chapter books, and novels for teens and tweens in a variety of genres, while also offering nonfiction, biographies, and anthologies.
Website: http://kids.simonandschuster.com

Freelance Potential

Published 90 titles in 2010: 60 were by agented authors. Receives 10,000 queries yearly.

- **Fiction:** Publishes toddler books and early picture books, 0–4 years; easy-to-read books, 4–7 years; story picture books, 4–10 years; chapter books, 5–10 years; middle-grade books, 8–12 years; and young adult books, 12–18 years. Genres include contemporary, historical, and multicultural fiction; mystery; fantasy; folklore; and fairy tales.
- **Nonfiction:** Publishes story picture books, 4–10 years; middle-grade books, 8–12 years; and young adult books, 12–18 years. Topics include social issues, science, nature, math, and history. Also publishes anthologies and biographies.
- **Representative Titles:** *The Rabbit Problem,* by Emily Gravett (4–8 years), is a funny story with a surprise pop-up ending about a growing brood of rabbits and how they cope with the challenges presented by the changing seasons. *The Book of Spells,* by Kate Brian (14+ years), takes the reader back 100 years to a private school that teaches a coven of witches; part of the Private series.

Submissions and Payment

Guidelines available. Catalogue available at website. Query with outline/synopsis. Accepts hard copy. SASE. Responds in 2 months. Publication in 2–4 years. Royalty; advance.

Editor's Comments

Your submission must be of award-winning quality to be considered for publication.

Small Horizons

34 Church Street
Liberty Corner, NJ 07938

Acquisitions Editor: P. Patty

Publisher's Interests
Established in 1992, this imprint of New Horizon Press publishes a "Let's Talk" series that uses stories and interesting characters to teach children crisis, coping, tolerance, and service skills. It also publishes books for parents and teachers.
Website: www.newhorizonpressbooks.com

Freelance Potential
Published 2 titles in 2010. Receives 192+ queries yearly.

- **Fiction:** Publishes story picture books, 4–10 years. Themes include coping with anger, anxiety, divorce, grief, and violence; understanding ADHD; and fostering tolerance.
- **Nonfiction:** Publishes easy-to-read books, 4–7 years; and story picture books, 4–10 years. Also publishes parenting books and books for adults who work with children. Topics include coping with anger, anxiety, divorce, grief, and violence; hyperactive and aggressive children; tolerance; and services.
- **Representative Titles:** *Paul the Pack Rat,* by Vickie J. Belmore & Corey Hoover (4–9 years), uses the story of a group of animal friends to teach the value of sharing. *My Stick Family,* by Natalie June Reilly & Brandi J. Pavese (4–9 years), is the tender story of a boy who comes to realize that the love of family doesn't disappear when parents divorce.

Submissions and Payment
Guidelines and catalogue available at website. Query with résumé, outline, 2 sample chapters, and market comparison. Accepts hard copy and email queries to nhp@ newhorizonpressbooks.com. Availability of artwork improves chance of acceptance. SASE. Responds in 3 months. Publication period varies. Royalty, 7.5% of net; advance.

Editor's Comments
Most of our titles are written by mental health professionals or educators. Please convey your professional expertise in your query.

Smith and Kraus

P.O. Box 127
Lyme, NH 03768

Editor: Marisa Kraus

Publisher's Interests
Smith and Kraus publishes the kinds of books that fill the bookshelves of working actors, theater professionals, and theater teachers. Its catalogue consists of essential books for the theater community, including collections of plays for community theater or classroom use, and books about acting and stage production.
Website: www.smithandkraus.com

Freelance Potential
Published 35 titles (10 juvenile) in 2010. Of the 35 titles, 17 were by authors who were new to the publishing house. Receives 100 queries yearly.

- **Fiction:** Publishes collections of plays, scenes, and monologues, grades K–12. Also publishes anthologies, translations, and collections of works by contemporary playwrights.
- **Nonfiction:** Publishes instructional books for teachers, grades K–12. Topics include theater history, stage production, Shakespeare, movement, and dramatizing literature.
- **Representative Titles:** *Meisner for Teens: A Life of True Acting,* by Larry Silverberg (YA), explains the Meisner acting technique to teen actors. *The Liar,* adapted by David Ives, features a new adaptation of the Pierre Corneille comedy, essays about the playwright, and full production information.

Submissions and Payment
Guidelines and catalogue available at website. Query with synopsis and writing sample; include reviews/production information if querying about a play. Accepts hard copy, email queries to editor@smithandkraus.com, and simultaneous submissions if identified. SASE. Responds in 1–2 months. Publication in 1 year. Royalty; advance. Flat fee.

Editor's Comments
We're always looking for practical, exciting books for young actors and their teachers or coaches.

Soho Press

853 Broadway
New York, NY 10003

Acquisitions Editor

Publisher's Interests
The focus of Soho Press is trade fiction, but autobiographies
and cultural historical accounts occasionally appear on its
list. Soho's preferred genres are mystery and suspense, particularly those set abroad. While it does not publish literature
or nonfiction for young adults per se, many of its titles have
crossover appeal to that audience.
Website: www.sohopress.com

Freelance Potential
Published 61 titles in 2010: 2 were developed from unsolicited submissions. Of the 61 titles, 8 were by unpublished
writers and 19 were by authors who were new to the publishing house. Receives 1,000 queries yearly.

- **Fiction:** Publishes literary fiction and mystery series with foreign or exotic settings.
- **Nonfiction:** Publishes autobiographies, biographies, and historical and cultural accounts.
- **Representative Titles:** *The Sand Box*, by David Zimmerman,
  is an intense mystery set at a military base in Iraq. *Rock Paper
  Tiger,* by Lisa Brackman, is a tale of international espionage
  set in China that features a physically and emotionally wound-
  ed female Iraq War veteran. *Gunshot Road*, by Adrian Hyland,
  features detective Emily Tempest investigating a murder in the
  Australian outback.

Submissions and Payment
Guidelines and catalogue available at website. Query with first
3 chapters, outline, and publishing credits. Accepts hard copy.
SASE. Responds in 3 months. Publication in 9+ months. Royalty; advance.

Editor's Comments
While many of our published works arrive through literary
agents, we place a high priority on publishing quality unsolicited materials from new writers.

Soundprints

353 Main Avenue
Norwalk, CT 06851

Submissions: Anthony Parisi

Publisher's Interests

Believing that educated and curious children grow into more aware and responsible adults, Soundprints publishes fact-based fiction and nonfiction titles that are as fun as they are educational. It also publishes middle-grade fantasy fiction.
Website: www.soundprints.com

Freelance Potential

Published 40–80 titles in 2010: 2–5 were by authors who were new to the publishing house. Receives several queries, 100+ unsolicited mss yearly.

- **Fiction:** Publishes easy-to-read books, 3–7 years; story picture books, 0–10 years; and middle-grade books, 8–12 years. Also publishes board books. Genres include fantasy and inspirational fiction and fact-based stories about nature and wildlife.
- **Nonfiction:** Publishes easy-to-read books, 4–7 years; story picture books, 4–10 years; and middle-grade books, 8–12 years. Topics include animals, history, nature, and the environment.
- **Representative Titles:** *Undersea City: A Story of a Caribbean Coral Reef,* by Dana Meachen Rau (5–7 years), follows a land hermit crab as he is swept into the new world of a coral reef. *I Love My Daddy,* by Laura Gates Galvin (18 months–3 years), presents the concept that even penguins, foxes, owls, and other baby animals love their daddies. *Quest for the Dragon Stone,* by Ami Blackford (8–12 years), is the story of a brother and sister who journey to a magical realm to find their father.

Submissions and Payment

Guidelines available. Catalogue available at website. Query or send complete ms. Accepts hard copy. SASE. Response time varies. Publication in 1–2 years. Payment policy varies.

Editor's Comments

We also produce books under license with the Smithsonian Institution, the African Wildlife Foundation, American Veterinary Medical Association, Disney, and Sesame Workshop.

Sourcebooks

1935 Brookdale Road, Suite 139
Naperville, IL 60563

Editorial Submissions

Publisher's Interests

Sourcebooks' children's imprint, Jabberwocky, produces fiction and nonfiction for children of all ages. Books for teens are published under its Fire imprint.
Website: www.sourcebooks.com

Freelance Potential

Published 300 titles (60 juvenile) in 2010: 5 were developed from unsolicited submissions, 200 were by agented authors, and 20 were reprint/licensed properties. Receives 2,400 queries yearly.

- **Fiction:** Publishes early picture books, 0–4 years; easy-to-read books, 4–7 years; story picture books, 4–10 years; chapter books, 5–10 years; middle-grade books, 8–12 years; and young adult books, 12–18 years. Genres include poetry, contemporary fiction, fantasy, and the classics.
- **Nonfiction:** Publishes toddler books, 0–4 years; middle-grade books, 8–12 years; and young adult books, 12–18 years. Topics include sign language, forensic science, and teen rights. Also publishes adult titles on pregnancy, parenting, special needs, and gifted education.
- **Representative Titles:** *The Tighty Whitey Spider,* by Kenn Nesbitt (7–12 years), is a collection of humorous animal poems. *Dear Teacher,* by Amy Husband (4–8 years), is a collection of funny letters from a boy explaining why he cannot go to class.

Submissions and Payment

Guidelines and catalogue available at website. Query with résumé, synopsis, table of contents, 2 sample chapters, and market analysis. Accepts hard copy and simultaneous submissions if identified. SASE. Responds in 4–6 months. Publication in 1 year. Royalty, 6–15%.

Editor's Comments

We are looking for strong writers who are excited about marketing their books and building a community of readers.

Square One Publishers

115 Herricks Road
Garden City, NY 11040

Publisher: Rudy Shur

Publisher's Interests
An independent publisher of nonfiction, Square One features self-help and how-to books on everything from legal issues to healthy eating—all written by authors with considerable expertise in their fields. Its list includes a variety of titles on child development and parenting.
Website: www.squareonepublishers.com

Freelance Potential
Published 15 titles in 2010: 10 were developed from unsolicited submissions. Of the 15 titles, 8 were by unpublished writers and 5 were by authors who were new to the publishing house. Receives 1,200 queries yearly.

- **Nonfiction:** Publishes self-help and how-to books for adults. Topics include pregnancy, childbirth, infant care, discipline, potty training, children with special needs, sports, and early childhood learning.
- **Representative Titles:** *Does Your Baby Have Autism?*, by Philip & Osnat Teitelbaum, outlines a prescreening program based on physical movement that can help with early diagnosis. *Hey! Who's Having This Baby Anyway?*, by Breck Hawk, helps moms-to-be understand how they can be actively involved in making decisions about their own care.

Submissions and Payment
Guidelines available at website. Query with synopsis, target audience, table of contents, and author bio. Accepts hard copy. SASE. Responds in 4–6 weeks. Publication period varies. Royalty.

Editor's Comments
We look for smart and illuminating books that make a difference. A deep knowledge of the subject matter you are addressing should be evident in your query. Send us something fresh on health, alternative health, parenting, or personal finance.

Standard Publishing

8805 Governors Hill Drive, Suite 400
Cincinnati, OH 45249

Editorial Director, Children's Products: Ruth Frederick

Publisher's Interests

Standard Publishing provides books and other Christian resources that meet the spiritual needs of the church and family. Its youth catalogue features books that introduce children to the Bible and help older readers grow in their faith.
Website: www.standardpub.com

Freelance Potential

Published 110 titles (10 juvenile) in 2010: 10 were developed from unsolicited submissions and 6 were by agented authors. Of the 110 titles, 10 were by new authors. Receives 200 queries, 300 unsolicited mss yearly.

- **Fiction:** Publishes board books, 0–4 years; story picture books, 4–10 years; and middle-grade books, 8–12 years. Genres include Christian fiction. Also publishes Bible stories.
- **Nonfiction:** Publishes board books, concept books, and early picture books, 0–4 years; middle-grade books, 8–12 years; and young adult books, 12–18. Topics include religion, faith, Christianity, and Christian values. Also publishes devotionals and resources for children's ministry leaders.
- **Representative Titles:** *Friends for Me Bible Storybook,* by Jodie McCallum, introduces children to Noah, Samuel, Esther, and Jesus. *Burn This Book,* by Garth Heckman (YA), is a 30-day devotional guide for high school students.

Submissions and Payment

Guidelines available at website. Query with outline and 1–2 sample chapters. Send complete ms for picture books. Accepts hard copy, email submissions to ministrytochildren@standardpub.com, and simultaneous submissions if identified. SASE. Responds in 4–5 months. Publication in 18 months. Royalty. Flat fee.

Editor's Comments

We are particularly interested in books about outreach, prayer, and the Bible, as well as educational resources.

Star Bright Books

30–19 48th Avenue
Long Island City, NY 11101

Publisher: Deborah Shine

Publisher's Interests

Star Bright's catalogue shows a focus on diversity and multi-ethnic views, with books featuring subjects and characters of varying cultural backgrounds and physical or mental abilities. Star Bright is interested in books for young people, from toddlers to young adults.
Website: www.starbrightbooks.com

Freelance Potential

Published 12 titles in 2010: 3 were reprint properties. Of the 12 titles, 3 were by unpublished writers and 1 was by an author who was new to the publishing house. Receives 360–480 queries, 240–360 unsolicited mss yearly.

- **Fiction:** Publishes concept books, toddler books, and early picture books, 0–4 years; easy-to-read books, 4–7 years; story picture books, 4–10 years; chapter books, 5–10 years; middle-grade books, 8–12 years; and young adult books, 12–18 years. Genres include contemporary, multicultural, and educational fiction. Also publishes board books.
- **Nonfiction:** Publishes concept books, toddler books, and early picture books, 0–4 years. Topics include families and animals.
- **Representative Titles:** *Carry Me,* by Rena D. Grossman (0–4 years), shows the many ways that babies are carried worldwide; part of the Babies Everywhere series. *How Do You Get a Mouse to Smile?,* by Bonnie Grubman (3–8 years), presents a young boy willing to go to silly lengths to get his mouse to smile.

Submissions and Payment

Guidelines available. Catalogue available at website. Query or send complete ms. Accepts hard copy. SASE. Responds in 6 months. Publication period varies. Royalty; advance.

Editor's Comments

Please note that we do not accept electronic submissions of any kind. Many of our books are bilingual or translated into several languages.

Stemmer House Publishers

4 White Brook Road
Gilsum, NH 03448

Editor: Becky Dalzell

Publisher's Interests
This publisher is interested in both fiction and nonfiction for children. For the former, it seeks "timeless" stories and poetry for young children. For the latter, it focuses on nature and science titles.
Website: www.stemmer.com

Freelance Potential
Published 6 titles (2 juvenile) in 2010: 2 were developed from unsolicited submissions and 2 were reprint/licensed properties. Of the 6 titles, 1 was by an unpublished writer and 2 were by new authors. Receives 180 queries, 240 mss yearly.

- **Fiction:** Publishes story picture books, 4–10 years. Genres include contemporary, historical, and multicultural fiction.
- **Nonfiction:** Publishes easy-to-read books, 4–7 years; story picture books, 4–10 years; chapter books, 5–10 years; middle-grade books, 8–12 years; and young adult books, 12–18 years. Topics include nature, science, natural history, art, music, and geography. Also publishes biographies, cookbooks, design books, and gardening books for adults.
- **Representative Titles:** *Tree House in a Storm,* by Rachelle Burk, is a touching tale about devastation caused by severe weather. *The Freshwater Alphabet Encyclopedia,* by Sylvester Allred, invites readers to learn about freshwater habitats.

Submissions and Payment
Guidelines and catalogue available with 9x12 SASE ($.77 postage). Catalogue also available at website. Send complete ms for picture books. Query with outline/synopsis and 2 sample chapters for longer works. Accepts hard copy and simultaneous submissions if identified. SASE. Responds in 2 weeks. Publication in 1–3 years. Royalty; advance.

Editor's Comments
We're proud of our growing list of new authors and hope to expand it. Children's fiction is our current need.

Sterling Publishing Company

387 Park Avenue South
New York, NY 10016

Children's Acquisitions Editor

Publisher's Interests
Sterling's children's catalogue includes picture books and
activity-based nonfiction titles. It also publishes a small number of history books and biographies for older children.
Website: www.sterlingpublishing.com/kids

Freelance Potential
Published 160 titles in 2010: 10 were developed from unsolicited submissions, 25 were by agented authors, and 25
were reprint/licensed properties. Receives 1,200–1,800
unsolicited mss yearly.

- **Fiction:** Publishes toddler books and early picture books, 0–4
  years; easy-to-read books, 4–7 years; and story picture books,
  4–10 years. Genres include fairy tales, fantasy, ghost stories,
  contemporary fiction, and stories about animals.
- **Nonfiction:** Publishes toddler books and early picture books,
  0–4 years; easy-to-read books, 4–7 years; middle-grade books,
  8–12 years; and young adult books, 12–18 years. Topics
  include routines, colors, sounds, shapes, numbers, animals,
  nature, science, holidays, seasons, cooking, crafts, activities,
  and games. Also publishes biographies.
- **Representative Titles:** *Chicken Dance,* by Tammi Sauer (4–7
  years), follows two feisty chickens as they enter a music contest. *The Secret Lives of Princesses,* by Rébecca Dautremer
  (7+ years), introduces a bevy of fairy tale princesses.

Submissions and Payment
Guidelines and catalogue available at website. Send complete ms. Accepts hard copy and simultaneous submissions
if identified. SASE. Response time varies. Publication in
1 year. Royalty; advance.

Editor's Comments
We are constantly reviewing new proposals, and given the
volume of submissions we receive it could take several
months for a reply. We appreciate your patience.

Stone Arch Books

Capstone Press
1825 Telegraph Road
Bloomington, MN 55438

Senior Editor: Beth Brezenoff

Publisher's Interests

This imprint of Capstone Press publishes contemporary, compelling fiction for reluctant readers in kindergarten through grade eight. Its catalogue includes high-interest novels as well as graphic novels designed to turn kids into readers one thrilling story at a time.
Website: www.capstonepub.com

Freelance Potential

Published 161 titles in 2010: 12 were by agented authors and 28 were reprint/licensed properties. Of the 161 titles, 8 were by unpublished writers and 32 were by authors who were new to the publishing house. Receives 600 queries each year.

- **Fiction:** Publishes chapter books, 5–10 years; and middle-grade books, 8–12 years. Genres include realistic and historical fiction, adventure, fantasy, horror, science fiction, mystery, sports, and humor. Also publishes graphic novels.
- **Representative Titles:** *Speed Camp,* by Jake Maddox (grades 4–8), tells how Dylan learns to respect his new partner—a girl!—at Top Speed Race Camp; part of the On the Speedway series. *Mud Mess,* by Mindy Crow (preK–grade 1), finds the truck friends helping each other when rain makes the track too muddy to drive; part of the Stone Arch Readers series.

Submissions and Payment

Guidelines and catalogue available at website. All topics are assigned. Send résumé and writing sample only. Accepts email to author.sub@stonearchbooks.com. Response time, publication period, and payment policy vary.

Editor's Comments

Please be aware that all topics are conceptually developed and assigned by our in-house editors and written by freelancers. Send us some samples if you would like to be considered for future projects.

Storytellers Ink Publishing Company

P.O. Box 33398
Seattle, WA 98133-0398

Editor-in-Chief: Quinn Currie

Publisher's Interests
Storytellers Ink uses books about animals and the environment to motivate children to read. Its fiction and nonfiction books—which are also designed to instill compassion, justice, responsibility, and a love for all living things—are for kids in preschool through the middle grades.
Website: www.storytellers-ink.com

Freelance Potential
Published 3 titles in 2010. Receives 120 unsolicited mss each year.

- **Fiction:** Publishes story picture books, 2–10 years; and middle-grade books, 8–12 years. Genres include adventure, folktales, fantasy, and multicultural and ethnic fiction; and stories about animals, nature, and the environment.
- **Nonfiction:** Publishes story picture books, 2–10 years; and middle-grade books, 8–12 years. Topics include animals, nature, the environment, and social issues.
- **Representative Titles:** *The Blue Kangaroo at the Zoo,* by Mary Jane Flynn (grade K), is a story about a kangaroo that returns to the zoo to teach children about wild animals and counting. *The Living Mountain,* by Rob Carson (grade 5), tells the dramatic story of the impact of the Mount St. Helens eruption and how certain bugs and animals are helping to return life to the area.

Submissions and Payment
Guidelines available. Catalogue available at website. Send complete ms. Accepts hard copy and simultaneous submissions if identified. SASE. Response time, publication period, and payment policy vary.

Editor's Comments
We look for books that teach important lessons about preserving the natural world and respecting animals, in addition to offering up engaging characters and storylines.

Tanglewood Press

P.O. Box 3009
Terre Haute, IN 47803

Acquisitions Editor: Kairi Hamlin

Publisher's Interests
Tanglewood Press is a small, independent publisher with a
large catalogue of fiction for children. Its list includes books
for kids of all ages, on all "kidcentric" topics.
Website: www.tanglewoodbooks.com

Freelance Potential
Published 2 titles in 2010: 1 was developed from an unsolicited submission. Receives 6,000 queries yearly.

- **Fiction:** Publishes early picture books, 0–4 years; story picture
  books, 4–10 years; middle-grade books, 8–12 years; and
  young adult books, 12–18 years. Genres include adventure,
  historical fiction, mystery, and humor.
- **Representative Titles:** *Wolf Camp,* by Katie McKy (4–8 years),
  is the story of a young girl who returns from camp behaving
  more like an animal than a human. *Blackbeard and the Gift of
  Silence,* by Audrey Penn (8–12 years), presents a tale of pirate
  loot, ancient mysteries, and four teens who learn the importance of keeping secrets. *You Can't Milk a Dancing Cow,* by
  Tom Dunsmuir (4–8 years), explores the many dilemmas faced
  by Farmer Pickett after his wife creates delightful fashions for
  the animals.

Submissions and Payment
Guidelines and catalogue available at website. Send complete ms for picture books. Query with 3–5 sample chapters
for middle reader and YA novels. Accepts hard copy. SASE.
Responds in 6–12 months. Publication in 2–3 years. Royalty,
6% of retail.

Editor's Comments
We look for books that kids want to read, which are different
from books that adults want children to read. A book on
table manners will never get published here. We pride ourselves on our author relationships and our support for the
select titles that we publish.

Teacher Created Resources

6421 Industry Way
Westminster, CA 92683

Editor-in-Chief: Ina Massler Levin

Publisher's Interests

The company name describes exactly what it is looking for: educational materials that have been written by credentialed professionals and successfully used in the classroom. It publishes workbooks, activities, and reproducibles for use in preschool through eighth grade classrooms.
Website: www.teachercreated.com

Freelance Potential

Published 70 titles in 2010: 4–6 were developed from unsolicited submissions. Of the 70 titles, 5 were by unpublished writers and 5 were by authors who were new to the publishing house. Receives 240 queries yearly.

- **Nonfiction:** Publishes workbooks and activity books, preK–grade 8. Topics include art, geography, history, social studies, science, mathematics, reading, phonics, spelling, writing, language arts, and technology. Also publishes teacher resource materials on student testing, multiple intelligences, assessment, and classroom management.
- **Representative Titles:** *Daily Warm-Ups: Language Skills* (grades 1–6) provides quick, easy, effective activities that support standards and help students improve skills they need for success in testing. *Paired Passages: Linking Fact to Fiction* (grades 1–8) helps students develop the skills they need to compare and contrast fiction and nonfiction passages.

Submissions and Payment

Guidelines and catalogue available at website. Query with synopsis, table of contents, and 10–12 manuscript pages. Accepts hard copy. SASE. Responds in 3–6 months. Publication in 3–12 months. Flat fee.

Editor's Comments

We are interested in ELL, technology as it applies to classrooms, reading, STEM (science, technology, engineering, and math), and early childhood education topics.

Teaching & Learning Company

1204 Buchanan Street
P.O. Box 10
Carthage, IL 62321

Vice President, Production: Jill Day

Publisher's Interests

Classroom resource materials for all the basic curriculum areas are available from Teaching & Learning Company. It develops products that help to make teaching and learning easier, and that reflect the needs of today's culturally and ethnically diverse schools.
Website: www.teachinglearning.com

Freelance Potential

Published 30–35 titles (11 juvenile) in 2010: 25–30 were developed from unsolicited submissions. Of the 30–35 titles, 3 were by unpublished writers and 6 were by authors who were new to the publishing house. Receives 1,200 unsolicited mss yearly.

- **Nonfiction:** Publishes educational teacher resource materials, preK–grade 8. Topics include language arts, social studies, current events, biography, mathematics, computers, science, nature, the environment, animals, holidays, arts and crafts, hobbies, multicultural and ethnic issues, and responsibility.
- **Representative Titles:** *Let's Read! Let's Talk! Let's Write! Let's Pretend!* (preK–K) is a literacy learning resource that teaches key academic skills through playful, enjoyable activities. *Explorers of the New World Time Line* (grades 4–8) complements textbook information and includes materials needed to launch whole-group discussions and small-group projects.

Submissions and Payment

Guidelines available. Send complete ms. Accepts hard copy and Macintosh disk submissions (Quark XPress or Microsoft Word documents). SASE. Responds in 6–9 months. Publication in 1–3 years. Royalty.

Editor's Comments

Our market reflects the diverse and culturally rich populations of the U.S. and Canada. Keep that in mind when preparing material—especially seasonal and holiday-related items.

TEACH Services

8300 Highway 41, Suite 107
Ringgold, GA 30736

Publisher: Bill Newman

Publisher's Interests
This full-service book producer—owned by Seventh-day
Adventists—publishes and distributes nonfiction books on
religious and health topics, as well as poetry and biographies
for young readers and young adults. 20% self-, subsidy, co-
venture, or co-op published material.
Website: www.teachservices.com

Freelance Potential
Published 60–80 titles (15 juvenile) in 2010: 65 were developed from unsolicited submissions. Receives 240 queries
each year.

- **Nonfiction:** Publishes easy-to-read books, 4–7 years; chapter
  books, 5–10 years; middle-grade books, 8–12 years; and
  young adult books, 12–18 years. Topics include Bible study,
  church doctrine and history, prayer, youth and children's ministry, health, education, and spiritual growth. Also publishes
  biographies, ministerial resources, and titles for adults.
- **Representative Titles:** *Best Buddies,* by Juanita Hamil, follows young Mikey and his best friend, Hound Dog, as they
  have good, clean fun on Grandma and Grandpa's farm. *The
  Beatitudes,* by David Meyer, uses an audiotape of songs to
  complement this book of Christian messages and questions
  designed to encourage readers to have spiritual discussions
  with their parents.

Submissions and Payment
Guidelines and catalogue available at website. Query with
outline. Accepts hard copy and simultaneous submissions if
identified. SASE. Responds in 2–3 weeks. Publication in 4–6
months. Royalty, 10%.

Editor's Comments
As a Christian organization, we're always seeking Bible-based
inspirational and educational works for parents and children.
We do not publish fiction or fantasy.

Texas Tech University Press

P.O. Box 41037
Lubbock, TX 79409-1037

Editor-in-Chief: Judith Keeling

Publisher's Interests
In addition to a variety of nonfiction titles for adults, Texas
Tech University Press produces fiction for middle-grade
readers and young adults. All of its books cover themes and
topics relating to the American West and the Great Plains.
Website: www.ttup.ttu.edu

Freelance Potential
Published 25 titles in 2010. Receives 200–250 queries
each year.

- **Fiction:** Publishes middle-grade books, 8–12 years; and young
  adult books, 12–18 years. Genres include regional and historical fiction; and folklore. Also publishes novels for adults.
- **Nonfiction:** Publishes books for adults. Topics include the natural sciences, history, and natural history of the Great Plains
  and American Southwest; costume and textile history; and
  Southeast Asia. Also publishes American Southwest regional
  biographies and memoirs.
- **Representative Titles:** *Hellie Jondoe,* by Randall Platt, is the
  story of a streetwise 13-year-old girl who heads west on a
  1918 orphan train and meets her match in unexpected ways.
  Get Along, Little Dogies, by Lisa Waller Rogers (8–12 years),
  chronicles one girl's journey along the Chisholm Trail as part
  of a 1878 cattle drive to Dodge City.

Submissions and Payment
Guidelines available at website. Query with brief author bio,
outline, table of contents, introduction, and 2 sample chapters. Accepts hard copy. SASE. Responds in 2 months. Publication in 1 year. Royalty, 10%.

Editor's Comments
Most of our titles are written for a general readership, so
please avoid getting deeply entrenched in theory, analysis,
or jargon. That said, we do expect submissions to pass a
rigorous review in terms of substance and accuracy.

Theytus Books

Green Mountain Road, Lot 45
RR 2, Site 50, Comp. 8
Penticton, British Columbia V2A 6J7
Canada

Submissions: Anita Large

Publisher's Interests
Owned and operated by the Aboriginal people of Canada, this publisher produces books by First Nations, Métis, and Inuit authors only. Its juvenile line includes story picture books and books for young adults.
Website: www.theytus.com

Freelance Potential
Published 10 titles (6 juvenile) in 2010. Of the 10 titles, 1–2 were by unpublished writers and 3 were by authors who were new to the publishing house. Receives 20 queries, 30–60 unsolicited mss yearly.

- **Fiction:** Publishes story picture books, 4–10 years; and young adult books, 12–18 years. Genres include contemporary, historical, and literary fiction; adventure; drama; and humor. Also publishes poetry and anthologies.
- **Nonfiction:** Publishes young adult books, 12–18 years. Topics include social history and policy relating to aboriginal issues. Also publishes humor.
- **Representative Titles:** *I See Me,* by Margaret Manuel, is a baby book that includes images of baby eating, sleeping, and playing, and includes blank lines for missing words that parents can fill in with their native languages. *The Rabbits' Race,* by Deborah L. Delaronde, provides a retelling of a story about a race between bush rabbits and jackrabbits.

Submissions and Payment
Canadian Aboriginal authors only. Guidelines and catalogue available at website. Query with synopsis, 4 sample chapters, and author bio. Send complete ms for story picture books and poetry. Accepts hard copy. SASE. Responds in 6–8 months. Publication in 1–2 years. Royalty, 10%.

Editor's Comments
The author biography you submit must include information about your tribal affiliation.

Third World Press

7822 South Dobson
P.O. Box 19730
Chicago, IL 60619

Assistant to the Publisher

Publisher's Interests
For more than 40 years, Third World Press has been offering black and African-centered books for a primarily African American audience. It creates books for the very youngest readers through young adults.
Website: www.thirdworldpressinc.com

Freelance Potential
Published 12 titles in 2010.

- **Fiction:** Publishes concept books, toddler books, and early picture books, 0–4 years; easy-to-read books, 4–7 years; story picture books, 4–10 years; chapter books, 5–10 years; middle-grade books, 8–12 years; and young adult books, 12–18 years. Features stories about African, African American, and Caribbean life; and the Diaspora.
- **Nonfiction:** Publishes easy-to-read books, 4–7 years; story picture books, 4–10 years; chapter books, 5–10 years; middle-grade books, 8–12 years; and young adult books, 12–18 years. Topics include African history and culture, and multicultural issues.
- **Representative Titles:** *I Look at Me,* by Mari Evans (3–5 years), is a beginning reader for preschoolers that introduces children to the African-centered concepts of unity and nation building. *The First: President Barack Obama's Road to the White House,* by Roland S. Martin, takes readers through the struggles and triumphs of the 2008 presidential campaign.

Submissions and Payment
Guidelines available at website. Send one-page query in July only with maximum 8-page synopsis, 2 sample chapters, and a copy of publisher's guidelines. Accepts hard copy and simultaneous submissions if identified. SASE. Response time varies. Publication in 1 year. Royalty.

Editor's Comments
Prospective authors must strictly adhere to our submission guidelines, or their submissions will not be reviewed.

Charles C. Thomas Publisher

2600 South First Street
Springfield, IL 62707

Editor: Michael P. Thomas

Publisher's Interests

This publisher offers books of interest to parents, educators, and professionals relating to the fields of behavioral science, speech-language pathology, early childhood education, and special education. Charles C. Thomas also develops textbooks on biomedical science topics.
Website: www.ccthomas.com

Freelance Potential

Published 60 titles in 2010: each was developed from an unsolicited submission. Receives 600 queries and unsolicited mss yearly.

- **Nonfiction:** Publishes titles for educators, preK–grade 12. Topics include early childhood, elementary, and higher education; reading; research and statistics; physical education and sports; special education; the learning disabled; teaching the blind and visually impaired; gifted and talented education; and speech-language pathology. Also publishes parenting titles and professional development books for the science and criminal justice fields.
- **Representative Titles:** *Behavior Management Strategies for Teachers,* by Joan C. Harlan & Sidney T. Rowland, presents proven methods that result in student motivation and success. *Media and Literacy,* by Dennis Adams & Mary Hamm, discusses ideas, issues, and teaching strategies for learning in the Information Age.

Submissions and Payment

Guidelines and catalogue available at website. Query or send complete ms. Accepts hard copy and disk submissions. SASE. Responds in 1 week. Publication in 6–8 months. Royalty.

Editor's Comments

We're looking for talented writers who have qualifications in the subject matter they are addressing. We try to respond to submissions in a prompt manner.

Thompson Educational Publishing

20 Ripley Avenue
Toronto, Ontario M6S 3N9
Canada

Submissions: Faye Thompson

Publisher's Interests

Educational resources for middle school, high school, and university classes are the focus of this publisher. It specializes in textbooks and scholarly titles in the fields of health, physical education, the social sciences, and the humanities. **Website: www.thompsonbooks.com**

Freelance Potential

Published 8 titles in 2010: 2 were by unpublished writers and 2 were by authors who were new to the publishing house. Receives 20 queries yearly.

- **Nonfiction:** Publishes middle-grade books, 8–12 years; and young adult books, 12–18 years. Also publishes single-author monographs for use in undergraduate education, as well as books for educators. Topics include social studies, sociology, social work, economics, communication, native studies, labor studies, and sports.
- **Representative Titles:** *Social Work in Canada: An Introduction,* by Steven Hick, introduces the fundamentals of Canadian social work practice in the context of challenges such as poverty, discrimination, violence, and economic globalization. *Seeing Ourselves: Exploring Race, Ethnicity and Culture,* by Carl James, uses a collection of students' personal comments and essays to examine what it means to participate in Canada's contemporary cultural mosaic.

Submissions and Payment

Guidelines and catalogue available at website. Query with outline and résumé. Accepts hard copy and email queries to faye@thompsonbooks.com. SAE/IRC. Response time, publication period, and payment policy vary.

Editor's Comments

We are particularly interested in Canadian scholars and books that feature a uniquely Canadian perspective to the subject at hand.

Tilbury House, Publishers

103 Brunswick Avenue
Gardiner, ME 04345

Associate Editor: Karen Fisk

Publisher's Interests
Tilbury House produces children's picture books that appeal
to kids and parents, but also offer enough learning content
to appeal to the educational market. Targeting middle-school
students, Tilbury focuses on cultural diversity, social justice,
and the environment.
Website: www.tilburyhouse.com

Freelance Potential
Published 5 titles in 2010: 3 were developed from unsolicited
submissions. Of the 5 titles, 3 were by unpublished writers
and 4 were by authors who were new to the publishing
house. Receives 960 unsolicited mss yearly.

- **Fiction:** Publishes middle-grade books, 8–12 years. Genres
  include realistic and multicultural fiction, and stories about
  nature and the environment.
- **Nonfiction:** Publishes middle-grade books, 8–12 years. Topics
  include nature, social studies, and multicultural and ethnic
  issues.
- **Representative Titles:** *Remember Me,* by Donald Soctomah
  & Jean Flahive (grades 3–6), tells a fictional story of Franklin
  Delano Roosevelt's boyhood relationship with a former chief
  of the Passamaquoddy tribe. *The Carpet Boy's Gift,* by Pegi
  Deitz Shea (grades 3–6), features a child laborer who tries to
  gain freedom for himself and other children.

Submissions and Payment
Guidelines and catalogue available at website. Send complete ms. Accepts hard copy and email submissions to
karen@tilburyhouse.com. SASE. Responds in 1 month. Publication in 1 year. Royalty; advance, negotiable.

Editor's Comments
Our current needs include books on water and social justice
issues. We do not publish general children's books about
animals, fables, or fantasy.

TokyoPop

5900 Wilshire Boulevard, Suite 2000
Los Angeles, CA 90036

Editor

Publisher's Interests
Using the Japanese graphic art of manga, this publisher
strives to engage children and young adults in storytelling
from a new perspective. It publishes manga-inspired graphic
novels in a broad spectrum of genres.
Website: www.tokyopop.com

Freelance Potential
Published 175 titles in 2010: 18 were developed from unsolicited submissions. Of the 175 titles, 158 were by unpublished writers and 88 were by authors who were new to the
publishing house. Receives 200+ queries and unsolicited
mss yearly.

- **Fiction:** Publishes chapter books, 5–10 years; middle-grade
  books, 8–12 years; and young adult books, 12–18 years. Genres include contemporary, historical, multicultural, Western,
  and science fiction; adventure; drama; fairy tales; fantasy; folktales; horror; humor; mystery; suspense; and romance.
- **Representative Titles:** *Warriors Volume 1: The Lost Warrior,*
  by Erin Hunter (YA), is the first in a series of action novels featuring Graystripe, the second in command of the ThunderClan
  of cats. *Stand By Chung Chun,* by Juder & Young-Bin Kim (YA),
  is a high school romance about a smart student who meets a
  beautiful girl in a college entrance exam prep class.

Submissions and Payment
Guidelines and catalogue available at website. Query with
outline; or send complete ms with résumé. Accepts hard
copy and disk submissions (Microsoft Word). SASE.
Responds to queries in 6–12 months; to mss in 3–6 months.
Publication in 1–2 years. Royalty; advance.

Editor's Comments
While all of our publications have a strong visual compo-
nent, you need not be an artist to write for us. Please
include the submission agreement found at our website.

Tor Books

Tom Doherty Associates
175 Fifth Avenue
New York, NY 10010

Senior Editor, Children's/YA: Susan Chang

Publisher's Interests
Tor Books, part of Macmillan, is a science fiction, fantasy, and horror publisher for adults and children. The Starscape imprint publishes fiction for grades five and up, and Tor Teen, grades seven and up.
Website: http://us.macmillan.com/Tor.aspx

Freelance Potential
Published 30 titles in 2010. Reviews tens of thousands of submissions a year.

- **Fiction:** Publishes chapter books, 8–10 years; middle-grade books, 8–10 years; and young adult books, 12–18 years. Genres are fantasy and science fiction. Also publishes thrillers, suspense, mysteries, paranormal romance titles for adults.
- **Representative Titles:** *The Web of Titan,* by Dom Testa (YA), is the second volume in a six-book series about 251 teens sent into space to save some of Earth's remaining population. *Goop Soup,* by David Lubar (8–12 years), is about a half-dead middle-schooler who deals with typical kid issues, but with a twist; part of the Nathan Abercrombie Accidental Zombie series.

Submissions and Payment
Guidelines and catalogue available at website. Send a cover letter that includes contact information; the genre of your work; your qualifications and credits, if any; a synopsis of the book; and the first 3 chapters. Do not send queries or disks. SASE. Responds in 4–6 months. Publication in 18–24 months. Royalty; advance.

Editor's Comments
Tor Books has an open submissions policy, and accepts unsolicited submissions but works with agents as well.

Toy Box Productions

Division of CRT, Custom Products, Inc.
7532 Hickory Hills Court
Whites Creek, TN 37189

President: Cheryl J. Hutchinson

Publisher's Interests
This publisher offers a line of read-along and interactive story picture books for children between the ages of 4 and 12. Each of its publications includes a CD, which is designed to help readers with literacy skills, memorization, and timing coordination. Its catalogue includes a number of books about the Bible, as well as stories about historical events.
Website: www.crttoybox.com

Freelance Potential
Published 3 titles in 2010: each was by an agented author. Of the 3 titles, 1 was by an unpublished writer and 1 was by an author who was new to the publishing house. Receives 1–2 queries yearly.

- **Fiction:** Publishes story picture books, 4–10 years; and chapter books, 5–10 years. Genres include historical, Western, multicultural, ethnic, and religious fiction.
- **Nonfiction:** Publishes story picture books, 4–10 years; and middle-grade books, 8–12 years. Topics include history, religion, and multicultural and ethnic issues.
- **Representative Titles:** *The Legend of Pocahontas and Captain John Smith* is a story about a group of children who travel back in time to learn about the English colonization of Virginia. *Thomas Jefferson* follows three children as they learn about the amazing life of the third U.S. president.

Submissions and Payment
Catalogue available at website. All work is assigned. Query with résumé and clips. Accepts hard copy. SASE. Response time, publication period, and payment policy vary.

Editor's Comments
While all of our titles are assigned, we'll consider hiring you if you have talents that fit in with our product line. We strongly believe in the power of "edu-tainment" to help children read and learn.

Tradewind Books

202-1807 Maritime Mews
Vancouver, British Columbia V6H 3W7
Canada

Submissions Editor: R. David Stephens

Publisher's Interests
Empowering kids to make a better world is the mission of
Tradewind Books. It publishes books for children and young
adults with an emphasis on North American folklore and
multicultural themes, as well as poetry books.
Website: www.tradewindbooks.com

Freelance Potential
Published 6 titles in 2010: 3 were developed from unsolicited
submissions. Of the 6 titles, 1 was by an unpublished writer
and 2 were by authors who were new to the publishing
house. Receives 900 queries, 600 unsolicited mss yearly.

- **Fiction:** Publishes early picture books, 0–4 years; easy-to-read
  books, 4–7 years; chapter books, 5–10 years; middle-grade
  books, 8–12 years; and young adult books, 12–18 years.
  Genres include multicultural and ethnic fiction, folklore, and
  stories about animals. Also publishes poetry.
- **Representative Titles:** *City Kids*, by X. J. Kennedy (8–11
  years), tells of the exciting adventures city kids can have.
  Once Upon a Bathtime, by Vi Hughes (3–6 years), features a
  child who takes a fairy tale bath with all her favorite tub toys.
  Shu-Li and Diego, by Paul Yee (8–11 years), follows the adventures of two friends as they take care of a neighbor's dog.

Submissions and Payment
Guidelines available at website. Query with résumé, outline,
and 3 sample chapters. Send complete ms for picture
books. Accepts hard copy. SAE/IRC. Responds in 3 months.
Publication in 3 years. Royalty; advance.

Editor's Comments
We accept young adult fiction from Canadian authors only.
Please note that we do not publish informational titles. We
strongly encourage you to read our guidelines carefully to
ensure that you follow the proper procedure for submitting
a proposal.

Tricycle Press

Random House
P.O. Box 7123
Berkeley, CA 94707

The Editors

Publisher's Interests
This imprint of Random House's Crown Publishing Group accepts fiction and nonfiction that inspire young readers of all ages to see the world in different ways.
Website: www.tricyclepress.com

Freelance Potential
Published 33 titles in 2010: 10 were by agented authors. Of the 33 titles, 4 were by unpublished writers and 8 were by new authors. Receives 480 queries, 5,000 mss yearly.

- **Fiction:** Publishes concept books, toddler books, and early picture books, 0–4 years; story picture books, 4–10 years; chapter books, 5–10 years; middle-grade books, 8–12 years; and young adult books, 12–18 years. Publishes contemporary and humorous fiction, stories that teach tolerance, character education books, and stories about nature.
- **Nonfiction:** Publishes concept books, toddler books, and early picture books, 0–4 years; story picture books, 4–10 years; and middle-grade books, 8–12 years. Topics include gardening, cooking, math, and real-life issues. Also publishes board books.
- **Representative Titles:** *Compost Stew: An A to Z Recipe for the Earth*, by Mary McKenna Siddals (3–7 years), presents an entertaining recipe for the home compost bin. *Brand-New Emily*, by Ginger Rue (11+ years), finds a girl trying to re-brand herself when she finds she's on the outs with the popular clique.

Submissions and Payment
Guidelines and catalogue available at website. Query with 2–3 sample chapters. Send complete ms for picture books only. Accepts hard copy and simultaneous submissions if identified. SASE. Responds in 2–6 months. Publication period varies. Royalty; advance.

Editor's Comments
Our detailed guidelines should help you determine if your work is right for us, and how to present it in the best light.

Turtle Press

P.O. Box 34010
Santa Fe, NM 87594-4010

Editor: Cynthia Kim

Publisher's Interests
Turtle Press focuses on books for the serious martial artist
and anyone who hopes to become one. Its titles target martial arts instructors, students, and those interested in self-
defense and protection.
Website: www.turtlepress.com

Freelance Potential
Published 10 titles in 2010: 3 were developed from unsolicited submissions. Of the 10 titles, 2 were by unpublished
writers and 3 were by authors who were new to the publishing house. Receives 480 queries yearly.

- **Fiction:** Publishes chapter books, 5–10 years; and middle-
  grade books, 8–12 years. Publishes stories about the martial
  arts, including adventure stories.
- **Nonfiction:** Publishes chapter books, 5–10 years. Topics
  include martial arts, Eastern philosophy, fitness, health,
  sports, and self-improvement. Also publishes books for adults,
  martial arts teachers, and martial arts students.
- **Representative Titles:** *A Part of the Ribbon,* by Ruth Hunter
  & Debra Fritsch (9+ years), takes the reader on a journey
  through Korean martial arts history through the eyes of two
  children. *The Martial Arts Training Diary for Kids!,* by Art
  Brisacher, is an activity book designed to help children get the
  most out of their martial arts classes and have fun doing it.

Submissions and Payment
Guidelines and catalogue available at website. Query.
Accepts hard copy. SASE. Responds in 2–3 weeks. Publica-
tion period varies. Royalty, 10%; advance, $500–$2,000.

Editor's Comments
We are now focusing more on the martial arts, their history,
and training than on children's books. Books that are appropriate for students, however, are still welcome. If you are
knowledgeable about the martial arts, send us your query.

Twenty-First Century Books

Lerner Publishing
241 First Avenue North
Minneapolis, MN 55401

Submissions Editor: Jennifer Zimian

Publisher's Interests
This division of Lerner Publishing Group produces supplementary educational materials for middle school and high
school students. Its titles cover a wide range of curriculum
areas, including history, current events, and science. It also
offers an extensive line of biographies. While it does not
accept unsolicited submissions, it will consider targeted
solicitations in specific areas for specific reading levels.
Website: www.lernerbooks.com

Freelance Potential
Published 100+ titles in 2010. Receives 100 queries yearly.

- **Nonfiction:** Publishes middle-grade books, 8–12 years; and
  young adult books, 12–18 years. Topics include science, technology, health, medicine, history, social studies, contemporary
  issues, language arts, government, politics, and sports. Also
  publishes biographies and multicultural titles.
- **Representative Titles:** *Green Energy: Crucial Gains or Economic Strains?*, by Matt Doeden (grades 9–12), examines the
  history of human energy and the latest energy developments
  in the U.S. *Seven Wonders of Communication,* by Donald
  Cleveland (grades 5–8), chronicles the history of human communication from the first use of spoken language, through
  hieroglyphs and the development of the written word, to tele-
  phones, cell phones, and the World Wide Web.

Submissions and Payment
No unsolicited submissions. See website for submission
details. Publication period and payment policy vary.

Editor's Comments
Please note that we do not publish textbooks. Our titles are
designed to supplement classroom lessons. We create
engaging books that will enthrall our readers, not dry recita-
tions of facts. We list targeted solicitations at our website
and in national newsletters, such as the SCBWI *Bulletin.*

Twilight Times Books

P.O. Box 3340
Kingsport, TN 37664

Publisher: Lida Quillen

Publisher's Interests

Producing books in electronic format as well as in print, Twilight Times specializes in general trade and young adult literary, historical, mystery, contemporary, and science fiction/fantasy fiction titles. It also publishes picture books for young children, as well as self-help and humor books.
Website: www.twilighttimesbooks.com

Freelance Potential

Published 15 titles (4 juvenile) in 2010: 8 were developed from unsolicited submissions. Of the 15 titles, 2 were by unpublished writers and 2 were by authors who were new to the publishing house. Receives 1,800+ queries yearly.

- **Fiction:** Publishes story picture books, 4–10 years; and young adult books, 12–18 years. Genres include historical, literary, and science fiction; mystery; suspense; realism; and stories about animals, magic realism, and New Age subjects.
- **Nonfiction:** Publishes young adult books, 12–18 years. Publishes self-improvement, how-to, and humorous books.
- **Representative Titles:** *Jeremy and the Dragon,* by Anne K. Edwards (4–10 years), is the story of a young dragon who discovers that his disability can be his weapon. *The Wolfman, the Shrink and the Eighth Grade Election,* by D. M. Nigro (YA), is the story of a teen girl asked to manage a popular boy's campaign for class president.

Submissions and Payment

Guidelines and catalogue available at website. Query with synopsis, first chapter, author bio, and marketing plan. Accepts email queries to publisher@twilighttimesbooks.com (no attachments). Responds in 1–2 months. Publication period varies. Royalty.

Editor's Comments

Please see our writers' guidelines for the latest information on our open submissions period.

Tyndale House Publishers

351 Executive Drive
Carol Stream, IL 60188

Acquisitions Director, Children & Family:
Katara Washington Patton

Publisher's Interests

Founded in 1962 as a means of publishing *The Living Bible*,
Tyndale now publishes Christian fiction, nonfiction, and various editions of the Bible. Its children's list includes fiction
and nonfiction books with a Christian perspective.
Website: www.tyndale.com

Freelance Potential

Published 15 titles in 2010: each was by an agented author.
Receives 240 queries yearly.

- **Fiction:** Publishes toddler books, 0–4 years; story picture
  books, 4–10 years; and middle-grade books, 8–12 years.
  Features fiction on general interest topics written from a
  Christian perspective.
- **Nonfiction:** Publishes toddler books and early picture books,
  0–4 years; easy-to-read books, 4–7 years; story picture books,
  4–10 years; middle-grade books, 8–12 years; and young adult
  books, 12–18 years. Topics include religion, spirituality, and
  the Christian faith. Also publishes parenting books.
- **Representative Titles:** *I Love God's Green Earth*, by Caroline
  Carroll & Michael Carroll, features devotions and Bible verses
  that help kids apply biblical and environmental lessons, plus
  "take-away" recycling activities. *Asking for Trouble: London
  Confidential #1*, by Sandra Byrd, finds an American teen moving to London with her family and learning to live out her faith
  while learning to love.

Submissions and Payment

Agented authors only. No unsolicited mss. Publication period
varies. Royalty; advance. Flat fee.

Editor's Comments

We no longer accept unsolicited manuscripts or queries. In
the past we had been inundated with them and published
very few. Now, we review material submitted through literary
agents or by previous Tyndale authors only.

Upstart Books

401 South Wright Street
Janesville, WI 53547

Editor: Kelly Loughman

Publisher's Interests

Upstart specializes in books about library use. Many of its titles introduce young children to the library; others teach library research skills to older children. Upstart also publishes resource books for librarians on professional development and children's library program ideas.
Website: www.upstartbooks.com

Freelance Potential

Published 10 titles (5 juvenile) in 2010: 3 were developed from unsolicited submissions. Of the 10 titles, 2 were by authors who were new to the publishing house. Receives 120 queries, 120 unsolicited mss yearly.

- **Fiction:** Publishes story picture books, 4–10 years; and chapter books, 5–10 years. Features stories that teach library skills.
- **Nonfiction:** Publishes professional resource books for librarians and teachers on library and research skills, story times, reading activities, and literature.
- **Representative Titles:** *There's Too Much Noise in the Library!*, by Susan Margaret Chapman (grades K–3), tells the story of the quiet-loving town mayor and how he grows to love the new— and noisy—media center at the library. *Liven Up Your Library*, by Jennifer Wetzel (librarians, grades K–5), is a professional resource designed to breathe new life into library lessons.

Submissions and Payment

Guidelines and catalogue available at website. Query with outline or sample chapters for mss longer than 100 pages; send complete ms for shorter works. Accepts hard copy and simultaneous submissions if identified. SASE. Responds in 2 months. Publication period varies. Royalty, 10–12%; advance.

Editor's Comments

We are specifically looking for books dealing with technology in the library, whether they be picture books for children or professional resource books for librarians.

URJ Press

633 Third Avenue
New York, NY 10017

Editor-in-Chief: Michael H. Goldberg

Publisher's Interests
This publishing arm of the Union for Reform Judaism produces an array of children's books dedicated to Jewish
history, values, and traditions. It also offers educational
resource materials for Torah and Hebrew study.
Website: www.urjbooksandmusic.com

Freelance Potential
Published 25 titles (12 juvenile) in 2010: 3 were developed
from unsolicited submissions. Of the 25 titles, 8 were by
unpublished writers and 4 were by authors who were new to
the publishing house. Receives 100 queries, 300 unsolicited
mss yearly.

- **Fiction:** Publishes early picture books, 0–4 years; story picture
  books, 4–10 years; and young adult books, 12–18 years. Genres include religious and historical fiction with Jewish themes.
- **Nonfiction:** Publishes toddler books and early picture books,
  0–4 years. Also publishes textbooks and educational resource
  materials for grades K–12. Topics include Jewish history and
  holidays, the Holocaust, and the Hebrew language.
- **Representative Titles:** *The Be a Mensch Campaign,* by
  Michelle Shapiro Abraham (grades 3–4), introduces children to
  five *middot,* or Jewish ethical behaviors. *Jeremiah's Promise,*
  by Kenneth Roseman (10–13 years), is an adventure set in
  modern Israel.

Submissions and Payment
Guidelines and catalogue available at website. Query with
résumé, outline, and 2 sample chapters. Send complete ms
for picture books. Accepts hard copy and email to press@
urj.org. SASE. Response time and publication period vary.
Royalty; advance.

Editor's Comments
We're looking for manuscripts that will fit into our line of
books for lifelong Jewish learning.

UXL

27500 Drake Road
Farmington Hills, MI 48331-3535

Editorial: Jim Person

Publisher's Interests
This publisher offers an extensive line of reference books
for students in the middle grades and high school. Primary
source volumes, encyclopedias, almanacs, chronologies, and
biographies can all be found in its catalogue, which covers a
broad range of academic subject areas.
Website: www.gale.cengage.com/uxl

Freelance Potential
Published 20 titles in 2010.

- **Nonfiction:** Publishes young adult books, 12–18 years. Topics
  include science, medicine, history, social studies, current
  events, multicultural issues, the arts, sports, and careers. Also
  publishes curriculum-based reference titles, encyclopedias,
  and biographies.
- **Representative Titles:** *Alternative Energy* (YA) is a three-
  volume set that reviews current energy sources, such as oil
  and gas, while introducing alternative energy options, including wind and solar energy, fuel cells, and geothermal power.
  Chemical Compounds (YA) features information on the ways
  different chemical elements combine, as well as 180 entries
  on organic and inorganic compounds and an overview of
  major discoveries and the scientists who made them.

Submissions and Payment
Guidelines and catalogue available at website. Accepts some
unsolicited material; most work is assigned on a work-for-
hire basis. Query with résumé and writing samples. Accepts
hard copy, simultaneous submissions if identified, and
queries submitted through website. SASE. Response time
and publication period vary. Flat fee.

Editor's Comments
While we prefer to assign topics to writers, occasionally an
unsolicited query that offers something new and intriguing
will grab our attention.

Viking Children's Books

Penguin Group
345 Hudson Street
New York, NY 10014

Editorial Assistant: Leila Sales

Publisher's Interests

This publisher offers a wide variety of fiction and nonfiction titles, including many award winners, for readers spanning the preschool to young adult years.
Website: www.us.penguin.com

Freelance Potential

Published 58 titles (38 juvenile) in 2010: 2 were developed from unsolicited submissions, 40 were by agented authors, and 6 were reprint/licensed properties. Of the 58 titles, 4 were by unpublished writers and 12 were by authors who were new to the publishing house. Receives 1,200 queries, 1,200 unsolicited mss yearly.

- **Fiction:** Publishes early picture books, 0–4 years; easy-to-read books, 4–7 years; story picture books, 4–10 years; chapter books, 5–10 years; middle-grade books, 8–12 years; and young adult books, 12–18 years. Genres include adventure; mystery; and contemporary, multicultural, and science fiction.
- **Nonfiction:** Publishes middle-grade books, 8–12 years; and young adult books, 12–18 years. Topics include animals, geography, history, sports, and science. Also publishes biographies.
- **Representative Titles:** *The Secret Year*, by Jennifer R. Hubbard (YA), tells of a girl and boy who are secretly dating until tragedy strikes. *Roly Poly Pangolin*, by Anna Dewdney (3–5 years), is about a shy pangolin who learns that new things don't have to be scary.

Submissions and Payment

Catalogue available at website. Agented authors preferred. Query or send ms. Accepts hard copy. Does not guarantee return of materials. Responds in 4 months if interested. Publication period varies. Royalty, 2–10%; advance. Flat fee.

Editor's Comments

Please don't contact us about your submission. We will contact you if we are interested.

Walch Education

40 Walch Drive
Portland, ME 04103

Submissions: Jill Rosenblum

Publisher's Interests

For more than 80 years, Walch Education has published educational materials, supplements, and curricula in all core subject areas for diverse learners in grades five through twelve. Its books are designed for use in classrooms or by homeschoolers.
Website: www.walch.com

Freelance Potential

Published 50 titles in 2010: 1 was developed from an unsolicited submission. Receives 24 queries yearly.

- **Nonfiction:** Publishes middle-grade and high school education books. Topics include reading, writing, vocabulary, grammar, geometry, algebra, critical thinking, world history, social science, chemistry, physics, money management, careers, and special education. Also publishes resource materials for teachers.
- **Representative Titles:** *100 Writing Starters for Middle School* (grades 6–8) reduces the terror of the blank page by providing students with high-interest topics and opening paragraphs designed to get them started on a writing project. *What's Next?* (grades 6–12) assists students transitioning into adulthood by guiding them through activities that teach life skills.

Submissions and Payment

Guidelines and catalogue available at website. Query with résumé, learning objectives, table of contents, sample chapter, and supporting material. Accepts hard copy and email queries to ideas@walch.com. SASE. Responds in 4–6 months. Publication period varies. Royalty. Flat fee.

Editor's Comments

Please be aware that we have a large, in-house team of educators that creates most of our books and material. We employ freelance writers only on large projects and commissioned titles. We will, at times, publish an unsolicited manuscript if it suits our needs perfectly.

Walker & Company

175 Fifth Avenue, 8th Floor
New York, NY 10011

Submissions

Publisher's Interests
Walker & Company's children's division, Walker Books for Young Readers, focuses on general interest fiction and non-fiction for children of all ages.
Website: www.walkeryoungreaders.com

Freelance Potential
Published 45 titles in 2010. Receives 8,000 queries, 5,000 unsolicited mss yearly.

- **Fiction:** Publishes toddler books, 0–4 years; story picture books, 4–10 years; middle-grade books, 8–12 years; and young adult books, 12–18 years. Genres include historical and contemporary fiction.
- **Nonfiction:** Publishes concept books, 0–4 years; story picture books, 4–10 years; middle-grade books, 8–12 years; and young adult books, 12–18 years. Topics include history, biography, and social issues.
- **Representative Titles:** *Off Like the Wind! The First Ride of the Pony Express*, by Michael P. Spradlin (grades 2–5), is a fictional but historically accurate account of the adventurous journey of the first Pony Express rider. *Poser*, by Sue Wyshynski (grades 7–12), is a novel of surfing, high school drama, and the discovery of true friendship.

Submissions and Payment
Guidelines and catalogue available at website. Query with outline/synopsis and 3–5 sample chapters. Send complete ms for picture books. Accepts hard copy and simultaneous submissions if identified. SASE. Responds in 5 months. Publication in 18–24 months. Royalty; advance.

Editor's Comments
Our current needs are for middle-grade and young adult novels and picture books for the preschool and early elementary age levels. Due to the limited number of titles we publish, we are extremely particular about the projects we take on.

Warner Press

1201 East Fifth Street
P.O. Box 2499
Anderson, IN 46016

Acquisitions Editor: Robin Fogle

Publisher's Interests
This publishing house of the Church of God produces a plethora of materials that communicate the message of Jesus Christ, including children's books and resources for church and religious education.
Website: www.warnerpress.org

Freelance Potential
Published 3–4 titles in 2010: 2 were developed from unsolicited submissions and 1 was by an agented author. Of the 3–4 titles, 1 was by an unpublished writer and 2 were by authors who were new to the publishing house. Receives 300+ queries, 120+ unsolicited mss yearly.

- **Fiction:** Publishes easy-to-read books, 4–7 years; story picture books, 4–10 years; and middle-grade books, 8–12 years. Features religious fiction and stories with biblical themes.
- **Nonfiction:** Publishes puzzle and activity books, 8–10 years. Topics include the Bible, religious history, and Christianity. Also publishes reference books for parents and teachers.
- **Representative Titles:** *The Princess and the Kiss: A Story of God's Gift of Purity,* by Jennie Bishop (8–12 years), is the story of a young princess who learns about the precious gift of purity. *Going Live in 3 . . . 2. . . 1!,* by Tina Houser (7–12 years), presents innovative techniques for Bible storytelling.

Submissions and Payment
Guidelines available at website. Query with synopsis and publishing credits for picture books. Send complete ms with illustration ideas for activity books. Accepts email queries to rfogle@warnerpress.org. Responds in 3–6 months. Publication in 12–18 months. Flat fee.

Editor's Comments
We look for authors who have a personal relationship with God and knowledge of the Bible. We are open to a multitude of non-denominational Christian subjects.

WaterBrook Multnomah Publishing Group

12265 Oracle Boulevard, Suite 200
Colorado Springs, CO 80921

Submissions Editor

Publisher's Interests
The evangelical division of Random House, WaterBrook Mult-
nomah offers books for Christian living and spiritual growth.
Its list includes books for children and inspirational novels
for young adults. Among its offerings for adults are titles
on parenting, love, and relationships—all from a Christian
perspective.
Website: www.waterbrookmultnomah.com

Freelance Potential
Published 65–70 titles in 2010. Receives 500 queries yearly.

- **Fiction:** Publishes story picture books, 4–10 years; and young
  adult books, 12–18 years. Genres include religious, inspirational, and contemporary fiction; and fantasy.
- **Nonfiction:** Publishes young adult books, 12–18 years. Topics
  include religion, Christianity, and personal faith. Also publishes
  parenting titles.
- **Representative Titles:** *This Little Prayer of Mine,* by Anthony
  DeStefano, uses rhymes and illustrations to teach young children that prayer can be a way to be closer to God. *Do Hard
  Things,* by Alex Harris & Brett Harris, challenges teens to rebel
  against the low expectations of today's culture by choosing
  to "do hard things" for the glory of God. *The Dragon and the
  Turtle,* by Donita K. Paul & Evangeline Denmark, is a novel
  about an unlikely friendship with unexpected rewards.

Submissions and Payment
Catalogue available at website. Accepts queries through literary agents only. Responds in 6–10 weeks. Publication in 1
year. Royalty; advance.

Editor's Comments
We are no longer giving consideration to unsolicited materials
unless presented to us by literary agents. Our website lists
several resources that may be helpful in putting your work in
front of a publisher that specializes in Christian books.

Watson-Guptill Publications

Random House
770 Broadway
New York, NY 10003

Senior Acquisitions Editor: Julie Mazur

Publisher's Interests

Books about art and graphic art, crafts, photography, design, architecture, film, and music fill the pages of this publisher's catalogue. An imprint of Random House and Crown Publishing Group, it has a line of books designed to inspire creativity in children and young adults. Many of its titles are illustrated "how-to" publications.

Website: www.watsonguptill.com

Freelance Potential

Published 77 titles in 2010: 25 were by agented authors.

- **Nonfiction:** Publishes middle-grade books, 8–12 years; and young adult books, 12–18 years. Topics include fine arts, drawing, painting, sculpture, cartooning, animation, graphic design, crafts, dramatic arts, music, photography, makeup artistry, architecture, and interior design.
- **Representative Titles:** *Superheroes and Beyond,* by Christopher Hart, provides step-by-step instructions for drawing a huge array of original superheroes. *A Rainbow of Stitches,* by Agnes Delage-Calvet et al., is a how-to guide that includes an extensive collection of stitches of all styles and types. *Cartoon Cute Animals,* by Christopher Hart, teaches young artists how to draw the most irresistible creatures on the planet.

Submissions and Payment

Guidelines and catalogue available. Query with table of contents, sample chapter, author bio, and market analysis. Accepts hard copy. SASE. Response time and publication period vary. Royalty; advance.

Editor's Comments

We look for beautifully designed and lavishly illustrated books that are as inspirational and aspirational as they are instructive. Your query should demonstrate your expertise in the area you are covering and your ability to provide clear, step-by-step instructions.

Wayne State University Press

The Leonard N. Simons Building
4809 Woodward Avenue
Detroit, MI 48201-1309

Acquisitions Editors: Kathryn Wildfong & Annie Martin

Publisher's Interests

Located in the heart of Detroit's cultural district, this mid-size university press features books for adults and students about the humanities, arts, and social sciences. Many have regional themes or are written by Michigan authors. It also offers titles for educators and books for young readers about Michigan and the Great Lakes.
Website: http://wsupress.wayne.edu

Freelance Potential

Published 35 titles in 2010: 2 were by agented authors and 2 were reprint/licensed properties. Receives 200 queries each year.

- **Nonfiction:** Publishes early picture books, 0–4 years; and middle-grade books, 8–12 years. Topics include the art, architecture, and culture of the Michigan region; the history of the Upper Peninsula and the Great Lakes; and historical Detroit personalities. Also publishes child development titles.
- **Representative Titles:** *Let's Read: A Linguistic Approach,* by Cynthia A. & Robert K. Barnhart (educators), is an update on a classic book about beginning reading. *Techno Rebels: The Renegades of Electronic Funk,* by Dan Sicko (YA–Adult), provides an overview of this musical genre and its roots in the Detroit music scene.

Submissions and Payment

Guidelines and catalogue available at website. Query with résumé, outline, table of contents, and sample chapters. Accepts hard copy and email queries to k.wildfong@ wayne.edu. SASE. Responds in 4–6 weeks. Publication in 15 months. Royalty, 6–7.5%.

Editor's Comments

We are dedicated to the discovery, discourse, and dissemination of ideas and knowledge and to the well-being of Detroit and Michigan.

Weigl Publishers

350 Fifth Avenue, 59th Floor
New York, NY 10118

Managing Editor: Heather Hudak

Publisher's Interests

Specializing in supplementary educational material, Weigl
publishes books for school libraries as well as for classroom
use. Its books cover all curriculum areas, especially science,
social studies, and language arts. All of its titles are written
on assignment.
Website: www.weigl.com

Freelance Potential

Published 88 titles in 2010. Of the 88 titles, 5 were by
authors who were new to the publishing house.

- **Nonfiction:** Publishes nonfiction series, 5–10 years; and
  middle-grade books, 8–12 years. Topics include global cultures, social and environmental issues, plant and animal life,
  biography, sports, science, and social studies.
- **Representative Titles:** *Budgeting* (grades 4–6) provides the
  foundation to understanding the role of budgeting in money
  management; part of the Everyday Economics series. *Sea
  Turtles* (grades 2–4) introduces young minds to these graceful
  undersea creatures; part of the World of Wonder: Underwater
  Life series.

Submissions and Payment

Catalogue available at website. All work is done on a work-
for-hire basis. Send résumé, publishing history, and subject
area of expertise only. No queries or unsolicited mss.
Accepts hard copy and email to linda@weigl.com. SASE.
Responds in 6–12 months. Publication in 2 years. Flat fee.

Editor's Comments

Do not bother to craft a query letter for a book idea you may
have—we will not read it. We assign book or series projects
to our stable of competent, experienced authors; however,
we will consider new writers if their expertise matches our
needs. Currently, we're looking for writers experienced in
science, biography, social studies, sports, and animals.

Weiser Books

500 Third Street, Suite 230
San Francisco, CA 94107

Acquisitions Editor: Pat Bryce

Publisher's Interests

Weiser Books publishes titles about esoteric or occult teachings from traditions around the world and throughout time, such as consciousness, new science, Wicca, and astrology. It does not publish children's titles, but some of its books may be of interest to young adults, especially its Weiser Field Guide series.

Website: www.weiserbooks.com

Freelance Potential

Published 30 titles in 2010: 5 were developed from unsolicited submissions and 5 were by agented authors. Receives 1,000+ queries yearly.

- **Nonfiction:** Publishes books on new consciousness, new science, coming Earth changes, magick, Wicca, Western mystery traditions, tarot, yoga, and astrology.
- **Representative Titles:** *The Weiser Field Guide to Ghosts,* by Raymond Buckland, examines categories of ghosts across time and cultures and offers stories of ghostly encounters and legendary ghosts. *Dreaming with the Archangels,* by Linda & Peter Miller-Russo, takes readers on a 30-night journey with the four Archangels as guides and reveals ways to understand and heal through dreams.

Submissions and Payment

Guidelines and catalogue available at website. Query with résumé, outline, table of contents, and 3 chapters. Accepts hard copy, email to submissions@redwheelweiser.com (Microsoft Word attachments), and simultaneous submissions if identified. Responds in 3 months. Publication in 18 months. Royalty; advance.

Editor's Comments

In addition to reviewing your proposal, we would be happy to add your email address to our mailing list and send you information about our publishing program from time to time.

Whitecap Books

351 Lynn Avenue
North Vancouver, British Columbia V7J 2C4
Canada

Editor: Taryn Boyd

Publisher's Interests
Through its children's imprint, Walrus Books, this publisher produces fiction and nonfiction for children and young adults. Its fiction list includes picture books and series fiction for teens, while its nonfiction list features titles on science, nature, and the environment.
Website: www.whitecap.ca

Freelance Potential
Published 43 titles (6 juvenile) in 2010: 2 were developed from unsolicited submissions and 3 were by agented authors. Receives 300 queries yearly.

- **Fiction:** Publishes easy-to-read books, 4–7 years; middle-grade books, 8–12 years; and young adult books, 12–18 years. Genres include contemporary fiction, adventure, fantasy, folklore, and stories about animals, nature, and the environment.
- **Nonfiction:** Publishes easy-to-read books, 4–7 years; and story picture books, 4–10 years. Topics include animals, natural history, science, the environment, and regional subjects.
- **Representative Titles:** *Accidental Alphabet,* by Dianna Bonder, features coughing camels, lazy llamas, and rowdy roosters who take children through the alphabet. *Fire Horse,* by Sharon Siamon, is an adventure tale in which three young heroines find self-discovery and friendship on Mustang Mountain; part of the Mustang Mountain series.

Submissions and Payment
Guidelines and catalogue available at website. Query with outline/synopsis, table of contents, and sample chapters. Accepts hard copy and simultaneous submissions if identified. SASE. Responds in 2–3 months. Publication in 1 year. Royalty; advance.

Editor's Comments
At this time, we're not accepting children's picture books, but we are open to receiving juvenile series-based fiction.

White Mane Kids

73 West Burd Street
P.O. Box 708
Shippensburg, PA 17257

Acquisitions Department

Publisher's Interests

White Mane Kids specializes in historical fiction for readers ages eight and up. Most of its titles feature themes relating to the American Civil War, although books about other eras in American history are also sometimes published. It looks for novels that offer engaging plot lines, while also providing accurate historical information. 30% self-, subsidy-, co-venture, or co-op published material.

Website: www.whitemane.com

Freelance Potential

Published 3 titles in 2010: 1 was developed from an unsolicited submission. Receives 100 queries yearly.

- **Fiction:** Publishes middle-grade books, 8–12 years; and young adult books, 12–18 years. Genres include historical fiction.
- **Representative Titles:** *No Girls Allowed,* by Alan N. Kay, uses fiction to depict the roles of women in the Civil War during the Battle of Antietam, as well as the frustrations doctors and nurses faced during the war; part of the Young Heroes of History series. *Divided Loyalties: A Revolutionary War Fifer's Story,* by Phyllis Haislip, tells of a boy in a fife and drum corps whose father is a Patriot and whose mother is a Loyalist.

Submissions and Payment

Guidelines and proposal submission form available. Query with proposal form, market analysis, and brief author biography. Accepts hard copy. SASE. Responds in 3–6 months. Publication in 12–18 months. Royalty, 7–10%.

Editor's Comments

Because we market our titles with additional educational resources for classroom use, it is very important that all stories be historically accurate. Your query should include information about the historical relevance and educational benefits of your work. Interesting characters and exciting situations are also a must.

Albert Whitman & Company

6340 Oakton Street
Morton Grove, IL 60053-2723

Editor-in-Chief: Kathleen Tucker

Publisher's Interests

For more than 90 years, Albert Whitman & Company has been creating books for children of all ages. Its catalogue features both fiction and nonfiction, and it has an extensive backlist that includes holiday books, concept books, and books in the Boxcar Children series.
Website: www.albertwhitman.com

Freelance Potential

Published 30 titles in 2010. Receives 300 queries, 4,500 unsolicited mss yearly.

- **Fiction:** Publishes early picture books, 0–4 years; chapter books, 5–10 years; middle-grade books, 8–12 years; and young adult books, 12–18 years. Genres include historical fiction, humor, and mystery.
- **Nonfiction:** Publishes early picture books, 0–4 years; chapter books, 5–10 years; and middle-grade books, 8–12 years. Topics include social, multicultural, ethnic, and family issues; history; and biography.
- **Representative Titles:** *If I Ran for President,* by Catherine Stier (6–9 years), explains the presidential election process in a kid-friendly way. *Lucy and the Bully,* by Claire Alexander (3–6 years), uses a simple story and bright illustrations to explain bullying and to show children how it can be stopped.

Submissions and Payment

Guidelines and catalogue available at website. Query with 3 sample chapters. Send complete ms for picture books. Accepts hard copy and simultaneous submissions if identified. SASE. Responds to queries in 6 weeks, to mss in 3–4 months. Publication in 18–24 months. Royalty; advance.

Editor's Comments

We are interested in reviewing picture book manuscripts, middle-grade novels, and chapter books and nonfiction for ages 3 through 12.

Windward Publishing

8075 215th Street West
Lakeville, MN 55044

President: Alan E. Krysan

Publisher's Interests

Windward Publishing markets children's stories and nonfiction books that focus on natural history, science, and exploring the outdoors. It is a division of Finney Company.
Website: www.finneyco.com

Freelance Potential

Published 4–5 titles (2–3 juvenile) in 2010: 4 were developed from unsolicited submissions. Of the 4–5 titles, 3 were by unpublished writers and 3 were by authors who were new to the publishing house. Receives 180–240 queries, 180–240 unsolicited mss yearly.

- **Fiction:** Publishes easy-to-read books, 4–7 years; and story picture books, 4–10 years. Genres include books about nature and the natural world.
- **Nonfiction:** Publishes easy-to-read books, 4–7 years; story picture books, 4–10 years; chapter books, 5–10 years; middle-grade books, 8–12 years; and young adult books, 12–18 years. Topics include nature, flowers, birds, reptiles, amphibians, fishing, seashells and sea life, and space.
- **Representative Titles:** *By the Light of the Moon,* by Julie Olsson Kenagy, tells readers about wild animals that hunt, run, and play by moonlight. *Space Station Science,* by Marianne Dyson, describes the systems that keep the International Space Station running.

Submissions and Payment

Guidelines available at website. Query with overview, table of contents, and up to 3 chapters; or send ms. Accepts hard copy and simultaneous submissions if identified. Artwork improves chance of acceptance. SASE. Responds in 10–12 weeks. Publication in 6–8 months. Royalty, 10% of net.

Editor's Comments

We're primarily interested in nonfiction books, but we will consider fiction, as long as it has some educational value.

Paula Wiseman Books

Simon & Schuster
1230 Avenue of the Americas
New York, NY 10020

Associate Editor: Alexandra Penfold

Publisher's Interests

This imprint of Simon & Schuster Children's Publishing focuses on picture books, novelty books, and novels for preschool kids through young adults.
Website: http://kids.simonandschuster.com

Freelance Potential

Published 25 titles in 2010. Of the 25 titles, 1 was by an unpublished writer and 2 were by authors who were new to the publishing house.

- **Fiction:** Publishes toddler books and early picture books, 0–4 years; easy-to-read books, 4–7 years; chapter books, 5–10 years; and young adult books, 12–18 years. Genres include contemporary and multicultural fiction; adventure; and humor. Also publishes board books.
- **Nonfiction:** Publishes easy-to-read books, 4–7 years; story picture books, 4–10 years; middle-grade books, 8–12 years; and young adult books, 12–18 years. Topics include animals, nature, the environment, history, and sports. Also publishes biographies and board books.
- **Representative Titles:** *Play Ball!,* by Jorge Posada (6–10 years), is the autobiographical story of a boy from Puerto Rico who worked hard to become a champion of the diamond. *Little Cloud and Lady Wind,* by Toni Morrison & Slade Morrison (4–8 years), tells the story of a young cloud who yearns to live on the Earth.

Submissions and Payment

Agented submissions only. Response time varies. Publication in 18–24 months. Royalty; advance.

Editor's Comments

We accept submissions from new and previously published authors—but only through agents, please. We like books that entertain while expanding the experience of children who read them, especially stories based on other cultures.

Woodbine House

6510 Bells Mill Road
Bethesda, MD 20817

Acquisitions Editor: Nancy Gray Paul

Publisher's Interests

Books for parents of children with developmental disabilities and the teachers and therapists who work with them fill the catalogue of this publisher. Woodbine also publishes books for the children themselves.

Website: www.woodbinehouse.com

Freelance Potential

Published 9 titles (1 juvenile) in 2010: 4 were developed from unsolicited submissions. Of the 9 titles, 3 were by unpublished writers and 5 were by new authors. Receives 50 queries, 250 unsolicited mss yearly.

- **Fiction:** Publishes concept books, 0–4 years; story picture books, 2–10 years; and chapter books, 8–18 years. Publishes stories for and about children with developmental disabilities.
- **Nonfiction:** Publishes guides and reference books for parents and professionals. Topics include autism spectrum disorders, Down syndrome, Tourette syndrome, executive dysfunction, and other developmental disabilities.
- **Representative Titles:** *Gravity Pulls You In*, by Kyra Anderson & Vicki Forman, eds., consists of slice-of-life essays and poems that depict the experiences of parents of children on the autism spectrum. *The Power to Spring Up*, by Diana M. Katovitch, explores the postsecondary education opportunities for special education students.

Submissions and Payment

Guidelines and catalogue available at website. Query with résumé, outline, and sample chapters. Send complete ms for picture books only. Accepts hard copy and simultaneous submissions if identified. SASE. Responds in 3 months. Publication in 1 year. Payment policy varies.

Editor's Comments

Our current needs include practical guides for parents and guides to specific issues related to a given disability.

Wordsong

Boyds Mills Press
813 Church Street
Honesdale, PA 18431

Editor: Joan Hyman

Publisher's Interests
Wordsong, part of Boyds Mills Press, is the only imprint
devoted solely to poetry for children. Wordplay, imagery,
lyricism, and humor are among the important qualities of
its books, which range from the serious to the lighthearted.
Website: www.wordsongpoetry.com

Freelance Potential
Published 9 titles in 2010. Receives 300–360 unsolicited
mss yearly.

- **Fiction:** Publishes story picture books, 6–9 years; and poetry
  collections, 3–17 years.
- **Representative Titles:** *Weekend Mischief,* by Rob Jackson
  (7–9 years), describes the comical antics of a boy on his days
  off from school. *An Egret's Day, by* Jane Yolen (9–11 years),
  follows the life of the majestic Great Egret with poems and
  photographs. *Becoming Billie Holiday*, by Carole Boston
  Weatherford (14–17 years), is a sequence of passionate,
  poignant poems about the life of the celebrated singer.

Submissions and Payment
Guidelines and catalogue available at website. Send complete,
book-length collection of your own poems. Accepts hard copy.
SASE. Responds in 3 months. Publication period varies. Royalty;
advance. Flat fee.

Editor's Comments
The fresh and contemporary voices in our poetry connect
with young readers to help them see the world with a new,
thoughtful perspective. The strongest collections demonstrate a facility with multiple poetic forms.

Workman Publishing

225 Varick Street
New York, NY 10014

Editorial Assistant: Natalie Rinn

Publisher's Interests

Workman, the home of the popular title, *What To Expect When You're Expecting*, publishes parenting and pregnancy guides, fun and educational children's fiction and nonfiction, and self-help books for adults.
Website: www.workman.com

Freelance Potential

Published 40 titles (7 juvenile) in 2010: 7 were by agented authors. Receives 1,000 queries, 360+ unsolicited mss each year.

- **Fiction:** Publishes toddler books, 0–4 years. Also publishes board books and novelty books for children.
- **Nonfiction:** Publishes concept books and toddler books, 0–4 years; middle-grade books, 8–12 years; and young adult books, 12–18 years. Topics include science, nature, humor, hobbies, and crafts. Also publishes books on pregnancy and parenting.
- **Representative Titles:** *Perfect Piggies!*, by Sandra Boynton (0–4 years), celebrates round noses, curly tails, floppy ears, and pleasing plumpness with whimsical verse and a download-able song. *Potato Chip Science*, by A. Kurzweil, features 29 child-friendly potato experiments and includes the tools neces-sary to complete them.

Submissions and Payment

Guidelines and catalogue available at website. Query with sample chapters and outline/synopsis; or send complete ms. Accepts hard copy. SASE. Responds in 3 months. Publication period varies. Royalty; advance.

Editor's Comments

Please note that we do not publish picture books or middle-grade and young adult fiction. Send those projects else-where. Each submission is reviewed by at least two editors, and this process takes time. Please be patient with us.

YouthLight

P.O. Box 115
Chapin, SC 29036

Vice President: Susan Bowman

Publisher's Interests
YouthLight publishes material on contemporary social issues designed to help counselors, teachers, parents, and mental health professionals who work with young people.
Website: www.youthlightbooks.com

Freelance Potential
Published 15 titles in 2010: each was developed from an unsolicited submission. Of the 15 titles, 10 were by unpublished writers and 5 were by new authors. Receives 48 queries, 48–72 unsolicited mss yearly.

- **Fiction:** Publishes easy-to-read books, 4–7 years; story picture books, 4–10 years; middle-grade books, 8–12 years; and young adult books, 12–18 years. Genres include multicultural fiction and stories about children dealing with social pressures.
- **Nonfiction:** Publishes easy-to-read books, 4–7 years; story picture books, 4–10 years; middle-grade books, 8–12 years; and young adult books, 12–18 years. Topics include self-help and social issues. Also publishes titles for adults.
- **Representative Titles:** *Kicky, the Mean Chick, Learns Her Lesson,* by Erika Shearin Karres (preK–grade 3), is the story of a young chicken who learns that being a bully is no fun. *Life Strategies for Teens,* by Jay McGraw (grades 6–12), guides teen readers through their pivotal years.

Submissions and Payment
Guidelines and catalogue available at website. Query for nonfiction. Send complete ms with table of contents for fiction. Accepts disk submissions and email to sbowman@youthlightbooks.com. Responds in 1–3 weeks. Publication in 6 months. Royalty, 10%.

Editor's Comments
We're looking for books on friendship for kindergarten through grade eight, and on empathy for kindergarten through grade 6. Activities for middle school students are needed as well.

Zephyr Press

814 North Franklin Street
Chicago, IL 60610

Acquisitions: Jerome Pohler

Publisher's Interests

This education publisher offers titles that can be used across the curricula in kindergarten through twelfth grade. It produces books on a broad spectrum of subject areas, including art and artists, science, nature, history, world cultures, and mathematics. Resources for gifted and talented education and school counseling are also available from Zephyr.
Website: www.zephyrpress.com

Freelance Potential

Published 6 titles in 2010. Receives 250+ queries yearly.

- **Nonfiction:** Publishes educational titles for use in grades K–12. Topics include art, brain compatible learning, counseling, critical thinking, cultural studies, history, gifted and talented education, math, engineering, multiple intelligences and differentiation, music, drama, dance, professional development, reading, writing, science, social and emotional development, Spanish, technology, new media, and testing.
- **Representative Titles:** *Great American Artists for Kids,* by MaryAnn F. Kohl & Kim Solga (preK–grade 4), presents hands-on art experiences in the styles of Great American Masters. *Take a Beach Walk,* by Jane Kirkland (grades 3–6), describes the waterfront ecosystem in a way that reconnects children with the outdoors; part of the Take a Walk series.

Submissions and Payment

Guidelines and catalogue available. Query with complete submissions packet included with guidelines. Accepts hard copy. Availability of artwork improves chance of acceptance. SASE. Responds in 3–6 months. Publication in 1–2 years. Royalty, 7.5–10%.

Editor's Comments

We're particularly interested in books that feature hands-on educational activities. Classroom-tested strategies are always the best.

Zumaya Publications

3209 South Interstate 35, #1086
Austin, TX 78741-6905

Executive Editor: Elizabeth K. Burton

Publisher's Interests
With titles appearing both in print and in electronic format, Zumaya publishes innovative fiction in a range of genres by new as well as aspiring authors. It has a children's catalogue as well as books for adults.
Website: www.zumayapublications.com

Freelance Potential
Published 36 titles (5–6 juvenile) in 2010: 20 were developed from unsolicited submissions. Of the 36 titles, 6 were by unpublished writers and 8 were by authors who were new to the publishing house. Receives 840 queries yearly.

- **Fiction:** Publishes chapter books, 5–10 years; middle-grade books, 8–12 years; and young adult books, 12–18 years. Genres include adventure; fantasy; folklore; folktales; romance; Westerns; horror; and historical, mainstream, seasonal, and science fiction.
- **Representative Titles:** *A Troll for Christmas,* by Harley L. Sachs, is an eclectic collection of stories that offers a loving look at the joys and pains of childhood and the lessons we learn when we aren't looking. *The Emerald City,* by Stephen S. Keeney, is an adventure tale featuring 13-year-old Spencer and his band of pre-teen detectives.

Submissions and Payment
Guidelines and catalogue available at website. Query with synopsis. Accepts email queries to acquisitions@zumayapublications.com (Microsoft Word or RTF attachments). Responds in 1–3 months. Publication period varies. Royalty, 20% for print books; 50% for e-books.

Editor's Comments
Because of a large backlog of projects, we had temporarily stopped reviewing queries. We are open again, however, as of summer of 2010. Please see the guidelines section of our website for the latest status information.

Additional Listings

We have selected the following publishers to offer you additional marketing opportunities. Most of these publishers have special submissions requirements or they purchase a limited number of juvenile titles each year.

For published authors, we include information about houses that produce reprints of previously published works. For writers who are proficient in foreign languages, we list publishers of foreign-language material. You will also find publishers that accept résumés only; who work with agented authors; or who usually accept unsolicited submissions, but due to a backlog, are not accepting material at this time.

As you survey these listings, you may find that a small regional press is a more appropriate market for your submission than a large publisher. Also, if you are involved in education or are a specialist in a certain field, consider sending your résumé to one of the educational publishers—you may have the qualifications they are looking for.

Publishers who usually accept unsolicited submissions but were not accepting unsolicited material at our press time are designated with an **X**.

Be sure to contact the publisher before submitting material to determine the current submissions policy.

As you review the listings that follow, use the Publisher's Interests section as your guide to the particular focus of each house.

Abbeville Family

137 Varick Street, 5th Floor
New York, NY 10013

Editor: Susan Costello

Publisher's Interests
Abbeville Family publishes parenting guides while its imprint, Abbeville Kids, produces books for children of all ages. It is currently not accepting unsolicited submissions, but it may open up in the future due to an expansion of its list. 50% self-, subsidy-, co-venture, or co-op published material.
Website: www.abbeville.com

Freelance Potential
Published 10–12 titles in 2010. Of the 10–12 titles, 4 were by authors who were new to the publishing house.
Submissions and Payment: Not currently accepting queries or manuscripts. Check the website for changes to this policy.

Abingdon Press

201 Eighth Avenue South
P.O. Box 801
Nashville, TN 37202-0801

Manuscript Submissions

Publisher's Interests
This imprint of the United Methodist Publishing House provides resources for those who seek, and seek to serve, God. These resources include both print and nonprint materials. The religious education materials it publishes are written on assignment by active members of the United Methodist Church. 50% co-op published material.
Website: www.abingdonpress.com

Freelance Potential
Published 10 titles in 2010. Receives 600 queries yearly.
Submissions and Payment: Guidelines available. Query with outline and 1–2 sample chapters. Accepts hard copy. SASE. No simultaneous submissions. Responds in 2 months. Publication in 2 years. Royalty.

Absey & Company

23011 Northcrest Drive
Spring, TX 77389

Editor-in-Chief: Edward Wilson

Publisher's Interests
This publisher offers fiction, poetry, and educational nonfiction titles for school-aged children. Resource books aimed at language arts teachers are also found on its list.
Website: www.absey.biz

Freelance Potential
Published 5–10 titles (1–2 juvenile) in 2010. Of the 5–10 titles, 4–7 were by unpublished writers and 4–9 were by authors new to the publishing house. Receives 10,000 queries yearly.
Submissions and Payment: Guidelines and catalogue available at website. Query with outline/synopsis and 2–3 sample chapters. Accepts hard copy. No simultaneous submissions. SASE. Responds in 6–9 months. Publication in 1 year. Payment policy varies.

Academic Therapy Publications

20 Commercial Boulevard
Novato, CA 94949

Acquisitions Editor

Publisher's Interests
This publishing company was formed to meet the needs of professionals in the fields of special education and learning disabilities, as well as the students and parents with whom they work. It produces standardized tests, reference books, curriculum materials, teacher/parent resources, and visual/perceptual training aids for all school-age children.
Website: www.academictherapy.com

Freelance Potential
Published 15 titles (12 juvenile) in 2010. Receives 50 queries each year.
Submissions and Payment: Catalogue available at website. Query with synopsis and author bio. Accepts hard copy. SASE. Response time varies. Publication period varies. Flat fee.

Accord Publishing

1130 Walnut Street
Kansas City, MO 64106

Book Submissions

Publisher's Interests
This publisher specializes in colorful, creative board books for babies and toddlers, and story picture books for very young children. It also produces calendars and gift books covering a wide range of themes.
Website: www.accordpublishing.com

Freelance Potential
Published 20 titles (17 juvenile) in 2010. Of the 20 titles, each was by an author who was new to the publishing house. Receives 72–144 queries, 120+ unsolicited mss yearly.
Submissions and Payment: Guidelines available at website. Query or send complete ms. No simultaneous submissions. Accepts hard copy. SASE. Response time, publication period, and payment policy vary.

Adasi Publishing

6 Dover Point Road, Suite B
Dover, NH 03820

Office Manager: Parvaneh Ghavami

Publisher's Interests
Educational books about math, physics, astronomy, and the history of science are available from Adasi Publishing, which targets an audience of adult readers only. It seeks books that reflect the viewpoint of individual authors. Books that are simply "politically correct" are not accepted.
Website: www.adasi.com

Freelance Potential
Published 1 title in 2010: it was developed from an unsolicited submission. Receives 12 queries yearly.
Submissions and Payment: Guidelines available at website. Query. Accepts hard copy and email queries to info@ adasi.com. SASE. Responds in 1 month. Publication in 6 months. Royalty, 5% (negotiable).

The Alternate Press

B2-125 The Queensway, Suite 52
Toronto, Ontario M8Y 1H6
Canada

Submissions Editor: Wendy Priesnitz

Publisher's Interests
The Alternate Press does not publish juvenile literature, but
does specialize in how-to books on natural parenting, homeschooling and unschooling, alternative education, green business, and environmentally conscious lifestyles.
Website: www.lifemedia.ca/altpress

Freelance Potential
Published 2 titles in 2010. Receives 40 queries yearly.
Submissions and Payment: Guidelines and catalogue available at website. Query with synopsis, 25 sample pages, and
author bio. Accepts hard copy, email to altpress@lifemedia.ca
(Microsoft Word attachments), and simultaneous submissions if
identified. SASE. Responds in 2 months. Publication period and
payment policy vary.

Ambassador International

427 Wade Hampton Boulevard
Greenville, SC 29609

Publisher: Samuel Lowry

Publisher's Interests
Toddler books and picture books are available from this
Christian publisher, which focuses primarily on titles for adults.
50% self-, subsidy-, co-venture, or co-op published material.
Website: www.ambassador-international.com

Freelance Potential
Published 45 titles (20 juvenile) in 2010: 22 were developed
from unsolicited submissions and 22 were by agented authors.
Of the 45 titles, 4 were by unpublished writers and 12 were by
new authors. Receives 1,800 queries yearly.
Submissions and Payment: Guidelines and catalogue available at website. Query. Accepts hard copy and email queries
to publisher@emeraldhouse.com. SASE. Responds in 3 weeks.
Publication in 6 months. Royalty, 10–18%.

American Girl Publications

8400 Fairway Place
Middleton, WI 53562

Submissions Editor

Publisher's Interests
This publisher solely accepts nonfiction titles of interest to
girls ages 8 to 12. It publishes activity, craft, and advice books,
with the goals of fostering curiosity, building self-confidence,
and encouraging dreams.
Website: www.americangirl.com

Freelance Potential
Published 30–40 titles in 2010. Receives 150 queries, 350
unsolicited mss yearly.
Submissions and Payment: Guidelines and catalogue available at website. Prefers query with sample chapters and clips;
will accept complete ms. Accepts hard copy and simultaneous
submissions if identified. SASE. Responds in 3–4 months.
Publication period and payment policy vary.

Anova Books

10 Southcombe Street
London W14 0RA
United Kingdom

Submissions

Publisher's Interests
Anova Books offers both fiction and nonfiction covering many
genres and topics. Genres include adventure, fantasy, humor,
and fairy tales; nonfiction topics include animals, nature, and
the environment. The titles from this publisher are geared
toward children and young adults.
Website: www.anovabooks.com

Freelance Potential
Published 175 titles in 2010. Receives 200 queries yearly.
Submissions and Payment: Guidelines and catalogue available at website. Query with synopsis. Accepts hard copy and
email queries to appropriate editor; list of editors and email
addresses available at website. SAE/IRC. Responds in 2
months. Publication in 15 months. Royalty; advance. Flat fee.

Association for Childhood Education International

17904 Georgia Avenue, Suite 215
Olney, MD 20832-2277

Director, Editorial Department: Anne Bauer

Publisher's Interests
The mission of this nonprofit organization is to provide resources that enhance childhood education programs throughout the world. To this end, its publishing arm offers books on education, literacy, early childhood development, parenting, special education, and curricula-related subjects.
Website: www.acei.org

Freelance Potential
Published 2–3 titles in 2010. Receives 120 unsolicited mss each year.
Submissions and Payment: Guidelines available at website. Send complete ms. Accepts hard copy and disk submissions (ASCII or Microsoft Word). SASE. Responds in 2 weeks. Publication in 1–3 years. No payment.

August House

3500 Piedmont Road NE
Atlanta, GA 30305

Editorial Department

Publisher's Interests
The mission of August House is to publish picture books, children's fiction, and multimedia products that focus on world folktales and the art and uses of storytelling. It seeks picture book manuscripts for children ages four to eight that feature traditional folktales; it is not interested in original stories written in fable or fairy-tale style.
Website: www.augusthouse.com

Freelance Potential
Published 20–40 titles in 2010.
Submissions and Payment: Guidelines and catalogue available at website. Query or send ms. Accepts hard copy and simultaneous submissions. SASE. Responds in 5 months if interested. Publication period and payment policy vary.

A/V Concepts Corporation

30 Montauk Boulevard
Oakdale, NY 11769

Editor: Janice Cobas

Publisher's Interests
A variety of educational materials are found in this publisher's
catalogue, including books, videos, CDs, and computer software for the preschool through high school years. It also
offers products for struggling students and special education.
Website: www.edconpublishing.com

Freelance Potential
Published 10 titles (5 juvenile) in 2010. Of the 10 titles, 3
were by unpublished writers. Receives 120 queries yearly.
Submissions and Payment: Guidelines available with 9x12
SASE ($1.75 postage). Catalogue available at website. Query
with résumé and clips or writing samples. Accepts hard copy.
SASE. Responds in 1 month. Publication in 6 months. Flat fee,
$300–$1,000.

Avocet Press

19 Paul Court
Pearl River, NY 10965-1539

Editor: Sally Williams

Publisher's Interests
This small, independent publisher seeks genre fiction with a
twist—for example, feminist mysteries. It is not interested in
romances or science fiction. Good stories told from an unusual
point of view are especially sought. Please note that it is not
the best market for novice writers.
Website: www.avocetpress.com

Freelance Potential
Published 4 titles in 2010. Of the 4 titles, 1 was by an unpublished writer and 2 were by authors who were new to the publishing house. Receives 600 queries yearly.
Submissions and Payment: Guidelines available at website.
Query. Accepts hard copy. SASE. Response time and publication period vary. Royalty; advance.

Azro Press

1704 Llano Street B
PBM 342
Santa Fe, NM 87505

Publisher: Gae Eisenhardt

Publisher's Interests
This small publishing company is dedicated to bringing to life
the works of authors and illustrators of the American
Southwest. Producing picture books, easy readers, and middle-
grade fiction, it currently seeks material about New Mexico
history for children in grades one to four.
Website: www.azropress.com

Freelance Potential
Published 2 titles in 2010: each was developed from an unso-
licited submission. Receives 360–480 queries yearly.
Submissions and Payment: Guidelines available at website.
Query with résumé. Accepts hard copy and simultaneous sub-
missions if identified. SASE. Responds in 3–4 months.
Publication in 2 years. Royalty, 5%.

Bantam Books for Young Readers

Random House
1745 Broadway
New York, NY 10019

Editor

Publisher's Interests
Among the numerous imprints of Random House Children's
Books, Bantam specializes in middle-grade and YA books, most
of them tied to movies and television. It also publishes com-
mercial original paperback series, and reprints.
Website: www.randomhouse.com/kids

Freelance Potential
Published several titles in 2010.
Submissions and Payment: Guidelines available at website.
Query. Accepts queries from agented authors only. No simulta-
neous submissions. Unagented writers are encouraged to enter
Random House's Delacorte Yearling contests. Response time
and publication period vary. Royalty; advance.

Barefoot Books

2067 Massachusetts Avenue
Cambridge, MA 02140

Submissions Editor

Publisher's Interests
Publishing fiction titles for children in preschool through
middle school, Barefoot Books chooses stories that help
nourish children's natural creativity and imagination while
making reading fun. At this time, the company is closed to
submissions.
Website: www.barefootbooks.com

Freelance Potential
Published 35–40 titles in 2010. Of the 35–40 titles, 2 were by
unpublished writers and 7 were by authors who were new to
the publishing house.
Submissions and Payment: Guidelines and catalogue available at website. Not currently accepting submissions. Check
website for changes to this policy.

Bay Light Publishing

P.O. Box 3032
Mooresville, NC 28117

Owner: Charlotte Soutullo

Publisher's Interests
This publisher specializes in books for Christian children, ages
four to ten, in the form of story picture books and series
titles. All of its books aim to teach Christian morals and values
through Bible-based stories that motivate, inspire, and educate
readers. Bay Light Publishing is currently not accepting freelance submissions.
Website: www.baylightpub.com

Freelance Potential
Published 1 title in 2010.
Submissions and Payment: Not reviewing queries or manuscripts at this time. Please check the website for changes to
this policy.

Beacon Hill Press of Kansas City

2923 Troost Avenue
Kansas City, MO 64109

Submissions: Judi Perry

Publisher's Interests
Books for Christian parents, homeschooling parents, pastors, and youth ministry workers are produced by this publisher.
Website: www.beaconhillbooks.com

Freelance Potential
Published 40 titles in 2010: 7 were developed from unsolicited submissions. Of the 40 titles, 10 were by unpublished writers and 10 were by authors who were new to the publishing house. Receives many queries and unsolicited mss yearly.
Submissions and Payment: Guidelines available via email request to bhinquiry@nph.com. Catalogue available at website or with 9x12 SASE ($1 postage). Query or send ms. Accepts hard copy. SASE. Responds to queries in 1 month, to mss in 3–6 months. Publication in 12–18 months. Payment policy varies.

Beckham Publications

P.O. Box 4066
Silver Spring, MD 20914-4066

Acquisitions Editor

Publisher's Interests
Fiction and nonfiction books that focus on multicultural, ethnic, and contemporary themes are published by this company. 20% co-venture published material.
Website: www.beckhamhouse.com

Freelance Potential
Published 60 titles (4 juvenile) in 2010: 50 were developed from unsolicited submissions. Receives 200 unsolicited mss each year.
Submissions and Payment: Guidelines and catalogue available at website. Send complete ms with illustrations. Prefers email to submit@beckhamhouse.com (Microsoft Word attachments); will accept hard copy. SASE. Responds in 6 weeks. Publication in 2 months. Royalty.

Behler Publications

22365 El Toro Road, Box 135
Lake Forest, CA 92630

Editor: Lynn Price

Publisher's Interests
This niche publisher produces mostly nonfiction titles for
young adults and adults on topics that relate to personal jour-
neys with social relevance. It occasionally reviews manuscripts
for fiction.
Website: www.behlerpublications.com

Freelance Potential
Published 12 titles in 2010. Receives 2,400 queries yearly.
Submissions and Payment: U.S. authors only. Guidelines
and catalogue available at website. Query with outline/
synopsis and author bio. Accepts hard copy and email to
acquisitions@behlerpublications.com (Microsoft Word attachments). SASE. Response time and publication period vary.
Royalty, 10%.

Alexander Graham Bell Association
for the Deaf and Hard of Hearing

3417 Volta Place NW
Washington, DC 20007-2778

Production/Editorial Manager: Melody Felzien

Publisher's Interests
The books, videos, and CDs produced by the Alexander
Graham Bell Association for the Deaf and Hard of Hearing are
designed to educate parents and professionals about hearing
loss and to promote the use of spoken language. Its catalogue
includes nonfiction as well as fiction titles, with fiction titles
featuring hearing impaired characters who use spoken language as their primary means of communication.
Website: www.agbell.org

Freelance Potential
Published 6 titles in 2010. Receives 150 queries yearly.
Submissions and Payment: Guidelines available. Query.
Accepts hard copy. SASE. Responds in 3 months. Publication
in 9–16 months. Royalty, to 10%.

The Benefactory

P.O. Box 213
Pembroke, MA 02359

Submissions: Cindy Germain

Publisher's Interests
The Benefactory seeks to appeal to the minds and hearts of
children—and encourage them to read—by publishing true
stories about animals. Queries for picture books for ages three
to nine are welcome; however, most work is assigned.
Website: www.thebenefactory.com

Freelance Potential
Published 20 titles in 2010: 1 was developed from an unsolicited
submission. Of the 20 titles, 6 were by authors who were new to
the publishing house. Receives 360 queries yearly.
Submissions and Payment: Guidelines available. Most work
is assigned. Query. Accepts hard copy and email queries to
cgermain@benefactory.biz. SASE. Responds in 6–8 weeks.
Publication in 2 years. Royalty, 5%; advance.

BePuzzled

University Games Corporation
2030 Harrison Street
San Francisco, CA 94110

General Manager: Elise Gretch

Publisher's Interests
Mysteries accompanied by puzzles related to the story are the
unique offering of this publisher. Each mystery story is 2,500
to 3,000 words in length, and is appropriate for children ages
seven to nine years. Submissions containing profanity, sex, or
other mature subject matter will not be considered.
Website: www.ugames.com/bepuzzled/default.asp

Freelance Potential
Published 5–7 titles (2–4 juvenile) in 2010: each was developed from an unsolicited submission. Receives 500 queries
each year.
Submissions and Payment: Guidelines available. Query with
short mystery sample. Accepts hard copy. SASE. Responds in
2 weeks. Publication in 1 year. World rights. Flat fee.

B & H Publishing Group

127 Ninth Avenue North
MSN 164
Nashville, TN 37234

Submissions

Publisher's Interests
Christian living is the focus of this publisher. It produces non-fiction titles that tackle issues related to parenting, home-schooling, history, and teens, as well as some children's fiction. It accepts submissions through literary agents only. All stories must have a Christian theme.
Website: www.broadmanholman.com

Freelance Potential
Published 100 titles in 2010. Receives 300 unsolicited mss each year.
Submissions and Payment: Agented authors only. Guidelines available. Responds in 3 months. Publication in 12–18 months. Royalty; advance.

Bick Publishing House

307 Neck Road
Madison, CT 06443

President: Dale Carlson

Publisher's Interests
This publisher's "books on living" are written to appeal to teens. Topics include relationships, psychology, science, and philosophy, in both fiction and nonfiction. Bick also publishes science fiction for young adults.
Website: www.bickpubhouse.com

Freelance Potential
Published 2 titles (both juvenile) in 2010: both were by agented authors. Receives 200 queries yearly.
Submissions and Payment: Guidelines and catalogue available at website. Query with outline/synopsis, table of contents, 3 chapters, and author biography. Accepts hard copy. SASE. Responds in 2 weeks. Publication in 1 year. Royalty, 10% of net; advance.

Birdsong Books

1322 Bayview Road
Middletown, DE 19709

President: Nancy Carol Willis

Publisher's Interests
This nonfiction children's publisher features natural science
titles that uncover the mysteries of North American animals and
their habitats. It currently seeks submissions on urban wildlife
for ages five to eight, and recent era extinction for ages eight to
twelve.
Website: www.birdsongbooks.com

Freelance Potential
Published 1 title in 2010: it was developed from an unsolicited
submission. Receives 120 unsolicited mss yearly.
Submissions and Payment: Guidelines available at website.
Send ms or book dummy with bio or market analysis. Accepts
hard copy and simultaneous submissions. SASE. Responds in 3
months. Publication in 2–3 years. Payment policy varies.

John F. Blair, Publisher

1406 Plaza Drive
Winston-Salem, NC 27103

Acquisitions Committee

Publisher's Interests
The books from John F. Blair focus on the southeastern region
of the U.S. Topics for nonfiction titles include history, travel,
and folklore. Biographies are also published. Fiction offerings
are few, and must have a tie-in with the American Southeast.
Website: www.blairpub.com

Freelance Potential
Published 15–20 titles in 2010.
Submissions and Payment: Guidelines and catalogue available at website. Query with synopsis, first 2 chapters, and
author bio for fiction; query with outline, 30 sample pages,
market analysis, and author bio for nonfiction. Accepts hard
copy. SASE. Responds in 2 months. Publication period and
payment policy vary.

Blooming Tree Press

P.O. Box 140934
Austin, TX 78714

Publisher/Managing Editor: Miriam Hees

Publisher's Interests
Blooming Tree Press publishes nonfiction and fiction, including graphic novels. It does not publish horror. Authors may query through their literary agents; unagented authors may submit material for the publisher's annual Bloom Award only. Check the website for details.
Website: www.bloomingtreepress.com

Freelance Potential
Published 5–10 titles in 2010: each was by an agented author.
Submissions and Payment: Guidelines available at website. Agented authors only. Query. Response time and publication period vary. Royalty, 10%.

Blue Bike Books

11919–125 Street
Edmonton, Alberta T5L 0S3
Canada

President: Nicholle Carriere

Publisher's Interests
Offering titles on "weird science" for readers ages 10 to 14, Blue Bike also publishes trivia books for a general audience.
Website: www.bluebikebooks.com

Freelance Potential
Published 5 titles (1 juvenile) in 2010: each was assigned. Of the 5 titles, 2 were by unpublished writers and 3 were by new authors. Receives 180 queries, 60 unsolicited mss yearly.
Submissions and Payment: Guidelines and catalogue available at website. Query with clips; or send complete ms with résumé. Accepts hard copy, disk submissions (Microsoft Word or PDF), and email submissions to info@bluebikebooks.com. SAE/IRC. Responds to queries in 2 weeks, to mss in 3–6 months. Publication in 6–12 months. Flat fee.

Blue Marlin Publications

823 Aberdeen Road
Bay Shore, NY 11706

Publisher: Francine Poppo Rich

Publisher's Interests
This publisher seeks middle-grade novels and historical fiction picture books about Long Island lighthouses.
Website: www.bluemarlinpubs.com

Freelance Potential
Published 2 titles in 2010: each was developed from an unsolicited submission. Of the 2 titles, each was by an unpublished writer and 1 was by an author who was new to the publishing house. Receives 300 queries yearly.
Submissions and Payment: Guidelines available at website. Query with synopsis and first 3 chapters; or send complete ms. Accepts hard copy and email queries to francinerich@ bluemarlinpubs.com. SASE. Responds in 3–9 months. Publication in 18 months. Royalty; advance, $1,000.

R. H. Boyd Publishing

P.O. Box 91145
Nashville, TN 37209-1145

Submissions

Publisher's Interests
The R. H. Boyd Publishing catalogue features books written from a Christian perspective, and includes both fiction and nonfiction. Nonfiction books on parenting, education, family issues, and religious history appear side by side with inspirational stories and poetry. Bible study aids and devotionals are also published.
Website: www.rhboydpublishing.com

Freelance Potential
Published several titles in 2010.
Submissions and Payment: Guidelines and catalogue available at website. Query with sample chapters; or send complete ms. Accepts hard copy. SASE. Responds in 2–4 months. Publication period varies. Royalty; advance.

Breakwater Books

100 Water Street, P.O. Box 2188
St. John's, Newfoundland A1C 6E6
Canada

Managing Director: Kim Pelley

Publisher's Interests
This company publishes fiction and nonfiction books that celebrate the unique culture of Canada's Newfoundland, Labrador,
and the Maritime provinces. Though it accepts manuscripts in
all genres, it rarely publishes science fiction or fantasy.
Website: www.breakwaterbooks.com

Freelance Potential
Published 14 titles (2 juvenile) in 2010. Receives 150 queries
each year.
Submissions and Payment: Guidelines available at website.
Query with author biography, synopsis, and 2–3 sample chap-
ters. Availability of artwork improves chance of acceptance.
Accepts hard copy. SAE/IRC. Responds in 6 months.
Publication in 1 year. Royalty, 10%.

Bridge-Logos Publishers

17750 NW 115th Avenue
Building 200, Suite 220
Alachua, FL 32615

Acquisitions Editor: Peggy Hildebrand

Publisher's Interests
This Christian publisher offers fiction and nonfiction titles for
children and adults alike. Picture books, chapter books, and
young adult fiction are among its many offerings. 40% self-,
subsidy-, co-venture, or co-op published material.
Website: www.bridgelogos.com

Freelance Potential
Published 30 titles (3–4 juvenile) in 2010: 5 were developed
from unsolicited submissions. Receives 120–180 queries
each year.
Submissions and Payment: Catalogue available at website.
Query with clips. Accepts email queries to phildebrand@
bridgelogos.com. Responds in 2–4 days. Publication in 1 year.
Payment policy varies.

Brook Farm Books

P.O. Box 246
Bridgewater, ME 04735

Owner/Manager: Jean Reed

Publisher's Interests
This small, family-run publisher specializes in educational resources, particularly homeschooling material, for young adults and adults. Its titles include *The Home School Source Book* and *The Lifetime Learning Companion*. Agented authors are especially encouraged to submit their work. 6% self-, subsidy-, co-venture, or co-op published material.
Website: www.brookfarmbooks.com

Freelance Potential
Published 2 titles in 2010. Receives 12 unsolicited mss yearly.
Submissions and Payment: Catalogue available. Send complete ms. Accepts hard copy. Availability of artwork improves chance of acceptance. B/W prints or transparencies. SASE. Responds in 6 weeks. Publication period varies. Royalty.

Brown Barn Books

119 Kettle Creek Road
Weston, CT 06883

Editor-in-Chief: Nancy Hammerslough

Publisher's Interests
Brown Barn Books, an imprint of Pictures of Record, Inc., publishes well-crafted fiction for children ages 12 and up. Its titles cover a wide variety of genres, including mystery, suspense, adventure, and romance. While it is currently not reviewing queries or unsolicited manuscripts, interested writers are advised to check its website for updates to this policy.
Website: www.brownbarnbooks.com

Freelance Potential
Published 20 titles in 2010.
Submissions and Payment: Guidelines and catalogue available at website. Not reviewing queries or unsolicited mss at this time. Please check the website for changes to this policy.

Caddo Gap Press

PMB 275
3145 Geary Boulevard
San Francisco, CA 94118

Publisher: Alan H. Jones

Publisher's Interests
Caddo Gap Press specializes in journals and books for professionals working in the fields of multicultural education, teacher education, and the social foundations of education. It is always on the lookout for innovative, out-of-the-box manuscripts for its periodicals. Freelance writers should note that more periodicals than books are published, and that published books are authored by experienced writers.
Website: www.caddogap.com

Freelance Potential
Plans to resume publishing (1 or more titles) in 2011.
Submissions and Payment: Catalogue available at website. Query or send complete ms. Accepts hard copy. SASE. Response time and publication period vary. Royalty, 10%.

Carolina Wren Press

120 Morris Street
Durham, NC 27701

Editor: Andrea Selch

Publisher's Interests
Carolina Wren Press focuses on publishing the work of historically underrepresented authors, including women, people of color, and writers with disabilities. Most published work is acquired through its biannual contests for emerging poets or women writers.
Website: www.carolinawrenpress.org

Freelance Potential
Published 3 titles (1 juvenile) in 2010: 1 was developed from an unsolicited submission.
Submissions and Payment: Guidelines available at website. Not currently reviewing queries or submissions. Do not submit unless website indicates an open reading or contest submission period. Check the website for the latest information.

Carolrhoda Lab

Lerner Publishing
241 First Avenue North
Minneapolis, MN 55401

Editor: Andrew Karre

Publisher's Interests
New in fall 2010, this young adult imprint of Carolrhoda publishes distinctive and provocative fiction. It wants books that push boundaries, including realistic, paranormal, dark fantasy, and dystopian fiction. Carolrhoda Lab will not publish high fantasy or graphic novels.
Website: www.carolrhodalab.com

Freelance Potential
Publishing six to eight titles a year.
Submissions and Payment: Editor Andrew Karre opens up the imprint to submissions periodically. Check the website for updates. Email a brief query or cover letter and manuscript to carolrhodasubmissions@lernerbooks.com, with QUERY in the subject line.

Carousel Press

P.O. Box 6038
Berkeley, CA 94706-0038

Publisher: Carole T. Meyers

Publisher's Interests
Focusing on travel books and guides, Carousel Press welcomes queries from experienced travel writers. Some of its popular titles cover the ins and outs of castle hotels, weekend trips in Northern California, traveling with children, and camping in Europe.
Website: www.carouselpress.com

Freelance Potential
Published 1 title in 2010. Receives 120 queries yearly.
Submissions and Payment: Writers' guidelines and catalogue available at website. Query with synopsis and table of contents. Accepts email to editor@carouselpress.com (no attachments). Responds in 1 month. Publication in 1 year. Royalty; advance.

Chaosium

22568 Mission Boulevard, Suite 423
Hayward, CA 94541

Editor-in-Chief: Lynn Willis

Publisher's Interests
A publisher of books, role-playing games, and game supplements for young adults and adults, Chaosium welcomes proposals for books in the following genres: horror, adventure, and fantasy fiction.
Website: www.chaosium.com

Freelance Potential
Published 15 titles in 2010. Of the 15 titles, 3 were by unpublished writers and 6 were by authors who were new to the publishing house. Receives 60+ queries yearly.
Submissions and Payment: Guidelines and catalogue available at website. Query with synopsis and writing samples. Accepts hard copy. SASE. Responds in 1–2 weeks. Publication in 1–2 years. Flat fee, $.03–$.05 per word.

Cinco Puntos Press

701 Texas Avenue
El Paso, TX 79901

Editor: Lee Byrd

Publisher's Interests
The bilingual fiction and nonfiction titles from this publisher focus on the history and folklore of the U.S./Mexico border region, the southwestern U.S., and Mexico. It targets children and young adults.
Website: www.cincopuntos.com

Freelance Potential
Published 10 titles in 2010.
Submissions and Payment: Writers' guidelines and catalogue available at website. Accepts phone calls to Lee Byrd at 915-838-1625 to discuss potential projects; manuscript must be completed prior to calling. No unsolicited queries or mss; no sample chapters before speaking with editor. Publication in 18–36 months. Royalty.

Conari Press

500 Third Street, Suite 230
San Francisco, CA 94107

Acquisitions Editor: Pat Bryce

Publisher's Interests
Conari Press publishes self-help and inspirational books for young adults and adults on topics such as spirituality, personal growth, parenting, and social issues.
Website: www.redwheelweiser.com

Freelance Potential
Published 45 titles in 2010: 9 were developed from unsolicited submissions, 36 were by agented authors, and 2 were reprint/licensed properties. Receives 1,200 queries yearly.
Submissions and Payment: Guidelines and catalogue available at website. Query with author bio, table of contents, 3 sample chapters, synopsis, market analysis, and sample artwork. Accepts hard copy. SASE. Responds in 3 months. Publication in 18 months. Royalty; advance.

Conciliar Press

P.O. Box 748
Chesterton, IN 46304

Acquisitions Editor: Katherine Hyde

Publisher's Interests
Orthodox Christianity is the focus of this publisher. Books are geared toward children of all ages, as well as young adults. Eastern Orthodox Christian writers are always encouraged.
Website: www.conciliarpress.com

Freelance Potential
Published 8–10 titles (3 juvenile) in 2010: 9 were developed from unsolicited submissions and 1 was a reprint/licensed property. Of the 8–10 titles, 2–3 were by unpublished writers and 3–4 were by authors new to the publishing house.
Submissions and Payment: Guidelines and catalogue available at website. Query with first 3 chapters. Send complete ms for picture books only. Accepts hard copy. SASE. Responds in 3 months. Publication period varies. Royalty.

Continental Press

520 East Bainbridge Street
Elizabethtown, PA 17022

Managing Editor: Megan Bergonzi

Publisher's Interests
Specializing in textbooks and other educational materials,
Continental Press is looking for fiction and nonfiction leveled
readers and state-specific test prep workbook materials.
Website: www.continentalpress.com

Freelance Potential
Published 50+ titles (40 juvenile) in 2010: 5 were developed
from unsolicited submissions. Receives 240 queries, 240
unsolicited mss yearly.
Submissions and Payment: Guidelines available at website.
Query with program rationale, author biography, outline, and
sample lesson, chapter, or unit; or send complete ms. Accepts
hard copy. SASE. Responds in 6 months. Publication period
and payment policy vary.

Course Crafters

P.O. Box 1058
Haverhill, MA 01831

CEO & Publisher: Lise Ragan

Publisher's Interests
Course Crafters specializes in English Language Learner and
English as a Second Language textbooks, and supplemental
products for students of all ages. It also publishes professional
development books for teachers and other education professionals. Freelance writers with a background in ELL or ESL
writing are encouraged to submit queries.
Website: www.coursecrafters.com

Freelance Potential
Published 10–12 titles in 2010. Receives 20 queries yearly.
Submissions and Payment: Guidelines available. Query with
clips. Accepts hard copy. SASE. Responds in 1 month.
Publication in 1–2 years. Flat fee.

Creative With Words Publications

P.O. Box 223226
Carmel, CA 93922

Editor & Publisher: Brigitta Geltrich

Publisher's Interests
Anthologies of all genres, written by authors of all ages, are the
focus of this publisher. It seeks submissions of folklore and
material on nature, the seasons, and relationships.
Website: www.creativewithwords.tripod.com

Freelance Potential
Published 6 titles (4 juvenile) in 2010: each was developed
from an unsolicited submission. Of the 6 titles, 3–4 were by
authors who were new to the publishing house. Receives
300–600 queries, 600 unsolicited mss yearly.
Submissions and Payment: Guidelines available. Query or
send complete ms. Accepts hard copy. SASE. Responds 1
month after anthology deadline. Publication period varies. No
payment; 20–40% discount on 10+ copies purchased.

Cricket Books

70 East Lake Street, Suite 300
Chicago, IL 60601

Submissions: Jenny Gillespie

Publisher's Interests
This division of Carus Publishing maintains a notable standard
of excellence in all of its titles for young readers. With a goal
of enticing kids to "fall in love with books and reading," Cricket
Books offers novels, nonfiction, picture books, chapter books,
and poetry.
Website: www.cricketmag.com

Freelance Potential
Published 2 titles in 2010: each was assigned. Receives 36
unsolicited mss yearly.
Submissions and Payment: Guidelines and catalogue available at website. Accepts submissions from authors previously
published by Cricket Books or Carus Publishing only.
Publication in 18 months. Royalty, to 10%; advance, $2,000+.

Dalmatian Press

3101 Clairmont Road, Suite C
Atlanta, GA 30329

Editor-in-Chief: Edward Wilson

Publisher's Interests
Dalmatian Press and its imprint Piggy Toes focus on fun
licensed and original books for birth to age eight. Recently,
the company moved all operations, including its novelty
imprint Intervisual Press, to Atlanta to redirect and develop its
lists through 2012. Dalmatian's other imprints are the Spanish-
language Sonrisas, and the religious Spirit Press.
Website: www.dalmatianpress.com

Freelance Potential
Published 6 titles in 2010.
Submissions and Payment: Catalogue available at website.
Send complete ms with novelty elements in dummy form, or a
written description. Accepts hard copy. SASE. Responds in
6–12 months. Payment policy varies.

May Davenport Publishers

26313 Purissima Road
Los Altos Hills, CA 94022

Publisher & Editor: May Davenport

Publisher's Interests
May Davenport Publishers offers student-readers in kindergarten through high school lighthearted stories and poetry in
anthology form. Stories should combine humor with learning
where possible. It also publishes free verse for young children's coloring books. It is always interested in work from
unpublished writers.
Website: www.maydavenportpublishers.com

Freelance Potential
Published 1 title in 2010. Receives 600 queries yearly.
Submissions and Payment: Guidelines available. Query.
Accepts hard copy. SASE. Responds in 1–2 weeks. Publication
in 1–2 years. Royalty, 15%. Flat fee.

Displays for Schools

1825 NW 22nd Terrace
Gainesville, FL 32605

Manager: Sherry DuPree

Publisher's Interests
Displays designed for classroom use at all grade levels are
the specialty of this publisher. Displays for special education,
religious education, and adult education classes are also produced. All of its products have been tested in the classroom
and cover a variety of subject areas.
Website: www.displaysforschools.com

Freelance Potential
Published 3 titles (2 juvenile) in 2010: 2 were developed from
unsolicited submissions. Receives 109 queries yearly.
Submissions and Payment: Guidelines available. Query with
outline, synopsis, sample chapters, and brief author biography.
Accepts hard copy. SASE. Responds in 1 month. Publication in
4–24 months. Royalty, varies.

Diversion Press

P.O. Box 30277
Clarksville, TN 37040

Acquisitions Editor

Publisher's Interests
This publisher's catalogue includes picture books for the
younger set, as well as middle-grade and young adult novels.
Its fiction titles center around inspirational and contemporary
stories while its nonfiction covers current events, history, and
social issues. All of its books depict childhood and adolescence in a positive light.
Website: www.diversionpress.com

Freelance Potential
Published 10–20 titles in 2010.
Submissions and Payment: Guidelines and catalogue avail-
able at website. Query with author bio and market analysis.
Accepts email to diversionpress@yahoo.com (no attachments).
Responds in 1–3 months. Publication period varies. Royalty.

DNA Press

P.O. Box 9311
Glendale, CA 91226

Nartea Publishing Editors

Publisher's Interests
All kinds of science books, for all ages and levels of readership, from children to scholars, are the province of this book and electronic publisher. It wants fiction touching on scientific issues, as well as nonfiction, and also publishes on business and self-help.
Website: www.dnapress.com

Freelance Potential
Welcomes new writers.
Submissions and Payment: Email queries to editors@dna-press.com. Include an outline of your book, the potential audience, and sales ideas. If interested, the editors will ask for a proposal, to include a tentative title, table of contents, and market and competition information.

Dog-Eared Publications

P.O. Box 620863
Middleton, WI 53562-0863

Publisher: Nancy Field

Publisher's Interests
Nonfiction books for children ages four to twelve are the specialty of this publisher. Topics include nature, animals, the environment, ecology, and biology. It is not accepting submissions at this time.
Website: www.dog-eared.com

Freelance Potential
Plans to resume publishing (1 or more titles) in 2011. Receives 240 queries, 120 unsolicited mss yearly.
Submissions and Payment: Not currently accepting submissions. Visit the website for the latest information concerning this policy.

Dragon Hill Publishing

5474 Thibault Wynd NW
Edmonton, Alberta T6R 3P9
Canada

President: Gary Whyte

Publisher's Interests
The titles from Dragon Hill target adults as well as teens seeking a better understanding of Canada's indigenous and traditional cultures. This company also publishes self-help guides.
Website: www.dragonhillpublishing.com

Freelance Potential
Published 4 titles in 2010: each was assigned. Of the 4 titles, 2 were by new authors. Receives 36 queries, 24 mss yearly.
Submissions and Payment: Guidelines and catalogue available at website. Query with clips; or send complete ms with résumé. Accepts hard copy, disk submissions (Microsoft Word or PDF), and email to info@dragonhillpublishing.com. SAE/IRC. Responds to queries in 2 weeks, to mss in 3–6 months. Publication in 6–12 months. Flat fee.

Dzanc Books

2702 Lillian Road
Ann Arbor, MI 48104-5300

Editors: Dan Wickett & Steve Gillis

Publisher's Interests
Literary fiction and poetry appear alongside creative nonfiction in this publisher's catalogue. As a nonprofit publisher, Dzanc offers books that defy traditional markets.
Website: www.dzancbooks.org

Freelance Potential
Published 25 titles in 2010. Of the 25 titles, 22 were by authors who were new to the publishing house. Receives 2,000 queries yearly.
Submissions and Payment: Guidelines and catalogue available at website. Query with 1–2 sample chapters. Accepts hard copy and email queries to submit@dzancbooks.org. SASE. Responds in 5–6 months. Publication period varies. Royalty; advance.

Eastgate Systems

134 Main Street
Watertown, MA 02472

Acquisitions Editor: Mark Bernstein

Publisher's Interests
This publisher specializes in stand-alone hypertexts on CD-ROMs and disks. As such, its offerings are interlinked, interactive works that would not normally appear in printed form. Eastgate's fiction and nonfiction titles are directed toward young adult readers. It also publishes poetry.
Website: www.eastgate.com

Freelance Potential
Published 2 titles in 2010. Receives 25 unsolicited mss yearly.
Submissions and Payment: Guidelines and catalogue available at website. Send complete ms. Accepts disk submissions, email submissions to info@eastgate.com, and simultaneous submissions if identified. SASE. Responds in 4–6 weeks. Publication in 1 year. Royalty, 15%; advance.

Ecopress

Finney Company
8075 215th Street West
Lakeville, MN 55044

President: Alan E. Krysan

Publisher's Interests
Enhancing awareness of the environment is the goal of this imprint of the Finney Company, an educational publisher that offers some titles suitable for young readers.
Website: www.ecopress.com

Freelance Potential
Published 4 titles (3 juvenile) in 2010: 3 were developed from unsolicited submissions. Of the 4 titles, 2 were by unpublished writers and 3 were by authors who were new to the publishing house. Receives 96–120 queries yearly.
Submissions and Payment: Guidelines available at website. Query with 3–4 sample chapters and marketing ideas. Accepts hard copy and simultaneous submissions. SASE. Responds in 10–12 weeks. Publication in 6–18 months. Royalty, 10%.

Educational Impressions

116 Washington Avenue
Hawthorne, NJ 07507

Creative Director: Barbara Peller

Publisher's Interests
Educational Impressions specializes in high interest/low reading level fiction and nonfiction for students ages four to twelve. Its curriculum-based books cover a variety of themes and school subjects. Libraries and schools are the main markets for this publisher, formerly listed as January Productions.
Website: www.edimpressions.com

Freelance Potential
Plans to resume publishing in 2010. Receives 20 queries, 20 unsolicited mss yearly.
Submissions and Payment: Catalogue available at website. Prefers query with outline/synopsis; will accept complete ms with résumé. Accepts hard copy. SASE. Response time and publication period vary. Flat fee, $325–$375.

Eschia Books

#218, 2323-119 Street
Edmonton, Alberta T6J 4E2
Canada

President: Kathy van Denderen

Publisher's Interests
Eschia Books publishes the work of Aboriginal writers. Fiction and books that delve into Aboriginal history are welcome.
Website: www.eschia.com

Freelance Potential
Published 2 titles in 2010: 1 was developed from an unsolicited submission. Of the 2 titles, 1 was by an unpublished writer and 1 was by a new author. Receives 60 queries, 36 mss yearly.
Submissions and Payment: Guidelines and catalogue available at website. Query with clips; or send complete ms with résumé. Accepts hard copy, disk submissions (Microsoft Word or PDF), and email to submissions@eschia.com. SAE/IRC. Responds to queries in 2 weeks, to mss in 3–6 months. Publication in 6–12 months. Flat fee.

Farrar, Straus and Giroux
Books for Young Readers

175 Fifth Avenue
New York, NY 10010
Children's Editorial Department

Publisher's Interests
The catalogue of this award-winning publisher features fiction
and nonfiction titles for toddlers to teens. Nonfiction topics
include science, history, and nature. Fantasy, humor, and
contemporary fiction are among the genres offered. In keeping
with the policy of the Macmillan Children's Publishing Group
of which it is a part, FSG is only accepting agented manuscripts
at this time.
Website: http://us.macmillan.com/fsgyoungreaders.aspx

Freelance Potential
Published 80 titles in 2010.
Submissions and Payment: Agented submissions only.
Please check the website for changes to this policy.

Feminist Press

The Graduate Center
365 Fifth Avenue, Suite 5406
New York, NY 10016

Associate Editor: Anjoli Roy

Publisher's Interests
This publisher offers fiction and nonfiction by and about
women and other underrepresented groups.
Website: www.feministpress.org

Freelance Potential
Published 16 titles in 2010: 2 were developed from unsolicited
submissions and 12 were reprint/licensed properties. Of the
16 titles, 10 were by authors who were new to the publishing
house. Receives 500 queries yearly.
Submissions and Payment: Guidelines and catalogue available at website. Query with sample chapter and author bio.
Prefers hard copy; will accept email queries to editor@
feministpress.org (include "Submission" in subject line). SASE.
Response time and publication period vary. Royalty; advance.

Margaret Ferguson Books

Farrar, Straus & Giroux
18 West 18th Street
New York, NY 10011

Editorial Director: Margaret Ferguson

Publisher's Interests
After 30 years at FS&G in various capacities, including the business side, Margaret Ferguson has returned to her editorial roots to launch this imprint in 2011. Among the authors contracted for the first lists were well-published and debut writers.
Website: http://us.macmillan.com/fsgyoungreaders.aspx

Freelance Potential
FS&G published 80 titles in 2010.
Submissions and Payment: Agented submissions accepted. Editorial queries may be directed to childrens.editorial@fsg-books.com. Please check the website for changes to submission policies.

Folklore Publishing

8025 102 Street
Edmonton, Alberta T6E 4A2
Canada

President: Faye Boer

Publisher's Interests
Books about Canada's history and culture and biographies of notable Canadians are featured in this publisher's catalogue.
Website: www.folklorepublishing.com

Freelance Potential
Published 8 titles in 2010: 1 was developed from an unsolicited submission. Of the 8 titles, 3 were by unpublished writers and 3 were by new authors. Receives 180 queries, 60 mss yearly.
Submissions and Payment: Guidelines and catalogue available at website. Query with clips; or send complete ms with résumé. Accepts hard copy, disk submissions (Microsoft Word or PDF), and email to submissions@folklorepublishing.com. SAE/IRC. Responds to queries in 2 weeks, to mss in 3–6 months. Publication in 6–12 months. Flat fee.

Forward Movement

412 Sycamore Street
Cincinnati, OH 45202

Editor & Publisher: Richard H. Schmidt

Publisher's Interests
Forward Movement is an Episcopal Church that produces
books and other materials to nourish people in their faith. Its
catalogue features a number of booklets related to parenting
and raising children in an atomosphere of faith in God.
Website: www.forwardmovement.org

Freelance Potential
Published 30 titles in 2010: 4 were developed from unsolicited
submissions, 10 were by unpublished writers, and 5 by
authors new to the house. Receives 24 unsolicited mss yearly.
Submissions and Payment: Guidelines and catalogue available at website. Sample pamphlet available. Mail complete ms
or email to rschmidt@forwarddaybyday.com. SASE. Responds
in 1 month. Publication period varies. Flat fee.

Gefen Kids

6 Hatzvi Street
Jerusalem 94386
Israel

Editor: Ilan Greenfield

Publisher's Interests
A leading Israeli publisher of Jewish books, Gefen Publishing
has a line of children's books that includes English-language
fiction and nonfiction. Gefen Kids books are about religious
holidays, the Holocaust, Shabbat, and Jewish traditions.
Website: www.gefenpublishing.com

Freelance Potential
Published 20 titles (4–5 juvenile) in 2010: most were devel-
oped from unsolicited submissions. Receives 240 queries,
100+ unsolicited mss yearly.
Submissions and Payment: Send complete ms with cover let-
ter, 1- to 2-page synopsis, author bio, and audience description.
Accepts hard copy and simultaneous submissions. SASE.
Response time, publication period, and payment policy vary.

The Globe Pequot Press

P.O. Box 480
Guilford, CT 06437

Editorial Administrator: Melanie Bugbee

Publisher's Interests
This publisher's books for parents and children focus on animals, nature, the environment, and outdoor recreation.
Website: www.globepequot.com

Freelance Potential
Published 440 titles in 2010: many were developed from unsolicited submissions and some were reprint/licensed properties. Of the 440 titles, 75 were by authors who were new to the publishing house. Receives 300+ queries yearly.
Submissions and Payment: Guidelines and catalogue available at website. Query with author biography, synopsis, table of contents, sample chapter, word count, and market analysis. Accepts hard copy. SASE. Responds in 3 months. Publication in 18 months. Royalty, 8–12%; advance, $500–$1,500.

Great Potential Press

P.O. Box 5057
Scottsdale, AZ 85261

Submissions: Janet Gore

Publisher's Interests
Books designed to help parents and teachers support the academic, emotional, and social needs of gifted children are the sole focus of Great Potential Press.
Website: www.giftedbooks.com

Freelance Potential
Published 4–8 titles (1 juvenile) in 2010. Of the 4–8 titles, 2 were by unpublished writers and 2–4 were by authors new to the publishing house. Receives 20–30 queries yearly.
Submissions and Payment: Guidelines and catalogue available at website. Query with introduction, table of contents, 3 sample chapters, and market analysis. Accepts hard copy and queries through form at website. SASE. Responds in 2 months. Publication period varies. Royalty.

Greene Bark Press

P.O. Box 1108
Bridgeport, CT 06601-1108

Editor

Publisher's Interests
A small, family-owned company, Greene Bark Press seeks colorful, imaginative books that enhance the growing and learning processes of young readers.
Website: www.greenebarkpress.com

Freelance Potential
Published 1 title in 2010: it was developed from an unsolicited submission and it was by an unpublished writer. Receives 2,400 unsolicited mss yearly.
Submissions and Payment: Guidelines available. Catalogue available at website. Send complete ms with illustrations and storyboard. One story per submission. Accepts hard copy and simultaneous submissions if identified. SASE. Responds in 2–6 months. Publication in 12–18 months. Royalty, 10–15%.

Greenwillow Books

HarperCollins
1350 Avenue of the Americas
New York, NY 10019

Editorial Department

Publisher's Interests
This imprint of HarperCollins publishes titles for children of all ages, from colorful picture books for the youngest child, to funny stories for middle-grade readers, to science fiction for young adults. It also offers many seasonal titles and books of poetry. This publisher is closed to submissions at this time.
Website: www.harperchildrens.com

Freelance Potential
Published 40 titles in 2010.
Submissions and Payment: Not accepting queries or manuscripts at this time. Please check the website for changes to this policy.

Grosset & Dunlap

Penguin Group
345 Hudson Street
New York, NY 10014

Editorial Department

Publisher's Interests
This imprint of Penguin Group focuses on licensed properties, in-house brands, series titles, and novelty books for children. It offers both fiction and nonfiction. Well-known characters include Strawberry Shortcake and Corduroy. Nonfiction books cover science topics such as nature and the environment.
Website: www.us.penguingroup.com

Freelance Potential
Published 175+ titles in 2010.
Submissions and Payment: Catalogue available at website. Query with outline/synopsis. Accepts hard copy. SASE. Responds in 4 months. Publication in 18–36 months. Royalty; advance.

Guardian Angel Publishing

12430 Tesson Ferry Road, #186
St. Louis, MO 63128

Submissions Editor

Publisher's Interests
This publisher offers print and electronic books, as well as DVDs, designed for children up to the age of 12. It seeks well-written fiction and nonfiction with positive principles.
Website: www.guardianangelpublishing.com

Freelance Potential
Published 50 titles in 2010. Of the 50 titles, 17 were by unpublished writers and 17 were by authors who were new to the publishing house. Receives 1,000 unsolicited mss yearly.
Submissions and Payment: Guidelines and catalogue available at website. Send complete ms stating genre and word count. Accepts email submissions to editorial_staff@ guardianangelpublishing.com. Responds in 2 months. Publication period varies. Royalty, 30%.

Harbour Publishing

4437 Rondeview Road
Madeira Park, British Columbia V0N 2H0
Canada

Editors: Howard White & Silas White

Publisher's Interests
Harbour Publishing focuses on fiction themes and nonfiction topics concerning the west coast of British Columbia. Its titles appeal to a wide range of age groups, and all are authored by Canadian writers.
Website: www.harbourpublishing.com

Freelance Potential
Published 25 titles (1–2 juvenile) in 2010. Receives 1,000 queries yearly.
Submissions and Payment: Canadian authors only. Guidelines available at website. Query with outline, brief author biography, publication credits, and sample chapter. Accepts hard copy. SASE. Responds in 2 months if interested. Publication period varies. Royalty; advance, negotiable.

Harcourt Religion Publishers

Houghton Mifflin Harcourt
6277 Sea Harbor Drive
Orlando, FL 32887

Submissions Editor

Publisher's Interests
Harcourt Religion Publishers offers books for Catholic education and faith formation. Titles are designed for children as well as adults in catechism classes and other programs, and are firmly grounded in the teachings of the Catholic Church.
Website: www.harcourtreligion.com

Freelance Potential
Published 30 titles (5 juvenile) in 2010. Of the 30 titles, 2 were by unpublished writers and 4 were by authors who were new to the publishing house. Receives 30–35 queries yearly.
Submissions and Payment: Guidelines available. Query with résumé, outline, and 3 sample chapters. Accepts hard copy. SASE. Responds in 3–6 months. Publication in 1 year. Royalty. Flat fee.

Hard Shell Word Factory

6470A Glenway Avenue, Suite 109
Cincinnati, OH 45211

Senior Editor: Skyla Dawn Cameron

Publisher's Interests
This publisher offers both print and electronic books. Its fiction titles are aimed at readers ages 8 to 18 and feature a variety of genres. Its nonfiction books are geared toward readers ages 12 to 18 and cover many topics, including biography.
Website: www.hardshell.com

Freelance Potential
Published 25–70 titles (5 juvenile) in 2010. Receives 200+ unsolicited mss yearly.
Submissions and Payment: Guidelines and catalogue available at website. Send complete ms with synopsis. Accepts email submissions to submissions@hardshell.com (RTF attachments). Responds in 2–3 months. Publication period varies. Royalty, 45% of e-book net; 15% of print net.

HarperFestival

HarperCollins
1350 Avenue of the Americas
New York, NY 10019

Editorial Department

Publisher's Interests
This HarperCollins imprint specializes in books for children under the age of seven. It offers board books, novelty books, picture books, and seasonal and easy-to-read titles, many featuring well-known licensed characters. Consistent with the policy of all imprints of HarperCollins, HarperFestival reviews submissions from agented authors only.
Website: www.harpercollinschildrens.com

Freelance Potential
Published 120 titles in 2010.
Submissions and Payment: Writers' guidelines available. Accepts queries through literary agents only. Accepts hard copy. SASE. Responds in 1 month. Publication in 18 months. Royalty; advance.

The Harvard Common Press

535 Albany Street
Boston, MA 02118

Senior Editor: Valerie Cimino

Publisher's Interests
In addition to cookbooks, this independent trade publisher
produces parenting and childcare titles that are renowned for
combining professional advice with nurturing support.
Website: www.harvardcommonpress.com

Freelance Potential
Published 9 titles in 2010: 5 were by agented authors.
Receives 240 queries yearly.
Submissions and Payment: Guidelines and catalogue available at website. Query with résumé, outline, 1–2 sample chapters, and market analysis. Accepts hard copy, email queries to
editorial@harvardcommonpress.com, and simultaneous submissions if identified. SASE. Responds in 1–3 months.
Publication period and payment policy vary.

Heyday Books

P.O. Box 9145
Berkeley, CA 94709

Acquisitions Editor: Gayle Wattawa

Publisher's Interests
This California publisher offers books for adults and children
about the Golden State. Most titles for children are picture
books, although Heyday publishes occasional middle-grade and
YA nonfiction. Books foster an understanding of California history, nature, arts, and culture. Picture books are of current interest.
Website: www.heydaybooks.com

Freelance Potential
Published 30 titles (3 juvenile) in 2010.
Submissions and Payment: Catalogue available at website.
Send complete ms for picture books; 3 chapters and a table
of contents with chapter-by-chapter summary for early readers.
Indicate writing background and market for the book in a
cover letter. Advance; royalty.

Hohm Press

P.O. Box 2501
Prescott, AZ 86302

Managing Editor

Publisher's Interests
Hohm Press seeks authoritative books on natural health and
nutrition for adults but is not interested in survival stories. It no
longer publishes children's books or contemporary poetry.
Website: www.hohmpress.com

Freelance Potential
Published 6–8 titles in 2010: 2 were developed from unsolicited submissions. Of the 6–8 titles, 1 was by an unpublished
writer and 1 was by an author who was new to the publishing
house. Receives 360 queries yearly.
Submissions and Payment: Guidelines and catalogue available at website. Query with sample pages. Accepts hard copy.
SASE. Response time and publication period vary. Royalty, 10%
of net.

Hyperion Books for Children

Disney
114 Fifth Avenue, 14th Floor
New York, NY 10011

Submissions Editor

Publisher's Interests
Titles for a wide range of ages, from toddler board and novelty
books to young adult novels, are featured in this publisher's
catalogue. It offers both fiction and nonfiction, series titles,
media tie-ins, and some bilingual titles. All queries and submissions must be made through literary agents.
Website: www.hyperionbooksforchildren.com

Freelance Potential
Published 100 titles in 2010: each was by an agented author.
Submissions and Payment: Guidelines and catalogue available at website. Accepts queries and manuscripts through
literary agents only.

Illumination Arts

13256 Northup Way, Suite 9
Bellevue, WA 98005

President: John Thompson

Publisher's Interests
Illumination Arts publishes children's picture books filled with
inspiring messages of peace, acceptance, and love. Its list is
full through 2011 and it is closed to submissions at this time.
The website will indicate when it opens again.
Website: www.illumin.com

Freelance Potential
Published 1 title in 2010: it was developed from an unsolicited
submission and it was by an unpublished writer.
Submissions and Payment: Guidelines available. Not accepting queries or manuscripts at this time. Check the website for
updates to this policy before submitting.

Images Unlimited

P.O. Box 305
Maryville, MO 64468

President: Lee Jackson

Publisher's Interests
This publisher of "books for cooks, children, parents, and
teachers" produces cookbooks, picture books, and other
educational titles. It is currently not accepting submissions.
Website: www.imagesunlimitedpub.com

Freelance Potential
Published 1 title in 2010: it was by an author who was new to
the publishing house. Receives 24 queries yearly.
Submissions and Payment: Not accepting unsolicited submissions at this time. Check the website for the latest information concerning this policy.

Innovative Kids

18 Ann Street
Norwalk, CT 06854

Publisher: Shari Kaufman

Publisher's Interests
Fun and learning come together in the books, puzzles, games, and toys offered by this publisher. As its website says, Innovative Kids is "where ha ha meets aha!" Its fiction and nonfiction titles are geared toward children up to age 12.
Website: www.innovativekids.com

Freelance Potential
Published 50 titles in 2010. Of the 50 titles, 20 were by authors who were new to the publishing house. Receives 200 queries, 200 unsolicited mss yearly.
Submissions and Payment: Guidelines available at website. Query or send complete ms with dummy. Accepts hard copy. Does not return mss. Response time and publication period vary. Flat fee.

Interlink Publishing Group

46 Crosby Street
Northampton, MA 01060

Editorial Director: Pam Thompson

Publisher's Interests
The global, cosmopolitan perspective of Interlink is represented in its catalogue of adult titles that delve into literature, history, travel, art, and world cuisine. Several children's books also appear on its list.
Website: www.interlinkbooks.com

Freelance Potential
Published 65 titles (8 juvenile) in 2010. Of the 65 titles, 11 were by unpublished writers and 24 were by authors new to the publishing house. Receives 1,800 queries yearly.
Submissions and Payment: Guidelines and catalogue available at website or with 9x12 SASE. Query. Accepts hard copy. SASE. Responds in 1–24 weeks. Publication in 18–24 months. Royalty, 6–7% of retail; small advance.

The Jewish Publication Society

2100 Arch Street, 2nd Floor
Philadelphia, PA 19103

Acquisitions Editor

Publisher's Interests
A publisher of books that embrace Jewish heritage and culture, the Jewish Publication Society produces fiction and nonfiction for children as well as adults. It is not accepting submissions for children or young adults at this time.
Website: www.jewishpub.org

Freelance Potential
Published 12 titles (4 juvenile) in 2010. Receives 500 queries each year.
Submissions and Payment: Not accepting submissions at this time. Check the website for the latest information concerning this policy.

Jonathan David Publishers

68-22 Eliot Avenue
Middle Village, NY 11379

Editor: David Kolatch

Publisher's Interests
This publisher specializes in Jewish-themed books for adults and children. Nonfiction topics include culture and history; works of fiction include folktales and stories about traditions.
Website: www.jdbooks.com

Freelance Potential
Published 11 titles in 2010. Of the 11 titles, 5 were by unpublished writers and 8 were by authors who were new to the publishing house. Receives 1,000 queries yearly.
Submissions and Payment: Guidelines available at website. Query with résumé, table of contents, synopsis, and sample chapter. Accepts hard copy. No simultaneous submissions. SASE. Responds in 1–2 months. Publication in 18 months. Royalty; advance. Flat fee.

Jossey-Bass

Wiley
989 Market Street
San Francisco, CA 94103

Education Editorial Assistant

Publisher's Interests
Jossey-Bass is a division of the large educational and business publisher Wiley. Its categories include titles for K-12 curriculum, teaching strategies, special education, psychology, and technology. It also has a series called Fantasy Sports and Mathematics that helps teachers get kids excited about math.
Website: www.josseybass.com

Freelance Potential
Publishes 15–20 titles a year.
Submissions and Payment: Accepts project proposals. Include the purpose in developing the project, the audience, why the topic is important, what new information will be included, research background, your relevant experience, outline, chapter descriptions, sample chapers, and competition information.

Journey Stone Creations

3533 Danbury Road
Fairfield, OH 45014

Editor: Patricia Stirnkorb

Publisher's Interests
Primarily a work-for-hire publisher, Journey Stone Creations offers fiction only—including early picture books, easy-to-read books, and chapter books. Check the website to see if the company is reviewing manuscripts before you submit a query. 10% self-, subsidy-, co-venture, or co-op published material.
Website: www.jscbooks.com

Freelance Potential
Published 16–20 titles in 2010. Of the 16–20 titles, each was by an unpublished writer. Receives 600 queries yearly.
Submissions and Payment: Guidelines and catalogue available at website. Query with author biography. Accepts email queries to info@jscbooks.com. Responds in 1 week. Publication period and payment policy vary.

Judson Press

P.O. Box 851
Valley Forge, PA 19482

Editor: Rebecca Irwin-Diehl

Publisher's Interests
Judson Press specializes in books for church leaders and
Christians. Titles for children are limited to ministry resources.
Website: www.judsonpress.com

Freelance Potential
Published 12 titles in 2010: 7 were developed from unsolicited
submissions, 2 were by agented authors, and 1 was a reprint/
licensed property. Of the 12 titles, 4 were by unpublished
writers and 3 were by authors who were new to the publishing
house. Receives 200 queries yearly.
Submissions and Payment: Guidelines and catalogue available at website. Query. Accepts hard copy and email to
JPacquisitions@abhms.org. SASE. Responds in 3–6 months.
Publication in 12–18 months. Royalty, 10%.

Jump at the Sun

Disney
114 Fifth Avenue
New York, NY 10011

Acquisitions

Publisher's Interests
An imprint of Disney Enterprises, Jump at the Sun is dedicated
to publishing books about the African American experience. It
publishes both fiction and nonfiction, including biographies
and photo-essays, for readers of all ages. Its list of titles features board and novelty books, picture books, chapter books,
and young adult novels. This publisher works with agented
authors only.
Website: www.jumpatthesun.com

Freelance Potential
Published 4 titles in 2010: each was by an agented author.
Submissions and Payment: Guidelines and catalogue available at website. Accepts submissions from agented authors
only. Royalty; advance.

Kaplan Publishing

1 Liberty Plaza, 24th Floor
New York, NY 10006

Editorial Department

Publisher's Interests
Kaplan Publishing has, in recent years, been expanding its
offerings for students in kindergarten through grade six. It publishes workbooks and study guides for history, math,
science, social studies, and language arts that are used by
students and professionals around the world. It also produces
books about college admission and special and gifted education, in addition to its test-preparation guides.
Website: www.kaplanpublishing.com

Freelance Potential
Published 200 titles in 2010.
Submissions and Payment: Guidelines available. Query.
Accepts email queries to kaplaneditorial@kaplan.com.
Response time and publication period vary.

Kregel Publications

P.O. Box 2607
Grand Rapids, MI 49501-2607

Acquisitions Editor

Publisher's Interests
Kregel Publications offers fiction and nonfiction books for
evangelical Christian readers of all ages. Topics covered
include Christian parenting and family life. It also publishes
Bible study materials for evangelical Christian leaders.
Website: www.kregel.com

Freelance Potential
Published 75 titles (2 juvenile) in 2010: 49 were by agented
authors and 2 were reprint/licensed properties. Of the 75
titles, 5 were by unpublished writers and 20 were by new
authors. Receives 200 queries, 125 unsolicited mss yearly.
Submissions and Payment: Guidelines available at website.
Query or send complete ms. Accepts email to acquisitions@
kregel.com. Response time varies. Royalty.

Laredo Publishing

465 Westview Avenue
Englewood, NJ 07631

Editor: Raquel Benatar

Publisher's Interests
This publisher's offerings include multicultural fiction,
biographies, and bilingual stories with North and South
American themes. Its readers are children ages 8 to 12. 50%
self-, subsidy-, co-venture, or co-op published material.
Website: www.renaissancehouse.net

Freelance Potential
Published 15 titles (8 juvenile) in 2010. Of the 15 titles, 2
were by unpublished writers and 4 were by new authors.
Receives 75 queries, 120 unsolicited mss yearly.
Submissions and Payment: Guidelines available. Catalogue
available at website. Query with synopsis; or send complete
ms. Accepts email to laredo@renaissancehouse.net (no attachments). Response time and publication period vary. Royalty.

Leadership Publishers

P.O. Box 8358
Des Moines, IA 50301-8358

Owner: Dr. Lois F. Roets

Publisher's Interests
The educational resources available from Leadership
Publishers address the needs of gifted and talented students,
their teachers, and their parents. Its list includes books written
by educators that offer instructional strategies, enrichment
activities, and personal support for teachers of gifted and talented programs. Leadership Publishers is not reviewing submissions at this time.
Website: www.leadershippublishers.com

Freelance Potential
Published 1 title in 2010.
Submissions and Payment: Catalogue available at website.
Not reviewing queries or manuscripts at this time. Check the
website for changes to this policy.

Leap Books

P.O. Box 112
Reidsville, NC 27320

Editor-in-Chief: Cat O'Shea

Publisher's Interests
Leap Books focuses on fiction for tweens and teens, especially inspirational, humorous, and multicultural stories. Only queries from agented authors, or from writers who have been solicited by the editors at a conference, will be considered.
Website: www.leapbks.com

Freelance Potential
Published 8 titles in 2010. Of the 8 titles, 4 were by unpublished writers and each was by an author who was new to the publishing house. Receives 48–60 queries yearly.
Submissions and Payment: Guidelines and catalogue available at website. Accepts email queries from literary agents and solicited writers only. Response time and publication period vary. Royalty.

Lighthouse Publishing

251 Overlook Park Lane
Lawrenceville, GA 30043

Submissions Editor: Chris Wright

Publisher's Interests
Books with a Christian message are offered by this publisher. 50% self-, subsidy-, co-venture, or co-op published material.
Website: www.lighthousechristianpublishing.com

Freelance Potential
Published 50 titles (30 juvenile) in 2010: 45 were developed from unsolicited submissions and 5 were by agented authors. Of the 50 titles, all were by authors who were new to the publishing house. Receives 144–180 unsolicited mss yearly.
Submissions and Payment: Guidelines available at website. Send complete ms. Accepts email submissions to info@lighthousechristianpublishing.com (Microsoft Word attachments). Responds in 6–8 weeks. Publication in 3–4 months. Royalty, 50% of net.

Lillenas Publishing Company

2923 Troost Avenue
Kansas City, MO 64109

Drama Editor

Publisher's Interests
A publisher of plays and resources for performers, directors, and playwrights, Lillenas targets those who use the dramatic arts in their Christian ministry. As such, all of its publications reflect a distinctly Christian perspective. Its plays deliver strong messages couched in scripts that entertain, but never sermonize. At this time, the company is closed to freelance submissions.
Website: www.lillenasdrama.com

Freelance Potential
Published 35+ titles in 2010.
Submissions and Payment: Not currently reviewing queries or manuscripts. Visit the website for the latest information concerning this policy.

The Love and Logic Press

2207 Jackson Street
Golden, CO 80401-2300

Publisher

Publisher's Interests
The Love and Logic Press publishes books and other media to help foster responsibility in children. To this end, its offerings include titles on practical parenting from birth to age six, helping underachieving school-aged children, and developing character in teens. Its material is designed for parents, educators, health care professionals, and anyone who works with children of any age.
Website: www.loveandlogic.com

Freelance Potential
Published 8 titles in 2010.
Submissions and Payment: Catalogue available at website. All work is assigned. Send résumé only. No queries or unsolicited manuscripts.

The Lutterworth Press

P.O. Box 60
Cambridge, CB1 2NT
United Kingdom

Managing Editor: Adrian Brink

Publisher's Interests
Lutterworth publishes nonfiction for adults, religious titles, and a small number of children's books. It is not currently accepting submissions for children's books. Check the website for updates to this policy. 2% self-, subsidy-, co-venture, or co-op published material.
Website: www.lutterworth.com

Freelance Potential
Published 2 titles in 2010: 1 was a reprint/licensed property. Of the 2 titles, 1 was by an author who was new to the publishing house. Receives 360 queries yearly.
Submissions and Payment: Guidelines and catalogue available at website. Not reviewing children's book queries or submissions at this time.

Mapletree Publishing Company

72 North WindRiver Road
Silverton, ID 83867-0446

Editor-in-Chief: Gail Howick

Publisher's Interests
Offering nonfiction only, Mapletree publishes books on homeschooling, child development, and the family.
Website: www.mapletreepublishing.com

Freelance Potential
Published 4 titles in 2010. Of the 4 titles, 1 was by an author who was new to the publishing house. Receives 48 queries each year.
Submissions and Payment: Guidelines available at website. Query with 3–4 chapters, synopsis, and market analysis. Prefers electronic queries through the website; will accept hard copy and simultaneous submissions if identified. SASE. Responds in 4–6 months. Publication period varies. Royalty, 15% of net.

Marlor Press

4304 Brigadoon Drive
St. Paul, MN 55126

Editorial Director: Marlin Bree

Publisher's Interests
In addition to its adult titles on boating and domestic and foreign travel, Marlor Press publishes books for kids on the go, such as trip diaries for young travelers. Other topics for children include magic tricks, family life, and crafts and activities. All of this publisher's books are nonfiction trade paperbacks; fiction and poetry are not part of its program.

Freelance Potential
Published 1 title in 2010. Receives 100+ queries yearly.
Submissions and Payment: Query with résumé, outline, description of target audience, and market analysis. No unsolicited mss. Accepts email queries to marlin.marlor@minn.net. Response time varies. Publication in 1 year. Royalty, 8–10% of net.

Maupin House

2416 NW 71 Place
Gainesville, FL 32653

Editor: Emily Raij

Publisher's Interests
Maupin House's educational resources are written by and for teachers of kindergarten through grade 12. Material covers literacy, writing, and the arts. Writers are encouraged to study the website to understand the publisher's niches.
Website: www.maupinhouse.com

Freelance Potential
Published 9 titles in 2010: 4–5 were developed from unsolicited submissions. Receives 240–350 queries yearly.
Submissions and Payment: Catalogue available at website. Query with résumé, publishing credits, table of contents, and sample chapter. Accepts email queries to publisher@ maupinhouse.com. Responds in 1 week. Publication in 12–18 months. Royalty, 10%.

Mayhaven Publishing

803 Buckthorn Circle
P.O. Box 557
Mahomet, IL 61853

Editor/Publisher: Doris Wenzel

Publisher's Interests
Children's print and audio books appear in this publisher's catalogue. Titles include biographies, illustrated novels, nonfiction, and poetry collections. 60% co-op published material.
Website: www.mayhavenpublishing.com

Freelance Potential
Published 14 titles (3 juvenile) in 2010: 13 were developed from unsolicited submissions. Of the 14 titles, 3 were by unpublished writers and 9 were by authors who were new to the publishing house. Receives 2,500 queries yearly.
Submissions and Payment: Guidelines available. Catalogue available at website. Query with 3 sample chapters. Accepts hard copy. SASE. Responds in 3–9 months. Publication in 9–12 months. Royalty.

Margaret K. McElderry Books

Simon & Schuster
1230 Avenue of the Americas
New York, NY 10020

Submissions Editor

Publisher's Interests
Margaret K. McElderry targets the teen, middle-grade, picture book, and poetry markets with a list that features fiction as well as nonfiction. High-quality literary fantasy, contemporary and historical fiction, character-driven picture books, and poetry are among its specialties. Please note that queries and unsolicited manuscripts are not accepted, as this publisher reviews work submitted through literary agents only.
Website: http://kids.simonandschuster.com

Freelance Potential
Published 50 titles in 2010: 49 were by agented authors and 1 was a reprint/licensed property.
Submissions and Payment: Agented authors only.
Publication in 2–4 years. Royalty; advance.

Milet Publishing

333 North Michigan Avenue, Suite 530
Chicago, IL 60601

Editorial Director

Publisher's Interests
Nontraditional, multicultural literature, characterized by a
bold, contemporary look, is the hallmark of the books offered
by Milet Publishing. It focuses mainly on picture books, particularly dual-language titles in Turkish, Polish, and Chinese.
Milet continues to be closed to submissions; changes to this
policy will be announced at the website.
Website: www.milet.com

Freelance Potential
Published 9 titles in 2010: 1 was by an agented author. Of the
9 titles, 2 were by authors new to the publishing house.
Submissions and Payment: Guidelines and catalogue available at website. Not accepting queries or manuscripts at this
time. Check website for changes to this policy.

Morning Glory Press

6595 San Haroldo Way
Buena Park, CA 90620-3748

President: Jeanne Lindsay

Publisher's Interests
Morning Glory Press publishes books written for teens who are
pregnant or parenting, and for the adults who counsel and
care for them. Its nonfiction titles cover topics including pre-
natal health, childbirth, parenting, relationships, child care,
adoption, teen fathers, and life skills. Fiction titles with
themes relevant to this group of teens are also published.
Website: www.morningglorypress.com

Freelance Potential
Published 1–2 titles in 2010. Receives 20 queries yearly.
Submissions and Payment: Query. Accepts hard copy. SASE.
Responds in 1–3 months. Publication in 6–8 months. Royalty;
advance, $500.

Natural Heritage Books

P.O. Box 95, Station O
Toronto, Ontario M4A 2M8
Canada

Publisher Emeritus: Barry Penhale

Publisher's Interests
The titles in this publisher's catalogue focus on the heritage, culture, natural environment, and history of Canada, and are geared toward middle-grade and high school readers. All of its titles are nonfiction.
Website: www.naturalheritagebooks.com

Freelance Potential
Published 20 titles in 2010. Receives 100+ queries yearly.
Submissions and Payment: Guidelines and catalogue available at website. Query with résumé, synopsis, table of contents, and 3 sample chapters. Accepts hard copy. SAE/IRC. Responds in 3–6 months. Publication in 1–2 years. Royalty; advance.

Nelson Education

1120 Birchmount Road
Scarborough, Ontario M1K 5G4
Canada

Submissions

Publisher's Interests
Nelson Education designs educational materials for use in Canadian classrooms. Its books and online resources cover the full range of kindergarten through high school curricula. It also publishes material for use in literacy programs for at-risk students. Submissions through literary agents are preferred; however, it will consider queries from highly qualified writers.
Website: www.nelson.com

Freelance Potential
Published 60 titles in 2010. Receives 100 queries yearly.
Submissions and Payment: Query. Prefers queries submitted through literary agents. Accepts hard copy. SAE/IRC. Responds in 6–12 months. Publication period and payment policy vary.

Newmarket Press

18 East 48th Street, 15th Floor
New York, NY 10017

Editor: Shannon Berning

Publisher's Interests
This publisher's catalogue features nonfiction books for children and teens, covering topics such as self-esteem, growing up, diet and health, and entrepreneurship. It also offers young adult novels, books with movie tie-ins, and biographies.
Website: www.newmarketpress.com

Freelance Potential
Published 45 titles in 2010: most were by agented authors. Receives 1,200 queries yearly.
Submissions and Payment: Guidelines available at website. Query with table of contents, sample chapters, market analysis, and credentials; or send complete ms. Accepts hard copy. SASE. Response time and publication period vary. Payment rates vary.

New Voices Publishing

P.O. Box 560
Wilmington, MA 01887

Editor

Publisher's Interests
As the publishing arm of KidsTerrain Inc., New Voices creates, acquires, and publishes books that address issues affecting children's lives. Its titles explore topics such as bullying, self-esteem, cultural sensitivity, and character. Its mission is to publish books that "make a difference." New writers are encouraged to submit to its subdivision, New Words Press.
Website: www.kidsterrain.com

Freelance Potential
Published 2 titles in 2010: 1 was developed from an unsolicited submission.
Submissions and Payment: Guidelines and catalogue available at website. Query. Accepts hard copy. SASE. Responds in 1–2 months. Publication in 12–18 months. Royalty, 10–15%.

New World Library

14 Pamaron Way
Novato, CA 94949

Submissions Editor: Jonathan Wickmann

Publisher's Interests
New World Library is known for publishing books on spirituality,
creativity, animals and nature, alternative health, consciousness,
well-being, personal growth, and multicultural issues. It offers
titles written for children and young adults, as well as adults,
including books on parenting and education issues.
Website: www.newworldlibrary.com

Freelance Potential
Published 35 titles in 2010. Receives many queries yearly.
Submissions and Payment: Guidelines available at website.
Query. Prefers email queries to submit@newworldlibrary.com;
will accept hard copy and simultaneous submissions. SASE.
Responds in 2–3 months. Publication in 12–18 months.
Payment policy varies.

Nickname Press

Box 454, 39 Queen Street
Cobourg, Ontario K9A 1M0
Canada

Editor: Heather Jopling

Publisher's Interests
This small, independent publisher offers books that celebrate
ethnic diversity, multiculturalism, the wide variety of lifestyle
choices, and nontraditional families. Its titles appear in the
form of easy-to-read and story picture books for children ages
four through ten.
Website: www.nicknamepress.com

Freelance Potential
Published 2 titles in 2010. Receives 12–20 queries yearly.
Submissions and Payment: Guidelines and catalogue avail-
able at website. Query with outline and synopsis. Accepts hard
copy and email queries to info@nicknamepress.com. SAE/IRC.
Responds in 2 months. Publication period varies. Royalty.

Nomad Press

2456 Christian Street
White River Junction, VT 05001

Editor: Susan Kahan

Publisher's Interests
This publisher offers books for children ages 6 through 13
who want to "discover, explore, and build it." Its titles cover
the sciences, social studies, and the environment.
Website: www.nomadpress.net

Freelance Potential
Published 10–12 titles in 2010. Of the 10–12 titles, 3 were by
unpublished writers and 7 were by authors who were new to
the publishing house. Receives 30 queries yearly.
Submissions and Payment: Guidelines and catalogue available at website. Query with résumé and list of publishing
credits. Accepts hard copy and email to info@nomadpress.net.
SASE. Responds in 2–4 weeks. Publication in 6–18 months.
Royalty. Flat fee.

Ocean Publishing

P.O. Box 1080
Flagler Beach, FL 32136-1080

Editor: Jake Wilson

Publisher's Interests
Ocean Press publishes nonfiction books about nature, the
environment, and conservation. Its titles for children and
young adults include how-to books and books about history,
as well as mystery fiction and picture books.
Website: www.ocean-publishing.com

Freelance Potential
Published 3 titles in 2010. Of the 3 titles, 1 was by an unpublished writer and 1 was by an author who was new to the publishing house. Receives 400 queries yearly.
Submissions and Payment: Guidelines available at website.
Query with clips. Accepts hard copy and simultaneous submissions if identified. SASE. Responds in 1 month. Publication in
6 months. Royalty, 5–8%; advance, to $250.

Orbit Books

Hachette Book Group
237 Park Avenue
New York, NY 10017

Editorial Department

Publisher's Interests
Orbit Books, an imprint of Hachette Book Group, focuses on
the science fiction and fantasy genres. While most titles are
geared toward adult readers, some are suitable for young
adults. Orbit Books will consider the work of new writers, but
accepts submissions only from writers who are represented
by literary agents.
Website: www.orbitbooks.net

Freelance Potential
Published 40 titles in 2010.
Submissions and Payment: Accepts submissions from
agented authors only. Responds in 2–6 months. Publication
period varies. Royalty; advance.

Orchard House Press

7419 Ebbert Drive SE
Port Orchard, WA 98367

Senior Editor: Chris K. A. DiMarco

Publisher's Interests
Orchard House is a small, independent press that publishes
books reflecting its commitment to human rights, equal rights,
freedom of religion, freedom of the press, and safety for all
children. It offers fiction books in many genres as well as
entertaining and enriching games. New writers are welcome.
Website: www.orchardhousepress.com

Freelance Potential
Published 100 titles in 2010: 95 were developed from unsolicited submissions. Receives 3,000+ queries yearly.
Submissions and Payment: Guidelines, required submission
form, and label available at website. Query with chapter-by-
chapter synopsis. Accepts hard copy. SASE. Responds in 1–3
months. Publication in 18 months. Royalty, 15%.

Our Child Press

P.O. Box 4379
Philadelphia, PA 19118

President: Carol Perrott

Publisher's Interests
Adoption is the focus of the fiction and nonfiction titles published by Our Child Press. Its books are geared toward children and adults alike.
Website: www.ourchildpress.com

Freelance Potential
Published 2 titles (1 juvenile) in 2010: both were developed from unsolicited submissions. Of the 2 titles, 1 was by an unpublished writer and 1 was by an author who was new to the publishing house. Receives 240 queries, 216 unsolicited mss yearly.
Submissions and Payment: Guidelines available. Query with outline/synopsis; or send complete ms. Accepts hard copy. SASE. Responds in 1–3 months. Publication in 1 year. Royalty.

Our Place Books

P.O. Box 1041
Darien, CT 06820

Founder: Chris Gorman

Publisher's Interests
Our Place Books seeks fiction picture books, preferably already illustrated, for children ages 4 to 10, that have creative, implied moral messages.
Website: www.ourplacebooks.com

Freelance Potential
Published 5–10 titles in 2010: 2 were developed from unsolicited submissions. Of the 5–10 titles, 2 were by unpublished writers and 2 were by authors who were new to the publishing house. Receives 100 queries, 50 unsolicited mss yearly.
Submissions and Payment: Catalogue available at website. Query or send complete ms. Accepts email to mail@ourplacebooks.com (Microsoft Word or PDF attachments). Response time and publication period vary. Royalty. Flat fee.

OverTime Books

#7, 1469 Galt
Montreal, Quebec J4Z 2J1
Canada

President: Jay Poulton

Publisher's Interests
This publisher specializes in sports-related books for older
teens and adults. It currently seeks biographies of athletes.
Website: www.overtimebooks.com

Freelance Potential
Published 6 titles in 2010: each was assigned. Of the 6 titles, 1
was by an unpublished writer and 1 was by a new author.
Receives 120 queries, 36 unsolicited mss yearly.
Submissions and Payment: Guidelines and catalogue available at website. Query with clips; or send complete ms with
résumé. Accepts hard copy, disk submissions (Microsoft Word
or PDF), and email to submissions@overtimebooks.com.
SAE/IRC. Responds to queries in 2 weeks, to mss in 3–6
months. Publication in 6–12 months. Flat fee.

Pacific View Press

P.O. Box 2897
Berkeley, CA 94702

Acquisitions Editor: Pam Zumwalt

Publisher's Interests
Pacific View Press is a small, cooperatively owned publisher of
books focusing on the Pacific Rim nations. Its catalogue features titles for adult and young teen readers on Chinese culture and history, as well as multicultural themes. 40% self-,
subsidy-, co-venture, or co-op published material.
Website: www.pacificviewpress.com

Freelance Potential
Published 2 titles in 2010. Receives many queries yearly.
Submissions and Payment: Guidelines available. Query with
outline and sample chapters. No unsolicited mss. Accepts hard
copy. SASE. Responds in 1 month. Publication period varies.
Royalty, 8–10%; advance, $500–$1,000.

Palari Books

P.O. Box 9288
Richmond, VA 23227-0288

Submissions Editor: David Smitherman

Publisher's Interests
Palari Books publishes both fiction and nonfiction titles, all highlighting the people and places of Virginia. Memoirs also appear in its catalogue of titles.
Website: www.palaribooks.com

Freelance Potential
Published 4 titles in 2010: 2 were developed from unsolicited submissions and 1 was by an agented author. Receives 1,200 queries yearly.
Submissions and Payment: Guidelines available at website. Query with synopsis/outline, intended audience, and author's credentials. Prefers hard copy; will accept email to dave@ palaribooks.com. SASE. Responds in 1 month. Publication period varies. Royalty.

PCI Education

P.O. Box 34270
San Antonio, TX 78265

Product Submissions Editor

Publisher's Interests
This publisher specializes in curriculum- and research-based educational materials. Its products are designed for students with special needs, including the intellectually and developmentally disabled and English language learners, and address both academic standards and life skills.
Website: www.pcieducation.com

Freelance Potential
Published several titles in 2010.
Submissions and Payment: Guidelines and catalogue available at website. Query or send complete ms with author bio, page count, description of target audience, and market analysis. Accepts hard copy. SASE. Responds in 2–4 months. Publication period varies. Payment policy varies.

Peartree

P.O. Box 14533
Clearwater, FL 33766

Publisher: Barbara Birenbaum

Publisher's Interests
Peartree publishes children's books on topics such as nature
and animals, as well as historical fiction. It offers referral assis-
tance to potential genre publishers for a fee. 50% self-, sub-
sidy-, co-venture, or co-op published material.
Website: www.peartreebooks.com

Freelance Potential
Published 5+ titles (2 juvenile) in 2010. Of the 5+ titles, 2 were
by unpublished writers and 1 was by a new author. Receives
30-50 queries, 25 unsolicited mss yearly.
Submissions and Payment: Guidelines available. Catalogue
available at website. Query or send complete ms. Accepts hard
copy. SASE. Responds in 5–8 weeks. Publication in 1 year.
Payment policy varies.

Pebble Books

Capstone Press
151 Good Counsel Drive
Mankato, MN 56001

Editorial Department

Publisher's Interests
This imprint of Capstone Press publishes mostly nonfiction
titles for readers in kindergarten through second grade. It
covers topics such as health, science and nature, and social
studies in colorful, entertaining formats. Biographies and
bilingual titles are also featured in its catalogue.
Website: www.capstonepub.com

Freelance Potential
Published 100 titles in 2010: several were reprint/licensed
properties.
Submissions and Payment: Guidelines available. Catalogue
available at website. Query with résumé and nonfiction writing
samples. Accepts hard copy. SASE. Responds in 1 month.
Publication period varies. Flat fee.

Penguin Books Canada

90 Eglinton Avenue East, Suite 700
Toronto, Ontario M4P 2Y3
Canada

Editorial Department

Publisher's Interests
Canadian authors, writing on Canadian themes, appear in the catalogue of Penguin Books Canada Limited. Titles include middle-grade fiction and young adult novels, as well as easy-to-read and picture books for younger children. Books on Canada's history also are offered.
Website: www.penguin.ca

Freelance Potential
Published 80 titles (14 juvenile) in 2010: each was by an agented author.
Submissions and Payment: Canadian authors only. Send complete ms. Accepts hard copy. SASE. Responds in 1 month. Publication in 1–2 years. Royalty, 8–10%.

Perspectives Press

P.O. Box 90318
Indianapolis, IN 46290-0318

Publisher: Patricia Irwin Johnston

Publisher's Interests
A niche publisher specializing in books about adoption and infertility, Perspectives Press is dependent on grant monies to meet some of its publishing goals. Those funds have slowed, as has the company's publishing schedule, which may change. Perspectives produces books for children and adults.
Website: www.perspectivespress.com

Freelance Potential
Publishing is currently on hold.
Submissions and Payment: Currently not accepting queries or mss. Changes to this policy will be posted at the website.

Phaidon Press

180 Varick Street, 14th Floor
New York, NY 10014

Editorial Submissions

Publisher's Interests
The Phaidon Press catalogue is comprised mainly of books for adults on art, architecture, music, theater, film, and the performing arts. It also includes some illustrated storybooks and arts and crafts titles for younger readers.
Website: www.phaidon.com

Freelance Potential
Published 20+ titles (3 juvenile) in 2010: 10 were developed from unsolicited submissions. Receives 120–240 queries each year.
Submissions and Payment: Guidelines available at website. Query with résumé, table of contents, and description of target audience. Accepts hard copy. SASE. Responds in 4 months. Publication period varies. Royalty; advance.

Piano Press

P.O. Box 85
Del Mar, CA 92014-0085

Owner/Editor: Elizabeth C. Axford

Publisher's Interests
Piano Press offers teaching materials for use in private studios and music classrooms, along with music-related picture books.
Website: www.pianopress.com

Freelance Potential
Published 6 titles in 2010: 3 were developed from unsolicited submissions and 3 were by agented authors. Of the 6 titles, 3 were by authors who were new to the publishing house. Receives 240 queries, 120 unsolicited mss yearly.
Submissions and Payment: Guidelines and catalogue available at website. Query for prose. Send complete ms for poetry. Accepts hard copy, disk submissions (Microsoft Word), and email submissions to pianopress@pianopress.com. SASE. Responds in 2–4 months. Publication in 1 year. Royalty.

Picture Me Press

1566 Akron-Peninsula Road
Akron, OH 44313

Submissions Editor

Publisher's Interests
By designing books that allow children to insert photos of themselves into the pages, Picture Me Press lets readers become the main characters of the story. In addition to these books, this publisher produces other interactive titles to help children develop their vocabulary and learn to count. Both fiction and nonfiction appear in the catalogue, and all titles encourage reading and foster the imagination.
Website: www.picturemepress.com

Freelance Potential
Published 10–15 titles in 2010.
Submissions and Payment: Query. No unsolicited mss. Accepts hard copy. SASE. Response time and publication period vary. Royalty; advance.

Pippin Press

Gracie Station Box 1347
229 East 85th Street
New York, NY 10028

Publisher/Editor-in-Chief: Barbara Francis

Publisher's Interests
Each year, Pippin Press produces a small list of chapter books for children ages 7 through 12. At this time, it is particularly interested in reviewing queries for fiction set in East Africa or for nonfiction on topics related to East African culture.

Freelance Potential
Published 4 titles in 2010: 2 were developed from unsolicited submissions. Of the 4 titles, 1 was by an unpublished writer and 1 was by an author who was new to the publishing house. Receives 600 queries yearly.
Submissions and Payment: Guidelines available. Query with 1-page synopsis and sample chapter. Accepts hard copy; mark envelope "Query Enclosed." SASE. Responds in 1 month. Publication in 1–2 years. Royalty; advance.

The Place in the Woods

3900 Glenwood Avenue
Golden Valley, MN 55422

Editor: Roger Hammer

Publisher's Interests
"Feel good" children's stories of triumph over adversity and multicultural fiction are the specialty of this small publishing program. It also features an adult list made up of nonfiction titles; topics include history and biography. An ongoing need is for stories that demonstrate sensitivity to people of all cultures who live in the U.S.

Freelance Potential
Published 1 title in 2010: it was developed from an unsolicited submission and it was by an unpublished writer. Receives 240 unsolicited mss yearly.
Submissions and Payment: Guidelines and catalogue available. Send complete ms. Accepts hard copy. SASE. Responds in 1 month. Publication in 2–3 years. Royalty. Flat fee.

Pogo Press

Finney Company
8075 215th Street West
Lakeville, MN 55044

President: Alan E. Krysan

Publisher's Interests
Minnesota is usually the focus of the books offered by this publisher. Topics covered include history, pop culture, the arts, and the travel odyssey.
Website: www.pogopress.com

Freelance Potential
Published 3 titles in 2010: each was developed from an unsolicited submission. Of the 3 titles, each was by an unpublished writer who was new to the publishing house. Receives 96–120 queries yearly.
Submissions and Payment: Guidelines and catalogue available at website. Query with 3–4 sample chapters and marketing plan. Accepts hard copy. SASE. Responds in 10–12 weeks. Publication in 6–18 months. Royalty, 10%.

Prep Publishing

1110½ Hay Street, Suite C
Fayetteville, NC 28305

Editor: Anne McKinney

Publisher's Interests
While its catalogue is predominantly focused on books concerning job hunting and careers, Prep Publishing also offers biographies, fiction, general nonfiction, and books with Judeo-Christian themes.
Website: www.prep-pub.com

Freelance Potential
Published 3 titles in 2010. Of the 3 titles, 1 was by an author who was new to the publishing house. Receives 1,000 queries, 400 unsolicited mss yearly.
Submissions and Payment: Guidelines and catalogue available at website. Query with synopsis; or send complete ms with $350 reading fee. Accepts hard copy. SASE. Responds in 3 months. Publication in 18 months. Royalty, 6–14%.

PUSH

Scholastic
557 Broadway
New York, NY 10012

Editor: David Levithan

Publisher's Interests
PUSH, a teen imprint of Scholastic, is dedicated to new writers with strong, authentic voices. It looks for aspiring authors who speak well to the young adult reader. Contemporary, historical, and multicultural fiction are featured. The PUSH Novel Contest also encourages teens, grades 7 to 12, to submit fiction.
Website: www.thisispush.com

Freelance Potential
Published 5 titles in 2010. Of the 5 titles, 2 were by authors who were new to the publishing house.
Submissions and Payment: Catalogue available at website. Accepts submissions from agented authors only. Young writers may submit to the PUSH contest. Response time varies.

QED

226 City Road
London, EC1V 2TT
United Kingdom

Editor: Amanda Askew

Publisher's Interests
QED offers books that combine entertainment with education, in both fiction and nonfiction. Its titles are designed for children up to 12 years of age.
Website: www.qed-publishing.co.uk

Freelance Potential
Published 80 titles in 2010. Of the 80 titles, 15 were by unpublished writers and 6 were by authors who were new to the publishing house. Receives 50–100 queries yearly.
Submissions and Payment: Guidelines available. Catalogue available at website. Query with clips. Accepts hard copy and email queries to amandaa@quarto.com. Availability of artwork improves chance of acceptance. SAE/IRC. Response time and publication period vary. Royalty. Flat fee.

Quagmire Press

#2, 11717–9B Avenue NW
Edmonton, Alberta T6J 7B7
Canada

President: Hank Boer

Publisher's Interests
The books from Quagmire Press fall into the categories of true crime, "strange but true" mysteries, or criminal biographies—and all are Canada-related. Freelancers may submit their own work or send a résumé with a list of publishing credits to be considered for assignments.

Freelance Potential
Published 3 titles in 2010: each was assigned. Receives 24 queries, 12 unsolicited mss yearly.
Submissions and Payment: Guidelines and catalogue available at website. Query with clips; or send complete ms with résumé. Accepts hard copy and disk submissions (Microsoft Word or PDF). SAE/IRC. Responds to queries in 2 weeks, to mss in 3–6 months. Publication in 6–12 months. Flat fee.

Rainbow Books

P.O. Box 430
Highland City, FL 33846-0430

Editorial Director: Betsy Lampe

Publisher's Interests
Books that help to build self-esteem and improve coping
mechanisms in tweens and teens are the focus of this publisher. Biographies of role models are also offered.
Website: www.rainbowbooksinc.com

Freelance Potential
Published 28 titles (4 juvenile) in 2010: 26 were developed
from unsolicited submissions and 2 were by agented authors.
Of the 28 titles, 18 were by unpublished writers and 20 were
by new authors. Receives 300–420 queries yearly.
Submissions and Payment: Guidelines and catalogue available at website. Query. Accepts hard copy and email to
submissions@rainbowbooksinc.com (no attachments). SASE.
Responds in 6 weeks. Publication in 1 year. Royalty; advance.

Randall House Publications

114 Bush Road
Nashville, TN 37217

Acquisitions Editor: Michelle Orr

Publisher's Interests
Randall House publishes Sunday school resources for children
of all ages, as well as fiction and nonfiction titles based on
Christian themes.
Website: www.randallhouse.com

Freelance Potential
Published 15 titles in 2010: 3 were developed from unsolicited
submissions and 2 were by agented authors. Of the 15 titles,
2 were by unpublished writers and 3 were by new authors.
Receives 1,000+ queries yearly.
Submissions and Payment: Guidelines available at website.
Query. Accepts hard copy and email queries via website.
SASE. Responds in 3 months. Publication in 12–14 months.
Royalty, 10–14%; advance, $1,000–$2,000.

Rand McNally

8255 North Central Park
Skokie, IL 60076

Editorial Director: Laurie Borman

Publisher's Interests
Well-known for its atlases, Rand McNally also produces a line of
educational materials for classroom use. These include travel
games, reference books, and interactive games for geography,
social studies, and history. Since it works by assignment only,
education writers are invited to send their résumés.
Website: www.randmcnally.com/education

Freelance Potential
Published 8–10 titles in 2010: most were by unpublished writers and 1–2 were by authors who were new to the publishing
house. Receives 12–24 queries yearly.
Submissions and Payment: Send résumé only. All work is
assigned. Response time, publication period, and payment policy vary.

Random House UK Children's Books

61-63 Uxbridge Road
Ealing, London W5 5DA
United Kingdom

Picture Books: Hannah Featherstone; Fiction: Naomi Wood

Publisher's Interests
From board books and picture books to novels and series, this
publisher is known for the award-winning titles it produces for
children of all ages. Accepting submissions from agented
authors only, it features fiction in a number of genres, such as
adventure, romance, and science fiction, as well as nonfiction.
Website: www.kidsatrandomhouse.co.uk

Freelance Potential
Published 200+ titles in 2010: most were by agented authors.
Receives 3,000 queries yearly.
Submissions and Payment: Guidelines available. Accepts
submissions from agented authors only. Publication in 1–2
years. Royalty; advance.

Rayo

HarperCollins
1350 Avenue of the Americas
New York, NY 10019

Executive Editor: Adriana Dominguez

Publisher's Interests
Rayo's list consists of culturally inspired Spanish, English, and bilingual books. It also includes translations of award-winning and highly popular English titles. Its mission is to publish stories that help children understand and learn more about the world in which they live. It works with agented authors only.
Website: www.harperchildrens.com

Freelance Potential
Published 20 titles in 2010: all were by agented authors. Receives 24 queries yearly.
Submissions and Payment: Accepts submissions through literary agents only. Response time, publication period, and payment policy vary.

Red Rock Press

459 Columbus Avenue, Suite 114
New York, NY 10024

Creative Director

Publisher's Interests
In addition to the entertaining gift books it produces for children and adults, Red Rock Press's children's imprint, Red Pebble, offers a list of fantasy titles. It prefers submissions from agented authors.
Website: www.redrockpress.com

Freelance Potential
Published 6 titles (1 juvenile) in 2010: 2 were developed from unsolicited submissions. Of the 6 titles, 1 was by an unpublished writer. Receives 800 unsolicited mss yearly.
Submissions and Payment: Prefers agented submissions. Send complete ms with marketing plan. Accepts hard copy. SASE. Responds in 2–4 months. Publication in 18 months. Royalty; advance. Flat fee.

Renaissance House

465 Westview Avenue
Englewood, NJ 07631

Editorial Director: Raquel Benatar

Publisher's Interests
Bilingual children's books and biographies are the focus of
Renaissance House. It also accepts poetry.
Website: www.renaissancehouse.net

Freelance Potential
Published 12 titles in 2010: 1 was developed from an unsolicited submission. Of the 12 titles, 1 was by an unpublished writer
and 2 were by authors who were new to the publishing house.
Receives 600 queries yearly.
Submissions and Payment: Catalogue available with SASE
($1.75 postage). Query. Accepts hard copy. Availability of art-
work improves chance of acceptance. Color prints or transparencies. SASE. Response time varies. Publication in 1 year.
Flat fee.

River City Publishing

1719 Mulberry Street
Montgomery, AL 36106

Editor: Jim Gilbert

Publisher's Interests
This publisher of books about the American South is currently
closed to children's submissions. Check its website for updates.
Website: www.rivercitypublishing.com

Freelance Potential
Published 6 titles in 2010: 2 were developed from unsolicited
submissions. Of the 6 titles, 5 were by unpublished writers
and 2 were by authors who were new to the publishing house.
Submissions and Payment: Guidelines and catalogue available at website. Not accepting queries or mss for children's
books at this time. Changes to this policy will be posted at
the website.

River's Bend Press

P.O. Box 606
Stillwater, MN 55082

Editor

Publisher's Interests
Although River's Bend Press is not a children's book publisher, it does accept work that appeals to young adult readers. Its fiction and nonfiction titles are typically about social issues, current events, and history, but humorous titles are also of interest.
Website: www.riversbendpress.com

Freelance Potential
Published 2 titles in 2010: each was developed from an unsolicited submission. Receives 600 queries yearly.
Submissions and Payment: Guidelines and catalogue available at website. Query with 3 chapters. Accepts hard copy. SASE. Responds in 2 months. Publication period and payment policy vary.

Robbie Dean Press

2910 East Eisenhower Parkway
Ann Arbor, MI 48108

Owner: Dr. Fairy Hayes-Scott

Publisher's Interests
Robbie Dean Press publishes books that tackle the issues most relevant to teens and young adults. It offers both fiction and nonfiction titles.
Website: www.robbiedeanpress.com

Freelance Potential
Published 5–10 titles (3 juvenile) in 2010: each was developed from an unsolicited submission. Of the 5–10 titles, each was by an unpublished writer. Receives 5 queries, 5 unsolicited mss yearly.
Submissions and Payment: Query for nonfiction. Send complete ms for fiction. Accepts hard copy and disk submissions (Microsoft Word). SASE. Responds to queries in 2 days; to mss in 2 months. Publication in 9 months. Royalty, 10–20%.

Robinswood Press

30 South Avenue
Stourbridge, West Midlands DY8 3XY
United Kingdom

Editor: Sally Connolly

Publisher's Interests
A publisher of children's books, parenting titles, and educational guides, Robinswood Press produces books that foster a love of reading and writing in children.
Website: www.robinswoodpress.com

Freelance Potential
Published 12 titles in 2010: 10 were developed from unsolicited submissions and 2 were by agented authors. Of the 12 titles, 2 were by unpublished writers and 3 were by authors who were new to the publishing house. Receives 360 queries yearly.
Submissions and Payment: Guidelines available at website. Query with synopsis and author bio. Accepts email queries to publishing@robinswoodpress.com (no attachments). Responds in 4–6 weeks. Publication period and payment policy vary.

Rose Publishing

4733 Torrance Boulevard, Suite 259
Torrance, CA 90503

Acquisitions Editor: Lynette Pennings

Publisher's Interests
Keeping within the conservative, evangelical Christian perspective, Rose Publishing produces Bible study and reference materials, including visual aids such as charts and timelines.
Website: www.rose-publishing.com

Freelance Potential
Published 25 titles in 2010. Of the 25 titles, 2–3 were by authors who were new to the publishing house.
Submissions and Payment: Catalogue available at website or with 9x12 SASE (4 first-class stamps). Query with sketch of proposed chart or poster. Accepts hard copy, email to rosepubl@aol.com, and simultaneous submissions if identified. Materials are not returned. Responds in 2–3 months. Publication in 18 months. Flat fee.

Running Press Kids

2300 Chestnut Street, Suite 200
Philadelphia, PA 19103-4399

Assistant to the Editorial Director

Publisher's Interests
Running Press Kids boasts a diverse selection of fiction for children through young adults, and nonfiction for kids up to age seven. Its nonfiction list includes books on science, nature, and arts and crafts, as well as biographies. Running Press Kids is not open to submissions at this time.
Website: www.runningpress.com

Freelance Potential
Published 50 titles in 2010. Of the 50 titles, 5 were by unpublished writers and 2 were by authors who were new to the publishing house.
Submissions and Payment: Guidelines and catalogue available at website. Not currently accepting submissions. Changes to this policy will be announced at the website.

Sandcastle Publishing

P.O. Box 3070
South Pasadena, CA 91031-6070

Acquisitions: Renee Rolle-Whatley

Publisher's Interests
Sandcastle Publishing designs books for school-aged children and young adults who are interested in learning about, and participating in, the performing arts. It publishes skits, read-aloud plays, and monologues, with the twin goals of improving acting skills and promoting literacy. It also offers some fiction titles for younger readers.
Website: www.childrenactingbooks.com

Freelance Potential
Published 2 titles in 2010. Receives 200 queries yearly.
Submissions and Payment: Writer's guidelines available. Query with résumé. No unsolicited mss. Accepts hard copy. SASE. Responds in 2–3 months. Publication period and payment policy vary.

School Zone Publishing

1819 Industrial Drive
P.O. Box 777
Grand Haven, MI 49417

Editor

Publisher's Interests
For more than 30 years, School Zone Publishing has produced educational workbooks, software, and flash cards geared to children in preschool through grade six. Each product contains research-based content with hands-on activities and games designed to entertain and challenge children. Written by leading educators, the workbooks cover reading, writing, mathematics, and bilingual studies; they are used by both teachers and parents.
Website: www.schoolzone.com

Freelance Potential
Published 5–6 titles in 2010. Receives 100 queries yearly.
Submissions and Payment: Query with résumé and writing samples. Response time and publication period vary. Flat fee.

Schwartz & Wade

Random House
1745 Broadway
New York, NY 10019

Editorial Directors: Anne Schwartz, Lee Wade

Publisher's Interests
Schwartz & Wade is a six-year-old imprint of Random House with a list that includes fiction and nonfiction in categories such as biography, sports, the arts, life skills, and contemporary retellings of fairy tales. It publishes concept books, picture books, early readers, chapter books, and middle-grade books. This imprint's titles are known for their creative blend of story and design.
Website: www.randomhouse.com/kids

Freelance Potential
Random House imprints publish hundreds of titles annually.
Submissions and Payment: Like other Random House imprints, Schwartz & Wade considers submissions only through literary agents.

Seven Stories Press

140 Watts Street
New York, NY 10013

Editorial Department

Publisher's Interests
Seven Stories Press publishes "works of imagination and political titles by voices of conscience." Its extensive catalogue features books on politics, human rights, women's issues, social and economic justice, literary fiction, and translations, many of which were shunned by mainstream publishers. It welcomes graphic novel submissions for young adults.
Website: www.sevenstories.com

Freelance Potential
Published 20–30 titles in 2010.
Submissions and Payment: Guidelines and catalogue available at website. Query with sample chapters. Accepts hard copy. SASE. Responds in 2–4 months. Publication in 18 months. Royalty.

Silver Moon Press

160 Fifth Avenue
New York, NY 10010

Submissions Editor

Publisher's Interests
In addition to test preparation guides, science books, and biographies, Silver Moon's catalogue also features historical fiction titles for grade-school children that portray significant eras in American history. It is most interested in the Revolutionary War, Colonial times, and New York State history.
Website: www.silvermoonpress.com

Freelance Potential
Published 2 titles in 2010. Receives 50–150 queries yearly.
Submissions and Payment: Guidelines available at website. Query with résumé, table of contents, and first chapter. Accepts hard copy and simultaneous submissions if identified. SASE. Responds in 6 months. Publication period and payment policy vary.

Silverton House Publishing

72 North WindRiver Road
Silverton, ID 83867-0446

Editor: Gail Howick

Publisher's Interests
Silverton House publishes story picture books for ages 4 to 10, as well as genre fiction and nonfiction for adults.
Website: www.silvertonhousepublishing.com

Freelance Potential
Published 4 titles (1 juvenile) in 2010: each was developed from an unsolicited submission. Of the 4 titles, 3 were by unpublished writers and each was by an author who was new to the publishing house. Receives 120 queries yearly.
Submissions and Payment: Guidelines available at website. Query with synopsis, 3–4 chapters, and market information. Prefers query via website; will accept hard copy and simultaneous submissions if identified. SASE. Responds in 4–6 months. Publication period varies. Royalty, 15% of net.

Skinner House

25 Beacon Street
Boston, MA 02108

Editor

Publisher's Interests
This imprint of the Unitarian Universalist Association of Congregations (UUA) publishes children's and adult titles on church adminstration, faith, and social issues. Juvenile titles include stories about Christian and pagan celebrations, contemporary parables, blessings, poetry, and books on principles such as forgiveness, love, and caring for the Earth. It wants authors and editors for worship resources and sermons for children, and for books on living faith, social justice, and confession and reconciliation.
Website: www.uua.org/publications/skinnerhouse

Freelance Potential
Publishes about 12 books annually.
Submissions and Payment: Send query or proposal, outline, two sample chapters. Check website for updates.

Smith & Sons

177 Lyme Road
Hanover, NH 03755

Editor: Marisa Kraus

Publisher's Interests
This relatively new imprint of Smith and Kraus is building its list of adventure, fantasy, and science fiction titles. It is seeking stories that engage the imagination of middle-grade and young adult readers.
Website: www.smithandkraus.com

Freelance Potential
Published 1 title in 2010: it was developed from an unsolicited submission.
Submissions and Payment: Guidelines available at website. Query with brief author bio, synopsis, and sample chapters. Accepts email queries to marisa@smithandkraus.com. Responds in 1–2 months. Publication in 1 year. Royalty; advance. Flat fee.

Southern Early Childhood Association

1123 South University, Suite 255
Little Rock, AR 72204

Editor: Janet B. Stivers

Publisher's Interests
Books published by Southern Early Childhood Association are read by early childhood professionals, including teachers, child care providers, social workers, and education policy makers. Titles cover topics such as professional development, classroom practices, program administration, relationships with families, special education, and social and behavioral issues.
Website: www.southernearlychildhood.org

Freelance Potential
Published 1–2 titles in 2010: each was assigned.
Submissions and Payment: Guidelines and calendar available at website. Query with clips. Accepts hard copy and email queries to editor@southernearlychildhood.org. SASE. Response time and publication period vary. Royalty, 10%.

Spinner Books

University Games Corporation
2030 Harrison Street
San Francisco, CA 94110

Product Manager

Publisher's Interests
This company publishes interactive children's books based
on its best-selling board games, as well as puzzle and brain
teaser books. Targeting children ages six and older, its books
combine imagination, social interaction, and learning. Spinner
Books is a division of University Games Corporation.
Website: www.universitygames.com

Freelance Potential
Published 8 titles (5 juvenile) in 2010: each was assigned.
Receives 20 queries yearly.
Submissions and Payment: Writers' guidelines available.
Catalogue available at website. Query. Accepts hard copy.
SASE. Responds in 3 months. Publication in 6–9 months.
Royalty, 5–10%.

Stackpole Books

5067 Ritter Road
Mechanicsburg, PA 17055

Publisher: Judith Schnell

Publisher's Interests
Stackpole Books' how-to and informational titles explore such
topics as outdoor sports, nature, crafts, history, travel, and
regional themes in the Mid-Atlantic states. It does not publish
children's books.
Website: www.stackpolebooks.com

Freelance Potential
Published 100 titles in 2010: many were developed from unsolicited submissions. Receives 1,000 queries yearly.
Submissions and Payment: Catalogue available at website.
Query with clips. Accepts hard copy and simultaneous submissions if identified. Availability of artwork improves chance of
acceptance. SASE. Responds in 1 month. Publication in 2
years. Royalty; advance.

Sumach Press

1415 Bathurst Street, Suite 202
Toronto, Ontario M5R 3H8
Canada

Submissions Editor

Publisher's Interests
Sumach Press is known as a feminist publisher with both fiction and nonfiction books written by and for women. Its young adult titles focus on contemporary teen issues in a nonracist and nonsexist way. Its goal is to expand its literary fiction offerings with the works of today's up-and-coming writers. Poetry and drama are not accepted.
Website: www.sumachpress.com

Freelance Potential
Published 9–10 titles in 2010.
Submissions and Payment: Send complete ms for young adult fiction. Query with sample chapter and outline for nonfiction. Accepts hard copy. SAE/IRC. Responds in 3–4 months. Publication period and payment policy vary.

The Templar Company

The Granary, North Street
Dorking, Surrey RH4 1DN
United Kingdom

Submissions: Rebecca Spiers

Publisher's Interests
Templar Publishing, best known for its *Ology* series of books, focuses on illustrated children's fiction.
Website: www.templarco.co.uk

Freelance Potential
Published 60 titles in 2010: 1 was developed from an unsolicited submission and 12 were by agented authors. Of the 60 titles, 6 were by unpublished writers and 12 were by authors who were new to the publishing house. Receives 300 queries, 400 unsolicited mss yearly.
Submissions and Payment: Guidelines available. Query with synopsis; or send complete ms. Accepts hard copy. SAE/IRC. Responds to queries in 2 weeks, to mss in 3–4 months. Publication period and payment policy vary.

Thistledown Press

633 Main Street
Saskatoon, Saskatchewan S7H 0J8
Canada

Submissions Editor: Allan Forrie

Publisher's Interests
Thistledown Press publishes fiction for middle-grade and young adult readers written by Canadian authors only.
Website: www.thistledownpress.com

Freelance Potential
Published 18 titles in 2010. Of the 18 titles, 7 were by unpublished writers and 10 were by authors who were new to the publishing house. Receives 600 queries yearly.
Submissions and Payment: Canadian authors only. Writers' guidelines and list of new titles available at website. Query with outline, sample chapter, and brief author biography. Accepts hard copy. SASE. Responds in 4 months. Publication in 1 year. Royalty.

Ticktock Media Limited

The Old Sawmill, 103 Goods Station Road
Tunbridge Wells, Kent TN1 2DP
United Kingdom

Editor: Melissa Fairley

Publisher's Interests
Ticktock Media Limited publishes nonfiction and fiction for children up to age 16, including read-aloud books for babies and toddlers. Ticktock's titles cover a broad spectrum of nonfiction topics, and it has recently inaugurated a search for works of fiction.
Website: www.ticktock.co.uk

Freelance Potential
Published 16 titles in 2010.
Submissions and Payment: All work is assigned. Guidelines available by email request to info@ticktock.co.uk. Query with résumé. Accepts hard copy and email queries to info@ticktock.co.uk. Response time varies. Publication in 1–2 years. Payment policy varies. Royalty.

TouchWood Editions

340-1105 Pandora Avenue
Victoria, British Columbia V8V 3P9
Canada

Associate Publisher: Ruth Linka

Publisher's Interests
Historical fiction, mysteries, and books about nature, garden-
ing, and art comprise this publisher's list of titles.
Website: www.touchwoodeditions.com

Freelance Potential
Published 15 titles in 2010: 5 were developed from unsolicited
submissions, 2 were by agented authors, and 1 was a reprint/
licensed property. Of the 15 titles, 4 were by unpublished writers and 4 were by new authors. Receives 200 queries yearly.
Submissions and Payment: Guidelines and catalogue available at website. Query with 200-word synopsis, market analysis, illustration list, author bio, table of contents, and 2–3
sample chapters. Accepts hard copy. SAE/IRC. Response time,
publication period, and payment policy vary.

Trumpet Media

72 North WindRiver Road
Silverton, ID 83867-0446

Editor: Gail Howick

Publisher's Interests
An imprint of WindRiver publishing, Trumpet Media produces
books for the Christian market. Topics covered include history,
apologetics, and doctrine. Study guides, biographies, autobiographies, and works of fiction also appear on its list, which
features titles for children, teens, and adults.
Website: www.trumpetmedia.com

Freelance Potential
Published 2 titles in 2010. Receives 24 queries yearly.
Submissions and Payment: Guidelines available at website.
Query with synopsis, 3–4 chapters, and market information.
Prefers query via website; will accept hard copy and simultane-
ous submissions if identified. SASE. Responds in 4–6 months.
Publication period varies. Royalty, 15% of net.

Tu Books

Lee & Low
95 Madison Avenue, Suite 1205
New York, NY 10026

Editorial Director: Stacey Whitman

Publisher's Interests
A new imprint at multicultural publisher Lee & Low, Tu Books specializes in fantasy, science fiction, mystery, and historical fiction for readers of color. The impetus behind the imprint was a gap in genre fiction for minority middle-graders and teens. The settings and worlds behind the fiction should be inspired by non-Western folklore or culture. Settings may be contemporary, historical, or futuristic.
Website: www.leeandlow.com/p/tu.mhtml

Freelance Potential
New imprint open to writers.
Submissions and Payment: Mail a cover letter, synopsis, and first three chapters for well-told, exciting, adventurous speculative fiction.

Tyrannosaurus Press

5486 Fairway Drive
Zachary, LA 70791

Submissions Editor: Roxanne Reiken

Publisher's Interests
This publisher's list covers the spectrum of speculative fiction for young adult and adult readers.
Website: www.tyrannosauruspress.com

Freelance Potential
Published 2 titles in 2010: 1 was developed from an unsolicited submission. Of the 2 titles, 1 was by an unpublished writer and 1 was by a new author. Receives 150+ queries yearly.
Submissions and Payment: Guidelines and catalogue available at website. Query with cover letter, author credentials, word count, and description of target audience. Prefers email to info@tyrannosauruspress.com (no attachments; include "Query" in subject line); will accept hard copy. SASE. Responds in 3 months. Publication in 1–2 years. Royalty, 10% of gross.

Unity House

Unity School of Christianity
1901 NW Blue Parkway
Unity Village, MO 64065-0001

Submissions

Publisher's Interests
Unity School of Christianity bases its teachings on metaphysical interpretation of scriptures with an emphasis on practical application. This imprint publishes books according to these teachings, offering nonfiction titles on topics including spirituality, parenting, and young adult issues. Fiction and children's material are not currently sought. Check website for updates.
Website: www.unityonline.org

Freelance Potential
Published 6 titles in 2010. Of the 6 titles, most were by new authors. Receives 450 queries yearly.
Submissions and Payment: Guidelines and catalogue available at website. Query with proposal. Accepts hard copy. SASE. Responds in 6 months. Publication in 11 months. Royalty.

VanderWyk & Burnham

1610 Long Leaf Circle
St. Louis, MO 63146

Acquisitions Editor

Publisher's Interests
An imprint of Quick Publishing, VanderWyk & Burnham specializes in nonfiction books that help make a difference in people's lives. Topics include self-improvement, aging, and social or contemporary issues. It is not accepting unsolicited submissions at this time.
Website: www.vandb.com

Freelance Potential
Published 1 title in 2010: it was developed from an unsolicited submission. Receives 60–240 queries yearly.
Submissions and Payment: Not accepting submissions at this time. Check the website for updates to this policy.

Volcano Press

P.O. Box 270
Volcano, CA 95689

Publisher Emerita: Ruth Gottstein

Publisher's Interests
The titles from Volcano Press generally focus on women's and children's issues, but some also cover California history. While most of the books in its catalogue are written for adult readers, particularly women, story picture books for children occasionally appear. Queries are always welcome.
Website: www.volcanopress.com

Freelance Potential
Published 4 titles in 2010.
Submissions and Payment: Catalogue available at website. Query with outline, sample chapters, and marketing analysis. Prefers email queries to ruth@volcanopress.com; will accept hard copy. SASE. Responds in 2 months. Publication period varies. Royalty; advance.

WestSide Books

60 Industrial Road
Lodi, NJ 07644

Submissions Editor: Evelyn M. Fazio

Publisher's Interests
WestSide Books publishes works of fiction for readers ages 14 to 18, particularly graphic novels and novels in verse. It is currently seeking edgy, contemporary books for urban teen boys.
Website: www.westside-books.com

Freelance Potential
Published 12 titles in 2010. Of the 12 titles, 3 were by unpublished writers and 3 were by authors who were new to the publishing house. Receives 10,000 queries yearly.
Submissions and Payment: Guidelines and catalogue available at website. Query with synopsis, first 25 pages, and brief author biography. Accepts email queries to submissions@ westside-books.com. Responds in 2 months. Publication period varies. Royalty.

Whiskey Creek Press

P.O. Box 51052
Casper, WY 82605-1052

Submissions Editor: Melanie Billings

Publisher's Interests
Whiskey Creek publishes genre fiction primarily for adults,
although some of its titles appeal to teens as well.
Website: www.whiskeycreekpress.com

Freelance Potential
Published 160–170 titles (6 juvenile) in 2010: 50–100 were
developed from unsolicited submissions, 5–10 were by agented authors, and 5–10 were reprint/licensed properties. Of the
160–170 titles, 5–10 were by unpublished writers and 10–20
were by new authors. Receives 120 unsolicited mss yearly.
Submissions and Payment: Guidelines and catalogue available at website. Send complete ms (60,000–80,000 words).
Accepts email submissions to subs@whiskeycreekpress.com.
Responds in 3–4 months. Publication period varies. Royalty.

Wild Child Publishing

P.O. Box 4897
Culver City, CA 90231-4897

Submissions: Marci Baun

Publisher's Interests
The titles from Wild Child Publishing span a broad range of
categories for a broad range of ages. Its nonfiction covers
most subjects. For fiction, it seeks stories with imaginative
plots and exciting characters.
Website: www.wildchildpublishing.com

Freelance Potential
Published 25–30 titles (1 juvenile) in 2010: 20 were developed from unsolicited submissions and 2 were by agented
authors.
Submissions and Payment: Guidelines and catalogue available at website. Query with synopsis. Accepts email queries to
mgbaun@wildchildpublishing.com. Response time and publication period vary. Royalty, 40% on e-books, 10% on print books.

Wiley

Professional and Trade Division
111 River Street
Hoboken, NJ 07030

Editor

Publisher's Interests
Wiley's children's books are nonfiction aimed at school-aged children. Categories include art and architecture, cooking, history, science, sports, careers, studying, activities, world holidays, pets, and family. The company also wants books on parenting, reference, self-help, technology, and many other topics.
Website: www.wiley.com

Freelance Potential
Published hundreds of titles in 2010.
Submissions and Payment: Mail a proposal, outline or table of contents, and résumé, with a discussion of why the book is needed, the primary and secondary markets, competitive works, and a partial or complete manuscript.

WindRiver Publishing

72 North WindRiver Road
Silverton, ID 83867-0446

Editor-in-Chief: Gail Howick

Publisher's Interests
Offering books for the Church of Jesus Christ of Latter-day Saints (LDS) market only, WindRiver offers Christian fiction as well as nonfiction on subjects such as LDS history, doctrine, and study. Queries for children's books are welcome.
Website: www.windriverpublishing.com

Freelance Potential
Published 1 title in 2010. Receives 48 queries yearly.
Submissions and Payment: Guidelines available at website. Query with 3–4 chapters, synopsis, and market analysis. Prefers electronic queries through the website; will accept hard copy and simultaneous submissions if identified. SASE. Responds in 4–6 months. Publication period varies. Royalty, 15% of net.

Wizards of the Coast

P.O. Box 707
Renton, WA 98057-0707

Submissions Editor

Publisher's Interests
Wizards of the Coast is primarily a publisher of role-playing
games, and also offers science fiction and fantasy for adults
under its YA imprint, Mirrorstone Books. Writers interested in
the world of fantasy fiction should send writing samples.
Website: www.wizards.com

Freelance Potential
Published 46 titles in 2010. Receives 200+ queries yearly.
Submissions and Payment: Guidelines and catalogue available at website. Check website for open submission periods.
Send a one-page cover letter, which indicates writing credits
and shared worlds of interest, and a hard copy writing sample
of about 10,000 words. SASE. Response time, publication
period, and payment policy vary.

World Book

233 N. Michigan Ave., Suite 2000
Chicago, IL 60601

Editor-in-Chief: Paul A. Kobasa

Publisher's Interests
World Book publishes reference books and nonfiction for all
ages, including children 3 to 14, teenagers, and adults. Topics
for children and teens include animals, careers, concepts,
geography, health, history, how-to, languages, multicultural,
reference, and science.
Website: www.worldbook.com

Freelance Potential
Published numerous titles in 2010.
Submissions and Payment: Catalogue available at website.
Query with outline/synopsis. Do not send mss. Accepts simul-
taneous submissions. Responds in 2 months. Publication in
18 months. Payment policy varies by product.

YMAA Publication Center

P.O. Box 480
Wolfboro, NH 03894

Director: David Ripianzi

Publisher's Interests
This publishing arm of Yang's Martial Arts Association offers books that illuminate the potential of martial arts and spiritual cultivation. Its nonfiction titles cover theory and practice, history, and philosophy. It also publishes martial arts fiction.
Website: www.ymaa.com

Freelance Potential
Published 8 titles in 2010: 2 were by agented authors. Of the 8 titles, 1 was by an author who was new to the publishing house. Receives 100+ queries yearly.
Submissions and Payment: Guidelines and catalogue available at website. Query with clips and sample chapter; or send complete ms. Accepts hard copy. SASE. Responds in 1–3 months. Publication in 12–18 months. Royalty, 10%.

Zaner-Bloser Educational Publishers

1201 Dublin Road
P.O. Box 16764
Columbus, OH 43216

Senior Vice President of Editorial: Marytherese Croarkin
Publisher's Interests
This publisher offers books designed to improve language arts skills—reading, writing, spelling, vocabulary, and fluency—all of which are curriculum-based for students in kindergarten through grade six. Its titles are leveled and suitable for literacy programs, and cover the subject areas of math, science, and social studies. Both fiction and nonfiction titles are published. Spanish language books are also featured.
Website: www.zaner-bloser.com

Freelance Potential
Published 200+ titles in 2010.
Submissions and Payment: Catalogue available at website. Query with résumé and clips. Accepts hard copy. SASE. Response time and publication period vary. Flat fee.

Zonderkidz

5300 Patterson Avenue SE
Grand Rapids, MI 49530

Acquisitions

Publisher's Interests
Zondervan/HarperCollins is the parent company of Zonderkidz,
a publisher of Christian board books, picture books, storybook
Bibles, chapter books, middle-grade and young adult titles, and
Bibles for teens. Nonfiction on topics such as nature, sports,
religion, and crafts appears on its list, along with fiction of
most genres. Agented authors are welcome to query.
Website: www.zondervan.com

Freelance Potential
Published 150 titles (60 juvenile) in 2010: most were by
agented authors. Receives 60–72 queries yearly.
Submissions and Payment: Catalogue available at website.
Query through literary agent only. Accepts hard copy. SASE.
Response time varies. Publication in 2–3 years. Royalty.

Agent Listings

Writers of books at some point face the question of whether or not to look for an agent. Some successful writers never work with an agent, while others prefer to find a strong representative for their work to deal with the business side. Some publishers will not accept unsolicited materials except through an agent. But a good manuscript will find its home with or without an agent, if you are committed to finding the right publisher to match your work.

How to find an agent: Look at listings in *Literary Marketplace* (LMP), or contact the Association of Authors' Representatives or go to its website (www.aar-online.org) for its member list. Other resources include the SCBWI Agents Directory (offered free to members) and the *2010 Guide to Literary Agents* (F & W Publications), which provides the names and specialties of agents around the world. If you'd prefer surfing the Web, the *Guide*'s editor's blog (www.guidetoliteraryagents.com/blog) is a wealthy resource, offering current information on agent needs and a wide variety of subjects related to working with and submitting to agents. Another site, Agent Query (www.agentquery.com/), is a free searchable database of agents that also includes specific information about each, including past and present clients and special interests. Be sure that any agent you contact works with writers for children.

What an agent does: An agent will review your work editorially before deciding to represent you, but the primary work of an agent is to contact publishers, market your material, negotiate for rights and licenses, and review financial statements. Although you don't need to be published to get an agent, most agents agree that an author should demonstrate commitment to the craft and a professional approach to writing in order to be considered for representation.

How to contact an agent: If the agent has a website, go online for specific contact requirements. If not, send a well-written, professional cover letter describing your work and background, accompanied by an outline or synopsis and sample chapter. Most agents will accept simultaneous submissions, as long as you inform them that you're querying other agents, and perhaps publishers, as well. Remember to tailor your query to individual agents just as you would to a publisher.

Fees: Be careful about agent fees. Increasingly, some will charge for readings and critiques, even without taking you on as a client. Compare the fees and the commissions to similar agents if you do enter into a contract. A typical rate is 15 percent for domestic sales, 20 percent for foreign.

What you need to know: Once you have an agent interested in representing you, compile a list of questions to ask him or her before getting on board. These might include:
- Why do you like my work?
- What should I expect of you, and you of me?
- What are the terms of the contract, including its duration?
- What is your track record, i.e. how many books have you sold?
- How does communication between us take place, via phone, email, or both?
- What can I do to help sell my work?
- What is required to end the agreement if it doesn't work out?

Adams Literary

7845 Colony Rd, C4 #215,
Charlotte, NC 28226

Agents: Tracey Adams, Josh Adams, Quinlan Lee

Representation
A boutique agency, Adams specializes in juvenile publishing
from picture books to YA novels. The agents "love debut au-
thors" and illustrators to welcome into their talented community.
Website: www.adamsliterary.com
Categories & Submissions
Current interests are middle-grade and YA fiction, including
timeless character-driven picture books, literary stories, fanta-
sy adventure, high-concept speculative fiction, and humor.
Query or send complete manuscript via the online form only.
Accepts simultaneous submissions, if indicated; inform the
agency of another offer of representation or publication.
Contract & Payment
One-page agreement, standard commissions: 15%, domestic;
20%, foreign, film, or television.

Miriam Altshuler

53 Old Post Road N.
Red Hook, NY 12571

Agent: Miriam Altshuler

Representation
Altshuler has worked with big-name authors, including Anne
Tyler and Nadine Gordimer. She represents adult, children's,
and YA work.
Website: www.miriamaltshulerliteraryagency.com
Categories & Submissions
YA, and very selectively, children's books. Considers how-to,
self-help, and spiritual books for adults if they focus on
women, children, mothering, or relationships. No science
fiction, fantasy, romance, mysteries, horror, or poetry. Mail
query with a brief bio and synopsis; include an email address.
Outline and sample chapters only on request. No unsolicited
manuscripts or electronic submissions.
Contract & Payment
Commission, 15% domestic; 20% foreign.

Anderson Literary Management

12 W. 19th Street
New York, NY 10011

Agents: Kathleen Anderson, Christine Mervart, Tess Taylor

Representation
An agency that works with wide-ranging subjects and genres,
Anderson Literary includes among its clients prestigious
"children's and young adult writers who have a penchant for
fantasy, leaps of imagination, and transformative stories
addressing the issues of our time."
Website: www.andersonliterary.com
Categories & Submissions
Middle-grade and YA, as well as adult. No picture books, adult
fantasy or science fiction, poetry, or Christian books. Mail a
query letter, the first 50 pages of the manuscript, and SASE.
Contract & Payment
Represents and negotiates all rights in all media, throughout
the world.

The Bent Agency

204 Park Place, Number Two
Brooklyn, NY 11238

Agents: Jenny Bent, Susan Hawk

Representation
The Bent Agency represents writers for adults and children.
Agent Susan Hawk, who was formerly an editor at Dutton,
specializes in books for children and teens.
Website: www.thebentagency.com
Categories & Submissions
Middle-grade and YA fiction and nonfiction, including mystery, historical fiction, fantasy, science fiction, realism,
humor, and boy books. Story—strong plotting—is key. Teen
nonfiction is a special interest. Query, with information on
your writing background, favorite authors, summary, and first
10 pages. Email to kidsqueries@thebentagency.com. No picture books, poetry, textbooks, sports, or reference.
Contract & Payment
Standard.

Meredith Bernstein Literary Agency

2095 Broadway, Suite 505
New York, NY 10023

Agent: Meredith Bernstein

Representation
Bernstein is a longtime, well-established agent who represents writers of YA and adult fiction and nonfiction. She is
open to new writers.

Categories & Submissions
YA fiction is among this agent's interests. Others are chick lit,
women's fiction, romance, science fiction, literary fiction,
humor, mainstream fiction, psychological suspense, medical
or legal thrillers, and love stories. Bernstein looks for commercial nonfiction in many categories. Regular mail queries
with an SASE only.

Contract & Payment
One-page agreement with an agency clause. Commission,
15% domestic, 20% foreign.

Andrea Brown Literary Agency

1076 Eagle Drive
Salinas, CA 93905

Agents: Andrea Brown, Laura Rennert, Caryn Wiseman, Jennifer Rofe, Kelly Sonnack, Jennifer Laughran, Jamie Weiss
Chilton, Jennifer Mattson, Mary Kole

Representation
A medium-sized agency on the West Coast specializing in
children's books, Andrea Brown also has agents with East
Coast publishing backgrounds.

Website: www.andreabrownlit.com

Categories & Submissions
Picture books, chapter books, middle-grade, and YA. Genres:
contemporary fiction, fantasy, graphic novels, science fiction,
humor, adventure, magical realism, thrillers, mysteries, narrative nonfiction. Email a three-paragraph query, with submission history and credits. For picture books, include full text;
fiction, 10 pages; nonfiction, proposal and sample chapter.

Contract & Payment
Commission, 15% domestic; foreign, 20%.

Dunham Literary

156 Fifth Avenue, Suite 625
New York, NY 10010

Agents: Jennie Dunham, Blair Hewes

Representation
Dunham Literary specializes in representing writers of children's books for all ages, and adult literary fiction and nonfiction. It welcomes first-time writers, and looks to develop writers' careers, not just books.
Website: www.dunhamlit.com
Categories & Submissions
Picture books, middle-grade, and YA. Seeks strong unique voices and fresh premises, especially character-driven fiction with a commercial hook. Query by mail. In one page, describe plot, themes, your credentials, and how you learned of the agency. If interested, an agent will request a manuscript or proposal, biography, synopsis, market statement.
Contract & Payment
Exclusive representation; agency clause. Commission, 15% domestic; 20%, foreign; 15% dramatic.

FinePrint Literary Management

240 W. 35th, Suite 500
New York NY 10001

Agents: Peter Rubie, June Clark, Colleen Lindsay, Suzie Townsend, Marissa Walsh

Representation
Agent Suzie Townsend is "specifically drawn to strong first-person narrators, and I'm a sucker for a good YA romance."
Website: www.fineprintlit.com
Categories & Submissions
Chapter books, middle-grade, YA fiction and nonfiction. No picture books. Genres include boy-oriented YA, teen nonfiction, paranormal, mainstream fiction, and books that tackle social issues or taboos. Match the genre to the agent profiles available on the website. Mail or email query and first 5-10 pages (no attachments).
Contract & Payment
Standard one-year contract initially, but the agency strives to represent authors throughout their careers. Commission, 15%.

Sheldon Fogelman

10 East 40th Street, Suite 3205
New York, NY 10016

Agents: Sheldon Fogelman, Marcia Wernick, Linda Pratt, Sean McCarthy

Representation
Founded in 1975, this agency was the first to specialize in children's books authors, among them Maurice Sendak.
Website: www.sheldonfogelmanagency.com
Categories & Submissions
All genres and ages of children's books, from picture books to YA. In particular, McCarthy looks for edgy narratives with flawed, multi-faceted characters, and graphic novels. Mail a one-page letter with a brief synopsis and credentials; indicate how you learned of the agency, and whether yours is a simultaneous submission. Also send first three chapters for novels, complete manuscript for picture books. No e-mail queries.
Contract & Payment
Not available.

Foundry Literary + Media

33 West 17th Street, PH
New York, NY 10011

Agents: Stephen Barbara, Hannah Brown Gordon, Mollie Glick, Brandi Bowles

Representation
A full-service agency, Foundry represents adult and children's authors. It includes a packaging division that produces books from concept to publication.
Website: www.foundrymedia.com
Categories & Submissions
Books for young readers from picture books through YA, as well as adult commercial and literary fiction and nonfiction. Mail or email a query, author bio, synopsis, and first three chapters for fiction; and sample chapters and table of contents for nonfiction. Address one agent.
Contract & Payment
Not available.

Sanford J. Greenburger Associates

55 Fifth Avenue
New York, NY 10003

Agents: Brenda Bowen, Faith Hamlin, Courtney Miller-Callihan

Representation
This is a large, prestigious agency founded in 1932. It has
represented Franz Kafka and Antoine de Saint-Exupéry, and
currently counts Dan Brown and children's author Robin
Preiss Glasser among its clients. Well-known children's book
publisher Brenda Bowen joined the agency in mid-2009.
Website: www.greenburger.com
Categories & Submissions
Children's books. Email query, the first three chapters for
fiction or a proposal for nonfiction, plus a synopsis, and brief
bio or résumé; attach as Word documents. Bowen wants the
full manuscript for picture books. She accepts mailed submissions but vastly prefers email to bbowen@sjga.com.
Contract & Payment
Commission, 15% domestic; 20% foreign.

Heacock Hill Literary Agency

1020 Hollywood Way, #439
Burbank, CA 91505

Agents: Catt LeBaigue, Tom Dark

Representation
The mission of Heacock Hill is to bring significant, uplifting
books into the marketplace. It is a new agency, founded in
2009 after Heacock Literary's owner/agent Rosalie Grace
Heacock Thompson semi-retired and stopped taking new
clients.
Website: www.heacockhill.com
Categories & Submissions
Picture books, chapter books, middle-grade fiction, YA fiction.
No children's nonfiction. Also interested in adult nonfiction.
Email a well-written query, with sample pages or chapters,
and for nonfiction, a proposal to agent@heacockhill.com. No
attachments. No unsolicited manuscripts.
Contract & Payment
No upfront fees.

Harvey Klinger, Inc.

300 W. 55th St., Suite 11V
New York, NY 10019

Agents: Sara Crowe, David Dunton, Andrea Somberg

Representation
"We are a highly selective, boutique agency and our clients all receive plenty of editorial advice and direction—from conception to publication," says Harvey Klinger. He represents only adult books, but other agents take on children's manuscripts.
Website: www.harveyklinger.com
Categories & Submissions
Middle-grade, but prefers YA in all categories. Query with a brief bio to queries@harveyklinger.com, or send by regular mail. Do not send full manuscript unless requested. Indicate simultaneous submissions.
Contract & Payment
Simple, to-the-point contract. Commission, 15%, domestic; 25%, foreign.

Knight Agency

570 East Avenue
Madison, GA 30650

Agents: Deidre Knight, Judson Knight, Pamela Harty, Elaine Spencer, Nephele Tempest

Representation
The Knight Agency has placed more than 2,000 books with large and small publishing houses. It represents all categories, with "white-glove management" and a hands-on approach.
Website: www.knightagency.net
Categories & Submissions
Middle-grade and YA. No books for younger children. Also specializes in romance, women's fiction, literary fiction, mysteries, science fiction, fantasy, and multicultural and inspirational fiction and nonfiction. Email a one-page query, without samples, to submissions@knightagency.net to the Submissions Coordinator, Melissa Jeglinski.
Contract & Payment
Not available.

Jean V. Naggar Literary Agency

216 E. 75th St, Suite 1E
New York, NY 10021

Agents: Jennifer Weltz, Alice Tasman, Jessica Regel

Representation
Founded more than 30 years ago by Jean V. Naggar, the
agency is behind a widely successful list of adult and chil-
dren's authors. The agency is open to debut authors.
Website: www.jvnla.com
Categories & Submissions
Accepts picture books, middle-grade, and YA fiction and non-
fiction; see the website for agents' individual preferences.
Email queries only, via the website. See specific guidelines,
but generally, include a brief description of the work, brief
bio, and paste the first three pages into the body of the
email. No attachments. Accepts simultaneous submissions.
Contract & Payment
Commission, 15%.

Nelson Literary Agency

1732 Wazee Street, Suite 207
Denver, CO 80202

Agents: Kristin Nelson, Sara Megibow

Representation
This Denver agency is full-service and hands-on in its representation of adult and children's books, and other media. It
is open to new authors.
Website: www.nelsonagency.com
Categories & Submissions
Middle-grade, YA, and adult. Genres: science fiction, fantasy
romance, women's fiction (including chick lit), commercial
fiction, and literary fiction with a commercial bent. Query via
email only to query@nelsonagency.com for completed works
of fiction. Do not send sample pages, synopses, links, or
attachments.
Contract & Payment
Commission, 15% domestic; 25% foreign and film.

Prospect Agency

551 Valley Road, PMB 377
Upper Montclair, NJ 07028

Agents: Emily Sylvan Kim, Teresa Keitlinski, Rachel Orr,
Becca Stumpf

Representation
Great books that are strong on storytelling fundamentals yet
boundary-breaking interest Prospect agents. Transport readers
through characterization, narrative, voice, and style.
Website: www.prospectagency.com
Categories & Submissions
Children's (including picture books), middle-grade, and YA; and
adult fiction. Genres: urban fantasy, science fiction, mysteries,
thrillers, romance; women's fiction, literary fiction. Query with
three chapters, synopsis, contact information, credits, writing
education. Upload via the website only. No mail or email.
Accepts simultaneous submissions; inform the agency if
another offer of representation is made.
Contract & Payment
At-will agreement. Commission, 15%.

Red Sofa Literary

2163 Grand Avenue #2
St. Paul, MN 55105

Agent: Dawn Michelle Frederick

Representation
Agent Dawn Frederick looks for "quirky, fun, smart, *and* commercial ideas," and to represent an author who has motivation and potential for a writing platform—talent and creativity
but also marketing promise.
Website: www.redsofaliterary.com
Categories & Submissions
Picture books (ages 3-12), graphic novels, YA fiction and
nonfiction. Also focusing on e-book publishing and social
marketing. Mail (with SASE) or email (no attachments) query
letter, full book proposal, and three sample chapters to
dawn@redsofaliterary.com.
Contract & Payment
Standard agency contract and commission.

Rodeen Literary Management

3501 N. Southport, #497
Chicago, IL 60657

Agent: Paul Rodeen

Representation
Rodeen Literary is a boutique agency specializing in children's book authors and illustrators. Founded in 2009, it welcomes new writers.
Website: www.rodeenliterary.com
Categories & Submissions
Actively looking for picture books, early readers, middle-grade fiction and nonfiction, graphic novels, comic books, YA fiction and nonfiction. Email submissions to submissions@rodeenliterary.com. Include a cover letter, contact information, the full text for picture books, and up to 50 pages of novels. Do not use regular mail for submissions.
Contract & Payment
Not available.

Schiavone Literary Agency

236 Trails End
West Palm Beach, FL 33413

Agents: James Schiavone, Jennifer DuVall, Kevin McAdams

Representation
Representing across many categories of adult and children's publishing, the Schiavone agency specializes in celebrity biographies, autobiographies, and memoirs.
**Website: http://schiavoneliteraryagencyinc.blogspot.
        com**
Categories & Submissions
Children's, YA, and adult books of high quality. No poetry. Query only to profschia@aol.com, jendu77@aol.com, or kvn.mcadams@yahoo.com.
Contract & Payment
Commission, 15% domestic; 20% foreign.

Susan Schulman Literary Agency

454 West 44th St.
New York, NY 10036

Agent: Susan Schulman

Representation
Schulman's boutique agency represents children's books, women's interests, and adult fiction and nonfiction. She looks for writers who "have thoroughly familiarized themselves in what constitutes good writing in their chosen genre," and welcomes new voices.
**Website: www.publishersmarketplace.com/members/
            Schulman**
Categories & Submissions
Children's and YA fiction and nonfiction; live stage, translation rights. Mail queries (with SASE), email to schulmanagency@ yahoo.com, or submit through Publishersmarketplace.com listing.
Contract & Payment
Agency agreement available for review. Commission, 15%.

Scovil Galen Ghosh Literary Agency

276 Fifth Avenue, Suite 708
New York, NY 10001

Agent: Ann Behar

Representation
This agency's list is eclectic and diverse, and the agents are open to any kind of book that is "first-rate." Behar is the juvenile publishing specialist. She looks for strong, distinct voices, vibrant characters, and beautiful writing. The agency is open to first-time authors.
Website: www.sgglit.com
Categories & Submissions
Children's and YA books for all ages. Also represents all genres of adult fiction and nonfiction. Email an "unadorned, unaccompanied" query, no attachments, to annbehar@ sgglit.com. Regular mail is accepted, but email is preferred.
Contract & Payment
Not available.

Serendipity Literary

305 Gates Avenue
Brooklyn, NY 11216

Agent: Regina Brooks

Representation
Children's publishing is a speciality of this boutique agency,
which also represents adult fiction and nonfiction. Regina
Brooks is very open to first-time authors with talent.
Website: www.serendipity.com
Categories & Submissions
Picture books to YA, fiction and nonfiction. Especially inter-
ested in urban YA. Currently not accepting picture books, but
check website for updates. Email queries with a one-page
synopsis detailing genre, theme, and plot to rbrooks@
serendipitylit.com. Or mail query, synopsis, and three sample
chapters; send entire manuscript for books under 32 pages.
For nonfiction, send a proposal detailing the target audience,
and a well-constructed outline. Exclusive submissions only.
Contract & Payment
Commission, 15% domestic; 20% foreign.

Stimola Literary Studio

306 Chase Court
Edgewater, NJ 07020

Agent: Rosemary B. Stimola

Representation
Rosemary B. Stimola has specialized in children's and YA
books throughout her 30-year career, first as a college teacher,
then as a bookstore owner, and since 1997, an agent.
Website: www.stimolaliterarystudio.com
Categories & Submissions
Picture books, fiction, graphic novels, nonfiction. Wants picture
books for the very young; middle-grade humor; middle-grade/
YA mysteries; YA thrillers, supernatural, and science fiction;
multicultural fantasy; graphic novels; nonfiction with adult
crossover appeal. No Revolutionary or Civil War historical fiction, poetry, institutional books. Mail or email a one-page query
with synopsis, credentials, and an indication of what makes the
book distinctive.
Contract & Payment
Commission, 15% domestic; 20% foreign.

The Strothman Agency

6 Beacon Street, Suite 810
Boston, MA 02108

Agents: Wendy Strothman, Lauren MacLeod

Representation
The Strothman Agency represents books in many categories
for middle-grade, YA, and adults. The agency "advocates for
authors of significant books."
Website: www.strothmanagency.com
Categories & Submissions
Middle-grade and YA; adult history, science, current affairs,
nature/environment, narrative nonfiction, arts, travel, business, memoirs. No commercial fiction, romance, science fiction, or self-help. Mail or email queries to strothmanagency@
gmail.com, with an outline of your qualifications and experience, a synopsis of the book, and, for fiction, 2 to 10 pages
of the manuscript. No attachments.
Contract & Payment
Commission, 15% domestic; 20% foreign.

Contests
and Awards

Selected Contests
& Awards

Whether you enter a contest for unpublished writers or submit your published book for an award, you will have an opportunity to have your book read by established writers and qualified editors. Participating in a competition can increase recognition of your writing and possibly open more doors for selling your work. If you don't win and the winning entry is published, try to read it to see how your work compares with its competition. Winning an award for a published book can increase sales, sometimes dramatically.

To be considered for the contests and awards that follow, your entry must fulfill all of the requirements mentioned. Most are looking for unpublished article or story manuscripts, while a few require published works. Note special entry requirements, such as whether or not you can submit the material yourself, need to be a member of an organization, or are limited in the number of entries you can send. Be sure to submit your article or story in the standard manuscript submission format.

For each listing, we've included the address, a description, the entry requirements, the deadline, and the prize. In some cases, the deadlines were not available at press time. We recommend that you write to the addresses provided or visit the websites to request entry forms and contest guidelines, which usually specify the current deadline.

Abilene Writers Guild
Monthly Contest

P.O. Box 2562
Abilene, TX 79604

Description
Open to guild members only, this monthly contest offers awards
in seven categories, among them children's stories for readers
ages three to eight; young adult novels; and inspirational fiction.
Website: http://abilenewritersguild.org
Length: Varies for each category.
Requirements: No entry fee for members. Accepts hard copy.
Author's name should not appear on manuscript. The cover letter should indicate the author's name, address, telephone, and
email in the upper left corner and the word or line count in the
upper right corner.
Prizes: First-place winners in each category receive $15. Second-
and third-place winners in each category receive $10 and $5,
respectively.
Deadline: Due the tenth of each month.

Arizona Authors Association
Literary Contest

Contest Coordinator
6145 W. Echo Lane
Glendale, AZ 85302

Description
Sponsored by the Arizona Authors Association, this contest's cat-
egories include published children's literature.
Website: www.azauthors.com/contest_index.html
Length: Varies for each category.
Requirements: Entry fee for a published children's book, $20.
Send two copies of each book with one entry form; multiple
submissions are accepted. Ebooks must be printed and bound.
Visit the website for a complete list of submission guidelines
for each category.
Prizes: First-place winners in each category receive $100. The
top three winners will be published or featured in *Arizona
Literary Magazine*.
Deadline: Entries are accepted between January 1 and July 1.

Atlantic Writing Competition

Writers' Federation of Nova Scotia
1113 Marginal Road
Halifax, Nova Scotia B3H 4P7
Canada

Description
This competition, open to writers living in Atlantic Canada, accepts unpublished young adult novels, short stories, poetry, writing for children, and magazine articles or essays.
Website: www.writers.ns.ca
Length: Varies for each category.
Requirements: Entry fees: novels, $35; all other categories, $25. WFNS members receive a $5 discount. Published authors may not enter the competition in any genre in which they have been published. Limit one entry per category. Accepts hard copy. Guidelines available at website.
Prizes: First- through third-place winners in each category receive awards ranging from $50 to $200.
Deadline: December 5.

Autumn House Poetry and Fiction Contests

Autumn House Press
P.O. Box 60100
Pittsburgh, PA 15211

Description
This annual contest is sponsored by Autumn House Press. It welcomes poetry collections and fiction, whether short stories, short shorts, novellas, or novels.
Website: www.autumnhouse.org
Length: Poetry collections, 50–80 pages. Fiction, 200–300 pages.
Requirements: Entry fee, $25. Accepts hard copy. Visit the website for complete competition guidelines. Include an SASE for contest results.
Prizes: Winning entries receive publication, a $1,500 advance, and a $1,500 travel grant. All entries are considered for publication by Autumn House.
Deadline: June 30.

AWP Award Series

Association of Writers & Writing Programs
George Mason University
Carty House MS 1E3
Fairfax, VA 22030-4444

Description
The annual AWP competition for book-length works of fiction,
creative nonfiction, and poetry is open to all writers. The evalua-
tion process is "of writers, for writers, by writers."
Website: www.awpwriter.org
Length: Poetry, at least 48 pages; short story and creative non-
fiction collections, 150–300 pages; novels, at least 60,000 words.
Requirements: Entry fee, $10 for AWP members; $25 for
non-members. Accepts hard copy with an AWP entry form.
Prizes: Winners receive awards from $2,000 to $5,000, and
publication of their book by the University of Pittsburgh Press,
University of Massachusetts Press, University of Georgia Press,
or New Issues Press.
Deadline: Entries accepted between January 1 and February 28.

Doris Bakwin Award

Carolina Wren Press
120 Morris Street
Durham, NC 27701

Description
This contest is sponsored by Carolina Wren Press, which publishes books by writers who are historically underrepresented by
mainstream presses. The Doris Bakwin Award is for unpublished
fiction or nonfiction on any subject, written by women. The
company's books include children's and adult titles.
Website: www.carolinawrenpress.org
Length: 150–500 pages.
Requirements: Reading fee, $20. Multiple entries are accept-
ed. Accepts hard copy. Visit the website in late summer for
complete, updated guidelines.
Prizes: Awards range from $150 to $600.
Deadline: December 1.

Geoffrey Bilson Award for Historical Fiction for Young People

The Canadian Children's Book Centre
40 Orchard View Boulevard, Suite 101
Toronto Ontario M4R 1B9
Canada

Description
Presented to outstanding historical fiction by a Canadian author published in the preceding year, this award values work that is historically accurate and based on primary research. The award winner is decided by a jury selected by the Canadian Children's Book Centre.
Website: www.bookcentre.ca/award
Length: Novels; no specific length requirements.
Requirements: No entry fee. Books must be published between January 1 and December 31 of the previous year. Send five copies of each title with a submission form.
Prizes: $5,000.
Deadline: December 18.

Waldo and Grace Bonderman Youth Theatre Playwriting Competition

Attn: Bonderman Administrator
140 W. Washington Street
Indianapolis, IN 46204-3465

Description
Playwrights who participate in the biennial Bonderman Workshop are eligible for this award, which encourages writers to create artistic theatrical scripts for youth.
Website: www.irtlive.com
Length: Grades one to three, 30 minutes; grades three and up, 45 minutes.
Requirements: Unpublished scripts, even those that have been commissioned, are eligible as long as they have never been produced. One submission per playwright; send three copies, a synopsis, and entry form. Musicals are acceptable.
Prizes: $1,000 and a staged reading.
Deadline: August 16.

The *Boston Globe–Horn Book* Awards

The Horn Book
56 Roland Street, Suite 200
Boston, MA 02129

Description
These prestigious awards honor excellence in literature for
children and teens. A three-judge committee evaluates in
three categories: picture books, nonfiction, and fiction and
poetry. Books must have been published in the U.S.
Website: www.hbook.com/bghb/submissions_bghb.asp
Length: No length requirements.
Requirements: No entry fee. Publishers may submit multiple
books, sending three copies of each. Books must have been
published between June 1 and May 31 of the preceding year.
No reprints, textbooks, audiobooks, e-books, or manuscripts
are eligible.
Prizes: Winner receives $500 and an engraved silver bowl.
Deadline: May 31.

Randolph Caldecott Medal

American Library Association
50 East Huron Street
Chicago, IL 60611

Description
The Caldecott is given annually to the American artist who
created the most distinguished original picture book of the
preceding year. Winners display excellence of execution in art
primarily, but also as the illustrations depict story, theme, con-
cept, setting, mood, and recognition of the child audience.
Website: www.ala.org/alsc/caldecott.html
Length: No length requirements.
Requirements: Must be an American picture book written in
English. Submit two copies, one to the Association for Library
Service to Children office and one to the committee chair.
Prizes: The winner is announced at the ALA Midwinter Meeting
and presented with the medal at an awards banquet.
Deadline: December 31.

California Book Awards

The Commonwealth Club of California
595 Market Street
San Francisco, CA 94105

Description
The California Book Awards, which began in 1931, honor
California writers and publishers who have demonstrated
exceptional literary merit. Awards are given in eight cate-
gories, including juvenile literature (to age 10) and young
adult literature (11–16).
Website: www.commonwealthclub.org/bookawards
Length: No length requirements.
Requirements: Entries must be written by a California resi-
dent and published in the award year. Authors or publishers
may mail six copies of the book with an official entry form,
which can also be found at the website.
Prizes: Medals are awarded in each category.
Deadline: December 17.

Delacorte Dell Yearling Contest for a First Middle-Grade Novel

Random House
1745 Broadway, 9th Floor
New York, NY 10019

Description
This annual contest is open to writers from the U.S. and Cana-
da only. All entries must have a North American setting.
Judges look for exemplary submissions of contemporary or
historical fiction targeting the 9 to 12 age group.
Website: www.randomhouse.com/kids/writingcontests
Length: 90–160 typewritten pages.
Requirements: No entry fee. Accepts hard copy. No simulta-
neous submissions or foreign-language translations. Include a
brief plot summary and cover letter. Include an SASE for
return of manuscript.
Prizes: A book contract, an advance of $7,500, and a prize
of $1,500.
Deadline: Entries must be postmarked between April 1 and
June 30.

Delacorte Press Contest for a First Young Adult Novel

Random House
1745 Broadway, 9th Floor
New York, NY 10019

Description
This contest is sponsored by Random House, which encourages writers to experiment in writing contemporary young adult fiction. The competition is open to residents of the U.S. and Canada who have not yet published a young adult novel.
Website: www.randomhouse.com/kids/writingcontests/
Length: 100–224 typewritten pages.
Requirements: Must have a contemporary setting and address readers ages 12 to 18. No entry fee. Accepts hard copy. No simultaneous submissions or translations. Include a brief plot summary and cover letter.
Prizes: A book contract, an advance of $7,500, and a prize of $1,500.
Deadline: Entries must be postmarked between October 1 and December 31.

Margaret A. Edwards Award

American Library Association
Young Adult Library Services Association
50 East Huron Street
Chicago, IL 60611

Description
The Margaret A. Edwards Award honors an author and his or her body of work for making a significant and lasting contribution to young adult literature. It recognizes "an author's work in helping adolescents become aware of themselves and addressing questions about their role and importance in relationships, society, and in the world."
Website: www.ala.org/yalsa/edwards
Length: No length requirements.
Requirements: The author must be living at the time of the nomination. Input on the nominee may be solicited from librarians and/or young adults.
Prizes: $1,000, and a citation presented during the annual ALA conference.
Deadline: December 31.

Excellence in Nonfiction
for Young Adults

American Library Association
50 East Huron Street
Chicago, IL 60611-2795

Description
The ALA honors the year's best nonfiction book written for
ages 12 to 18. Winners display excellent writing, research,
and readability. All forms of print, including graphic formats,
are eligible.
Website: www.ala.org
Length: No length requirements.
Requirements: The book must have been published between
November 1 and October 31, and the publisher must have
designated it as a YA book. Publishers, authors, or editors may
not nominate their own titles. Entries should be submitted
through the online nomination form.
Prizes: The award is conferred at the annual ALA conference.
Deadline: December 1.

Shubert Fendrich Memorial
Playwriting Contest

Pioneer Drama Service
P.O. Box 4267
Englewood, CO 80155

Description
This annual contest encourages the development of high-quality
drama for educational and community theaters. It is open to
playwrights who have not been published by Pioneer Drama
Service.
Website: www.pioneerdrama.com
Length: Running time 20 to 90 minutes.
Requirements: No entry fee. Accepts hard copy and email
submissions to playwrights@pioneerdrama.com. See website
for further guidelines.
Prizes: Winners are announced on June 1. Prizes include a
publication contract and a $1,000 advance.
Deadline: Ongoing.

Don Freeman Grant-in-Aid

Society of Children's Book Writers & Illustrators
c/o Judy Enderle
3646 Wood Lake Road
Bellingham, WA 98226

Description
SCBWI established this grant to help picture book artists grow in their abilities and understanding of the genre. SCBWI members and associate members are eligible.
Website: www.scbwi.org
Length: No length requirements.
Requirements: Applicants should supply either a book dummy with two illustrations and the picture book text, or 10 completed illustrations. The book dummy should show your ability to convey story mood, show action and pacing, and reveal characters. Include four copies of the application.
Prizes: One grant of $2,000 is awarded annually, as is a runner-up grant of $500.
Deadline: Entries must be postmarked no earlier than January 2 and received no later than February 2.

Theodor Seuss Geisel Award

American Library Association
50 East Huron Street
Chicago, IL 60611-2795

Description
First given in 2006, the annual Dr. Seuss awards honor the author and illustrator of the year's best beginning reader book in the U.S. Winning books provide a "stimulating and successful reading experience" for preschool to second-grade readers, through excellence of plot, rhythm, language, sensibility, and illustration.
Website: www.ala.org
Length: To 96 pages.
Requirements: Winners must be citizens or residents of the U.S. Submit one copy to the ALA office and one to the award committee chair.
Prizes: Plaque presented at the annual ALA conference.
Deadline: December 31.

Genesis Contest

American Christian Fiction Writers
Camy Tang, Coordinator
genesis@acfw.com

Description
Members of the American Christian Fiction Writers may enter
this annual contest if they have not published young adult or
adult fiction in the last seven years. It accepts manuscripts
in several categories including young adult, suspense/thriller,
historical fiction, and chick lit.
Website: www.acfw.com
Length: Projected final word count of 45,000 words minimum.
Requirements: Entry fee, $35. Multiple entries are allowed.
Enter with the online form only; include the first 15 pages of
the manuscript. No hard copy submissions.
Prizes: Winners receive a plaque and first choice for an editor/
agent appointment at the annual ACFW conference.
Deadline: March 1.

Golden Kite Awards

Society of Children's Book Writers & Illustrators
8271 Beverly Boulevard
Los Angeles, CA 90048

Description
Presented by the SCBWI, the Golden Kite Awards annually recognize excellence in children's literature. They are given to
published authors and illustrators in four categories: fiction,
nonfiction, picture book text, and picture book illustration.
Website: www.scbwi.org
Length: Varies for each category.
Requirements: Current SCBWI members are eligible, and may
enter themselves or be entered by their publishers. All entries
must be in final form, having been published and copyrighted
within the calendar year. Send four copies with a letter indicating the category. Picture books may be submitted for both text
and illustration; in that case, eight copies are required.
Prizes: $2,500.
Deadline: December 17.

The Barbara Karlin Grant

Society of Children's Book Writers & Illustrators
Barbara Karlin Grant Committee, c/o Q. L. Pearce
884 Atlanta Court
Claremont, CA 91711

Description
The SCBWI established this grant to encourage aspiring picture
book writers. It is open to SCBWI members who have not yet
published a picture book. Original short stories, nonfiction, or
re-tellings of fairy tales, folktales, or legends are eligible.
Website: www.scbwi.org
Length: 8 pages.
Requirements: One SCBWI grant submission per applicant. Six
copies of the application and six copies of the picture book
manuscript (text only) should be submitted.
Prizes: Grant of $1,500; runner-up grant, $500.
Deadline: Entries are accepted between February 15 and
March 15.

Coretta Scott King Award

American Library Association
50 East Huron Street
Chicago, IL 60611-2795

Description
Outstanding children's and young adult books by African
American authors and illustrators are honored by this annual
award. The winning titles express—and encourage the literary
and artistic expression of—the black experience in the U.S.
Check the guidelines for category information.
Website: www.ala.org
Length: No length requirements.
Requirements: Submit three copies of the published book to
the ALA Office for Literacy and Outreach Services, along with an
author-illustrator information form, and one copy to each of the
jury members.
Prizes: Award is conferred at the Coretta Scott King Award
Breakfast at the annual ALA conference.
Deadline: December 1.

Maryland Writers' Association Contests

P.O. Box 128
1009 Bay Ridge Avenue
Annapolis, MD 21403

Description
This contest encourages aspiring authors by providing a reputable literary critique and contest experience in the categories of short story, poetry, playwriting, and children's literature. It is open to all writers. The novel category includes young adult fiction.
Website: www.marylandwriters.org
Length: Novels, 50,000 words minimum. Short works contest, to 3,000 words; poetry, to 50 lines.
Requirements: Entry fee: novels, $35 for MWA members, $45 for non-members; short works, $10 and $15 respectively. Visit the website or send an SASE for complete guidelines. Entries must be original and not currently under contract.
Prizes: First place, $150; second place, $100.
Deadline: February 22.

Milkweed Prize for Children's Literature

1011 Washington Avenue South, Suite 300
Minneapolis, MN 55415-1246

Description
Publication of high-quality middle-grade fiction is the ultimate goal of this annual competition, held by Milkweed Editions. Entries for readers ages 8 to 13 should reflect humane values and cultural understanding.
Website: www.milkweed.org
Length: 90–200 typewritten pages.
Requirements: All manuscripts submitted to Milkweed by writers the company has not previously published are considered for the prize. Picture books and story collections are not eligible. Follow Milkweed's regular submission guidelines.
Prizes: Publication and a $10,000 advance on royalties.
Deadline: Ongoing.

Mythopoeic Fantasy Award for Children's Literature

306 Edmon Low Library
Oklahoma State University
Stillwater, OK 74078

Description
This award honors fantasy picture books, early readers, and middle-grade or young adult novels that are written in the tradition of C. S. Lewis or J. R. R. Tolkien, and published in the previous year.
Website: www.mythsoc.org
Length: No length requirements.
Requirements: Members of the Mythopoeic Society nominate books, and a membership committee selects the winners. Questions about the society or its contests should be directed to the awards administrator at awards@mythsoc.org. Authors may not nominate their own titles.
Prizes: A statuette.
Deadline: February 28.

National Book Award for Young People's Literature

National Book Foundation
95 Madison Avenue, Suite 709
New York, NY 10016

Description
Publishers submit books for the prestigious National Book Awards, which include a prize for an outstanding original work of young people's literature. Fiction, nonfiction, and single-author collections of stories or essays for young readers are eligible.
Website: www.nationalbook.org
Length: See guidelines at website.
Requirements: Entry fee, $125. All books must be published in the U.S., and written by a U.S. citizen. Re-tellings of folk-tales, myths, or fairy tales are not eligible.
Prizes: $10,000 and a crystal sculpture. Short-list prizes, $1,000.
Deadline: June 15.

National Children's Theater Festival Competition

Actors' Playhouse at the Miracle Theater
280 Miracle Mile
Coral Gables, FL 33134

Description
This competition, in its sixteenth year, welcomes original, unpublished scripts for musicals targeting ages 5 to 12. Plays should, however, appeal to children and adults. The judges prefer scripts that have not been widely produced, staged, or workshopped.
Website: www.actorsplayhouse.org
Length: Running time, 45–60 minutes.
Requirements: Entry fee, $10. Multiple entries are accepted. Accepts hard copy. Include an SASE for return of manuscript.
Prizes: $500, full production of the play, and travel expenses to the theater festival.
Deadline: April 1.

Newbery Award

American Library Association
50 East Huron
Chicago, IL 60611

Description
The Newbery Award is presented annually to an author who has made a distinguished contribution to American literature for children. The Newbery was the first children's book award in the world. It values interpretation of theme, clarity and accuracy, plot development, well delineated characters and setting, and appropriate style.
Website: www.ala.org
Length: No length requirements.
Requirements: No entry fee. All entries must have been published in the U.S. in the preceding year. Authors must be U.S. citizens or residents.
Prizes: The Newbery Medal is awarded to the winner. Honor books may also be named.
Deadline: December 31.

New Voices Award

Lee & Low Books
95 Madison Avenue
New York, NY 10016

Description
To nurture new talent, Lee & Low Books sponsors this annual
award for picture book manuscripts by writers of color. Fiction, nonfiction, or poetry, all submissions should offer readers ages 5 through 12 stories with which they can identify,
and promote mutual understanding.
Website: www.leeandlow.com
Length: To 1,500 words.
Requirements: No entry fee. Limit 2 entries per competition.
Include cover letter, brief biographical note with cultural and ethnic information, and manuscript. Open to U.S. residents who
have not published a picture book. No folklore or animal stories.
Prizes: $1,000 and a standard publishing contract. An honor
grant of $500 is also awarded.
Deadline: December 31.

Scott O'Dell Award for Historical Fiction

Hazel Rochman
5429 Eastview Park
Chicago, IL 60615

Description
Author Scott O'Dell established this award to encourage others,
particularly new writers, to focus on historical fiction. He hoped
to interest young readers in learning more about the historical
background that has shaped our country and our world.
Website: www.scottodell.com
Length: No length requirements.
Requirements: Published historical fiction intended for an audi-
ence of young readers, set in the New World (North, Central, or
South America), from a U.S. publisher, and written in English by
a U.S. citizen.
Prizes: $5,000.
Deadline: Ongoing.

Orbis Pictus Award for Outstanding Nonfiction for Children

National Council of Teachers of English
Orbis Pictus Committee Chair
1111 West Kenyon Road
Urbana, IL 61801

Description
The Orbis Pictus Award honors outstanding U.S. children's nonfiction for kindergarten to grade eight. The winning titles are factually accurate, balanced, well-structured, attractive and readable, stimulating, rich in language, and appealing to a range of ages.
Website: www.ncte.org
Length: No length requirements.
Requirements: Nominations may come from NCTE members or the educational community. Nonfiction or informational books intended to share information are eligible. Textbooks, historical fiction, folklore, and poetry are not.
Prizes: A medal is presented at the annual NCTE convention. Honor books are also recognized.
Deadline: December 31.

Pacific Northwest Writers Association Literary Contests

PMB 2717
1420 NW Golman Boulevard, Suite 2
Issaquah, WA 98027

Description
These annual contests offer prizes in 12 categories, including juvenile/young adult novel; nonfiction book; juvenile memoir; and short story. Only original, unpublished material is eligible for submission.
Website: www.pnwa.org
Length: Varies for each category.
Requirements: Entry fee, $35 for PNWA members; $50 for non-members. Multiple entries are accepted. Accepts hard copy. Submit 2 copies of each entry; all entries must include an official entry form.
Prizes: Awards range from $150 to $600.
Deadline: February 19.

Pikes Peak Writers Fiction Contest

Pikes Peak Writers
427 E. Colorado, #116
Colorado Springs, CO 80903

Description
This annual contest is open to short stories and book-length fiction in the categories of mystery, romance, historical, mainstream fiction, science fiction, and children's and young adult novels. Its purpose is to help unpublished writers focus on marketable projects, and benefit from feedback.
Website: www.ppwc.net
Length: Varies for each category.
Requirements: Entry fee, $30 for PPW members; $40 for non-members. Accepts electronic submissions only at pgcontest@gmail.com.
Prizes: First place in each category, $100. Second place, $50. Third place, $30.
Deadline: November 15.

Edgar Allan Poe Awards

Mystery Writers of America
1140 Broadway, Suite 1507
New York, NY 10001

Description
The Edgar Allan Poe Awards, considered the most prestigious awards in the genre, are sponsored by the Mystery Writers of America. These awards, presented annually, include prizes for best juvenile mystery and best young adult mystery.
Website: www.mysterywriters.org
Length: Varies for each category.
Requirements: No entry fee. All books, short stories, television shows, and films in the mystery, crime, suspense, and intrigue fields are eligible for Edgar® Awards in their respective category if they were published or produced for the first time in the U.S. during the preceding calendar year. See guidelines for details.
Prizes: An Edgar and cash award, presented at an annual banquet.
Deadline: November 30.

San Antonio Writers Guild Annual Contest

P.O. Box 100717
San Antonio, TX 78201-8717

Description
This contest, open to all writers, offers five different categories in fiction and nonfiction. Prizes are given to unpublished work.
Website: www.sawritersguild.com
Length: Novel, first 15 pages. Short story, 4,000 words. Nonfiction memoir, 2,500 words. Essay, 2,500 words. Flash fiction, 1,000 words.
Requirements: Entry fee, $10 for SAWG members, $20 for nonmembers. Multiple entries are accepted in up to three different categories. All entries must meet submission guidelines or they will be rejected and the entry fee forfeited.
Prizes: First place, $100. Second place, $50. Third place, $25.
Deadline: October 1.

SCBWI Work-in-Progress Grants

Society of Children's Book Writers & Illustrators
8271 Beverly Boulevard
Los Angeles, CA 90048

Description
Each year, SCBWI presents five grants that assist children's book writers in the completion of a project. Grants are awarded in the categories of general work-in-progress; contemporary novel for young people; nonfiction research; and unpublished author.
Website: www.scbwi.org
Length: 750-word synopsis and writing sample from a manuscript that is no longer than 2,500 words.
Requirements: No entry fee. Applications available no earlier than February 15. Instructions and complete guidelines are sent with application forms.
Prizes: Cash grants of $2,000 and $500 in each category.
Deadline: March 15.

Schneider Family Book Award

American Library Association
50 East Huron Street
Chicago, IL 60611-2788

Description
This award honors an author or illustrator whose book artistically embodies a child or adolescent's experience of physical, mental or emotional disability. It includes three categories: birth through age eight, middle school, and teens. In fiction, the person with the disability may be the protagonist or a secondary character. Nonfiction is also considered.
Website: www.ala.org
Length: No length requirements.
Requirements: Must be published in English. Submit eight copies of the application and eight copies of the book.
Prizes: $5,000 and a plaque.
Deadline: December 1.

Kay Snow Writing Contest

Willamette Writers
9045 SW Barbour Boulevard, Suite 5A
Portland, OR 97219-4027

Description
This annual contest looks to help writers reach professional goals. It offers awards in several categories including juvenile writing, fiction, nonfiction, and screenwriting.
Website: www.willamettewriters.com
Length: Varies for each category.
Requirements: Entry fee, $10 for WW members; $15 for non-members. Student writers (18 or under), no fee. Submit two copies of each entry. Author's name must not appear on manuscript.
Prizes: Range from $50 to $300 in each category. The Liam Callen award, $500, is presented to the best overall entry.
Deadline: April 23.

SouthWest Writers Contests

SouthWest Writers Workshop
3721 Morris NE
Albuquerque, NM 87111

Description
SouthWest Writers sponsors a quarterly and an annual contest
in many categories, including middle-grade novel, young adult
novel, children's picture book, and nonfiction book. The web-
site indicates the changing specifications for each quarterly
contest.
Website: www.southwestwriters.com
Length: Varies for each category.
Requirements: Entry fees vary. SWW members receive a dis-
count. Submit 2 copies of each entry and an entry form.
Author's name should appear on the entry form only. Multiple
entries are accepted.
Prizes: Prizes range from $50 to $150.
Deadline: May 1.

John Steptoe Award for New Talent

American Library Association
50 East Huron Street
Chicago, IL 60611-2795

Description
Affiliated with the Coretta Scott King awards, the John Steptoe
award was created to encourage new talent among writers and
illustrators whose work depicts the African American experience.
It focuses on original books that otherwise might not be formally
acknowledged because they fall outside other award criteria.
Website: www.ala.org
Requirements: Must be written/illustrated by an African American, and published in the U.S. in the preceding year. The award
is given in three categories: preK to grade 4, grades 5 to 8, and
grades 9 to 12.
Prizes: A plaque is awarded at the annual ALA conference.
Deadline: December 1.

Surrey International Writers' Conference Writing Contest

Unit 400, 9260-140 Street
Surrey, British Columbia V3V 5Z4
Canada

Description
Open to all writers over the age of 18, this annual contest offers awards in the categories of nonfiction, short story, poetry, and writing for young people.
Website: www.siwc.ca
Length: Nonfiction and writing for young people, to 1,500 words. Short stories, 3,500–5,000 words. Poetry, to 40 lines.
Requirements: Entry fee, $15. Multiple entries are accepted. Accepts hard copy and email entries to contest@siwc.ca. Author's name should not appear on manuscript. Include a cover letter with author's name and contact information.
Prizes: First-place winners in each category, $1,000. Honorable mentions, $150.
Deadline: September 10.

Sydney Taylor Manuscript Competition

Aileen Grossberg
204 Park Street
Montclair, NJ 07042

Description
The Sydney Taylor Manuscript Award was established to encourage aspiring authors of Jewish children's books for ages 8 to 11. The books should deepen young readers' understanding of Judaism.
Website: www.jewishlibraries.org
Length: 64–200 pages.
Requirements: No entry fee. One entry per competition. Short stories, plays, and poetry are not eligible.
Prizes: $1,000.
Deadline: December 15.

Laura Ingalls Wilder Medal

American Library Association
Association for Library Service to Children
50 East Huron Street
Chicago, IL 60611

Description
A bronze medal is presented every other year to an author
or illustrator whose body of work over the years has made
a substantial and lasting contribution to American literature
for children.
Website: www.ala.org
Requirements: Nominations are made by ALSC members,
and the winner is selected by a team of children's librarians.
Criteria for judging includes whether the books have been
notable examples of the genre they represent, or have forged
a new direction in children's books.
Prizes: The medal is presented at the annual ALA conference.
Deadline: December 31.

Writers-Editors Network Writing Competition

CNW/FFWA
P.O. Box A
North Stratford, NH 03590

Description
This annual competition is open to all writers and accepts
entries in four divisions: nonfiction, fiction, children's literature,
and poetry. Children's literature entries may be unpublished or
self-published, and may include a short story, nonfiction article,
book chapter, or poem.
Website: www.writers-editors.com
Length: Varies for each category.
Requirements: Entry fee, $3–$10 for CNW members; $5–$20
for non-members. Multiple entries are accepted. Author's
name should not appear on manuscript. Send an SASE or visit
the website for category-specific guidelines and entry forms.
Prizes: First place, $100. Second place, $75. Third place, $50.
Deadline: March 15.

Writers' League of Texas Book and Manuscript Contests

611 S. Congress Avenue, Suite 130
Austin, TX 78704

Description
The Writers' League of Texas honors published books and also welcomes unpublished manuscripts in two annual contests. Categories include middle-grade and young adult fiction, as well as mainstream fiction, mystery/thriller, science fiction, historical/Western, and romance.
Website: www.writersleague.org
Length: No length restrictions.
Requirements: Entry fee, $50. Send a one-page synopsis, the first 10 pages of your unpublished work, and an entry form. Send an SASE or visit the website for guidelines.
Prizes: Manuscript contest, a one-on-one meeting with an agent at a June conference. Book contest, $1,000 and an award.
Deadline: February 15.

Writing for Children Competition

90 Richmond Street, Suite 200
Toronto, Ontario M5C 1P1
Canada

Description
Canadian citizens who have not yet published a book are encouraged to submit to this annual children's writing competition. Sponsored by the Writers' Union of Canada, its purpose is to discover new talent in any genre.
Website: www.writersunion.ca
Length: To 1,500 words.
Requirements: Entry fee, $15. Multiple entries are accepted. Unpublished Canadian citizens or landed immigrants writing in English are eligible. Send hard copy with a cover letter; manuscripts will not be returned.
Prizes: $1,500. Winning entries will be submitted to three children's publishers.
Deadline: April 24.

Paul Zindel First Novel Award

Hyperion Books for Children
114 Fifth Avenue
New York, NY 10011

Description
Sponsored by Jump at the Sun, a multicultural imprint of
Hyperion Books for Children, the Paul Zindel First Novel Award
is given to contemporary middle-grade fiction that reflects the
ethnic and cultural diversity of the U.S.
Website: www.hyperionchildrensbooks.com
Length: 100–240 typewritten pages.
Requirements: Unpublished U.S. writers may submit an origi-
nal work of fiction appropriate for ages 8 to 12. Submit the
manuscript with an entry form.
Prizes: A book contract; $7,500 advance; $1,500 cash.
Deadline: December 31.

Indexes

2011 Market News

New Listings: Publishers, Agents, Contests

Adams Literary
Miriam Altshuler
Anderson Literary
The Bent Agency
Meredith Bernstein Agency
Geoffrey Bilson Award
Blue Bike Books
Waldo and Grace Bonderman
  Youth Theatre Award
Bridge-Logos
Brook Farm
Andrea Brown Agency
Randolph Caldecott Medal
California Book Awards
Candy Cane Press
Dalmatian Press
Dragon Hill Publishing
Dunham Literary
Educational Impressions
Margaret A. Edwards Award
Egmont USA
Eschia Books
Excellence in Nonfiction for
  Young Adults
Margaret Ferguson Books
FinePrint Literary
Sheldon Fogelman
Folklore Publishing
Foundry Literary + Media
Don Freeman Grant-in-Aid
Theodor Seuss Geisel Award
Golden Kite Awards
Sanford J. Greenburger
Hammond Publishing
Heacock Hill
Heyday Books
Kaplan Publishing
Coretta Scott King Award
Harvey Klinger
Knight Agency

Leap Books
Magical Child Books
MuseItUp
Mythoepeic Fantasy Award
Jean V. Naggar Literary
Nelson Literary
National Book Award
Scott O'Dell Award
Orbis Pictus Award
Our Place Books
OverTime Books
Pikes Peak Writers Contest
Edgar Allan Poe Awards
Prospect Agency
Quagmire Press
Red Sofa Literary
Renaissance House
Rodeen Literary
Rourke Publishing
Rubicon Publishing
Schiavone Literary
Schneider Family Book Award
Schwartz & Wade
Susan Schulman Literary
Scovil Galen Ghosh Literary
Serendipity Literary
Silverton House
John Steptoe Award
Stimola Literary Studio
The Strothman Agency
Sydney Taylor Competition
Trumpet Media
Tu Books
Laura Ingalls Wilder Medal
Wiley
World Book
Writers-Editors Network
  Writing Competition
Paul Zindel First Novel Award

2011 Market News

Deletions

The following publishers have been removed from this year's directory for a variety of reasons, whether they have ceased publishing, are unresponsive to submissions, or have proven too small a niche or too little interested in juvenile books.

A & B Publishers Group: No longer publishing.

Alaska Northwest Books: Parent company, **Graphic Arts Publishing**, declared bankruptcy twice and liquidated.

Avari Press: No longer publishing.

Avocus Publishing: Not responding to letters or emails.

Baker Trittin Press: No longer publishing.

Baylor University Press: Not publishing children's or YA.

Cascadia Publishing: Mennonite press; limited YA interest.

Creative Bound International: Charges a fee to publish.

Encounter Books: Political publisher with limited YA interest.

Exclamation!: Very limited publishing.

Faith Kidz: Defunct imprint of Cook Ministries.

Five Leaves Publications: Small, niche, U.K. publisher.

Graywolf Press: Does not publish children's or YA.

Hampton-Brown Books: Not accepting submissions.

History Publishing Company: Publisher on history for adults, with limited YA interest.

Hodder Education: Publisher for the British curriculum.

Immortal Books: Australian niche publisher redirecting its publishing program.

InQ Publishing: No longer publishing.

The Liturgical Press: Not publishing children's books.

MacAdam/Cage: No longer publishing.

Manor House: Small Canadian publisher; occasional family, but no children's, titles.

National Resource Center for Youth Services: An adolescent outreach program that offers limited publications, such as manuals and workbooks.

New Canaan Publishing: Not accepting manuscripts; may no longer be publishing.

Optimum Publishing: No longer publishing.

Oxford University Press: No longer publishing children's or YA books.

Pick-a-WooWoo: Small, Australian spirituality publisher with a limited list.

Pitspopany Press: Website has dated titles and submission information; editors did not respond to information requests; may require author investment to co-publish.

Pleasant St. Press: Moratorium on manuscripts; unclear whether the company will continue to publish.

Purple Sky Publishing: No longer publishing.

Quixote Press: Not responding to information requests; has no website.

Sandcastle Books: No longer a separate imprint of the Dundurn Group. Not the same as Sandcastle Publishing.

Santillana USA Publishing: Has not accepted queries or manuscripts for two years; Spanish-language education books.

Scholastic Canada: Has not accepted queries or manuscripts for two years.

Silver Dolphin Books: Uses content from packagers only.

Success Publications: No longer publishing.

Turtle Books: No longer publishing.

Category Index

T o help you find the appropriate market for your query or manuscript, we have compiled a selective index of publishers according to the types of books they currently publish.

If you do not find a category that exactly fits your material, try a broader term that covers your topic. For example, if you have written a middle-grade biography, look through the list of publishers for both Middle-Grade (Nonfiction) *and* Biography. If you have written a young adult mystery, look under Mystery/ Suspense *and* Young Adult (Fiction). Always check the publisher's listing for explanations of specific needs.

For your convenience, we have listed the categories that are included in this index.

Activities
Adventure
Animals/Pets
Arts
Bilingual
Biography
Board Books
Canadian
   Publishers
Careers
Chapter Books
   (Fiction)
Chapter Books
   (Nonfiction)
Concept Books
Contemporary
   Fiction
Crafts/Hobbies
Current Events/
   Politics
Drama/Plays
Early Picture Books
   (Fiction)
Early Picture Books
   (Nonfiction)
Easy-to-Read
   (Fiction)
Easy-to-Read
   (Nonfiction)
Education/Resources
Fairy Tales
Fantasy

Folklore
Geography
Gifted/Special
   Education
Graphic Novels
Health/Fitness
High-Lo/Reluctant
   Readers
Historical Fiction
History
Holidays
Horror
How-to
Humor
Inspirational Fiction
Language Arts
Mathematics
Middle-Grade
   (Fiction)
Middle-Grade
   (Nonfiction)
Multicultural/
   Ethnic (Fiction)
Multicultural/Ethnic
   (Nonfiction)
Mystery/Suspense
Nature/Outdoors
Parenting
Picture Books
   (Fiction)
Picture Books
   (Nonfiction)

Poetry
Reference Books
Regional (Fiction)
Regional
   (Nonfiction)
Religious (Fiction)
Religious
   (Nonfiction)
Romance
Science
Science Fiction
Self-Help
Series
Social Issues
Social Skills
Social Studies
Sports (Fiction)
Sports (Nonfiction)
Story Picture Books
   (Fiction)
Story Picture Books
   (Nonfiction)
Technology
Toddlers (Fiction)
Toddlers (Nonfiction)
Travel
Westerns
Young Adult
   (Fiction)
Young Adult
   (Nonfiction)

577

Publisher, Agent, and Contest Index

★ indicates a newly listed publisher, agent, or contest